WITHDRAWN

Churchills in Africa

By the same Author
LADIES IN THE VELD
CECIL RHODES AND THE PRINCESS

Winston Churchill standing beside the overturned armoured train. This photograph was taken when he returned to Natal after escaping from Pretoria

Daily News, Durban

Churchills in Africa

BRIAN ROBERTS

Illustrated

TAPLINGER PUBLISHING COMPANY
NEW YORK

First Published in the United States in 1971 by
TAPLINGER PUBLISHING CO., INC.
New York, New York

Copyright © 1970, Brian Roberts

All rights reserved. No portion of this book may be reproduced in any form without the written permission of the publisher, except by a reviewer who may wish to quote brief passages in connection with a review for a newspaper or magazine. No part of this publication may be reproduced, stored in a retrieval system, or transmitted in any form or by any means, electronic, mechanical, photocopying, recording or otherwise, without the prior permission of the copyright owner.

International Standard Book Number 0-8008-1580-7

Library of Congress Catalog Card Number 79-148405

DA
566.9
C5
R58
1971

Printed in Great Britain

FOR MY BROTHERS

FOR MY BROTHERS

Contents

Preface — xi
Acknowledgements — xiii

PART ONE: THE QUARREL

1. 'To the Land of Ophir' — 3
2. Trouble in the Transvaal — 19
3. Looking for Gold — 41
4. Going Home — 66

PART TWO: THE RAID

5. Enter Lady Sarah — 87
6. The Aftermath — 104

PART THREE: THE WAR

7. An Ambitious Young Man — 119
8. Lady in Waiting — 143
9. 'Everyone is talking about Mr Churchill' — 162
10. Betrayed by a Pigeon — 181
11. Over the Garden Wall — 197
12. Swopped for a Horse Thief — 216
13. 'Churchill, Dead or Alive . . .' — 235
14. Shut up in Mafeking — 255
15. Churchills in the *Maine* — 271
16. 'The Good Genius of the Siege' — 292
17. Marching to Pretoria — 309
18. The Leave Taking — 323

Epilogue — 337
Bibliography — 339
References — 344
Index — 360

Illustrations

Winston Churchill standing beside the overturned armoured train. (A photograph taken when he returned to Natal after escaping from Pretoria.) *Frontispiece*

1	Lord Randolph Churchill in 1891	*facing page* 18
2	Lord Randolph arrives in Africa	19
3	Kruger and Lord Randolph—a Pretoria cartoon	50
4	In Mashonaland: Lord Randolph and Hans Lee encounter a troop of lions	51
5	Lady Sarah Wilson as a war correspondent in South Africa	146
6	The wrecked armoured train at Chieveley, Natal.	147
7	(a) School at Pretoria where Winston Churchill was imprisoned.	178
	(b) John G. Howard, manager of the colliery where Churchill was hidden after his escape	178
8	General Snyman and Commandant Botha, Boer commanders of the force besieging Mafeking	179
9	Petrus Viljoen is exchanged for Lady Sarah	210
10	(a) £25 reward for Churchill's capture, dead or alive	211
	(b) Churchill's arrival at Durban	211
11	(a) Lady Sarah at the entrance to her Mafeking bombproof shelter	242
	(b) Inside her shelter	242
12	Lady Sarah in her Mafeking outfit	243
13	Lady Randolph and John Churchill on board the hospital ship *Maine* at Durban	274
14	Churchill as an officer of the South African Light Horse	275

ILLUSTRATIONS

15 Churchill at Hlangwane Hill, Natal, shortly before
    the relief of Ladysmith   306
16 Release of captive British officers in Pretoria   307

MAP

(by Patrick Leeson)

Southern Africa circa 1899   120

Preface

FOR THE Churchill family, the 1890s were fateful years. The first half of the decade saw the tragic decline and death of Lord Randolph Churchill; the second half launched his son, Winston, on his spectacular career. Both events were set against, and influenced by, the turbulent state of affairs in Africa. This is hardly surprising. The period was one in which the African continent—particularly the south—was attracting the attention of ambitious men throughout the world. Kimberley's diamonds, the Transvaal's gold and the opening up of Rhodesia all played a part in luring the adventurous to Africa. The continent offered not only riches but the chance of political involvement and military renown: for behind the glitter of its mineral wealth a situation was developing which, as many forsaw, led inevitably to the Anglo-Boer war at the close of the century. Such a set of circumstances was bound to prove irresistible to the spirited Churchills.

This book is concerned mainly with three members of the Churchill family—Lord Randolph Churchill, his sister, Lady Sarah Wilson, and his son, Winston Churchill—whose adventures in Africa reflect the mounting tensions which culminated in the outbreak of war. All three have recorded their African experiences but, being autobiographical, these accounts are selective, somewhat biased and two of them have been largely forgotten. Lord Randolph's book *Men, Mines and Animals in South Africa* was an immediate success when it was published in 1892 and was reprinted several times. No one, reading it today, would, however, appreciate what widespread controversy his tempestuous journey provoked. In 1909 Lady Sarah Wilson described her experiences in *South African Memories*. This created a certain amount of interest when it was published but its tone was so understated that both the book and its author were soon forgotten. The adventures of this redoubtable woman are here resurrected in full for the first time. Winston Churchill wrote several accounts of his adventures during the Anglo-Boer war, the best known being the simplified version given in *My Early Life*. Stimulating as this classic piece of autobiography undoubtedly is, it too is somewhat lacking in objectivity. Some of the gaps left by Churchill in his account created resentment among his former colleagues and resulted in unsavoury rumours about his activities in South Africa. His escape from the Staatsmodelskool, for instance, appears as little more than a risky leap over a fence: the part played in the escape by his fellow prisoners, the confusion he left behind him and the effect of the escape on the prison organization is largely ignored. Only recently have private memoranda written by Churchill and Sir Aylmer Haldane, in an attempt to clarify the circumstances surrounding the escape, been published: these, together with documents released by the Transvaal Government, make it possible to take a more complete view of the episode. Other unanswered questions proved more damaging: they were to plague Churchill throughout his career. Was he armed when he was captured? Did he break his parole by escaping when he did? Did the Boers deliberately allow him to get away? Such accusations were repeatedly levelled at him and, while it is not possible to give categorical answers to all these accusations, an attempt has been made to put them into perspective. Further points throughout his narrative have needed to be corrected or amplified in order to relate them to contemporary reports of his activities or to authoritative accounts of the war. The story told in these pages differs considerably from that of *My Early Life*.

Acknowledgements

IN WRITING this book I have received help from a great many people. My chief debt of gratitude is to Mr Theo Aronson whose interest, advice and encouragement have been of inestimable value. I would also like to thank Mrs S. Minchin for lending me Thomasina Cowan's unpublished diary and for her help and hospitality during my stay in Mafeking; Mr A. J. P. Graham for kindly sending me his interesting account of Winston Churchill's capture and escape; Mrs A. B. Ferguson for her recollections of Witbank and those concerned with Winston Churchill's escape; Mrs E. M. Johnstone (*née* Keeley) of Setlagole for making available the papers and cuttings related to the Keeley family; the Mother Superior of the Convent of Mercy, Rosebank, Johannesburg, for use of the correspondence of the Mafeking convent at the time of the siege; Mrs C. Cassidy of Maseru, Lesotho, for extracts from her mother's diary; Mr John Fuller of Johannesburg for the unpublished diary of his grandfather (Trooper W. R. Fuller) and Mr W. Hillcourt of New Brunswick, U.S.A., for sending me photostat extracts from Lord Baden-Powell's Staff Diary.

My sincere thanks are due to Mr John Nicholson who, together with Mother Columba and Mother Joseph of the Convent of Mercy, supplied me with many details concerning Lady Sarah Wilson and the siege of Mafeking; to Miss Julie Mullard for her useful advice and interest; to Miss Joy Collier and Miss Norah Henshilwood for the timely loan of books which were difficult to obtain and to Miss Ann Seeliger for her valuable help with translations.

For answering queries, offering advice and assistance, I would like to record my thanks to Olave, Lady Baden-Powell, Dr Thelma Gutsche, Mrs C. Webster, Miss Elizabeth Dey, Mrs Eira Parker, Mrs R. G. Keeley, Mr W. S. Keeley, Mr John McIntosh, Mr Alex Kiddie, Mr Peter Tomlinson and Mr D. MacAndrew. I am extremely grateful for the assistance given to me by the staff at Blenheim Palace, by Mr Snyman of the Transvaal Archives and by the Librarian of the Killie Campbell Africana Museum in Durban, as well as for the

ACKNOWLEDGEMENTS

co-operation I have received when working at the British Museum, the Cape Archives, the Johannesburg Africana Library, the Parliamentary Library, Cape Town, and the South African Library, Cape Town.

I am greatly indebted to the following newspapers for supplying me with photographs from their files: *Daily News*, Durban, *Cape Argus*, Cape Town, and *The Star*, Johannesburg.

My thanks are also due to His Grace the Duke of Marlborough for permission to quote from the Blenheim papers; to William Heinemann Ltd for permission to quote from Randolph Churchill's Companion Volume 1 to his *Winston S. Churchill, Volume 1, Youth: 1874–1900*; to the Hamlyn Publishing Group Ltd for permission to quote from the following books by Winston S. Churchill: *My Early Life, London to Ladysmith via Pretoria, Ian Hamilton's March and The River War*; to Chatto & Windus Ltd for permission to quote from J. B. Atkins' *Incidents and Reflections* (Christophers, London, 1947).

PART ONE

THE QUARREL

CHAPTER ONE

'To the Land of Ophir'

ONE DAY in February 1891 Cecil Rhodes and Lord Randolph Churchill were poring over a map of Africa in a London hotel. They were discussing the possibility of Lord Randolph visiting Mashonaland.

The map was either new or had recently been revised for, prominent upon it, to the north of the Limpopo river, were pin-points marking the outposts of the British South Africa Company: outposts which had been established less than a year before by the Company's pioneer force. Upon these outposts the attention of the two men was focused. Rhodes, who had only briefly visited the territory over which the outposts were scattered, nevertheless knew each of them in detail. More than any other man, he was responsible for them being on the map at all. At his instigation the British South Africa Company had been formed and through his untiring efforts the enterprise had been blessed by the British Government, in the form of a Royal Charter. For Rhodes, the pin-points represented the realization of a vision; a vision that had been born when, as an unknown diamond digger in Kimberley, he had flattened his hand on another map of Africa and declared: 'All this to be painted red; that is my dream.'

The idea of Imperial expansion in Africa had obsessed Rhodes throughout his astounding career. His achievements in amalgamating the diamond mines of Kimberley, in gaining a firm foothold in the goldfields of the Witwatersrand and, more recently, in being elected Prime Minister of the Cape Colony, he regarded simply as stepping stones to the fulfilment of his ultimate desire. He saw himself as the precursor of a crusade which was destined to make, not only Africa, but the entire world subject to the benevolent influence of the British Empire.

The outposts that had sprung up beyond the Limpopo were but the beginnings of this grandiose dream.

Shortly before coming to England, Rhodes had paid a flying visit to the southern-most fort in Mashonaland. He now pointed to the spot on the map. 'There is Fort Tuli,' he informed Churchill, 'the first station of the Chartered Company.' Then taking a pencil he drew a straight line linking the fort with Pretoria, the capital of the Transvaal. 'And that,' he added, 'is the road you must travel.'

Some four months later, Churchill, riding beside an officer of the Bechuanaland Police, crested a slight rise in the barren bushveld. 'There,' said his companion, pointing to a group of white tents in the distance, 'is Fort Tuli.' The sight of the neat, staring camp perched on a desolate koppie came as something of an anti-climax. Removed from Rhodes's contagious enthusiasm and tired after weeks of travelling, Lord Randolph could have found little about the camp to cheer his flagging spirits. Indeed, it must have seemed like nothing more than a humourless caricature of the glowing picture painted by Rhodes. The Union Jack which fluttered limply above the handful of tents might have been placed there by a bad cartoonist parodying the might of the British Empire. It was yet another disappointment in what was proving to be a disastrous expedition.

*

It had all started on a very different note. From the moment that *The Times* had announced, on 28 February 1891, that 'Lord Randolph Churchill has definitely decided to visit Mashonaland in the spring' and that preparations were under way for the 'arduous journey he is about to undertake', the expedition had been treated as one of the most colourful and hilarious events of the year. To set off on a well-publicized journey to the wilds of Africa was the sort of spectacular venture that the public had come to expect of Lord Randolph. Impetuous, high-handed and completely unpredictable, he was liable to create a sensation by everything he said and did. Africa would provide the ideal setting for his flamboyant personality. Not for a long time had his admirers been able to anticipate so much fun. Newspaper columnists and cartoonists had a field day. With great glee, they forecast the likely and unlikely situations which would confront the intrepid Lord Randolph. He was depicted hacking his way through palm-tree jungles, pursuing wild animals (all looking remarkably like his political opponents) and enduring comical discomforts in a semi-tropical climate. That the newspaper jokers had not the remotest idea of the region he was about to visit only served to encourage their bizarre inventions. Friends and foes alike were looking forward to several months of amusing reading.

There were others who greeted the announcement with a different brand of optimism. The South African expedition would, they hoped, herald a new chapter in the erratic Churchill saga. Lord Randolph's reputation as the *enfant terrible* of British politics had, it was thought, diminished his stature as a statesman: for too long he had allowed himself to be ridiculed as a political eccentric. Far from relishing the prospect of further indiscretions, his more serious friends felt that the time had come for him to assert himself as a politician of real purpose. He was no longer a young man. On 13 February he had celebrated his forty-second birthday. He was of an age to turn his back on the capricious behaviour that had both marked and marred his early career. He should now claim his rightful place in the affairs of the nation.

There were signs that this was his intention. Of late he had begun to talk of making his parliamentary come-back: he had hinted to his friends that he would soon return to the Treasury Bench in the House of Commons. In December 1890 he had paid a short visit to Egypt and returned radically changed in appearance. To the despair of political cartoonists, his familiar handlebar moustache had disappeared and been replaced by a stubbly, grey-flecked beard. This was surely an indication that the publicity-conscious Lord Randolph was intent on creating a new role for himself. 'He has grown a beard,' it was reported. 'The much-twisted moustachios have had to hide their diminished ends, and, consequently, a considerable change has taken place in Lord Randolph's personal appearance. The "Member for Woodstock" has quite disappeared, and in his place we see a "grave and reverend seignior" who feels his responsibilities as a leader of men.' If this were true, his well-wishers had good cause to be hopeful. The long-delayed promise of his early years was, it seemed, at last to be fulfilled.

For few young politicians had displayed more promise. The second surviving son of the seventh Duke of Marlborough, Lord Randolph Churchill had made his political debut in 1874, when, at the age of twenty-five, he had taken his seat in the House of Commons as the Tory member for Woodstock. Something of a dandy, with a fondness for coloured shirts and jewellery, he was by no means a typical member of the Churchill family. Perhaps this was to his advantage. Since the death of the great Duke of Marlborough, a century or so earlier, the participation of the house of Churchill in national events had produced little of significance. The gloss that Lord Randolph was to give to the family's lack-lustre image was long overdue. Already he had made an important departure from the traditions of Blenheim Palace. At the age of twenty-four he had met, and immediately fallen in love with, the daughter of a self-made American millionaire. Young Jennie Jerome was dark and lovely, an accomplished musician, graceful dancer and, as Lord Randolph told his father, quite suited to any position. He was determined to marry her. The proposal was not popular with either the Churchills or the Jeromes, but he wore down all opposition and the couple were married at the British Embassy in Paris shortly after Lord Randolph's election as the Member for Woodstock. Having revitalized the Churchill stock, he set about rejuvenating the House of Commons. His maiden speech, on 22 May 1874, lacked polish but created a significant stir. Writing to Queen Victoria, Disraeli, the ageing Prime Minister, noted: 'Lord Randolph said many imprudent things, which is not very important in the maiden speech of a young member and a young man; but the House was surprised and then captivated, by his energy, and natural flow, and his impressive manner. With self-control and study, he might mount. It was a speech of great promise.'

Self-control and study were not to be his strong points. He was emotional, self-willed and pugnacious: from the very outset his turbulent nature threatened his political promise. While he was still finding his parliamentary feet he became involved in a serious quarrel. The quarrel was not of his making but he made it his own. His elder brother, the Marquis of Blandford, was entangled with a married woman and the affair earned him the enmity of the Prince of Wales. So vigorously did Lord

Randolph champion his brother that the Prince demanded that the Churchills be ostracized. Society obeyed the royal decree and Lord Randolph and his young wife became outcasts. Partly to offset the chilling effect of the Prince's anger, Disraeli renewed an offer made to the Duke of Marlborough to become Viceroy of Ireland. The Duke accepted and took his younger son with him as an unofficial secretary. At the Little Lodge in Phoenix Park, Dublin, the Randolph Churchills set up house and it was here that their two-year-old son, Winston Leonard, formed his earliest memories: Viceregal pomp, ceremonial gunfire, scarlet-coated soldiers on horseback, an elegant, fairy-like mother in a riding habit, an ogre of a governess, struggles with a reading-primer and dark warning of wicked Fenians. Of his father he remembered little.

In 1880 Lord Randolph returned to England to fight a General Election. With him went his wife, his son Winston and a second son, John, born in February that year. The election marked another turning point. Although Lord Randolph retained his seat with a reduced majority, elsewhere the Tories were defeated and Mr Gladstone became Prime Minister. The Duke of Marlborough's term as Viceroy came to an end and Lord Randolph took his place on the Opposition benches at Westminster. The change was very much to his taste: he was born to oppose. Some three years were to pass before he won back the Prince of Wales's favour but the opportunities now open to him were such that little else mattered. The Liberals had won the election with a large majority. Gladstone, recently retired, had plunged back into politics at the age of seventy-one in the full flood of his moral indignation over the Bulgarian atrocities. Disraeli, now Lord Beaconsfield, was ensconced in the House of Lords and the leadership of the Tory party in the House of Commons was uninspired. The situation was ripe for an astute, ambitious mischief-maker. The impish Lord Randolph quickly made the most of it. Backed by three lively companions—John Gorst, Henry Drummond Wolff and Arthur Balfour—he nightly harried the Government and lampooned the elderly 'Goats' of his own party. The Government's secure position provoked his rebelliousness, the Prime Minister's rectitude invited his sarcasm and the timidity of his own leaders encouraged his audacity. He soon made his mark. So assertive and independent was the campaign waged by himself and his friends that an Irish Nationalist dubbed them 'the Fourth Party'; the title was gladly accepted.

An independence of attitude bred an independence of thought. Dissociating himself from the conventional doctrines of his party, Lord Randolph was soon proclaiming his own brand of conservatism: he called it Tory Democracy. It was aimed at winning over the working class. Revolutionary as it at first appeared, many came to regard it as little more than a political gimmick. Churchill seemed to admit as much. 'Tory Democracy,' he explained wryly, 'is a democracy which supports the Tory party.' Even so, it was too much for his more orthodox colleagues. A creed designed to appeal to the masses bordered dangerously upon the Radical. When the members of the Fourth Party established themselves on the front bench below the gangway, some of their immediate neighbours fled. 'I found it getting a little too hot for me,' one of them explained to Henry Drummond Wolff.

But the diehards tended to exaggerate. If Lord Randolph was a radical, he was—at least, at this stage of his career—very much a radical of the right. The implications of Tory Democracy were feudal rather than progressive. Like many another conservative romantic, Lord Randolph was merely embellishing the myth that a natural bond existed between the aristocracy and the working class: he saw the bourgeoisie as the common enemy. 'The career of Lord Randolph Churchill,' says E. T. Raymond, 'was founded on a hatred and an illusion. The hatred was for the middle class. The illusion was that the Conservative Party was still the party of the aristocracy, that the old quarrel between the landowner on the one side and the banker, the manufacturer and the tradesman on the other, yet persisted. He failed, not because he was before, but because he was behind his time.' Certainly he took no pains to hide his dislike for the middle class. His speeches were peppered with slighting references to bourgeois pretentiousness. 'It is remarkable,' he observed of Mr Sclater-Booth, a Tory minister, 'how often we find mediocrity dowered with a double-barrelled name!' He dubbed two other prominent tradesmen of his own party the 'Marshall and Snelgrove of debate'. And he was contemptuous about the 'lords of suburban villas, owners of vineries and pineries'. The only self-made men he appeared willing to tolerate were millionaires.

He offended the stolid Conservatives but made himself the idol of the working class. His attacks upon Gladstone—'the people's William'—were greeted with delight. In Parliament he taunted the Prime Minister with being 'an old man in a hurry'; and in a public speech he poked fun at the 'Grand Old Man's' peculiar relaxation as a wood-cutter. 'The forest laments, he declared, 'in order that Mr Gladstone may perspire, and full accounts of these proceedings are forwarded by special correspondents to every daily paper every recurring morning.' In turn, he earned a variety of nicknames for himself. To his admirers he was 'Little Randy' or 'Cheeky Randy'; *Punch* depicted him as 'Grandolph'; and his opponents hit back with 'Yahoo Churchill'. But whether loved or loathed, there was no denying his impact. His notoriety became a rare asset to the Conservative cause and the Tory leaders were forced to take his popularity into account. It brought its rewards.

Gladstone's Government fell on 8 June 1885. On a seemingly harmless amendment to the Budget, which the Prime Minister had made an issue of confidence, the Liberals were defeated. When the results of the division were announced, the triumphant Churchill was the first to leap on the bench, wave his handkerchief and cheer. In Lord Salisbury's short-lived Conservative administration, which followed Gladstone's defeat, Lord Randolph was made Secretary of State for India. The following year, after a General Election in which he was returned as the Tory member for South Paddington, he received further promotion. To the dismay of some of his colleagues he was appointed, at the age of thirty-seven, Leader of the House of Commons and Chancellor of the Exchequer. Within six months he had resigned both posts and his political career was at an end.

The dramatic rise and fall of Lord Randolph Churchill is without parallel in British politics. His startling resignation at the height of his career has been the subject of endless debate. It was as much a matter of tactics as of politics and for once his tactics were misplaced. In preparing his first Budget he demanded cuts in the army and navy estimates; cuts which were to prepare the way for the social reforms of Tory Democracy. His proposals were opposed by the chiefs of the War Departments. To force the issue he resigned. He was staying at Windsor Castle and penned his letter of resignation on royal writing paper: he did not seriously expect it to be accepted but, to his astonishment, Lord Salisbury allowed him to relinquish his posts. Whether, as was claimed, he considered himself to be irreplacable is debatable. When told that Mr Goschen was to succeed him as Chancellor, he said: 'I forgot Goschen.' But it is unlikely that a man of his intelligence thought it would be impossible for the Prime Minister to find another Chancellor. It seems more reasonable to suppose that he had simply overestimated the strength of his position. His advocacy of Tory Democracy had done much for his reputation; his mistake was in trying to implement such a policy. The panjandrums of the Tory party were prepared to accept a new vote-catching slogan, but they drew a line at legislating for it. In resigning from the Cabinet Lord Randolph had expected to be recalled on his own terms; instead he was shrugged off as an embarrassment. He had too many enemies in high places. 'He made the clever man's mistake of under-rating dull men,' says a historian of the period, 'forgetting the patience of their malice and the perfection of their hypocrisy. There were people with great names and claims, but little brains, who had cried "Hosannah!" as loudly as any in public, but never ceased to mutter "Crucify him" in the Carlton Club arm-chairs.' He would not allow his friends—and he had influential friends—to interfere and he ignored the taunts of those who cried 'I told you so.' His stand might be the result of clumsy tactics but he was determined to maintain it.

This had been his position for a little over four years. He was still the Member for South Paddington, he could still command a large audience and was considered by many to be biding his time. He had left the Cabinet in a startling manner and his return was expected to be equally dramatic. His trip to Mashonaland might well be the beginning of the big things which lay ahead. 'We may notice with satisfaction,' wrote a political columnist, 'that so keen an observer, and, in spite of some eccentricities, so able a statesman as Lord Randolph Churchill purposes going to South Africa to examine the state of affairs for himself. He will find plenty of materials to interest him, and very much promise for the future . . .'

*

A few days after *The Times* announced his intention of visiting Mashonaland, Lord Randolph agreed to be interviewed by a newspaper. The journal he chose for this interview was the then influential magazine *South Africa*. Started a little over a year earlier, *South Africa* was regarded by many as the London mouthpiece of Cecil Rhodes and the mining magnates of the Witwatersrand. By selecting this paper for his first interview, Lord Randolph created the suspicion that there was more to his expedition than the professed sporting holiday in an exotic new country. Some of his opponents hinted that he was being used to further the interests of South African millionaires.

The reporter who interviewed Lord Randolph was fully conscious of his privilege. From the moment he was ushered into the hall of Churchill's London house, 2 Connaught Place, he displayed a deference rarely accorded to the rumbustious Lord Randolph by newspapermen. 'We are in his Lordship's library and he is greeting us with gentle courtesy,' he gushed. 'How unlike the man one is accustomed to expect, say, from the comic papers!' Not surprisingly, the interview amounted to little more than a Churchillian monologue. Lolling back in an easy chair, a cigarette in one hand and stroking his new beard with the other, Lord Randolph gave his reasons for visiting South Africa. He intended to sail in the *Garth Castle* on 24 April, he said. The expedition was to be partly private, partly public. He had a few free months and was interested to explore the new territory.

'I think, on the whole,' he went on, 'that perhaps South Africa is the most interesting of all the British possessions in many ways and naturally I am very anxious to see what I can of a country likely to excite a great share of public attention in this country within the next few months. I am specially interested not only to see the Cape and the Cape Colony and Kimberley, and perhaps the Rand, but I am very interested indeed to penetrate into Mashonaland. From all I can learn, I think it is very probable that Mashonaland offers possibly the best and most attractive field for British emigration that has been opened up since the development of the Australian Colonies. . . In the present overcrowded state of our great towns, it would probably be a matter of State importance to discover some foreign territory suitable for State-aided emigration. Then I am very anxious to see for myself whether the accounts I have read of

Mashonaland are true, and whether in that part of the world we may expect to find a home for our surplus population.'

His talks with Rhodes and the fact that he held shares in the Chartered Company were not mentioned. Anxious to present it as a patriotic undertaking, he was reluctant to discuss the more private aspects of the trip. The reporter timidly enquired whether he intended prospecting for gold. 'Well—ah—certainly,' he replied, 'we shall be on the look-out for any advantage in that way which may turn up.' However, at the end of the interview, the newspaper man noted that included in Lord Randolph's equipment there was a small gold-crushing machine. Mention of this machine immediately attracted the attention of Churchill's critics. 'It appears,' remarked one of them, 'that Lord Randolph is intent on extracting from the soil of Mashonaland substantial compensation for the political fortune he has lost in England.'

That Lord Randolph possessed a gold-crushing machine was no surprise to his friends. For months the Churchill circle had talked of little else. Invented by a Scotsman named Crawford and championed by Lady Randolph's ever-optimistic brother-in-law, Moreton Frewen (husband of Lady Randolph's elder sister, Clara Jerome) the machine may well have played a part in Lord Randolph's decision to visit South Africa. It was no ordinary gold-crusher. It had been designed to extract gold from refuse ore surrounding derelict mines. Moreton Frewen, whose life was dedicated to the possibility of making a quick fortune from outlandish schemes, had seized upon the idea of salvaging huge quantities of discarded gold. He had persuaded his family and friends to take shares in the company he formed to exploit the invention: his mother-in-law, old Mrs Jerome, had even sold a precious diamond necklace in order to invest. Of more importance was the support he had received from Alfred Beit, the South African millionaire. Not only had Beit shown a flattering interest in the machine but he had supplied Frewen with a bag of South African ore with which to experiment. The success of this experiment may well have aroused Lord Randolph's interest. Usually extremely wary of his brother-in-law's erratic enthusiasms, he appears to have been completely captivated by the gold crusher.

Unfortunately, as was often the case with Moreton Frewen's schemes, just when excitement over the machine was at its height, some of the more influential business men behind the venture began to back out. Alfred Beit had second thoughts about its commercial soundness and Lord Randolph became discouraged. He decided to drop both Frewen and the gold crusher. Shortly after the reporter from *South Africa* had spotted the machine, Churchill wrote to his brother-in-law declining shares in the proposed company. He also abandoned the idea of taking Frewen and the gold-crusher with him. News of this family rift leaked out. 'It is a pleasant omen,' remarked a newspaper, 'that Randolph has quarrelled with his brother-in-law before they have set out. The other members of the party must be looking forward to a nice friendly time.'

By opting out of Frewen's gold-crushing scheme, Lord Randolph had by no means given up hope of finding riches in South Africa. Like the thousands of other fortune hunters who sailed south at this time, he was fascinated by the wealth of Africa. He was desperately in need of money. He had been out of office for over four years and his social position made heavy demands upon him. With two sons to educate (the sixteen-year-old Winston's poor progress at Harrow providing cold comfort) his financial worries increased by the year. He could not afford to ignore South Africa's gold. In order to exploit his opportunities he had formed a gold-prospecting syndicate, the controlling interest of which was kept firmly within his own family. To his own contribution of £5,000, his mother had added £1,000, his sister and brother-in-law, Lord and Lady Wimborne, had each contributed £1,000, and his youngest sister, Lady Sarah Spencer Churchill, had invested £1,000—an investment which was destined to bring Lady Sarah some unexpected dividends. The other members of the syndicate were two financiers, Baron de Hirsch and Sigismund Neumann; two journalists, Sir Algernon Borthwick, proprietor of the *Morning Post*, and H. H. Marks, editor of the *Financial News*; and two soldiers, Colonel North and Major Warde, all of whom contributed £1,000 each, while the last member of the syndicate, the Marquise of Breteuil (an admirer of Lady Randolph) invested the odd sum of £944: thus providing the Churchill expedition with a capital of £15,994. For all his talk of *lebensraum*, Lord Randolph clearly intended to explore more than the possibility of British settlement in Mashonaland.

The syndicate was not Lord Randolph's only financial backing. At the beginning of April 1891, it was announced that: 'LORD RANDOLPH CHURCHILL has accorded to the proprietors of the *Daily Graphic* the exclusive right to publish a Series of Letters signed by himself, giving a detailed account of his experiences in SOUTH AFRICA . . . It is a source of great satisfaction to the conductors of the paper that a statesman of Lord Randolph Churchill's high reputation has chosen the *Daily Graphic* to be the medium of his views and opinions of a New Continent.' The newspaper proprietors had good reason to be pleased with their catch. Although the *Daily Graphic*'s offer to pay two thousand guineas for twenty letters had been considered an astonishing bid for an amateur journalist, other newspapers had not been deterred. The *Daily Telegraph* had immediately tried to go one better with a flat offer of £100 a column. But Churchill remained loyal to the *Graphic* and, having signed the contract, set about arranging for his letters to be published in book form on his return.

*

As the time for departure drew nearer, so did public interest in the expedition increase. Almost every day news items concerning the proposed visit 'to the Land of Ophir' appeared in the popular press. It was announced that the expedition would be under the command of Captain George Edward Giles of the Royal Artillery, a thirty-six-year-old officer—'perhaps the tallest and handsomest man in the British Army'—who had served in various African campaigns and was said to be 'a master of all the wrinkles of South African travel'. Besides supervising the travel arrangements, Captain Giles was to act as the official artist of the party. The *Daily Graphic* was able to inform its readers that Lord Randolph's letters would be fully illustrated 'by Sketches by Captain Giles, R.A.' (leaving them to decide for themselves whether R.A. stood for Royal Academician or Royal Artillery). As his aide-de-camp, Lord Randolph chose Captain Gwynydd Williams, a young officer of the Royal Horse Guards who, despite a promising army career, resigned his commission in order to travel to Mashonaland. The doctor chosen to accompany the party was also a soldier. He was Dr Hugh Rayner, a surgeon of the Grenadier Guards who had been given special permission to join the expedition by the Duke of Cambridge, Commander-in-Chief of the British Army. 'Besides acting as medical officer,' it was officially explained, 'Surgeon Rayner will report generally on the climate of the country traversed and on other matters which may be of military value.' As far as Lord Randolph's critics were concerned, the most interesting addition to the expedition was Henry Cleveland Perkins, an American mining expert who, the *Manchester Guardian* later pointed out, 'is, in fact, employed by Messrs Rothschild, and the commercial success or failure of the expedition really turns upon the character of his reports.' Messrs Rothschild were, as was widely known, closely associated with the financial concerns of Cecil John Rhodes.

The tall and handsome Captain Giles sailed for the Cape at the beginning of April. He was sailing in advance of the main party in order to complete arrangements for the overland journey. No sooner had he arrived at Lisbon, on his voyage south, than he was sending long reports to the *Daily Graphic* to explain precisely what those arrangements were. The members of the expedition, he said, would be equipped with everything they could possibly want: 'tables and chairs, washstands, baths, looking-glasses, mosquito curtains, gauze head nets proof against flies, felt-covered ebonite water-bottles, which can be padlocked when in charge of native servants, pocket filters of the newest pattern, enamelled iron plates, Punkah lamp shades, cork mattresses and air-tight tin-cases—in short, no article of camp equipment that suggested itself to Messrs Silvers' veteran experience has been forgotten.' In addition to these luxury items he had arranged for the transportation of an unspecified number of 90 lb portable fly tents, ordinary 100 lb bell tents, specially designed saddles, saddle bags and holsters and an armoury of revolvers, repeating rifles, big-bore elephant rifles, deer-shooting rifles and shot-guns. The expense of all this was borne by the Churchill syndicate. When the financial report of the expedition was later published, it was estimated that Lord Randolph's personal equipment had cost £1,750, while Captain Giles's expenditure was £131 and Henry Perkins, the mining engineer, completed the journey on a mere £15.

Not all the publicity attending the expedition was welcomed. As a conscientious Tory Democrat, Lord Randolph did not want his working-class constituents to think that he was off on a pleasure jaunt. Two weeks before he was due to sail, he explained the purpose of the trip to the South Paddington Conservative Association at a dinner given in his honour. Once again his theme was emigration. 'It is true that I am shortly to commence a journey into, perhaps, the greatest possession of the British Crown,' he said. 'I like to think that the journey possibly may not be altogether unattended in useful results, should I return, with public advantage... It is possible that our dominions in South Africa, by climate, by soil, and by natural resources, may offer to hundreds and thousands of our fellow countrymen who are seeking with difficulty their livelihood here, a means of employing their labour profitably, and making themselves a happy and prosperous home... I cannot conceive that a member of Parliament—a member, moreover, representing such a constituency as South Paddington—is at all straying from his duty when he endeavours to find out for himself in a reliable manner the nature and resources of that great possession of the Crown.' His speech was greeted with cheers but he appears to have remained uneasy. Rumour had it that he had left a 'species of political will' with the Chairman of his Committee, to be consulted should a General Election occur during his absence. For those who hoped that he was about to make a political comeback the signs looked favourable.

A week later he was the principal guest at a more lighthearted dinner. Organized by his political associates, it was held at the then fashionable Amphitryon Club. In a room garlanded with pink roses, primroses, violets and white lilac, between forty and fifty of Lord Randolph's male friends gathered to bid him farewell. Among the guests were two members of the now defunct Fourth Party—Henry Drummond Wolff and Arthur Balfour—some members of the South Paddington Committee and an odd assortment of Liberals, including Herbert Asquith, Joseph Chamberlain and Lord Rothschild. The after-dinner speeches were brief. Amid loud cheers the Chairman wished Lord Randolph 'God-speed' and Herbert Asquith leapt to his feet to propose a toast. 'Having regard to the character of the occasion,' he said, '... I think we cannot do less than drink in solemn silence to the undying memory of the Fourth Party.' He was answered by Arthur Balfour who caused more laughter by denying that the Fourth Party had ever had a leader and making a particular point of disclaiming leadership for himself.

Churchill left from Paddington station on the Castle Express on Friday, 24 April. From eight o'clock in the morning, crowds of his constituents had been pouring into the station. An hour later, when Lord Randolph arrived with his wife, the platform was so packed that a special police cordon was formed to protect friends and members of the family who had come to say their goodbyes. Prominent within the ring of policemen were the discarded Moreton Frewen and his wife, Lord Randolph's young sister Sarah and Mr Bourchier Hawkesley, Cecil Rhodes's London solicitor. Lord Randolph had some difficulty in reaching his railway carriage. 'Everyone,' it was reported, 'appeared anxious to have a final hand-shake with him, and to get a glimpse of his beautiful wife.' The lovely Lady Randolph, it was noted, looked very tear stained.

There was good reason for Lady Randolph's tears. A few weeks earlier her father, old Leonard Jerome, had died and now her husband was setting out on a journey about which she was far from happy. She was worried about the state of Lord Randolph's health: this was an aspect of the expedition that had not been publicized. For some time Lord Randolph had been suffering from an illness which his doctors professed themselves unable to diagnose; their only advice was that the patient should rest and cut down his cigarette smoking. It seems probable, however, that both Lord Randolph and his wife were aware of the hopelessness of his condition. They knew he was living on borrowed time. Lady Randolph might even have feared that she was saying goodbye to him for the last time. Although their marriage had not been particularly happy, because of circumstances forcing them to lead separate lives, Lady Randolph was still fond and proud of her husband. The poignancy of their parting was unmistakable.

In the excitement surrounding Lord Randolph's departure, the other passengers received scant attention. 'Mr Alfred Beit, quiet and retiring as usual,' noted a reporter, 'and Sir Charles Metcalfe, slipped into their carriage almost unnoticed.' This was probably just as well. Shy little Alfred Beit was Cecil Rhodes's financial adviser and his burly companion, Charles Metcalfe, was one of Rhodes's closest friends. Both, in a way, were unofficial members of the Churchill expedition but nobody wished to emphasize the Rhodes connection.

This did not prevent the inevitable speculation. 'While wishing him [Lord Randolph] all possible success in his quest,' remarked a suspicious political columnist, 'and recognizing the comparative lightness of his luggage, we cannot help feeling some apprehension for his future under the weight of such an overpowering personality as Mr Cecil Rhodes.'

Lord Randolph Churchill in 1891

South African Library

Lord Randolph's first step on African soil—landing at Cape Town

South African Library

CHAPTER TWO

Trouble in the Transvaal

THAT Cecil Rhodes had great hopes of Lord Randolph's visit there can be no doubt. In spite of the initial enthusiasm aroused by his march into Mashonaland, Rhodes still had a great deal of public scepticism to overcome before he could hope for a real show of confidence in the country. Reports sent back by early pioneers had been conflicting. Exuberant announcements of large gold deposits had, more often than not, been followed by flat denials or complete silence. The hardships encountered by the pioneer force were well known and the possibility of taming the country and making it habitable for European settlement was open to doubt. On all sides there were suspicions of Rhodes's purpose and of the Chartered Company's integrity.

Of more immediate concern was Rhodes's difficulty in defining the borders of the new territory. The coast which separated Mashonaland from the Indian ocean in the east was occupied by the Portuguese. On their march northwards the pioneer force had discovered Portuguese concessionaires working gold claims in parts of the country which the Chartered Company intended to occupy. Rhodes was determined, not only to keep the Portuguese out of Mashonaland but, if possible, to take over the coastal strip which they already occupied. For this he needed help. There had been several indecisive clashes between the Chartered Company's force and the Portuguese and Rhodes realized that, if the final outcome was to be in his favour, it would be necessary to involve the British Government in his struggle. An influential and popular politician like Churchill could be invaluable in helping him gain the support he needed.

When Lord Randolph arrived at Cape Town, on 14 May 1891, there was nothing to show that his visit was in any way connected with Rhodes. He was met on board by his advance agent, Major George Giles (whose promotion from the rank of captain had been announced shortly after he left England) and greeted at the docks by the Mayor and Town Clerk of Cape Town. After telling local reporters that he 'was much struck by the beauty of the Bay and the mountain scenery' he entered a carriage and, acknowledging the cheers of the crowd gathered at the harbour gate, was driven to Government House. The *Cape Times* dismissed his arrival as 'a somewhat tame affair' and concluded its report by saying that 'during his stay in Cape Town, which may extend some little time, he will be the guest of His Excellency the Governor. It is said that Lord Randolph Churchill will decline to make any public statement during his stay in Cape Town.' Both these statements were to be proved wrong.

Churchill stayed at Government House only a few days. Then he moved to Rhodes's house, 'The Grange', in the suburb of Rondebosch. In contrast to the publicity given to other aspects of the trip, this change of residence passed almost unnoticed. Those who met him in public at this time found him strangely subdued. 'Grandolph is in our midst,' noted J. X. Merriman, the Treasurer General, 'quiet and even shaky but no doubt taking in a good deal more than he lets out. What a curious expedition for an ex-leader of the House of Commons.' This shakiness was an early indication of the spasmodic attacks which were to torture Churchill for the remaining years of his life; they seem, on this occasion, to have resulted from his somewhat unhappy sea voyage. Every effort had been made to ensure his comfort on the *Grantully Castle*. Sir Donald Currie, the head of the shipping line, had gone so far as to take the ship out of its scheduled turn so that Churchill would not have to travel in an older vessel. But the voyage had proved more than his constitution could stand: the heat, sea-sickness, boredom and, above all, the food, which he found unpalatable, had all taken their toll. He had been left feeling weak and bad tempered. Shortly before reaching Cape Town a fire had mysteriously broken out in the ship and lifeboats had been ordered to emergency stations; the alarm had proved to be false but the scare had provided a fitting climax to a disastrous passage. 'The voyage has been a pleasant and uneventful one,' Lord Randolph had said when he landed. Later he was to have some scathing remarks to make about the performance of the *Grantully Castle*.

A few days in Cape Town and Rhodes's hospitality seem to have restored him to better health. Harry Currey—who was then Rhodes's private secretary—was to remember Churchill as the most interesting guest to stay at The Grange. Soon it became obvious that he was indeed 'taking in a great deal' and that his information was not uninfluenced by the views of this host. His first public statement from the Cape created quite a stir. It dealt with an explosive situation which directly concerned Cecil Rhodes.

Three days before the *Grantully Castle* docked at Cape Town there had been another clash between the Portuguese and the Chartered Company's force in Mashonaland. The tension that had been building up on the Mashonaland border came to a head on 11 May 1891. A small band of Chartered Company policemen, under the command of a Captain Heyman, had advanced to a fortified outpost, Macequece (or Massi Kessi as the English spelt it), which was just within the Portuguese border. They had been attacked by a Portuguese army contingent. The Chartered Company force, although greatly outnumbered, had repulsed the attack and frightened their enemy into deserting the fort under the cover of night. Heyman, acting on Rhodes's instructions ('Take all you can and ask me afterwards') had then set off towards the coast, where he intended to occupy the port of Beira. Unfortunately for Rhodes, the British authorities decided to intervene and a Major Sapte was despatched to warn off the Chartered Company's men. Rhodes was furious when he heard what had happened. 'Why,' he wired to Heyman, 'didn't you put Sapte in irons and say he was drunk!'

News of the engagement at Macequece was made public in Cape Town shortly before Lord Randolph was due to leave; it was accompanied by details of further violence in Portuguese East Africa. From Delagoa Bay, the capital of the territory, it was reported that a British doctor had been surrounded by a gang of Portuguese soldiers while out riding and had been severely wounded. Another British resident was said to have been attacked in his house and wounded three times before he was rescued by the British Consul. Lord Randolph, as correspondent to the *Daily Graphic*, immediately cabled a report of the incidents to his paper. He did not confine himself to straight reporting. His cable to the *Daily Graphic* was belligerent. He detailed the assaults at Delagoa Bay, upbraided the Portuguese authorities, and concluded by declaring: 'The immediate occupation of the coast by a British naval force seems to be imperative.' This, from a former Chancellor of the Exchequer and Leader of the House of Commons, was strong language.

It took some time for this message to be relayed back to South Africa. By the time it was made public, Lord Randolph had left Cape Town. His visit to the city had been a distinct disappointment. Insisting that his tour was a private one, he had managed to keep newspaper reporters at bay and the only news of him to leak out had been about the telegrams he had sent to the Mayors of Kimberley and Vryburg declining invitations to attend public banquets. 'It is abundantly clear,' observed the *Cape Times*, 'that Lord R. Churchill will maintain a discreet silence during his journey north.'

*

The first shock came the day after his departure. On 28 May the Cape papers published a cable from London: 'Lord Salisbury, speaking in the House of Lords, announced that Lord Randolph Churchill telegraphed from the Cape stating that he considered the occupation of the Mozambique Coast by Great Britain to be imperative.' Even Rhodes's supporters found this demand a little difficult to swallow. Attempts were made to dismiss the report as false. 'The cable message attributed to Lord Randolph was really despatched by Mr Churchill, Consul at Mozambique,' it was said, 'the title and christian name being added by the telegraphic agency.' It was not a very convincing explanation. The embarrassment remained even after it had been established that Lord Randolph had cabled his newspaper and not the British Prime Minister. 'The message,' observed the *Cape Argus*, 'is a testimony to his lordship's fine British spirit, but it is, to say the least, hasty. The occupation of the coast may some day be forced upon Great Britain, but the collision west of Massi Kessi scarcely calls for such a measure.' Concern over the incident was so great in England that young Winston Churchill wrote to his father from Harrow begging him not to try to conquer the Portuguese.

TROUBLE IN THE TRANSVAAL

More genuine alarm was expressed in other parts of South Africa. The *Daily Graphic*'s special correspondent was now headed for the Transvaal, a Boer republic whose relationship with Britain was anything but easy. The Transvaal burgers had good reason for being apprehensive of suggestions that Britain should occupy further African territory. 'There is no knowing what effect this opinion will have upon a great many of the people of England...' declared *De Volksstem*, a leading Transvaal newspaper. 'Truly a Jingo only has to journey over land and sea to announce suddenly that all countries belonging to other nations should be annexed to the British Empire.' This was written from bitter experience. Some fourteen years earlier the Transvaal, then a struggling near-bankrupt country, had itself been annexed to the British Empire. For three years Britain had ruled the Transvaal, ignoring all internal opposition. Finally the Boers had risen and after a series of military encounters, culminating in the defeat of a British force on Majuba Hill in February 1881, they had succeeded in reinstating their republic. The success of the Boers at the battle of Majuba said much for the excellence of their guerrilla tactics. They were never to forget this victory. They tended to exaggerate its significance. Had the British followed up their defeats with a more determined campaign—employing the reinforcements then being directed to South Africa—there can be little doubt that, at that time, they could have crushed the Transvaal rebellion. That Gladstone, the British Prime Minister, had decided to sue for peace was due more to the conciliatory policies of his Liberal Government than to the Boer show of arms. The peace had not been popular in Britain. The Conservative Opposition had severely criticized Gladstone for yielding in what appeared to be humiliating circumstances. Lord Randolph Churchill, then a rising and vocal Opposition member, had played a prominent part in criticizing the conciliation policy. Now this declared enemy of Transvaal independence was about to visit the country. Moreover, he was publicly demanding further annexations. The Transvaalers could hardly be expected to welcome him.

Unbeknown to the Boers, Lord Randolph had already begun to air his views on the Transvaal. While he was in Cape Town he had despatched his first two letters to the *Daily Graphic*. One of these letters detailed his uncomfortable experiences on board the *Grantully Castle* and the other gave his impressions of Cape Town. In the second letter he had broached the problem posed by the Transvaal. He had compared the situation in the Boer republic with that which existed in the Cape Colony.

He had been very taken with the Cape. The Cape Afrikaners (Dutch) had particularly impressed him. He was delighted to find that they harboured no animosity towards Great Britain and lived in 'respect, friendship and mutual trust' with their English-speaking fellow citizens. What is more, he considered that this harmonious state of affairs was largely due to Gladstone's conciliatory policies. To the surprise of friends and enemies alike, he now came out in support of the peace that had followed Majuba. Closer contact with the South African situation had made him revise his opinions. Had Gladstone continued with the war, he said, his Government 'would indeed have regained the Tranvaal, but it might have lost the Cape Colony. The Dutch sentiment in the Colony had been so exasperated by what it considered to be the unjust, faithless and arbitrary policy pursued towards free Dutchmen of the Transvaal . . . that the final triumph of the British arms mainly by brute force would have permanently and hopelessly alienated it from Great Britain.' Thanks to Mr Gladstone's 'magnanimity' this had not happened. On the other hand, he was forced to admit that the South African problem was far from being solved. There was still the Transvaal to be considered. 'The peace thus concluded with the Transvaal,' he went on, 'carried with it some grave disadvantages. The re-erection of the South African Republic contributed another powerful factor in the forces of disunion in South Africa; the Boers of the Transvaal, wanting altogether the common sense of their kinsmen in the colony, have since the war been inflated with an overweening pride, foolishly eager to seek quarrels and sustain disputes with the English power, and will continue, possibly for generations, to be a formidable obstacle to either political or commercial federation in South Africa.'

This had been written while he was staying at The Grange. His views were very much in line with those of Cecil John Rhodes. From the moment that Rhodes had assumed the Premiership of the Cape he had set about working for the unification of the various states in southern Africa. It was all part of his vision. A United States of South Africa was to provide the base for British expansion throughout the continent. He had wooed 'Dutch' opposition in the Cape and attempted to strengthen the economic ties between the British dependencies and the neighbouring Boer republics. The Transvaal had proved to be the greatest hindrance to his schemes. Suspicious of the hated British connection and determined to maintain their hard-won independence, the Transvaal Boers had resisted all Rhodes's overtures. They had obstinately refused to co-operate with the Cape, levied heavy taxes on goods coming from the Colony, discriminated against Cape citizens in civil employment and obstructed attempts at forming a railway juncture between the two countries. Rhodes could not hope to realize his ambitions until he had eliminated this opposition from the Transvaal. Lord Randolph claimed that his views had been formed from 'better and more precise information'. There could be little doubt as to where he had obtained that information.

But, Rhodes or no Rhodes, there was more than a grain of truth in Lord Randolph's arguments. The Transvaal Boers were certainly different from the Cape Afrikaners and the theory that the Transvaal Republic was an encumbrance to South African unity was a popular one: it appealed to British colonists as well as British politicians. An upright, rugged and stubborn people, the Boers were difficult neighbours. As individuals they were kindly and hospitable, but as a nation they were the victims of a fundamentalist religion which made them appear self-righteous, even Pharisaical. The victory at Majuba had indeed gone to their heads: they saw it as a triumph of arms vouchsafed them by the holiness of their cause. The Cape papers were full of stories of Englishmen who had been insulted by sanctimonious burgers crowing over the ineptitude of the British army. These stories were no doubt exaggerated, but were not without foundation. The intolerant attitude of the Boers undoubtedly added weight to the tendentious attacks of their enemies.

And they had no shortage of enemies. The situation outlined by Lord Randolph ignored a pertinent factor in the Transvaal controversy. In the Volksraad at Pretoria, many a Boer orator could justify his country's stand in very different terms. If the Boers were obstructing a South African federation, it was a federation desired more by high-powered finance than by high-minded politics. Had the Transvaal remained the same impoverished country it had been at the time of Majuba, it is doubtful whether Rhodes's demands for unification would have been so urgent or so widely supported. But the situation had changed with a suddenness which was equalled only by its decisiveness. If the Boers now appeared to be grasping and intractable, there was a definite method in their meanness.

In the year 1886, the rumours of the huge gold deposits which were said to lie under the ochre-coloured hills of the Transvaal were confirmed. The discoveries of the gold-bearing rock, coming as they did in startling and rapid succession, galvanized the Republic's British neighbours and reverberated around the world. The once austere and backward little country was suddenly transformed into a nineteenth-century Eldorado. Prospectors of every nationality flocked to it by the thousands. It is said that, in September 1886 alone, some four thousand people came rushing to the Transvaal goldfields. The glorious isolation so dear to Boer hearts was shattered by the odd assortment of carts and wagons that came rumbling over their borders.

President Paul Kruger, watching these revolutionary developments from his homely stoep in Pretoria, regarded the invasion of foreigners—or Uitlanders, as they were called—with characteristic shrewdness. Pleased as he was at this staggering Godsend to his country's economy, he had no intention of allowing the new-found wealth to corrupt his people. For him the Calvinistic doctrine of the elect applied with special significance over the people he ruled. His philosophy was that of the Old Testament: the Boers, like the Israelites, were a chosen people and if they had been sent manna in their wilderness it must be used to further their God-appointed mission. The forces of Mammon must be kept at bay. The Uitlanders were welcome to seek their fortunes in the Transvaal and add to the country's prosperity but they could not be allowed to interfere with the destiny of the Boer nation. To this end he set about hemming in the newcomers with restrictions: he granted them mining rights but safeguarded himself by withholding concessions for transport and vital mining equipment; he burdened them with heavy taxes but allowed them no say in municipal affairs. Having insufficient burgers to handle the concessions, he granted monopolies to outsiders whom he could trust; control of the mining towns was left in the hands of inefficient appointees. In this way he hoped to regulate the life blood of the mining community: but his grip soon became a stranglehold.

In the first headlong stampede for gold, not knowing how long their luck would last, many of the miners had been willing to submit to the impositions placed upon them by the Transvaal Government. However, when it became clear that the first rush had merely scraped the surface of the immense reef and that a stable industry would replace these early scratchings, they began to chafe at the restrictions which hampered them at every turn. They began to agitate for a greater control of their own affairs. They wanted a say in the Government which was supported by their money and labour. Kruger found that his financial godsend had turned into a hydra-headed monster. He found himself on the defensive. 'Wealth cannot break laws,' he had protested. 'Though a man has a million pounds he cannot alter the law... Is it a good man who wants to be master of the country, when others have been suffering for twenty years to conduct its affairs? ... It is the unthankful people to whom I have given protection that are always dissatisfied, and, what is more, they would actually want me to alter my laws to suit them.' This was the side of the Transvaal situation that Lord Randolph had ignored: the Boers could also talk of ingratitude and trouble makers.

The Uitlanders, like Rhodes, had great hopes of Lord Randolph's visit. The predominantly British mining community looked to this well-known English statesman to bring influence to bear on their behalf. If *De Volksstem* in Pretoria regarded Lord Randolph's contentious cable with apprehension, its counterpart in the mining town of Johannesburg, *The Star*, saw it as a promise of better things to come. 'There is nothing very remarkable in the fact that Lord Randolph Churchill should have cabled Lord Salisbury the strong impressions upon the South African situation which he has formed on the spot,' observed the Uitlander newspaper in an editorial headed 'The Beginning of the End'; 'but it is significant that Lord Salisbury should, at this juncture, have published the fact to the world. His doing so can only mean that he is resolved on vigorous action... What will now, in all possibility, happen should serve as an object lesson for the irresponsible politicians nearer home . . .' Fighting talk was contagious.

*

Having left the lush Cape by the Kimberley mail train, Lord Randolph spent his first night up-country at the little village of Matjesfontein. He was accompanied by his aide-de-camp, Captain Williams, and his shipboard companion, Sir Charles Metcalfe. Matjesfontein was a curious settlement. Situated at the edge of the vast, arid, scrub-covered Karoo, it had been established by an enterprising Scotsman and consisted of a single British-suburban-like street, complete with a row of ornamental lamp-posts. Lord Randolph considered it an excellent example of British initiative. Remembering his promise to his constituents (one of whom he discovered was driving his train) he recommended the forbidding countryside to young English farmers 'with a good training, an active disposition, and a small capital' as a likely spot in which to seek a home and fortune.

Kimberley, which was reached after a gruelling twenty-four-hour train journey across the empty lunar landscape of the heat-hazed Karoo, proved a disappointment. The straggling corrugated-iron and wood houses, which had sprung up haphazardly as a result of the diamond 'rushes' some twenty years earlier, struck Churchill as unworthy of the mining town's wealth and fame. The renowned Diamond City had, he admitted, a number of excellent shops, a comfortable club and an admirable racecourse, but was entirely lacking in 'municipal magnificence'.

That Lord Randolph should have formed this unfavourable impression was not the fault of Kimberley's leading citizens. For weeks the town had been looking forward to his visit. Plans to entertain him had been the subject of much public discussion. Unfortunately most of these plans had had to be abandoned after Churchill's firm refusal to be fêted. However, this had not prevented his being met at the station by a delegation of local worthies and welcomed by an effusive speech by the Mayor. Also at the station to meet him was Alfred Beit. As a director of De Beers, the all-powerful, Rhodes-inspired diamond organization, Beit had travelled ahead of Lord Randolph in order to prepare his reception and act as his host. From now on Alfred Beit, one of Rhodes's closest friends, was to be an inconspicuous but watchful figure in the background of Churchill's well-publicized tour.

'At Kimberley,' wrote Lord Randolph, 'the diamond is everything.' It was an observation made from tedious experience. Apart from a day's organized hunting in the veld he saw little of the town other than the diamond industry. He was taken on tours of the De Beers sorting sheds, conducted through the mine compounds, bombarded with statistics and photographed at the bottom of a 900-ft.-deep mine shaft. He found it extremely boring. The letters he wrote from Kimberley were, on the whole, painfully dull. Most of his information was taken from a recent report of the General Manager of De Beers and was of little interest to the readers of the *Daily Graphic*. Only when dealing with the trade in illicit diamond buying did he manage to work up a little enthusiasm. The precautions taken to prevent African workers from stealing diamonds fascinated him. 'On returning from their day's work,' he wrote, 'they have to strip off all their clothes, which they hang on pegs in a shed. Stark naked, they then proceed to the searching room, where their mouths, their hair, their toes, their armpits, and every portion of their body are subjected to an elaborate examination. White men would never submit to such a process, but the native sustains the indignity with cheerful equanimity, considering only the high wages which he earns . . . During the evening, the clothes they have left behind them are carefully and minutely searched, and are restored to their owners in the morning. The precautions which are taken a few days before the natives leave the compound, their engagements being terminated, to recover diamonds which they may have swallowed, are more easily imagined than described.'

No less remarkable was the rigorous law which applied to diamond smugglers. Under a special statute passed by the Cape Parliament, a person accused of illicit diamond trading was obliged to prove his innocence, instead of his accuser having to prove his guilt. A person found in possession of an undeclared diamond was liable to fifteen years' penal servitude. 'It must be admitted,' wrote Lord Randolph, 'that this tremendous law is in thorough conformity with South African sentiment, which elevates [illicit diamond buying] almost to the level, if not above the level, of actual homicide.'

Everyone visiting Kimberley came away with a story which illustrated the lengths to which men would go to smuggle diamonds out of the town. Churchill had his. He was told of a notorious diamond thief who was seized by the police when he was leaving Kimberley for the Transvaal. A thorough search of the man revealed nothing and he was allowed to go on his way. A detective, still suspicious, followed him until he had crossed the Transvaal border where he immediately shot his horse and extracted a large parcel of diamonds from the animal's intestines. There was nothing the detective could do. Once across the border thieves were no longer subject to Cape law. It was another irritation of an independent Transvaal.

Interesting though they were, these were the sort of details that were familar fare from South African travellers. Not until he came to make his final remarks on Kimberley did Lord Randolph show any originality. Summing up his views on the diamond industry, he found little to say in its favour. Unlike the mining of gold, coal, tin, copper and lead, the unearthing of diamonds, in his opinion, brought no real benefit to mankind. 'At the De Beers mine,' he said, 'all the wonderful arrangements I have described are put in force in order to extract from the depths of the ground, solely for the wealthy classes, a tiny crystal to be used for the gratification of female vanity in imitation of a lust for personal adornment essentially barbaric if not altogether savage. Some mitigation of cynical criticism might be urged if the diamonds only adorned the beautiful, the virtuous and the young, but this, unhappily, is far from being the case, and a review of the South African diamond mines brings me coldly to the conclusion that, whatever may be the origin of man, woman is descended from an ape.'

This rather weak attempt at humour was to bring a storm about his head when it was published. With all the solemnity that Victorians could bring to a flippancy, outraged editors of quite serious journals denounced Churchill as an unutterable cad. Indignant letters poured into the offices of the *Daily Graphic.* 'It is,' fumed one angry correspondent, 'an unmitigated insult to woman and her Creator.' In the *Spectator* and the *Speaker* Lord Randolph's views were unfavourably compared with those of Darwin. His more determined opponents rejoiced over the effect it would have on his political standing. 'Lord Randolph

Churchill has "done for himself" this time,' crowed the *St James's Gazette*. 'His popularity with men of sense has long been inconsiderable; his popularity with the other sex has been utterly and hopelessly extinguished by the alleged libel which he has committed upon it in his latest letter from South Africa... We tremble for Lord Randolph's future more than we ever trembled for it before, and that is saying a good deal.' Even his friends found it difficult to defend him. They argued that a man with such a beautiful wife could not possibly hold such jaundiced views. 'It will probably be found to be the drunken freak of some Kimberley misogynist who has had access to his lordship's correspondence,' it was said. Churchill, astonished at the seriousness with which his 'lightly turned off' speculation was treated, eventually agreed to withdraw the final offending sentence.

It took Lord Randolph's party five days to travel the 450 miles between Kimberley and Johannesburg, passing, as he said, 'from the region of diamonds into the region of gold'. It also meant passing from the Cape into the Transvaal. This no doubt accounted for the asperity with which Churchill now viewed his surroundings. Once he had left the British territory his comments upon the South African scene became decidedly more critical.

The slowness of the journey was due largely to a change of transport. The railway line extended only to Vryburg in British Bechuanaland. There travellers were obliged to exchange their comfortable railway carriage for cumbersome horse-drawn coaches. It was not an encouraging introduction to the Boer Republic. Jolting along the deeply rutted tracks which passed for roads in the Transvaal—'shaken up inside like an omelet in a frying pan'—fording rocky river beds, with the coach heeling over at a perilous angle, and travelling at an average speed of six miles an hour, proved a nerve-racking experience for the urbane Lord Randolph. He was amazed that both he and the coaches completed the journey in one piece. However, it was the unpleasantness of the overnight stops that he found most exasperating. 'The hotel accommodation in the Transvaal,' he grumbled, 'is of the roughest description, the Dutch scarcely appreciating either cleanliness or comfort.' On being offered a menu at one hotel, which listed no fewer than thirty different courses, he was unable to find that a dish was edible. He ended his meal longing for 'a quarter of an hour at the Amphytrion'. At another hotel he denounced the proprietor as rapacious and insolent and complained that the guests were 'tormented by excessive dirt and discomfort'.

Trivial and biased as much of his carping was, it did not pass unremarked. Everything he said and did was a matter for public comment and that comment was now becoming more and more hostile. As his coach lumbered its way across the tawny, rock-studded highveld it left behind it a trail of affronted citizens who lost no time in blazoning their grievances abroad. The Boers soon felt that the suspicion with which they had anticipated Lord Randolph Churchill's visit was fully justified.

*

His entry into Johannesburg resembled a royal progress. His earlier pleas for privacy were not taken seriously. All work in the town appears to have stopped early in the afternoon and by the time he arrived the main streets were crowded with Uitlanders. There was nothing accidental about this welcome. The people of Johannesburg were determined to bring their plight to his notice. Great things were expected of Lord Randolph. In an editorial that morning *The Star* had prepared the ground for its readers. 'Lord Randolph Churchill, whose arrival is expected today,' it had explained, 'is the first English politician of Cabinet rank who has penetrated so far into the recesses of the Transvaal . . . Lord Randolph Churchill is something more than an average politician, something very much more than an average nobleman. His personality is no common force, which has exerted not a little influence in England, and will certainly not fail to be appreciated in this part of South Africa. . . . Lord Randolph has much to learn from us. In the Transvaal he will find himself confronted with political conditions which can hardly fail to strike him with amazement . . . He will see a community, industrious, intelligent and enterprising, wholly excluded from those political functions which Englishmen have been conspicuously disposed in all ages to regard as an inalienable birthright. He will see a Republic to which the principles usually associated with corrupt oligarchies are applied. He will observe an over-taxed class which is unrepresented, and a relatively untaxed class which is dominant.' None of this was new to readers of *The Star;* nor, for that matter, could the editor have thought that Lord Randolph needed his promptings. However, it did provide Johannesburgers with an excuse for a demonstration and they were only too ready to make the most of it.

Churchill's reception started a few miles outside the town. At Klip River he was met by a group of mining magnates. After brief introductions, the party was arranged in three carriages and proceeded at a leisurely pace to Johannesburg. In the first carriage, Lord Randolph and Alfred Beit were accompanied by Hermann Eckstein, the son of a Lutheran pastor, who was Beit's representative on the Witwatersrand; Sir Charles Metcalfe and Captain Williams followed in a carriage with Lionel Phillips, a leading figure in the Beit-Eckstein organization; while Lord Randolph's mining expert, Henry Perkins, was entertained in the third carriage by Eckstein's younger brother, Friedrich. *The Star's* lecture on the Transvaal situation seemed superfluous indeed.

On entering the town the calvalcade proceeded through the main streets to loud cheering which was particularly vociferous as they drove 'past the Stock Exchange'. Much to everyone's disappointment Churchill refused to allow his carriage to stop until it reached the house in which he and his party were to stay. The newspapers referred to this house as 'the residence of Mr Goldman, facing the Wanderer's Pavilion'. In fact, it was the home of Lionel Phillips, Alfred Beit's chief lieutenant. Not everybody was fooled. 'Lord Randolph is the guest of the Eckstein gentlemen,' observed *De Volksstem* in Pretoria.

The influence of the mining magnates was to become more apparent during Churchill's short stay in Johannesburg. Once again, apart from a few days' hunting in the veld, his time was mainly taken up with visits to various mines. His host, Lionel Phillips, accompanied him on his tours of inspection and there were long financial discussions between Churchill and the leaders of the mining community. It was noticed that his attitude towards the Uitlanders' newspaper was in marked contrast to his usual dealings with the press. 'It was only when his lordship met someone on *The Star* newspaper,' wrote a jealous journalist, 'that he really talked with ease and *abandon* which is only possible where there exists complete oneness of idea, congeniality of soul and intellectual sympathy.'

A legend later grew up that during his Johannesburg visit Lord Randolph discussed the possibility of a position being found on the Witwatersrand for his son Winston. But as he had just learned that Winston stood a good chance of entering Sandhurst this seems highly unlikely. He did, however, write to Winston from Johannesburg telling him that he was making investments for the family's future and this seems to have been the main point of his talks with the mining magnates. The result was that the Uitlanders acquired a confirmed, if somewhat unpredictable, champion.

The first *Daily Graphic* letter which Lord Randolph sent from the Transvaal reads like a paraphrase of *The Star*'s leading articles. He considered Johannesburg to be a bustling progressive city, rather like an English manufacturing town without the noise, smoke and dirt. The inhabitants were an active, keen and intelligent-looking community, hamstrung only by the perversity of the Boer Government. The streets were unpaved and unlit by night, stalked by housebreakers and thieves. The police provided by the Government were few and inefficient; they could not begin to cope with the rising crime rate. Public sanitation was poor and transport to and from the town extremely precarious. For all this, and despite the high taxes paid by the mining community, control of municipal matters was confined to 'Dutch-speaking citizens'—few of whom contributed to the town's welfare. 'It is not to be supposed,' he said ominously, 'that the inhabitants of Johannesburg will long tolerate their absolute servitude in municipal matters.'

Socially his stay in Johannesburg was a disaster. Everywhere he went he was followed by large, gaping crowds. He made no effort to conceal his annoyance at the way he was being pestered both in public and in private. His tactlessness became a by-word, even among the loyal English community. Stories about his rudeness were legion. 'His Lordship was asked out to dinner and went,' ran a popular example, 'but finding his humour that way inclined, was silent and preoccupied. Next morning his host of the night before ran against him in the street, when there ensued the following conversation:

Host: How d'ye do, Lord Randolph.
Lord R: Ah! Good morning. Let me see, have I met you before?
Host: We—er—I er—you—er
Lord R. Oh yes, of course! We met at that old buffer's house last night. Pleasant day, isn't it? Goodbye.'

Johannesburg's socially conscious *nouveaux riches* were distinctly disappointed. He was dismissed as an irritable, snobbish middle-aged man whose blasé attitude warranted all the abuse that was being showered upon him.

He did, however, agree to become the honorary president of the Johannesburg Chess Club, and many years later Lionel Phillips was to recall his visit with warmth. According to Phillips, Lord Randolph was one of the most attractive companions he had ever met. He looked back fondly to their long talks which often lasted until the early hours of the morning. 'Poor man!' he says, 'I think his health was already failing, and this may have accentuated his intolerant attitude towards people at large, but particularly towards that section he deemed of no use to him.'

For all its drawbacks, the Transvaal did help to improve his health. At the end of his stay in Johannesburg a hunting expedition was organized for him on the estate of Sammy Marks, a well-known Transvaal entrepreneur. Marks allowed the Churchill party four days' unrestricted shooting on his huge game reserve and, to Lord Randolph's delight, provided an excellent French chef to supervise the cooking of their daily bag. Camping in the veld, stimulated by the sparkling atmosphere of a Transvaal winter and revelling in the excitements of the chase, Churchill appears to have recovered much of his lost energy.

But Sammy Marks's estate was an isolated Eden. Even away from the towns Lord Randolph was unable to restrain his criticism of the Boers. He claimed that by their indiscriminate destruction of wild life they had denuded the veld of buck and left the sportsman little to pursue beyond feathered game. How different things would have been if 'God had only given a glimmer of intelligence to the Boer'. This did not prevent him from listing two springbok, as well as four duck, fifty partridge, four hares, two hundred and fifty quail, eight koran, eleven snipe, one dikkop, one wild turkey and one blue crane, among his party's meaningless slaughter.

He left Johannesburg reflecting on the opportunities offered by the gold mining industry to enterprising Englishmen. Young men arriving in the Transvaal with hardly a penny were making fortunes, he claimed. Everyone was needed: miners, artisans, clerks, accountants, even domestic servants. He emphasized the necessity for immediate emigration, pointing out that: 'It can hardly be a matter for doubt that the goldfields of Johannesburg are destined to attract and support a population which will ultimately dominate and rule the Transvaal.' If this was meant as an enticement for his Paddington constituents, it was a thought which must have appealed to his new South African friends. The arguments of Cecil Rhodes and the mining magnates had undoubtedly been persuasive.

*

Travelling the thirty-five miles from Johannesburg to Pretoria, Churchill was mainly concerned with the dreadful road. That such a busy, important highway was so badly maintained provided him with further evidence against the Transvaal Government. But the Boer capital itself he found extremely pleasing. Lying in a hollow, its cottages set well back from the road in flower-filled gardens, Pretoria had a relaxed, complacent atmosphere which was refreshing after the bustle and brashness of the mining city. Like most visitors he was impressed not only by Pretoria's tranquillity but by its simple dignity.

By leaving Johannesburg he had by no means freed himself of the attentions of the mining community. One of his first visitors at the Transvaal Hotel, where his party was staying, was J. B. Taylor, an associate of Beit and Eckstein. Taylor undertook to act as Lord Randolph's escort in the Boer capital. They were soon joined by friends from Johannesburg. On the afternoon following his arrival, Churchill and Taylor went to Irene, just outside Pretoria, where they spent the night in conference with Alfred Beit and Hermann Eckstein. It was Taylor and Beit also who employed a new transport officer for the expedition: a young, red-headed South African of Irish descent named Percy Fitzpatrick.

Lord Randolph had travelled from the Cape to Pretoria

without his main supply wagons: these, in the charge of Major Giles and Surgeon Rayner, were proceeding to Mashonaland by a separate route and were to meet him at Fort Tuli. In the meantime he needed assistance to complete his journey through the northern Transvaal. Taylor and Beit produced Percy Fitzpatrick. Then an unsuccessful speculator in the Eastern Transvaal, Fitzpatrick was later to distinguish himself as a South African politician and as the author of the children's classic, *Jock of the Bushveld*. He was in his late twenties, had had a good deal of experience as a transport rider and was more than capable of acting on his own initiative. What was perhaps of greater importance, he possessed a robust sense of humour. This was to prove very necessary. The situation with which he was faced when he arrived in Pretoria was beyond anything he had previously experienced. Lord Randolph's travelling arrangements had, in fact, become a standing joke throughout South Africa. Only a confirmed optimist would have undertaken to supervise his cumbersome progress.

Some weeks earlier Major Giles had sent one of his periodic reports to the *Daily Graphic*. In it he had detailed the difficulties he had experienced on reaching the Cape. 'From all sorts and kinds of people came applications to go with us,' he wrote, '—city clerks who had been three months in the colony, broken-down ex-members of the various colonial corps, gentlemen— excellent fellows too—who had come out to visit the new Eldorado, and who had no idea how to compass the 1,300 miles that still lay between them—dealers in horses (for the most part worthless) for which exorbitant prices were asked, and which you were told were "salted", namely, had been through the terrible horse sickness. . .' Having warded off the place-seekers, Giles had set about assembling the equipment that had been sent from England. As crate after crate was unpacked, so the amazement of experienced veld travellers increased. Not only were there the tents, cooking utensils, camp furniture and bedding supplied by Messrs Silvers of London, but other English firms had provided boxes of fruit, ham, tea and coffee, pressed vegetables and tinned meats—all of which could easily have been obtained in South Africa at half the price. Major Giles, ignoring his critics, gamely assured readers of the *Daily Graphic* that he was prepared for any eventuality. Every detail had been planned, he said, 'so that nothing should be found wanting when we were 500 to 1,000 miles from comparative civilization'. His assurance does not appear to have convinced his employer. As Lord Randolph made his own way northwards he was plagued with misgivings. In almost every South African town through which he passed he felt impelled to restock.

'The wonderful thing was that they could never buy enough,' wrote Fitzpatrick. 'If a bottle of beer was wanted—they secured a case. If they fancied chipped potatoes they bought a bag! Weight was nothing. Bulk was a joke! . . . they put in some supplementaries at Cape Town, and some "after-thoughts" at Kimberley, and etceteras at Johannesburg, and extras at Pretoria, and replenishments at Pietersburg, till they looked like a commissariat of a continental army. A forty-gallon Kaffir pot took their fancy—a thing you could boil pigs in—"Capital notion! Hot baths night and morning!" They bought it. There seemed to be no security as long as there was a store in the country.'

In addition to assisting with Lord Randolph's over-loaded wagons, Fitzpatrick had to organize Alfred Beit, who was trekking to Mashonaland at the same time. Ostensibly the Churchill and Beit expeditions were separate concerns; in fact, they were never far removed from each other.

Before leaving Pretoria, Lord Randolph had a brief meeting with President Kruger. On a visit to the Volksraad he was introduced to the President during an adjournment of a debate. He was surprisingly impressed by the grave-faced, pipe-puffing old man whose manner he found 'extremely gracious and genial'. But this did not alter his opinion of the Boer administration. Everywhere he looked he seemed to find fresh evidence of its smug and inefficient workings. What he could not discover for himself was readily pointed out by his Transvaal friends. His reports from Pretoria were full of second-hand stories of Boer incompetence; stories which he rarely bothered to check and which, in some cases, were to be heatedly refuted.

For instance, in giving an illustration of the Boers' inhumanity towards the Africans of the Transvaal, he quoted at great length from a newspaper report of a glaring miscarriage of justice. A local Boer official in the district of Rustenburg had been accused of beating an African prisoner to death after prolonged torture.

TROUBLE IN THE TRANSVAAL

When the official was first arrested the magistrate had refused to admit him to bail. A delegation of local Boers had then gathered outside the court-house and assumed such a menacing attitude that the magistrate was forced to withdraw his refusal. At the subsequent trial the jury—which consisted largely of members of the same church as the accused—had found the man not guilty, despite a mass of evidence to the contrary. The pro-Boer paper reporting the case had said that the verdict was a popular one as the accused was 'a man who understands how to deal with a Kaffir.' 'Such,' exclaimed Lord Randolph, 'is Boer justice.' Unfortunately for Churchill, when his comments were published, the Transvaal Government was able to issue an effective denial. It was pointed out that the trial had taken place weeks before Lord Randolph had arrived in the Transvaal and that a State investigation into the case had been proceeding for some time. While this did not exculpate the original offenders, it did take some of the sting out of the taunt of 'Boer injustice'.

It was not only the Transvaal Government that Churchill vilified: everything and anything to do with the Boers he treated with contempt. Stories of his churlishness grew with every mile he travelled. Shortly after leaving Pretoria a report appeared in *De Volksstem* detailing his renewed offensive against the hoteliers of the Transvaal. His wagons had arrived at Nylstroom, a small town in the northern Transvaal, at eleven o'clock one morning and halted outside the local hotel. 'In a flash,' said *De Volksstem*'s report, 'the hotelkeeper was ready to offer the gentlemen his fatted calf: fried chicken and ducks were waiting to tempt the gentlemen to the table. Imagine the host's surprise when the said gentlemen carried several large cases into the dining room, lit a paraffin stove, requested the hotelkeeper to remove his "little dinner" and to supply a leg of mutton, and then, like regular cooks, began to grill meat and prepare their own meal. After standing admiringly round the stove until the meal was cooked, they partook of a little here and there. Then they repacked their boxes, inspanned the coach, and departed, having rather grudgingly paid the hotelkeeper for the rooms they had booked as well as the dinner.' Churchill's own version of the incident was somewhat different. The hotelkeeper, he said, was a 'rascally fellow' who first informed them that they would have to wait two hours for their meal and then charged them £2 10s. for an hour's use of the 'common dining-room'. Naturally the Boers preferred to believe their own newspaper.

However, there can be no doubt about Lord Randolph's hostile attitude. Even his Uitlander friends became concerned about it. They appear to have done their best to get him to differentiate between Boer politicians and the simple country folk he met on his travels, but it was to no avail. According to Fitzpatrick the one visit he paid to a local farm was disastrous. Churchill had expressed a wish to see a typical Boer homestead and preparations were immediately made for him to inspect a near-by farm. The farmer was away but his wife, having been suitably primed, came out to welcome the English Lord. The English Lord was unimpressed. No sooner had his carriage drawn up at the farm and he had taken one look at the starched and smiling *vrouw* than he thumped his driver on the back and ordered him to drive away. 'Ugh! go on, get away! drive off,' he shouted. 'Awful people! drive on! get along! I won't stay here.'

This was at Pietersburg, halfway between Pretoria and the Mashonaland border. By this time his every prejudice had been confirmed. He could not get out of the country quickly enough. 'I rejoice,' he wrote, 'after all I have seen in the Transvaal, that the country of the Matabele and the Mashona have been rescued in the nick of time, owing to the genius of Mr Rhodes and the tardy vigour of the British Government, from the withering and mortal grasp of the Boer.'

CHAPTER THREE

Looking for Gold

MASHONALAND, the country towards which Lord Randolph was heading, was a land of legends. From the time the first European—a Portuguese convict attempting to earn his pardon—had been sent into the recesses of this central African territory at the beginning of the sixteenth century, and had returned with reports of huge gold deposits, rumours of its mineral wealth had been as persistent as they were fabulous. It was said to be the Land of Ophir, the Kingdom of Prester John, the source of the Queen of Sheba's riches and the location of King Solomon's mines. The rumours had continued to circulate despite the failure of the Portuguese to unearth any significant treasure. In the second half of the nineteenth century they had become more pertinent. With the discovery of diamonds in the north Cape, and of gold in the Transvaal, the mineral potential of central Africa seemed to be more than a romantic possibility. Optimistic prospectors began to explore the region. Their findings, if not conclusive, were far from discouraging. What *was* discouraging were the restrictions imposed by the rulers of the country. For, at that time, the entire area was under the sway of the Matabele, one of the most fearsome black tribes in Africa.

In the 1830s Mzilikazi, founder of the Matabele nation, had led his people to the high fertile plains beyond the Limpopo river. The Matabele were of Zulu origin; Mzilikazi had once been a high-ranking warrior in the army of Shaka, the famous Zulu king. Expelled from Zululand after a rebellious clash with Shaka, Mzilikazi and his followers had marched northwards. The name Mzilikazi means *The Path of Blood* and this is an apt description of his progress from Zululand. Aggressive, ruthless and dedicated to the arts of war, the Matabele had subjugated every Bantu tribe they had encountered. They had left a desolate trail of bloodshed and plunder in their wake. But in the Transvaal they had met their match. Pitted against the skilful guerrilla tactics of the early Boer trekkers they had themselves been defeated. They were forced to abandon their kraals and flee the Transvaal. Once across the Limpopo they had little trouble in reasserting their military might. They had quickly vanquished the enfeebled tribes inhabiting the region; as vassals of the Matabele, these tribes were to become known as the Mashona—the lost ones. However, the collision with the Transvaal Boers had taught Mzilikazi a lesson. He was wary of the white man. Fortune hunters seeking to mine the Matabele king's country found themselves regarded with suspicion and their activities were frustratingly circumscribed. It was not the mineral wealth that Mzilikazi was guarding, but his right to the land he had conquered. As far as the concession hunters were concerned it amounted to the same thing: they became more persistent in their demands.

Mzilikazi was dead when Cecil Rhodes's agents joined the petitioners at the royal Matabele kraal. In his stead ruled one of his sons, Lobengula, an astute and able politician. His astuteness served him well, but not well enough; when it came to dealing with Rhodes he had been outwitted. By a subtle admixture of bribery and pressure, Rhodes's men had succeeded in obtaining a concession which forced their rivals from the field. After signing an agreement, which he imagined would allow a small body of men to mine his vassal state, Lobengula had been confronted with an army of white settlers moving into Mashonaland. He had regarded the invasion with apprehension; his young warriors had grown restive. The Pioneer Column of 1890 had avoided Matabeleland and, on the march into adjacent Mashonaland, they had kept a searchlight blazing at night to frighten off the half-expected attack.

A year later the Chartered Company was still concerned with the need to placate the Matabele monarch. Lord Randolph Churchill was fully aware of this. Somewhere in his bulging wagons was a peace offering which he intended to send to Lobengula: a scarlet and gold bath chair, said to be, 'capacious enough to hold the great King stretched at half length in full ease', and surmounted by a fixed umbrella. Lobengula, fat and gout-ridden, was to treasure this wheelchair. So much so that when, in 1893, the Chartered Company moved against him, his flight from his kraal was seriously impeded by his refusal to be parted from it. But at the time it was presented, Churchill's gift was regarded as an amusing sop to the formidable old king.

Churchill's party splashed across the Limpopo at Rhodes's Drift on 11 July. Lord Randolph was delighted to be met by a contingent of the Bechuanaland Border Police and to see the British flag again. 'To feel that at last one was well out of Boerland,' he says, 'was truly pleasant and refreshing.' In fact, his last few days in the Transvaal had given him little cause for complaint. Travelling from Pietersburg in a light four-wheeled 'spider' he had managed to get in a good deal of shooting and, once he had left the hotels behind, he thoroughly enjoyed the outdoor life. The last evening had been spent in camp some 400 yards from the Limpopo. Here he had strolled along the river bank and had come upon a scene which held him enraptured. It appeared to him as an indescribable combination of the tropics, Windsor forest and a fine reach of the Tay or Tweed. 'The setting sun threw on this enchanting spot a light of inconceivable loveliness,' he wrote. 'It was absolutely fairyland, but the fairies were a a few ugly naked Kaffirs.' The only trouble, of course, was that this little paradise was in the hands of the Boers; he felt that had it been located in Europe it would have become a holiday resort for thousands. The Boers had no appreciation of such things. Sadly reflecting on this waste, he had returned to camp and a 'wonderful dinner' of baked partridges, fried partridge liver, minced kudu, vegetables and hot stewed prunes. Life in the Transvaal had its compensations.

But now the frustrations of the Boer republic were well and truly behind him. Once across the river and surrounded by Bechuanaland policemen—looking trim in their buff corduroy, cocked slouch hats and high black boots—the prospects looked altogether more hopeful. At the near-by encampment he received further reassurance. The commanding officer, Major Goold-Adams, was able to give him details of how his men had recently turned back a party of Boers who had tried to invade the Chartered Company lands. Lord Randolph was able to report to the *Daily Graphic* that a 'great calamity' had been averted.

The following day he arrived at Fort Tuli. If, at first sight, this isolated outpost looked unimpressive, the men stationed there gave the place a definite tone. They were a mixture of the Bechuanaland and Chartered Company's police forces; all men, Churchill was delighted to note, of 'good education, and in many cases of good family'. To illustrate their undoubted quality he was able to tell the story of one trooper who turned to another and remarked: 'I say, Bill, I don't think much of this new fellow. I don't remember having met him in White's or Boodle's.' The Transvaal must have seemed a million miles away.

At Tuli Churchill found Major Giles and Surgeon Rayner waiting for him with the supply wagons. When assembled, the entire expedition was an impressive sight. Besides the members who had travelled from England, there was now the Hon. Charles Coventry, on leave from the Bechuanaland Police, Hans Lee, a well-known big game hunter, three white servants—including Thomas Walden, Lord Randolph's devoted personal servant—two 'Cape boys', four grooms, two cooks (each with an assistant) two herd boys and fourteen transport drivers. They were to travel in an odd assortment of vehicles which included Lord Randolph's spider, a large mule wagon, four half-tented wagons, an uncovered wagon, a Scotch cart and a two-wheeled ox-wagon. Leading and trailing this caravan was to be an equally impressive collection of livestock: 103 oxen, 19 horses, 18 mules, 14 donkeys and 11 mongrel dogs. It is hardly surprising that hardened travellers, accustomed to arriving at Tuli with little more than a horse and the clothes they stood up in, found these elaborate preparations for a few weeks in the veld a source of endless wonder and amusement.

Not so Lord Randolph. He was both pleased and proud of the efficient foresight shown by his transport officers. In his *Daily Graphic* letter from Tuli he gave a detailed account of his travelling arrangements for the benefit of 'those at home who may be contemplating or may undertake a similar journey'. He also made a point of warning would-be travellers against merchants in London and South Africa who, if left to themselves, would not scruple at palming their customers off with shoddy, badly assembled equipment. The mountains of crates which filled his wagons were full, he said, of second-rate and incomplete apparatus, badly damaged owing to careless packing. As many of the merchants had been previously named, or were well known, this letter did nothing to increase Churchill's popularity.

A little more relevant was the advice he offered as a guard against the dreaded horse-sickness. This disease was the cause of great anxiety among African travellers; even 'salted' horses were not entirely immune from a second attack. Churchill's remedy—a mixture of common sense and 'elementary sanitary science'—was based on the experience of his assistants. A reliable groom should be employed, he said; the animal should be kept clear of river water which might be tainted, its nostrils should be tarred inside three times a week and a weekly dose of two wine-glasses of gin and enough quinine to cover a shilling administered. Like everything he wrote, this suggested treatment was to become the subject of much controversy.

Lord Randolph was delayed at Tuli waiting for various items of luggage to catch up with him. Already the rutted tracks and boulder-strewn river beds had proved too much for his overloaded wagons. Percy Fitzpatrick, who was bringing up the rear with Alfred Beit's expedition, was witness to the desperate attempts made to lighten Lord Randolph's load. 'The first day of trekking,' he says, 'they bore it patiently only wondering what was wrong. Next day off went the "piano" case in the morning trek—followed quickly by the "reserved stores" in the afternoon. Then went two portmanteaux, a box of cooking utensils and some sundries. Then—awful wrench—the paraffin stove went overboard, and the day after the case of paraffin. Day by day as we went along we overtook transport waggons, with something belonging to "de Lord" as the Dutchmen call him.' Even so, nothing was to be abandoned. Now that extra transport was available, messengers were despatched to pick up the off-loaded goods. Fitzpatrick stayed at Tuli for four days and, he says, 'they were still waiting to recover jettisoned cargo for two days after we left'.

Shortly before the Churchill party departed a camp concert was arranged. A huge bonfire was lit, a piano was hoisted on to one of the wagons and an oddly assorted company—ranging from spruce policemen to Africans in blankets—gathered round to sing songs and applaud heroic recitations. The highlight of the evening was a speech from Lord Randolph. Silhouetted against the fire, dressed in a black Inverness cape, he was, it is said, 'a striking and rather picturesque figure'. Unfortunately, except to those close to him, he was inaudible. But his thoughts were attuned to the drama of the occasion. 'Here,' he was to recall, 'some thousands of miles away from England, in a country inhabited by a numerous tribe of savages of noted ferocity, not a hundred miles from the kraal of the great Lobengula, was a tiny group of men holding their own, maintaining their authority partly by their own reputation, partly because they represent the might and the prestige of the Empire; never dreaming for a moment that a shadow of danger could approach them, never doubting their ability to dissipate any danger should it arise.'

A few days later he set off for the interior. Now, as he said, the hard travelling was to begin.

*

By disappearing into Mashonaland when he did, Lord Randolph escaped the full blast of the storm gathering in his wake. It had taken some weeks for his controversial letters to reach England and a little longer for reports of them to be relayed back to South Africa. Disapproving murmurs had reached him by cable while he was in Johannesburg, but it was not until he had left the Transvaal that full accounts of the outcry he had produced appeared in the South African papers.

The trouble had started with the publication of his first letter. This, like all his letters, was published in two instalments: the first part dealing with his voyage as far as Madeira, the second covering the rest of the voyage to the Cape. As a shipboard log, it was remarkable only for the incessant complaints about the *Grantully Castle*'s catering arrangements. The meals served, he said, were 'unworthy of any description'; a little later he disdained 'to notice the infamous productions of the galley'; and when describing the day-to-day life on board ship, he remarked: 'At half-past six the bell for dinner sounds (for the third time I think of the cook only to curse him). After this ungrateful meal...' And so it goes on. Every mention of food is accompanied by a derogatory remark. These remarks were to be returned in full. For the host of journalists waiting to criticize the *Daily Graphic*'s highly paid, amateur correspondent, such petty complaints were heaven-sent. The controversy which resulted was out of all proportion. There was hardly a newspaper in England which did not find space to comment on Lord Randolph's indigestion. 'Those who have had occasion to travel to or from the Cape,' ran a typical example, 'know how excellent is the *cuisine* on board the Castle Company's steamers. . . . Perhaps the stomachs of "men of high degree" are more tender than others, but it was surely ungraceful for Lord Randolph, considering the special attention paid to his wants by the Castle Company, to complain of their *menu*.' This charge of ingratitude gave substance to what otherwise might have been dismissed as an exaggerated newspaper squabble. Even the more serious journals found it necessary to take Churchill to task for his lack of common courtesy. 'Sir Donald Currie,' said the *Speaker*, 'having put the *Grantully Castle* on the berth out of her turn so as to afford him the best possible chance to be comfortable, Lord Randolph might fitly have considered himself under the restraints incumbent on a guest in criticizing the arrangements of the vessel.' It added: 'For ourselves, we are sorry that Lord Randolph should have taken this opportunity of laying bare the seamy side of his character—due, we believe, almost entirely to physical depression and ill-health.' Such excuses did not curb other critics. Letters to the newspapers kept the controversy alive for weeks. On the next voyage of the *Grantully Castle* a deputation, headed by two M.Ps., subscribed to a testimonial addressed to Mr W. Sullivan, the Chief Cook. 'We the undersigned first saloon passengers,' it read, 'have much pleasure in asking you to accept this assurance of our entire satisfaction at the admirable manner in which our wants have been anticipated by your excellent cuisine. . .' It was signed by forty-two passengers.

The gastronomical battle was raging when Lord Randolph's second letter appeared. To the ranks of the Castle Company's defenders was added a veritable army of indignant Tories. The cause was twofold. While in Cape Town Churchill had seized the opportunity of hitting at his old enemies at the War Office. He had inspected the defences at the Cape and assured his readers that much public money was being wasted by the Conservative Government in sending obsolete guns to South Africa. This was immediately questioned in Parliament by Henry Labouchere, the Radical M.P., and flatly denied by the War Secretary, Mr Stanhope. Churchill stuck to his statement and made himself popular with the Liberal Opposition. Even more infuriating to the Tories was his defence of Gladstone's Majuba policy. 'Lord Randolph has deeply wounded the Tories by confessing that the so-called Majuba surrender was one of the wisest acts of statesmanship in our time,' it was said. 'He now believes that if we had not made that surrender we should have lost South Africa. The Tory organs are livid with rage, and fling upon their one-time leader much abuse.' It was probably this that later caused delegates at the annual Conservative conference to hiss the mention of Churchill's name.

These first two letters set the pattern for the rest. From now on whatever Churchill wrote—whether it be political or personal —he was attacked from all sides. He had only to make a casual remark about tropical fauna, to be put right by botanists; his observations on a new rifle warranted a detailed report from two leading authorities on small arms; his speculations on the origins of the female sex produced a national uproar. Having successfully alienated the Tories, he was roundly denounced by the Radicals for his repeated attacks on the Boers. 'If the Boers have not created a very favourable impression on Lord Randolph,' observed Labouchere, 'even more unfavaurable is the impression produced by his lordship on the Boers, who have got a clear idea that civilization does not consist solely of water-carts and high-class cookery.'

The bickering was not confined to England. So heated were the arguments which followed Churchill's proposed treatment for horse-sickness that the *Daily Graphic* sent a reporter to France to obtain the views of Louis Pasteur. 'Lord Randolph Churchill,' explained the reporter, 'has been drawing attention to the terrible illness which befalls horses and mules in South Africa.' 'I have heard of the illness,' replied the bewildered M. Pasteur. 'And then?' After some more prodding, the distinguished Frenchman refused to be drawn into the controversy. 'Seeing,' he said, 'that I have not studied the disease.' In Berlin there was a more positive reaction to Churchill's letters. 'They are like those of some wild schoolboy,' the Kaiser told a South African visitor.

Journalists everywhere kept up their sniping. They all agreed that the *Daily Graphic* was getting poor value. The letters were judged to be dull and entirely lacking in perception and political shrewdness. 'There is, it is generally admitted,' reported the London correspondent of the *Cape Times*, 'an emptiness about Lord Randolph's letters denoting, if nothing more, a wrong conception on his part of what is expected from a "special correspondent" . . . As a politician he was a shining light among the stars of Conservatism. As a journalist, it would be idle to deny his inability.' A rumour was spread that the letters were not being sent from South Africa but had been concocted in Paddington before Churchill left. With the appearance of the third letter (written from Kimberley) even Lord Randolph's former champions deserted him. 'Really Lord Randolph must wake up,' declared *South Africa*. 'At present he has the best of the bargain—those 2,000 guineas will be easily earned by 20 letters such as this. We hope the *Daily Graphic* likes them. Candidly we don't.'

The *Daily Graphic* most certainly did like them. Whatever rival newspapers might say, there was no denying the popularity of the series. The general public adored them. In the weekly edition of the *Graphic* they vied for pride of place with the serialization of *Tess of the D'Urbervilles*; *Punch* ran a parallel series from 'Grandolph the Explorer;' and the personal column of *The Times* broke out in a rash of advertisements from 'Gentlemen' offering to conduct gold-prospecting expeditions to Mashonaland. After Lord Randolph's description of the 'fairyland' he discovered on the banks of the Limpopo, it was reported that: 'Lord Randolph Churchill's "fairies" is the latest gutter wheeze in Cheapside. It refers to a tiny model of a Zulu damsel—in her habit as she lives—sold by enterprising itinerant merchants for a penny. And it sells well.'

The most popular attraction of the 'Churchill boom' was a skit produced at the Gaiety Theatre. In the middle of a musical burlesque, *Joan of Arc* (set in medieval France) a castle courtyard suddenly sprouted palm-trees and Arthur Roberts, the leading comedian, strutted on stage wearing a slouch hat, shirt and breeches, twirling unmistakable Churchillian moustaches and singing:

> 'I'm a regular Randy Pandy, oh!
> A swell and a toff and a dandy, oh!
> With a big moustache that's all the mash
> In the great Mashonalandy, oh!

> I've a temper sweet as candy, oh!
> And a book and pencil handy, oh!
> And you never met such a social pet
> As the correspondent Randy, oh!'

This incongruous interlude invariably stopped the show. 'The song was encored half-a-dozen times a night,' it was reported. 'Everyone laughed. The Duke of Marlborough heard it, and laughed. Lady Randolph Churchill has been twice. She was there one evening last week, and laughed louder than ever.' But what amused Churchill's wife and brother did not please others. His mother, the old Duchess of Marlborough, had been against his accepting the *Daily Graphic*'s commission, which she considered a cheap publicity gimmick. The fun poked at Churchill in the comic papers (which she posted on to him) confirmed her disapproval. It was probably the Duchess who put a stop to the Gaiety skit. Complaints were made to the Lord Chamberlain who, in turn, wrote to George Edwardes, the producer, prohibiting the song. A few days after Lady Randolph's second visit, Arthur Roberts was obliged to change Randy Pandy to Jack the Dandy: this did not deter the public who, having read the original version in the *Daily Graphic*, continued to pack the Gaiety for the rest of the show's run.

Young Winston Churchill was one of the few who refused to be unduly impressed by the rumpus created by his father; even though the *Harrow Gazette* had joined in the attack on Lord Randolph. He was extremely tickled by the fuss that was made over the criticism of the *Grantully Castle* but, when reporting it to his father, dismissed it as boring compared with the excitements of Africa. He was keen to have news from the 'land where the Rudyards cease from Kipling and the Haggards ride no more'. He was anxious to know whether his father had shot a lion. Above all, he was insistent in his pleas for a small antelope. Letters from Winston for, at least, the head of an antelope to decorate his room, are said to have followed Lord Randolph throughout his long journey and when his open pleadings failed he resorted to embellishing his letters with reproachful drawings of antelope heads. In the end he was forced to settle for a collection of African stamps.

The reaction to the *Daily Graphic* letters in England was as

LORD RANDOLPH CHURCHILL IN SOUTH AFRICA.

After those letters in the Daily Graphic you could not expect anything else, my lord.

This cartoon of President Kruger kicking Lord Randolph Churchill out of the Transvaal appeared in a Pretoria shop window soon after Lord Randolph left the Boer capital

South African Library

Lord Randolph Churchill and Hans Lee encounter a troop of lions in Mashonaland

South African Library

nothing compared to the outcry they produced in South Africa. Friends and foes alike were staggered at Churchill's tactlessness. At first the letters were accepted philosophically. J. X. Merriman considered that they contained nothing more than frightful piffle which might have been written 'in Pall Mall for all they tell us'. This mood did not last long. The publication of the sixth letter—ferociously attacking the Boers—made even the editor of *The Star* blanch. In a leader headed 'Randolph at Random' the misguided champion of the Uitlanders was severely taken to task. It was pointed out that his attitude towards the Boers was bound to revive prejudices which had begun to disappear. His slighting remarks about their lack of education was considered most unfortunate. 'We are fain to admit,' confessed *The Star*, 'that men who have been trekking, hunting, fighting from youth upwards, rendering the country safe for us to inhabit and possibly for Lord Randolph to travel in had not many opportunities brought within their reach of education as the modern Englishman understands the term.' There was much in Churchill's sixth letter, it concluded, which the English-speaking inhabitants of the Transvaal would agree with as little as the Boers themselves.

The Boers were far more emphatic. Not only in the Transvaal but in the neighbouring republic of the Orange Free State, Lord Randolph Churchill was vehemently denounced. He was regarded as a typically arrogant representative of British Imperialism. 'We have written—year in, year out—with the view of showing the irresponsible folly of responsible statesmen, who, at a distance of 6,000 miles, assume to direct the destinies of this continent,' declared a Bloemfontein paper, 'and we have failed, mostly by reason of the illusionary notions that a good many people have of the goodness, and the sincerity, and the abilities, and the statesmanship of politicians over the water. Now the smartest of the crew has come among us, and proved himself a howling cad, a superficial scoffer—utterly unable to read the history of the past, as any right-minded and sensible person would read it, and appreciate and treat with seriousness the political problems of the day—we shall have a much lighter task in persuading the yet wavering elements that there is nothing to be expected for South Africa so long as that class of men have a word to say in our affairs.' In Pretoria, *De Volksstem*'s response was more concise but equally concerned with the lessons of history. 'The hasty, ill-tempered and unjust criticism which Lord R. Churchill has passed on this republic and the Boers,' it thundered, 'can be answered in one word—Majuba.'

The anger of the Press was echoed by the rantings of the mob. In Pretoria an infuriated crowd paraded an effigy of Lord Randolph through the town, halting every now and then to allow spectators to hiss and give three cheers for President Kruger, finally burning the tattered figure on a bonfire in one of the main streets. How this demonstration started is not certain: some reports claimed that one of the hotelkeepers whom Churchill had offended had arrived in the capital to organize a protest, while others maintained that it had been sparked off by indignant English-speaking residents of Pretoria. However, there can be no doubt that the spectacle of Lord Randolph being roasted was enjoyed by all. The following day a cartoon showing Churchill being kicked out of the Transvaal by Kruger, wearing a boot labelled 'public opinion', was displayed in the window of a leading bookshop. 'We very much hope,' commented *De Volksstem*, 'that the sentiment thus expressed will soon become a reality.'

And indeed it seemed as if it would. Public speakers willing to abuse the English Lord found themselves in demand; the mere mention of Churchill's name was sufficient to set an audience booing. The number of his enemies increased with the appearance of each *Daily Graphic* letter. 'Lord Randolph,' it was said, 'will evidently have to find some other route home again. He certainly cannot go back *via* Pretoria... The Cape also does not regard his lordship favourably.'

Inevitably, Cecil Rhodes was held partly responsible for his guest's surly behaviour. Rhodes's dislike of the Kruger régime was well known. A pro-Boer newspaper in Johannesburg even hinted that Churchill was being paid to attack the Boers and that 'the spoor of the Cape sorcerer, Mr Rhodes, can be seen in this'. This is most unlikely. Churchill was undoubtedly influenced by Rhodes and the Uitlanders, but he was not a man to allow himself to be used by anyone. In fact, Rhodes was acutely embarrassed by Churchill's behaviour. He had little to gain by encouraging such clumsy tactics. The ways of Cecil Rhodes were more devious.

LOOKING FOR GOLD

But as long as Lord Randolph was in the Transvaal, Rhodes was content to remain in the background. Only after the Churchill expedition had crossed the Limpopo did he become obviously perturbed. He had good reason to be. It could not have been long after Lord Randolph had left Fort Tuli that the most disturbing reports were relayed back to Cape Town. Not content with attacking the Boers, the fault-finding visitor had launched out in a new direction. He had committed the unforgiveable sin of criticizing Mashonaland. This was more than Rhodes had bargained for. He decided that the time had come for him to pay his first real visit to the Chartered Company's territory.

*

One of the reasons why Mashonaland had remained isolated for centuries was its peculiar geography. The pestilent terrain between the Limpopo and the high, invigorating plateau where the Chartered Company had centred its outposts had provided an effective barrier against the encroachments of civilization. Explorers, missionaries and a few hardy traders had succeeded in penetrating the country but, until the march of Rhodes's pioneer column in 1890, the hazards facing white settlers had been daunting. The Company's force had hacked a road through the unhealthy lowveld but trekking north of Fort Tuli remained a treacherous undertaking. For Lord Randolph Churchill it proved a hell.

The first few days were pleasant enough. Once he had been persuaded to allow the ox-drawn vehicles to travel ahead during the night (instead of exhausting the animals in the heat of the day) his spider was able to follow in the wake of the main expedition at a leisurely pace. Most of the day was spent on horseback with the squat, black-bearded Hans Lee, whose stories of the veld Churchill found enchanting. Lord Randolph's own performance in the field was, at first, disappointing. His early letters from Mashonaland were full of near misses and accounts of wounded animals pathetically escaping into the bush. Hunting in Africa, he was forced to admit, was very different from deer-stalking in Scotland. But, after a few days, game became so plentiful that even the poorest shot in the party could boast an impressive bag. Kudu, roan-antelope, quagga and waterbuck were dragged back to the camp each evening to be skinned, preserved or roasted. So proficient did they become that it was necessary to make a pact to try only for sable antelope and giraffe and not to shoot at hornless buck.

A climax was reached a week after they had left Fort Tuli. While in camp one night, lions were heard roaring on the opposite side of the river. The following morning, after pursuing a wounded kuku, Churchill and Hans Lee stumbled upon the pride, much nearer to the camp than they had imagined. 'There they were,' reported Churchill, 'trooping and trotting along ahead of us like a lot of enormous dogs, great yellow objects, offering such a sight as I had never dreamed of.' Following them was a risky business. Lee appears to have been in two minds about it but Churchill insisted. On catching up with them Lee managed to wound two before they disappeared into the long grass. Churchill, on a strange horse, thought it inadvisable to shoot from the saddle and wisely decided against dismounting. Although they could hear the growling sobs of the wounded lions, Lee warned against entering the long grass to finish them off. He said that there was a strong possibility that the rest of the pride would attack. They returned to the spot later that day with some dogs. One of the wounded animals had recovered sufficiently to escape, but the other was still there and still alive. After climbing some trees and shooting into the grass they managed to kill the growling beast: they discovered it to be an old lioness with worn teeth but a perfect skin. This somewhat inglorious episode stood out as memorable in Lord Randolph's tour. 'I had thought when I came to Africa that I would try and shoot a few nice buck,' he wrote, 'but I had never bargained to come across such a posse of lions. On reviewing the incidents of that day, I came to the conclusion that all had ended very fortunately, and that I had had an exciting experience such as is known to few, and had escaped unscathed.'

Shortly after leaving 'lion camp' the dangers of Mashonaland travelling were revealed. The hunting party was separated from the main expedition by some thirty miles and, with provisions running short, it was necessary to make a speedy trek to catch up with their supplies. But speed proved impossible. They were forced to hack their way through the bush to reach the main road; two of the mules pulling Lord Randolph's spider died of sickness; unseasonable rains set in and one of the mule wagons stuck fast in a rocky river bed. Luckily they met other expeditions from whom they were able to beg bread and this, together with the game they shot, enabled them to push on without going hungry. However, on joining the main expedition they discovered that the delay entailed in waiting for them at an unhealthy camping spot had resulted in several of the horses contracting horse-sickness. From then on—until they reached the bracing highveld—they were dogged by disaster. Not only horses but mules and oxen and even Lord Randolph's favourite shooting pony succumbed to the fatal sickness. To top everything a raging bush fire nearly destroyed their wagons. Churchill's opinion of Mashonaland became as jaundiced as his views on the Transvaal. He considered the country unfit for human habitation and was forced to change his mind about the preventive measures he had suggested for horse sickness. 'This horse sickness is a terrific scourge,' he declared, 'either for the settler or the traveller. I am surprised that the Cape Government or the Chartered Company do not endeavour to cope seriously with this malady.'

The sparkling highveld air helped to alleviate the sufferings of Lord Randolph's animals; it did nothing to soothe Lord Randolph's temper. Travelling in the highlands presented new hazards and produced a fresh crop of complaints. The soil was sandy, the water was bad, the sour grass contained no nourishment for the overworked livestock and the roads were so rutted that after a few hours' trekking the mules were exhausted. Churchill found it all very discouraging. Where, he wanted to know, was the fine country of the Mashona about which he had heard so much? In the lowveld the soil was fertile but fever and horse sickness made it uninhabitable; in the highveld the country appeared to be barren and worthless. Nor was he particularly impressed by the Chartered Company's settlements. He considered both Fort Victoria and Fort Charter 'miserably weak constructions'—useless if attacked by the unpredictable Matabele. Neither place could boast a doctor. There was a complete lack of medicines or medical comforts. He found the complacency of the Chartered Company officials disquieting. 'Having now travelled upwards of two hundred miles through Mashonaland,' he wrote after leaving Fort Victoria, 'I have, as yet, seen no place suitable for prosperous European settlements.' This was hardly the sort of report that Rhodes, or the electors of South Paddington, had been hoping for.

His accounts of the perils facing would-be settlers were undoubtedly coloured by his own lack of experience. A great many of the obstacles he encountered resulted from the unwieldy nature of his expedition. Instead of ensuring his comfort, his bulging wagons were a hindrance and a constant source of irritation. On one occasion, as his oxen strained along a particularly bad stretch of road, he had to admit his envy of two Englishmen who gaily strode along beside them, equipped with nothing more than a couple of blankets and a small bundle of goods for trading with the local Africans. To men like these Churchill's crawling wagons were a huge joke. Travellers returning to Pretoria delighted audiences with exaggerated accounts of Lord Randolph's difficulties. A parson, lecturing the Young South African Society, claimed that: 'He had met Lord Randolph Churchill near Fort Salisbury cursing everything African. All his mules and horses were dead, and his oxen were knocked up by the weight of the provision wagons.' Of course things were not as bad as that; but it made a good story and was enthusiastically received.

At Fort Salisbury, the Chartered Company's 'capital', Lord Randolph began to unwind. He was pleasantly impressed by the ramshackle little town with its makeshift hotel, general stores, chemist, dentist, solicitor and 'not least among the many signs of civilization, a tolerably smart perambulator'. He thought the settlers were content and confident and formed a busy, industrious community. An added attraction was the excellent hunting in the surrounding countryside. Soon he was sending home glowing reports of his days in the veld which he hoped would encourage the *jeunesse dorée* of London to come to Mashonaland. He estimated the costs of such an expedition at £2,000 and strongly recommended prospective hunters to provide themselves with champagne which, in his opinion, was the most refreshing drink after a day's hunting in the sun.

While Churchill spent his days hunting, his aide-de-camp, Captain Williams, and his mining expert, Henry Perkins, set off to explore the gold reefs near the Mazoe river. Rumours concerning the mineral potential of this area were circulating in Fort Salisbury and, although Lord Randolph professed to have little faith in them, he agreed to allow Perkins to join Alfred Beit who, accompanied by his own mining expert, was investigating the claims. The result was far from encouraging. For the optimistic pioneers of the Mazoe valley, the sight of Lord Randolph's mining engineer riding pessimistically back from one gold mine after another became painfully familiar. His verdict was invariably the same: the reefs were of such a limited extent and depth that they could not be expected to yield more than a small profit. There was no general formation to enencourage workings by a large company or syndicate. Mr Perkins's gloomy predictions caused almost as much offence as did his employer's bad temper. According to one of the pioneers, the impression he gave was that he had 'started with antagonistic feelings towards Mashonaland, and was prepared to damn every property he saw after the most rapid and perfunctory inspection. Mine after mine was casually looked at—and then turned down as a possible investment.'

His findings more or less convinced Churchill. Shortly after the return of his mining engineer, he did purchase a half share in a gold mine but he had no great hopes of it. The mine was at Hartley Hill, some fifty miles from Fort Salisbury. Lord Randolph was persuaded to share the property—the Matchless Mine—with Alfred Beit, whom he had joined on a hunting expedition. Frank Johnson (the leader of Rhodes's pioneer column), who held an option on the mine, says that he was reluctant to forgo his option and did so on orders from Rhodes. When Rhodes heard that Johnson was holding out for a higher price, he sent off a terse, peremptory telegram: 'You will part at once,' he commanded. Somewhat against his will, Johnson did.

Rhodes's intervention, together with the backing of a shrewd business man like Alfred Beit, may have removed some of Churchill's misgivings about the Matchless Mine, but nothing could change his opinion of conditions in Mashonaland. Some time before leaving for Hartley Hill he had received a message to say that the main body of his expedition, which was following in his wake, had come to a standstill between Fort Victoria and Fort Salisbury. Major Giles was reported to be incapacitated by a broken collarbone. Considering the country they had to cover, this news had not surprised Churchill. However, at Hartley Hill both Major Giles (surprisingly recovered) and the rest of the expedition caught up with him. The difficulties they had encountered were nowhere as great as Churchill had imagined, but he remained pessimistic. 'The truth has to be told,' he wrote. 'Mashonaland, so far as is at present known, and much is known, is neither Arcadia nor an El Dorado.'

His name became a by-word for despondency throughout the territory. Those who, acting on Rhodes's strict instructions, were bound to attend him found his prickly company very difficult to bear. Frank Johnson described him as an impossible person and a woman visiting the country wrote: 'Randolph Churchill . . . has been making himself ridiculous here, and . . . has written such tactless things that the Chartered Company is trying to shake him off.' Percy Fitzpatrick was scathing. 'Besides his lisp and one or two other attractions,' he wrote, 'there is one particularly charming trait in Lord Randolph's character—if I might put it that way—and that is his candour. "Perfectly Candid," "transparently open," these are the terms his friends apply to him. Other people call it other names, and by degrees it gets tapered off into "infernally candid," "beastly rude," and so on into the unprintable; but that, of course, is a matter of individual opinion or experience. It is this trait which impresses his strong personality on one, and prevents one from ever forgetting the fact of having once come in contact with him.

'There will never be any need to mark in red ink the route Lord Randolph took through South Africa. There is no doubt that he left a good strong trail behind him, and from Cape Town to Salisbury and back one hears of characteristic anecdotes of how the noble Lord maintains his dignity and position, rebukes the too colonial spirit of independence, or lapses unaffectedly into personal details—about the food and liquor, the fit of his pants, or the way mules scratch each other. To me there is something welcome in the knowledge that a well-cooked dinner can "mark an epoch," or make a place "ever memorable"; it makes one feel that after all he is but human, and I own to having picked up with real interest every detail I could about our distinguished "special".'

But neither Churchill's rudeness nor his scepticism bothered hopeful gold seekers arriving in Mashonaland. Rumours of new finds continued and little notice was taken of Lord Randolph's gloomy expert. So convincing were the reports reaching Fort Salisbury that, shortly after his return there, even Lord Randolph threw Mr Perkins's caution to the wind. News of promising reefs discovered by experienced miners near Fort Victoria decided him to abandon his plan of returning to the Cape by sea from Portuguese East Africa and to retrace his steps as far as Fort Victoria. From there he hoped to avoid the Transvaal and travel south through British Bechuanaland.

Before his party left Fort Salisbury, it was agreed that they should sell some of their supplies. The disposal of these provisions by auction created a sensation among the luxury-starved community; it became a memorable event in the town's history. For four days a jostling crowd of pioneers—waistcoats unbuttoned and shirt sleeves rolled up—vied with each other to buy a variety of goods, ranging from cans of paraffin at £2 a gallon to a £1 bottle of eau-de-cologne. Churchill was amazed at the prices paid: cotton shirts costing 9s. 6d. in London sold for 33s., a new pair of boots fetched £4 and an old shooting jacket £1 5s. 'During this sale,' said Lord Randolph, 'I realized with some regret that a large and well-conducted trading expedition into this country would have been a far more profitable speculation than gold prospecting.' The high cost of living was a sore point with the settlers at Fort Salisbury; a week or so before Churchill's sale a protest meeting had been called to express the general discontent. Not surprisingly Lord Randolph and his friends had come in for some of the blame. Angry questioners wanted to know why he had been allowed to bring liquor when it was forbidden to others and more than one questioner had blamed Mr Perkins for the poor gold finds. It was officially explained that Lord Randolph had obtained the necessary magistrate's permission to import alcohol and the fact that he had more liquor than he required did not prevent bidders at the sale buying his English ale at 3s. 6d. a bottle, and selling it at 6s. 6d. immediately afterwards. 'As money was plentiful,' says Frank Johnson, 'and there was nothing else to spend it on, such prices did not seem to matter greatly.'

Less successful, as far as Churchill was concerned, was the first horse-race to be held at Fort Salisbury. A keen student of the turf, Lord Randolph entered a horse against one belonging to a Chartered Company official. Churchill, who felt certain that his horse would win, was somewhat put out to find that the betting was against him. He was even more discouraged when his horse appeared on the field looking extremely woebegone. His suspicion that the animal had been nobbled might well have been justified: he was not the most popular person at Fort Salisbury.

The horse-race was to have marked the end of Lord Randolph's stay. Having auctioned off his stores and sent some of his wagons ahead, he was ready to start on his homeward journey. However, he was obliged to stay a few more days: on the eve of his departure Cecil Rhodes, accompanied by the Administrator of Mashonaland, Dr Jameson, arrived at Fort Salisbury.

*

This was Rhodes's first purposeful visit to the territory which was to bear his name. A year earlier, at the end of October 1890, he had travelled to the southern border of Mashonaland intending to follow the pioneer column which had recently hoisted the Union Jack at Fort Salisbury. He had been dissuaded from continuing his journey. Rumour had it that the Matabele were spoiling for a fight and Sir Henry Loch, the British High Commissioner in South Africa, had forbidden Rhodes to endanger his life. As Prime Minister of the Cape, said Loch, he had no right to take such risks. Despite this warning, Rhodes had crossed the border and proceeded as far as Fort Tuli. Here, the combination of river floods and further ominous reports from Matabeleland had finally decided him to heed Loch and return to the Transvaal. Since then his duties at the Cape had prevented him making a second attempt.

Not until the end of the Parliamentary session in 1891 did he feel free to travel north. He left Cape Town on 14 September and sailed to Beira in Portuguese East Africa. His main concern was to inspect the new country and to negotiate a settlement with a particularly refractory concessionaire. His attempts to clear Mashonaland once and for all of rival claimants had been under attack and matters had not been helped by a series of articles written by F. J. Dormer, the editor of *The Star*. 'What between that fool of a Churchill and that idiot of a Dormer,' he was heard to say, 'we are getting into a nice mess in the newspapers.' There can be no doubt that talks with Lord Randolph were high on his list of priorities. His arrival in Mashonaland was awaited with apprehension. 'We are told to expect the Premier by the 30th or before,' wrote the *Cape Times*'s correspondent, 'and Dr Jameson and Lord Randolph Churchill may be here simultaneously. Nobody knows what to expect.'

He arrived in a bad temper but this soon disappeared. By the time he had reached Umtali, the first outpost of the Chartered Company, he was in high spirits. 'He was besieged with petitions of all sorts,' wrote one of the settlers. 'Malcontents and chronic grumblers went to his hut and came away cheerful and satisfied. Not that anything was altered in the condition of affairs: the man's personal magnetism wrought the change.' So infectious was Rhodes's optimism that, when he arrived at Fort Salisbury, even Churchill began to look at the country with new eyes. There was a distinct change of tone in the letter he wrote to the *Daily Graphic* immediately after Rhodes's arrival. He praised the Chartered Company's administration, held out hopes of further improvements once the telegraph reached Fort Salisbury and noted that the high prices had already begun to fall. 'Thus,' he concluded, 'as I looked all round on the eve of my departure on my journey south, I thought I could see much that was bright and smiling in the present condition of Mashonaland.' All that was needed was the discovery of some rich goldfields and even this he thought might occur with patience and hard work. Unfortunately this hopeful attitude did not last long.

A second excursion to the Mazoe valley was arranged. The party included Rhodes, Churchill and Dr Jameson. It took them a day to cover the thirty miles between Fort Salisbury and the Mazoe mining area; they arrived just as evening was setting in. Tired after their long ride, they drew a wagon and cart together, spread a canvas and settled down to supper round a camp fire. Among those at the camping spot was D. C. de Waal, a member of the Cape Assembly and an ardent Afrikaner supporter of Rhodes. It was not long before he and Churchill were at each other's throats.

'After supper Lord Randolph began to express his views on certain South African political points,' says de Waal, 'and during the course of his remarks he railed against the Boers for being lazy people! Though I was already disgusted with the man, owing to the letters he had written to the *Daily Graphic*, I quietly and attentively sat listening to all he said. The more he spoke the more he exposed his ignorance on the subject he was trying to handle, and it appeared only too plain by his utterances that he cherished a bitter animosity towards the Boers. Having listened to his absurb talk, I begged him to tell me what were his actual reasons for his aversion to the Boers.

"They are lazy, dirty, and barbarous," was his cutting reply.
"How do you know that? Have you been to their farms?"
"Yes," he replied, "at a couple of them."
"But surely you can't judge the whole country by a couple of farms in it!"
"Well," he said, "I have seen and heard enough of them."
"No," I told him frankly; "you fancy that because you have seen a few farms—the worst in the country, for all I know—you have gathered sufficient knowledge to write a lengthy article in one of the leading London newspapers about the Transvaal and its inhabitants. I would draw a black stroke through every line of that article, and don't be angry with me if I declare its contents for the greater part to be untrue and slanderous. To judge from that letter, I must say, you have as little knowledge of the Transvaal as a sucking baby has."'

Churchill certainly did get angry. The argument became more heated. Things were not helped when Lord Randolph tried to distinguish between the Transvaal Boers and the Cape Afrikaners. De Waal refused to be side-tracked. He insisted upon taking every remark about the Transvaal as a personal insult. 'You are entirely ignorant as to what South African farmers are,' he stormed.

Churchill must have realized that his criticisms were making little impression. Not a man sitting round the fire agreed with him. Finally, when it was obvious that De Waal's temper was getting out of control, Rhodes decided to intervene. Calmly but forcibly he told Lord Randolph that his controversial letters to the *Daily Graphic* had created ill feeling throughout South Africa. They had stirred up fresh hatred between the English and Afrikaners in the Cape as well as antagonizing the Boers. The harm caused, he said, was the last thing he had expected from an ex-Chancellor of the Exchequer.

It made no difference to Churchill. 'The stubborn man,' declared de Waal, 'would not give in.' It was late when the ill-tempered little party went to bed. The high spirits produced by Rhodes's arrival had dissolved; more than ever Churchill was anxious to start for home.

The following morning Rhodes and Lord Randolph made a quick tour of the mines. They found little to offset Mr Perkins's estimate. Promising surface quartz invariably petered out once shafts were sunk. Rhodes appears to have remained optimistic; Churchill said nothing. 'He was afraid, I dare say, to expose himself,' observed de Waal, 'for there was already on its way to England a letter of his to the *Daily Graphic*, wherein he condemned Mashonaland as far as its auriferous character was concerned.' It was to take some time before Lord Randolph's doubts were seen to be justified.

On returning to Fort Salisbury the two parties separated. Rhodes and Jameson went off on further explorations and Churchill started for the Cape. He spent two months and a week at the Chartered Company's capital and left it with a tinge of regret. He considered the Fort Salisbury area the most promising for would-be settlers and hoped that his descriptions of the climate and hunting there would arouse sympathy for the fledgling town.

The mellow mood in which he started his homeward trek did not last long. By now he had abandoned his spider and was travelling in a sturdy coach, especially designed for rough roads: drawn by twelve mules and capable of carrying eight people as well as three thousand pounds of baggage. It was able to average a speed of thirty miles a day. All the same, the return trip was no joy ride. The sandy roads were as treacherous as ever, the heat was oppressive and summer storms were sweeping the country. It was not long before Churchill was again cursing the Chartered Company, its administration, its officials and its police. 'While I was in the country,' he declared, 'I was wondering what this most costly force had done, what it was doing, or what it was going to do. It is true that some thirty of the Company's police rendered great service in routing the Portuguese near Massikessi, but the spasmodic energy of a few does not excuse the normal sluggishness and uselessness of the many.'

They arrived at Fort Victoria on 26 October. All along the

road they had received good reports of the gold discoveries in this region but closer inspection proved them to be somewhat fallacious. For once Churchill did not entirely despair. He was interested to note that prospectors were no longer concentrating on ancient workings in the hopes of unearthing King Solomon's mines. It now appeared likely that the old diggings had been abandoned not, as was previously supposed, because the ancients had lacked skill or knowledge but because the mines had been exhausted. There was a possibility, thought Lord Randolph, that the new approach might prove successful.

They had been at Fort Victoria a week when Rhodes and his party caught up with them. Once again tempers on both sides became frayed. In an attempt to patch things up, Jameson and de Waal suggested that Lord Randolph accompany them to the Zimbabwe ruins, some twenty-five miles away. These mysterious ruins, bearing as they did indications of an unexplained civilization in an otherwise primitive country, were regarded as one of the sights of Mashonaland. They would make good copy for a *Daily Graphic* letter. But Churchill would have none of it. He said he had seen enough old débris heaps in his day and had no desire to see more. 'But,' he added, 'if you can take me to a reef bearing two ounces of gold to the ton, I will go and see it.'

However, he did agree to inspect one of the modern wonders of Mashonaland. The telegraph line had been brought within two miles of Fort Victoria on the day Rhodes arrived and they all rode out to send messages to Cape Town and London. The operator was seated in a covered wagon, behind which stretched the line connecting him with the outside world. 'The scene,' says Lord Randolph, 'was peculiar and very African.' Having sent their messages, Churchill suggested that Rhodes accompany him back to the Cape. By this time Rhodes appears to have given up hope of influencing his guest and, after consulting the rest of his party, politely declined.

De Waal recorded Lord Randolph's departure with ill-concealed delight. 'At two o'clock in the afternoon,' he wrote, 'he left with his spider drawn by four horses and four mules, with a coach drawn by twelve mules, and with a waggon drawn by sixteen oxen.

'I dare say the noble correspondent of the *Daily Graphic* burnt with anger and disgust when he had to drive away without the

Premier, seeing that he had waited for us at Fort Victoria fully six days . . . Lord Randolph's drivers and "reinholders" had a thousand complaints to make against their master. According to them the nobleman must possess a very bad temper.'

CHAPTER FOUR

Going Home

THE JOURNEY back, although not without mishaps, was nowhere near as exhausting as the northward trek had been. Despite the approach of summer and the rainy season, Churchill had fewer complaints as he travelled south. This may have been a matter of luck or the thought of heading towards home; it could have been the result of his new method of travelling or simply that experience had hardened him to African conditions. Whatever the reason, his outlook was decidedly more philosophic.

The hazardous crossing of the lowveld was accomplished in five and a half days, with the loss of only one horse from sickness. Churchill claimed this as a record. He said it would be a long time before anyone covered the 197 miles between Fort Victoria and Fort Tuli in so short a time. Reaching Fort Tuli was like coming home again. He was delighted to find the camp much as he had left it and pleased to be among the Bechuanaland Police again. More than anything else, he was relieved to have put Mashonaland behind him. Looking back, he was able to appreciate the more fortunate aspects of his excursion: the fact that he had met with no real trouble, that none of his party had fallen ill and that, compared with other travellers, his losses had been small. Nevertheless, his failure to discover 'the great gold mine' still rankled; 'this fact,' he said, 'stamped itself somewhat disappointingly and sourly on my mind.'

Shortly before his arrival at Fort Tuli, an ominous report had appeared in the South African papers. It came from Pretoria. 'The general opinion here,' it said, 'is that Lord Randolph Churchill will be well advised in taking another route than that by the Transvaal home. His uncalled for remarks against this country have not yet been forgotten, either in official or public circles.' Similar warnings had been sounded throughout his stay in Mashonaland. Not everyone took them seriously. It was thought that the worst that could happen to him was that the bulk of Transvaalers would ignore him. How much importance Churchill attached to the growlings from Pretoria it is not possible to say: his decision to bypass the Transvaal may well have been due to his intense dislike of the country. However, this dislike did not prevent him sending his mining expert on a further tour of the Witwatersrand. At Fort Tuli Mr Perkins left the party and travelled south to Johannesburg; Lord Randolph and the others headed west to Macloutsie in the Bechuanaland Protectorate.

Churchill's homeward route was the old Missionaries Road: a comparatively fertile strip of Bechuanaland between the western Transvaal and the Kalahari desert. Rhodes once described this route as the 'Suez Canal' to the north: it had been used for many years by missionaries, traders, explorers and big-game hunters. But, although long established and used regularly by the transport wagons of the Bechuanaland Exploration Company, travelling the Missionaries Road was by no means easy: at times it could prove as hazardous as the primitive tracks in Mashonaland. But for once Lord Randolph was lucky. He survived what could have been a thoroughly unpleasant journey in relatively good spirits.

He was kept fully occupied. Not only did he involve himself in the transport arrangements but he assumed responsibility for feeding the party. At Fort Tuli the cook had been dismissed and Churchill seized the opportunity to take charge of the kitchen. He found it extremely diverting. He had to admit that the daily menu of mutton, bully beef and preserved vegetables was monotonous, but he provided some variety with tinned soup which, he says, was 'excellent when flavoured with Harvey or Worcester sauce'. His only regret was that he had not mastered the art of baking bread.

It took them two days to reach Macloutsie. Here, Churchill was again impressed by the efficiency and *esprit de corps* of the Bechuanaland Border Police. Unlike the Chartered Company's force they kept themselves busy, sober and alert. He thought they would be more than a match for the Matabele. Two officers had just returned from a spying expedition in Lobengula's country and Churchill was fascinated by their reports. He left the outpost feeling that British interests were well guarded in Bechuanaland: it was all very different from the alien Transvaal and the muddle of Mashonaland.

Four days later they arrived at Palapye where Churchill exchanged gifts with Khama, the teetotal chief of the Bangmangwato. He admired the severe but just way in which Khama ruled, but this did not prevent him sharing an illicit bottle of brandy with his hosts (agents of the Bechuanaland Exploration Company) in defiance of the chief's strict prohibition.

The road got worse after Palapye and a few days later they were held up by a swollen river. This was their only serious set-back. It was made more annoying by the news that Rhodes and his party, supervised by the Bechuanaland Exploration Company, had overtaken them and crossed the river with ease. The efficiency of this professional transport company made Churchill finally admit the faults of his own organization. 'If I were again going to Fort Salisbury,' he said, 'I should make arrangements with this company for my journey, instead of resorting to the large, very costly and cumberous expedition which ignorance of the country let me in for.'

Once across the river their troubles were over. They travelled to Mafeking, the first sizeable town in Bechuanaland, in high spirits. Churchill was so pleased to reach this outpost of civilization that for once he had nothing but praise for his accommodation. He stayed at Dixon's Hotel and pronounced it 'an establishment of the greatest merit'. Newspaper reporters found him surprisingly affable. He told them that he was 'much pleased with the Bechuanaland route'. When asked for his opinion of the future prospects of Mashonaland he refused to comment.

At Mafeking he received disturbing news of political developments in England. Arthur Balfour, who had coyly declined to speak about the leadership of the Fourth Party at Churchill's farewell dinner, had, during his absence, accepted leadership of the House of Commons. The news threw Lord Randolph into black despair. Writing from Dixon's Hotel, he told his wife that Balfour's appointment marked the end of his own political career. All his hopes for Tory Democracy were ended; his long sojourn in the political wilderness had left him with a feeling of hopelessness; he could no longer support the Tories and had no wish to join the Opposition; he felt he would be happier away from the House of Commons and intended to spend what life he had left working for the benefit of his family.

Two days later he left for Kimberley where he spent a few days as the guest of Alfred Beit. Then, accompanied by Cecil Rhodes, he travelled by rail to Cape Town. 'Lord Randolph Churchill, who seemed in remarkably good health,' announced the *Cape Times* on his arrival, 'will proceed to England by next week's mail steamer; meanwhile his lordship is the guest of His Excellency the Governor.'

*

He did not leave by the next steamer nor did he stay long at Government House. His return to Cape Town followed the pattern of his previous visit. After spending a few days with Sir Henry Loch—who accompanied him when he sailed up the coast to visit the British warship, H.M.S. *Raleigh*—he discreetly removed himself to Rhodes's house. It was announced that he had postponed his departure and would sail to England three weeks later. The reason for the delay, Churchill explained (although he made no mention of staying with Rhodes), was that he had to wait for Mr Perkins to join him from Johannesburg.

His mining expert's second examination of the Transvaal goldfields produced favourable results: Churchill was finally convinced of the country's potential. 'The most sanguine dreamer can hardly overestimate the agricultural and mineral resources of the Transvaal...,' he wrote. 'Probably in the history of mining no goldfield more important than the Witwatersrand has ever been discovered.' Since his visit to Johannesburg, six months earlier, the monthly output of gold had risen considerably and was still rising; with the introduction of modern mining methods and machinery he saw no reason why the boom should not continue. It was unfortunate that such a country was controlled by the 'feeble, corrupt and almost insolvent Boer Government', but this was something which the prosperity of the mining community and a further influx of Uitlanders was bound to remedy. The Transvaal offered greater scope for investment than Mashonaland. Acting upon Mr Perkins's advice, Churchill acquired shares in a promising gold mine on the Witwatersrand.

Shortly after his return to England it was announced that 'certain claims adjoining the Meyer and Charlton property have been bought by Lord Randolph Churchill for £5,000.'

Accounts of Churchill's second visit to Cape Town vary. Esme Howard (later Lord Howard of Penrith), who had met him earlier in Mashonaland and had thought that he looked 'very unwell', says that when they met again at Rhodes's house Lord Randolph 'looked more out of tune with life than even at Salisbury'. But Howard's account was written many years later. Contemporary descriptions make no reference to Churchill's ill-health; on the contrary, it was generally thought that the Mashonaland trip had done him good. He was bright-eyed, sun tanned and full of his old bounce. In his last letter to the *Daily Graphic* he described his three weeks in Cape Town as 'enjoyable beyond description'. Guests at Rhodes's house—where Churchill would sit cross-legged on the drawing-room sofa, recalling his Parliamentary triumphs—found him agreeable and amusing, although it was obvious that he was still brooding over Balfour's appointment. 'There is only one position in England where you are really in full command and can dictate even to Royalty,' he declared one evening, 'and that is as leader of the House of Commons.'

For all his affability, his acceptance of Rhodes's hospitality after he had roundly denounced the Chartered Company puzzled many people. When he was tackled about this, his reply—according to a story told to Esme Howard—was: 'My dear fellow, its the only place in this God-forsaken country where I can get Perrier Jouet '74.' It is typical of the many stories current about Lord Randolph in Cape Town at this time. His reputation for rudeness was such that everybody felt free to add their own version. But there can be no doubt that his presence at The Grange was embarrassing. Reports from London stated that certain English newspapers had taken up his criticisms and were doing their best to dissuade would-be settlers 'against any rush to Mashonaland'. Even more serious was the effect which the *Daily Graphic* letters were having on the London Stock Exchange. Shortly after Lord Randolph moved into Rhodes's house, the *Cape Times* reported: 'London, December 15—The London share market was today in a very depressed condition, especially for South African land shares. The stock of the British South Africa Company has dropped to 15s., the lowest yet touched, and this great decline is attributed to the adverse report of Lord Randolph Churchill upon conditions in Mashonaland, as disclosed in his last letter to the *Daily Graphic*. De Beers also show a decline, but not nearly to the extent exhibited in the case of the Chartered Company's stock. Shortly after noon today De Beers were quoted at £13 7s. 6d. Lord Randolph Churchill's adverse report is much commented upon, and has caused a great sensation.' It is hardly surprising that Churchill was regarded as a cuckoo in Rhodes's nest.

There seems, in fact, to have been a jinx on Rhodes as far as Lord Randolph's visit was concerned. Everything had gone wrong. Instead of enlisting an ally, Rhodes found himself saddled with an encumbrance. De Waal's opinion that Churchill 'had written in bitter malignity against my fellow Africanders' was shared by several of Rhodes's Afrikaans supporters. It was difficult for them to reconcile Rhodes's pleas for unity with his friendship for a man who seemed intent upon alienating the Transvaal. Now, with the shares of the Chartered Company plummeting and Mashonaland under fire in England, Rhodes had real cause for regret. But the final blow had yet to fall.

On the morning of 22 December—the day before Churchill was due to sail—Rhodes was out riding with J. X. Merriman. It was his habit to take an early morning ride with members of his Government and he was usually too engrossed in talk to pay attention to his horse which, in any case, he handled badly. On this occasion, as the two men cantered across the Rondebosch flats, Rhodes's Irish mare stumbled over a tuft of grass and threw her rider. By the time Merriman reached him, Rhodes was unconscious and bleeding profusely. Some German settlers who lived near by rushed to Merriman's assistance and Harry Currey, Rhodes's secretary, who had been bringing up the rear, rode off in search of a vehicle. When Currey returned with a spring cart Rhodes had recovered consciousness and was able, with assistance, to climb on to the vehicle. He was driven back to The Grange and a doctor was sent for. 'Upon examination,' says a report of the accident, 'the doctor found that Mr Rhodes had broken his collarbone and had sustained a cut on the temple from which blood was running. The patient, though he had recovered consciousness, was still in a dazed state, and he was ordered complete quiet.'

The following day it was announced that the accident was less serious than was at first supposed. The shoulder was successfully set but Rhodes suffered from the after effects for a long time. It is said that the shock was largely responsible for his prematurely aged look of later years. He had cause to remember Lord Randolph's visit.

Merriman and Sir Charles Metcalfe, who were booked to sail in the s.s. *Scot* with Churchill, postponed their departure. Lord Randolph sailed on schedule. His leavetaking was appropriately subdued. 'A number of people saw the distinguished visitor off,' it was reported, 'and although there was some handshaking no demonstration was attempted.'

*

Southampton was blanketed in snow when the s.s. *Scot* docked on the morning of 8 January 1892. A group of newspaper reporters, who had been huddled in a tender throughout the night, watched the ship drop anchor with intense relief. It was over ten hours late. The newspaper men were joined by Lady Randolph and her son John. Winston, much to his annoyance, had been bundled off to Versailles for his winter holiday in order to brush up his shaky French.

When the tender pulled alongside the *Scot* the reporters scrambled on board and rushed to interview the crew. The entire catering staff was lined up to meet them. Everyone knew what to expect. The stewards had their answers prepared. Lord Randolph Churchill had been the most sociable and agreeable of passengers. He had eaten all his meals with gusto and had had no complaints. 'Apparently,' noted a disappointed journalist, 'he had forgotten how to swear at anybody!' The reporters then turned to Churchill, who was busy embracing his wife and son. They found him 'looking remarkably brown and well, notwithstanding that a great beard almost hid his face.' (The neat beard with which he had left England had grown so bushy that his wife and son were horrified by it.) In answering the questions fired at him, Lord Randolph was disarmingly affable. The South African expedition had been thoroughly enjoyable, he said. The *Scot* was a comfortable ship and the food excellent. The homeward voyage had been most pleasant. He refused to retract anything he had written about Mashonaland but admitted that he had a small investment in the country. On his own political prospects he was more reticent. While in South Africa he had applied for an Ambassadorship and news of his request had leaked out. When taxed about it he refused to be drawn. 'I really cannot say what I shall do politically.' he said, 'as I am quite in the dark as to all recent reports about me. And now you must excuse me, for I have a wife here to look after.' With that he disappeared behind a pile of luggage which was being offloaded on to the tender.

Lord Randolph's trip was a popular topic of fashionable conversation for weeks after his return. 'Everyone,' it was said, 'makes fun of it and of him.' His critics were joined by a member of his expedition. Major Giles gave a Press interview in which he flatly contradicted everything his employer had said about Mashonaland. He announced that he intended returning to the country. 'There is not the slightest doubt,' he said, 'about the existence of plenty of gold in Mashonaland . . . sufficient development has not been done to state a positive opinion as to its payable character.'

But Churchill stuck to his guns. Later that year his controversial letters were reprinted in book form. The book, *Men, Mines and Animals in South Africa*, was an immediate success. In a preface which he wrote in March 1892, he explained that he had taken out the offending paragraphs relating to the cook of the *Grantully Castle* and the 'origin of the female sex'. There were also a few other minor alterations but his comments on the Transvaal Boers and the condition of Mashonaland were left intact. The controversy, which was beginning to die down, started up all over again.

But soon all attacks on Lord Randolph were to cease. He was so obviously ill that even his most hostile critics fell silent. His decline was slow and tragic. On his return from South Africa he appeared well; his family found him in great spirits and his doctor thought that the holiday had done him good. His reappearance in the House of Commons, a month after his return, caused political commentators to remark on his improved health. Apart from an unexplained attack of giddiness in March this improvement seemed to continue. There was no need for him to exert himself unduly. He did not speak in the House and, apart from addressing his constituents, refused most invitations to speak in public (including a plea from Winston for him to give the boys at Harrow a 'jaw' on South Africa). In the General Election of July—which brought the Liberals to power—he was returned unopposed as the Conservative member for South Paddington. During that summer he was subject to bouts of irritability but, for the most part, he appeared to have recovered much of his rare charm. By the end of the year he had been persuaded to forsake his back-bench seat in the House and take his place on the Front Opposition Bench.

This outward display of well-being was deceptive. As those close to him knew only too well, Churchill was making a tremendous effort to conceal his failing powers. For instance, after taking great pains over a speech he intended to deliver to the House in August, he decided, surprisingly, not to take part in the debate. He later confided to friends that he had lost his nerve at the last minute; an admission that was as ominous as it was uncharacteristic. As the winter months approached, the distressing symptoms of his illness—deafness, giddiness, partial paralysis and difficult articulation—became more apparent. His doctors were much concerned but the public knew little of his sufferings. Not until 17 February 1893, a year after his return, did the seriousness of his illness become a matter for public comment. Rising to address a crowded House on the Second Home Rule Bill, he was seen to be a mere shadow of his former self: his face was white and drawn, his hands shook and his voice trembled as he tried valiantly to complete his speech. He was then forty-four years of age; he looked and sounded like a decrepit old man.

His appearance on this occasion started a fresh spate of rumours concerning the nature of his disease. He was well aware of the gossip and it may well have been an attempt to silence it that made him agree to consult another doctor. This was Dr Thomas Buzzard, a specialist in diseases of the nervous system, who had attended Churchill earlier but had not seen him for a year or two. On examining him in the early summer of 1893, Dr Buzzard diagnosed the incurable General Paralysis. It was not then possible to determine the stage of the disease but it was obvious that Lord Randolph was beyond medical assistance.

With the doctor's consent, Churchill, accompanied by his wife, spent several weeks at a fashionable health resort in Germany. He was trying to build up his strength for the political campaign he had planned for the end of the year. But his holiday did him no real good.

He lingered on for little over a year, his voice growing weaker, his memory more feeble and tortured by encroaching paralysis. For friends and enemies alike, the sight of this once brilliant man being steadily deprived of his faculties was harrowing. In June 1884, against doctor's orders, he set out on a world tour. With him went his wife and a personal physician. They sailed to America and continued on to Canada, Japan, Hong Kong, Singapore and Burma. At first his health seemed to improve but soon after leaving America there was a noticeable deterioration. On arriving in Japan he became so violent at times that neither his wife nor his doctor could control him. The hopelessness of his case was apparent even to casual acquaintances. 'He is travelling with a doctor, much broken down in body and mind,' noted Maurice de Bunsen, who met him on board ship between Japan and Hong Kong. 'He is far too ill to recognize his condition, and talks of a round of visits in India, which will certainly be too much for him. Lady Randolph is going through a terrible ordeal and devotes herself entirely to him.' The proposed tour of India did indeed prove more than his health could stand. On reaching Madras he collapsed completely and was forced to return home. He was given six months to live.

He did not last that long. Early in the morning of 24 January 1895, a few weeks after his return to England, he died at his mother's house in Grosvenor Square. An impressive memorial service, attended by political friends and opponents, was held in Westminster Abbey and he was buried in the village churchyard at Bladon, a short distance from his childhood home, Blenheim Palace.

*

South Africa is a country that attracts criticism. Its turbulent colonial history, its racial divisions, its isolation as a white outpost at the tip of a predominantly black continent has, rightly or wrongly, rendered it a target for every type of attack. Visitors to the country—particularly political visitors—have rarely been able to resist the temptation to side with one section of the community at the expense of the others and such partisanship has inevitably intensified existing friction. But rarely have the opinions of an outsider created more controversy than did those expressed by Lord Randolph Churchill in 1891. During the seven months he spent in South Africa, the smouldering antagonisms of the uneasy country were fanned into flames: warning was given of the conflagration to come.

It would be a mistake to exaggerate the effects of his much publicized visit but, on the other hand, his position as a prominent, popular British politician was such that his influence cannot be ignored. His damning comments on Mashonaland undoubtedly played a part in cooling the enthusiasm of investors and gave scant encouragement to prospective emigrants; his hostility towards the Chartered Company proved an adverse factor in Rhodes's plans for central Africa; and, perhaps most important of all, he was regarded by the Boers as the embodiment of the high-handed British Imperialism which threatened their very existence. For these reasons alone, his brief excursion into South African affairs warrants consideration.

That Lord Randolph's biographers have tended to play down his visit to South Africa is understandable. The acceleration of his illness after his return and his death three years later have, retropectively, cast a shadow over the furore surrounding his activities in 1891. However, tragic as his early death was, it is by no means certain that the opinions he expressed during his South African tour were entirely the result of his ill-health. To understand his attitude at that time it is necessary to examine both the nature of his illness and the validity of his judgements.

For many years the disease which caused Lord Randolph's premature death was the subject of much ill-informed, often vicious, speculation. During his lifetime there was no shortage of scandalmongers willing to hint at, or even explain in detail, the origin of this disease. Many of the stories found their way into the more scurrilous memoirs of the Victorian era. Often written anonymously, and invariably unreliable, these books aimed at disclosing the dark secrets of eminent public figures. Few Victorian statesmen escaped their innuendoes. The mystery of Lord Randolph's illness provided plenty of scope for such writers. For example, Julian Osgood Field in *Uncensored Recollections* (published anonymously) claims that Churchill's illness 'first seized him during his Oxford days' and that he refused to follow the treatment prescribed by a French physician. Frank Harris in his *pot-pourri* of pornography, *My Life and Loves*, is more explicit. He tells a story—obtained, he says, from one of Lord Randolph's friends—of how Churchill got hopelessly drunk at Oxford one evening and woke the following morning in the bed of a hideous old crone from whom he contracted syphilis. He was supposedly treated for the infection with mercury but the treatment proved ineffective. Such stories are run-of-the-mill stuff for the books in which they appear. Were they the only available evidence they would have to be ignored. However, as far as Lord Randolph's fatal disease is concerned, there would seem to be, if not truth, at least some foundation for the accounts given by Field and Harris.

The publication of Churchill's family papers has brought to light detailed doctors' reports on the final stage of Lord Randolph's illness. The symptoms revealed by these reports are significant. Dr Thomas Buzzard describes the disease unequivocally as GP (General Paralysis) and GP—or GPI (General Paralysis of the Insane) to give it the more commonly used term—is the medical description of an ultimate stage of syphilis. The symptoms of GPI—the slurring of the tongue, creeping paralysis, an uncertain jerky gait, grandiose ideas, alternating fits of depression and unnatural bonhomie—are unmistakable. During the last year of Churchill's life these symptoms could be applied to his condition with text-book precision. Lady Randolph appears to have known that her husband had syphilis. The psychological effect of this knowledge on both husband and wife must have been profound. It could well explain their mutual need for escapism and their partial neglect of their two sons.

Syphilis is a progressive disease and in its early stages the symptoms are variable. It would, therefore, be idle conjecture to attempt an interpretation of Lord Randolph's career on the assumption that he contracted the disease while at Oxford. There is no certain way of telling how a person afflicted with syphilis would behave at any given stage other than the final one.

However, it seems unlikely that the disease had seriously affected Churchill's political judgement while he was in South Africa. When the mental symptoms of General Paralysis begin to manifest themselves they are said to be so slight 'as to be apparent only to those who know the patient well'. That Lord Randolph's condition had not passed this stage in 1891 is evidenced by the reports of his doctors and by a study of his more considered pronouncements. As late as the summer of 1893, Dr Buzzard was able to report that the mental symptoms 'have hitherto been of comparatively slight character,' and Winston Churchill, in his two-volume life of his father, was to claim that the quality of a speech Lord Randolph made that year (when he looked a physical wreck) 'showed no signs of intellectual failing'. So it would appear that while the bouts of irritability which plagued him throughout his African venture, two years earlier, can be attributed to the incipient stage of his fatal paralysis, it is by no means certain that his political acumen was impaired. Impulsiveness and a highhanded disregard for the opinions of others characterized his entire career; while allowance must be made for the vehemence with which he expressed his prejudices, there seems no reason why his controversial *Daily Graphic* letters should be treated as exceptional. Moreover his judgement, by and large, has stood the test of time.

It was probably his negative verdict on the mineral potential of Mashonaland that earned Churchill the most heated abuse. 'In my opinion,' he wrote shortly after his arrival at Fort Salisbury, 'at the present time all that can be said of Mashonaland from a mining point of view is that the odds are overwhelmingly against the making of any rapid or large fortune by any individual.' He insisted that South Africa's greatest attraction lay in the wealth of the Transvaal. He was soon shown to be correct. In September 1894, Cecil Rhodes engaged an American mining expert, John Hays Hammond, to survey the Chartered Company's territories. Hammond's report was far from favourable. 'If he cannot say anything stronger than that,' remarked one of Rhodes's associates on reading the report, 'I have not much hope for the future of the Chartered Company.' Rhodes accepted the report philosophically but there is reason to think that it contributed in no small way to his decision to embark on his disastrous campaign against the Transvaal. Like

Churchill, he was obliged to recognize the superior attractions of the Boer Republic.

Lord Randolph's wisdom in heeding his mining expert, in face of widespread criticism, was made apparent by his South African investments. In June 1892, five months after his return to England, a full account of his dealings on behalf of the 'Churchill syndicate' was published. The names of the original subscribers were listed together with details of expenditure and investments. The balance sheet was greeted with a great deal of cynical amusement. The expenses of the expedition were seen to be enormous and Lord Randolph's investments looked far from promising. It was explained that work on the Matchless mine—which Churchill and Alfred Beit had acquired in Mashonaland—had been suspended owing to 'the influx of water' and the syndicate's investments on the Witwatersrand depended on the success of deep-level mining (regarded at that time as a somewhat uncertain novelty). Publication of the balance sheet was followed by an announcement of Lord Randolph's proposal to convert his syndicate into a limited liability company. The syndicate's capital was to be raised from £16,000 to £30,000 and the subscribers were to receive £1 shares equivalent in amount to their original subscriptions. On the 14,000 new shares to be issued *pro rata* 12s. a share would at once be called up. 'For this capital,' observed a technical journal, 'the shareholders would have half a flooded mine, and the option of a share amounting to £5,000 in a scheme for working deep-level mines at Johannesburg.' But once again Churchill was shown to be right. While the Matchless mine never amounted to much—despite the backing of Alfred Beit—Mr Perkins's assessment of the Witwatersrand was more than justified. Churchill was forced to sell some of his deep-level shares but the remainder fetched some £70,000 when they were disposed of to pay his outstanding debts at the time of his death. The other members of the syndicate must have been well pleased with Lord Randolph's 'foolish investments'.

The suggestion that Churchill was being used by Rhodes and his financier friends was of course inevitable. And at one stage this seemed to be more than idle political gossip. On his arrival in South Africa Lord Randolph appeared to be giving uncritical support to Rhodes; in Johannesburg he had no hesitation in backing the Uitlanders. This, together with his reluctance to acknowledge the hospitality of Rhodes and Beit in his *Daily Graphic* letters, was bound to create suspicion. It was soon proved groundless. By the end of the visit no one was more disillusioned than Rhodes, and the Uitlanders were acutely embarrassed by their champion's lack of tact. Whatever support Churchill gave to his South African friends was occasioned more by his Imperial ardour than by any sinister influence. He was perfectly prepared to speak up for the rights of English colonists, but he was not prepared to support any dubious undertakings. His change of heart once he arrived in Mashonaland was not, as was claimed, a sign of his political instability: if anything it was evidence of his political integrity. Nor was his behaviour in South Africa, as is sometimes supposed, entirely at variance with his earlier career. Faced with a choice between factional collusion and personal conviction he invariable plumped for the latter—however mistaken he might be. His often impulsive decisions had lost him friends and followers; he was never a good party politician.

Churchill's reluctance to acknowledge the hospitality of Rhodes and Beit was probably a matter of politeness to his hosts. For obvious reasons Rhodes did not want their close association publicized and Alfred Beit was notoriously shy. Certainly Churchill made no secret of his own financial dealings. What mystery existed about his gold-prospecting syndicate before he left England was dispelled after his return. If Rhodes and the mining magnates had indeed expected to win Churchill over it soon became clear that they had placed their hopes on the wrong man.

However, some of the political opinions he expressed were undoubtedly influenced by Rhodes. It was these opinions that angered his enemies in the Conservative party. His praise of Gladstone (and, later, his prediction in Johannesburg that the Liberals would win the next election) helped to widen the gulf between himself and orthodox Tories. But there was much to be said for the support he gave to Rhodes. It was important for Britain to win the support of the Afrikaners and, as later events proved, this could not be done by crushing the Transvaal. For all Churchill's hostility towards the Boers, he was never an advocate of armed intervention in the Transvaal. Indeed,

Winston Churchill was to claim that had his father lived he would have been an active opponent of the Anglo-Boer war. His attitude earned him much abuse from his own party but it was by no means as wrongheaded as it was made to appear.

For all that, it was his unbridled attacks upon the Boers that produced the loudest outcry. This was not as contradictory as it seems. A potentially dangerous situation existed in the Transvaal. It was aggravated as much by Boer intransigence as by Tory jingoism. For a conciliatory policy to work, both sides needed to make concessions. The Boers showed no signs of yielding. Incensed by the unjust conditions imposed on the Uitlanders and convinced that Gladstone would soon be returned to power, Churchill regarded the Kruger régime as the main obstacle to a peaceful solution of the South African problem. Moreover, he saw the dominance of the Boers in the Transvaal as a threat not only to the Uitlanders but to the indigenous African population. 'The Boer does not recognize that the native is any degree raised above the level of the lower animals,' he wrote. 'In conversation he describes the native as a "creature". His undying hatred for the English arises mainly from the fact that the English persist in according at least in theory equal rights to the coloured population as are enjoyed by the whites. In the Transvaal no native may travel from one place to another unless he is provided with a pass. In the towns no native may be out at night, unless he is similarly protected. Neither can any native in the Transvaal acquire a title to land.' Unfortunately this line of argument alienated many of his new-found friends. There were very few Uitlanders who were prepared to accept the theory of racial equality when it was extended to the Africans.

If Churchill was often rude, tactless and overemphatic, his arguments, for all their one-sidedness, were not devoid of reason or consistency. He repeated his hope that the Uitlanders would increase in such numbers that the Boers would have to yield to their demands. The reactionary government of the Transvaal would then be replaced by a more enlightened administration and the Boers would be absorbed in the new progressive community. This was his answer to those who advocated force. 'The natural events of the future,' he said, 'will probably peacefully retrieve the losses occasioned by the errors of the past.' Nevertheless he was fully aware of the effect which mounting frustration was having on the Uitlanders. If the Transvaal Government continued with what he considered to be its perverse and obstinate policies the situation could get out of hand. The failure of political pressure could easily lead to the adoption of more violent methods. Realization of this might well have added to his vehemence in condemning the Boers.

Protests against Lord Randolph's anti-Boer onslaught came mainly from the radicals of the Liberal party. To them the Transvaal was a small vulnerable republic struggling against the sinister designs of foreign capitalists and the might of British Imperialism. There was much to be said for this view. Churchill's own role seemed to support it. After all, he was a Tory and a friend of the Johannesburg mining magnates; for all his new-found admiration of Mr Gladstone's settlement his motives for attacking the Transvaal were extremely suspect. The idea of the Boers as a reactionary, oppressive force in southern Africa seemed absurd. What sort of threat could this pastoral community offer to the wealth and stealth of their opponents? The plight of the Africans was conveniently ignored. Henry Labouchere, the radical editor of *Truth*, took refuge in the comforting view that it was beyond human possibility 'to get at the truth on any question where the evidence comes from the other side of the globe'. However, he only applied this to questions concerning the Africans; he had no hesitation in pontificating on the righteousness of the Boer cause. Many years were to pass before the irony of this Liberal standpoint became apparent. The Boers—and their descendants—were to reject the political philosophy of their champions with a cynicism which not only made mock of Liberal efforts on their behalf but greatly intensified one of the major dilemmas of twentieth-century Africa. It would be a bold Liberal today who could dismiss the strictures of Lord Randolph Churchill as lightly as did Henry Labouchere.

Churchill refused to be swayed. Liberal wrath could not move him any more than could Conservative spleen. On leaving Johannesburg he had summed up his feelings about the Boers. 'The days of the Transvaal Boers,' he wrote, 'as an independent and distinct nationality in South Africa are numbered; they will pass away unhonoured, unlamented, scarcely remembered either by the native or by the European settler. Having had given to them great possessions and great opportunities, they will be written of only for their cruelty towards and tyranny over the native races, their fanaticism, their ignorance, and their selfishness; they will be handed down to posterity by tradition as having conferred no single benefit upon any single human being, not even upon themselves, and upon the pages of African history they will leave a shadow, but only a shadow, of a dark reputation and an evil name.' These were powerful, uncompromising words; but he refused to modify them. *Men, Mines and Animals in South Africa* was reprinted several times before his death. The damning passage remained unaltered.

*

Things worked out not as he had hoped but as he feared. Tension in Johannesburg built up and finally exploded. Lord Randolph did not live to witness the events that followed; many of his family did. The Churchills, in fact, were destined to play no small part in the repercussions which attended the Johannesburg upheaval. Unknowingly Lord Randolph had, in a way, forged a link between South Africa and the next Churchill to make a mark there.

On his way back from Mashonaland he had sent a congratulatory telegram to the youngest member of his syndicate, his sister Sarah. She received it on the afternoon of 21 November 1891. That morning, at a smart pink-and-white wedding in St George's Church, Hanover Square, London, attended by the Prince of Wales and the Duke of Cambridge, she had married Mr Gordon Wilson of the Royal Horse Guards. Lord Randolph was one of the few members of his family not present. Instead he was battling his way along the Missionaries Road towards the little town of Mafeking. In the years ahead, the name of that isolated town was to echo around the world: when it did, one of the names most closely and dramatically connected with it would be that of Lord Randolph's sister, the then unsuspecting bride—Lady Sarah Wilson.

PART TWO

THE RAID

CHAPTER FIVE

Enter Lady Sarah

'I HAD a letter yesy. from my child Sarah [dated] the 16th of Decr., just after her landing at Cape Town,' wrote the Dowager Duchess of Marlborough to a friend in January 1896, 'she described that state of ferment existing in the Transvaal and the bad feeling of the Boers, and she said that she and Mr Beit and others had been talking over what Randolph had written in his 1891 letters to the *Graphic*, for which he was so abused, as likely to check enterprise and speculation in Africa, and they all noticed how wise and quite prophetic had been his remarks.'

The Duchess's child, Sarah, was then a married woman of thirty with two children of her own. Her arrival at Cape Town in December 1895 marked the beginning of her long and exciting association with South Africa, an association which, she claimed later, provided her with everything of interest in her life. And she led a very interesting life.

Born the Lady Sarah Isabella Augusta Spencer Churchill, the youngest of the Churchill children, there had been little, before she arrived in South Africa, to distinguish her from any other young society woman. Her childhood, apart from a short sojourn in Ireland when her father had been Viceroy, had been spent amid the Palladian splendours of Blenheim Palace. Here, surrounded by reminders of her great ancestor the first Duke of Marlborough and his formidable Duchess (whose name she bore) she had been educated in all the pursuits and virtues proper to a well-born Victorian girl. It was not an upbringing which made for excitement. A high-spirited, self-willed girl, she must, in fact, have resented the restraints imposed upon her. Her father—described by his biographer as a 'complete, full-blown Victorian prig'—was a man of serious-minded, if narrow principles. A stalwart churchman and extreme Tory, he devoted most of his life to the worthy, but limited, cause of ecclesiastical legislation. Despite his wife's social assertiveness, life at Blenheim seems to have been stiff and formal. Mornings spent reading the newspapers, afternoon drives to visit neighbours, and full-dress dinners, heavily larded with political talk, formed an unvarying pattern for every day. Newcomers found the rituals of Blenheim overwhelming. 'At luncheon,' wrote Lady Randolph Churchill, who joined the family when Sarah was a child, 'rows of *entrée* dishes adorned the table, joints beneath massive silver covers being placed before the Duke and Duchess, who each carved for the whole company, and as this included governesses, tutors and children it was no sinecure.' After the meals whatever food was left was distributed by the children among the sick and poor. In the evenings, not until the 'sacred hour of eleven had struck' would anyone dream of suggesting bed. The family would then line up, their candles lit, to peck dutifully at the cheeks of the Duke and Duchess before retiring to their rooms. It was a staid, august and, above all, assured way of life: the household at Blenheim was unequivocably aristocratic. Against this background Sarah gained her first impressions of her place in life. It was something she never forgot. Like the rest of her family she was always conscious of being a Churchill: a member of the house of Marlborough.

She was a late child. By the time she was born, in 1865, her parents were middle-aged; and by her eighth birthday two of her sisters had married and two more come out. It was therefore to the fifth daughter, Georgiana—five years her senior—that Sarah became most attached. Thrown together under the severe régime of their elderly parents the two girls formed an intimacy that lasted throughout their lives. Of her two brothers, Randolph was undoubtedly the favourite. Although the younger of the two boys, the life of the family tended to centre on his career. He exercised a great influence over his sisters, following their careers with obsessive interest. He was, says his son, 'petted and beloved by his mother and sisters to whom in return he showed the gay and affectionate sides of his nature'. Sarah idolized him.

Together with her brother and sisters, Sarah accompanied her parents to Ireland. The move made little difference to her circumscribed life. Apart from attendance at church and an occasional visit to the theatre she was rarely seen in public. Like her young nephew Winston, she was confined to the schoolroom and diverted only by dark warnings from the servants against murderous Fenians.

She was fifteen by the time the family returned to England. Three years later she was presented at Court. The year of her début, 1883, saw a radical change in her way of life. In June her sister Georgiana married Viscount Curzon, the only son of the 4th Earl Howe. Sarah, dressed in white, was one of the nine bridesmaids. Georgiana's marriage, at the age of twenty-three, had been considered a rare stroke of luck. Suitable young men were not plentiful. 'When I look round here it seems to me the chances of *any* girl are very small,' Lady Randolph had written some three years earlier, '—there are so few *partis*, and when I see a girl like Georgie, with everything that money, dress and position can do for her, hanging on year after year! and she is not the only one . . .' In Sarah's case the going was to prove tougher.

More than her emergence in society, the marriage of her sister marked the end of Sarah's childhood. She was now the only daughter at home. When her father died of a heart attack a month later she lost her childhood home as well. Her brother, the Marquis of Blandford, became the 8th Duke of Marlborough, and her mother, unable to accept the changes made at Blenheim, moved to her house in Grosvenor Square, taking Sarah with her. From this house the Dowager Duchess of Marlborough worked to further the career of her favourite son, Randolph. 'She lived for nobody else,' says Lady St Helier, 'and when, after the death of her husband, she came to settle in London, the whole of her life was devoted to helping his political career, as far as she could, with all the might of her deep passionate admiration, great ability, and social influence. . . . She had a family of devoted daughters, and the whole-hearted way in which they espoused each other's cause and threw themselves into their mutual interests was a great example of the old saying, *L'union fait la force.*'

Sarah's position in this formidable band of females (known to society as 'the Churchill lot') was an unfortunate one. The only unmarried daughter of a domineering mother, she was forced into the role of a Victorian widow's constant companion. She was the spinster daughter who arranged the flowers, fetched the mother's shawl and accompanied aspiring tenors and amateur violinists on the piano (an accomplishment which she was said to perform 'beautifully'). 'The Dowager Duchess of Marlborough accompanied by Lady Sarah Spencer Churchill' began to appear on guest lists with ominous frequency. A Victorian girl was given eight seasons in which to find a husband; if she had not married at the end of that time she was considered to be 'on the shelf'. As season after season passed, it began to look as if the shelf—elevated as it might be—would be Sarah's fate.

But by no stretch of the imagination could Sarah be described as a carbon copy of the retiring Victorian spinster. Her personality was far too definite for that.

She was not a particularly pretty girl. In years to come she was to be considered good looking—a handsome woman—but these were looks more suited to maturity. Short and rather squat, she was unmistakably a Churchill. She had the wide-set, protuberant eyes, the short snub nose and the firm downslanting mouth. However, on her the familiar features were softened, giving her the appearance of a haughty pekinese rather than an aggressive bull-dog. If her features were muted her manner was not. Young men found her abrupt, schoolmistressy approach off-putting. In a family noted for its brusque, caustic humour Sarah was said to have 'more than her share of Churchill wit and acumen'. Proud and authoritative, she could never resist a pungent comment or a withering jibe delivered in 'her own inimitably slashing, straight-from-the-elbow style'. Amusing as all this might be, it was hardly a talent likely to attract a husband. In her case there was no need to study the mother to discover how domineering the daughter would become.

Like her sisters, Sarah entered heart and soul into the campaign for promoting Lord Randolph's career. With the exception of her sister Fanny, who had married Edward Marjoribanks, a Liberal MP, the family were nominally Conservative. But like Lord Randolph's, their Toryism was unpredictable. On the one hand they supported Tory Democracy while on the other hand they clung to their old-fashioned prejudices. When the editor of the *Nineteenth Century* launched an anti-suffragette campaign, it was the Dowager Duchess of Marlborough and her daughters who headed the list protesting against women's rights. Outlandish as Sarah's behaviour could often be, she respected such die-hard conventions throughout her life.

She was involved in most of the crises of her brother's turbulent career. When Lord Randolph resigned from the Cabinet, for instance, she was able to follow events from close range. Sarah and her mother were at a ball given by Lord Salisbury at his country house, Hatfield, when the news broke. It was a grand pre-Christmas affair with the Duchess of Teck and her daughter, Princess May (the future Queen Mary), as guests of honour. Shortly before half-past one in the morning, while Lord Salisbury was chatting to the Duchess of Teck, it was noticed that he was handed a red despatch box containing a single letter. As, after reading it, he continued his conversation, no importance was attached to the incident. Not until the following day did Sarah and her mother realize the importance of that letter. They were due to catch an early train and the Duchess was extremely annoyed when they were allowed to leave without their host and hostess seeing them off. This apparent breach of good manners was explained in that day's *Times*, which announced Lord Randolph's resignation. This was the first indication that the family had had of Lord Randolph's intention; it was left to Sarah to comfort her mother who, on learning the news, is said to have 'wept large tears of fury and mortification'.

But as Lord Randolph's political horizons darkened, so did Sarah's matrimonial prospects brighten. For it was in the years following her brother's resignation—the desperate years of her sixth and seventh seasons—that her friendship with an acceptable young man developed. He was Gordon Wilson, a lieutenant of the Blues (the Royal Horse Guards) and the eldest son of a neighbouring family. His parents were friendly with Sarah's sister Fanny. Living close and being of the same age, it was natural that Sarah and Gordon should be brought together (although it is said that Lady Randolph was largely responsible for the match). Unlike other suitors, Gordon Wilson was not intimidated by Sarah. A good-natured, easy-going young man—but with a mind of his own—Gordon ignored her acid tongue and recognized her more solid virtues: her sense of loyalty, her lack of affectation and her uncomplicated approach to life. He saw in her hearty, out-going nature the makings of an ideal wife for a soldier. He proposed and, although he might not have measured up to the family's expectations, he was accepted.

It has been said of Sarah that 'her brothers possessed genius, her sisters stately homes'. By accepting Gordon Wilson, Sarah altered the family pattern. The Wilsons did not own a stately home; in fact, when they were in England they had to lease Disraeli's old home, Hughenden, as a country residence. Gordon's father, Sir Samuel Wilson, had started life as a farmer's son at Ballycloughan, in Ireland. In 1852, at the age of twenty, he had been persuaded by his brother to emigrate to Australia. Here, after working as a miner, he had made his fortune cattle ranching. In 1861 he had married a daughter of the Hon. William Campbell and from that time on the family of four sons and three daughters had divided their time between England and Australia. Having made a name for himself in the Legislative Assembly of Western Australia—for which he was knighted in 1875—Sir Samuel returned to England to settle more or less permanently. In 1886 he was elected Conservative MP for Portsmouth.

While his family were in Australia, Gordon had been at Eton. His educational career was not particularly distinguished but he was to be remembered at Eton for the records he set as a runner and for his singular feat in saving his sovereign's life. One day in March 1882, as Queen Victoria was about to leave from Windsor station, a madman named Maclean fired a gun at her; only young Gordon Wilson's prompt action in striking the assailant's arm saved the Queen from being killed. On leaving Eton, Gordon completed his academic education at Christ Church, Oxford, and entered the army in 1887. He was a dedicated soldier; his only interest outside his career was his passion for horse-racing. Homely looking, with laughing eyes and an untidy walrus moustache, he combined sound judgement and strong will with a gentle manner and unassuming nature.

Although seemingly ill-assorted, it is not difficult to understand the attraction which Sarah and Gordon held for each other. Each supplied the other's defects. Her cutting assertiveness was complemented by his imperturbable good-nature; his insouciance was off-set by her determination. Between them they built a comfortable, if somewhat prosaic, relationship.

Their marriage, on 21 November 1891, was one of the social

events of the year. It attracted an almost embarrassing amount of publicity. Sarah's portrait featured on the covers of society magazines; sketches of her dress, the bridesmaids' dresses and her mother's dress filled the inside pages. Reports of the ceremony and the reception filled columns of tiny print in all the leading newspapers. The only person to express disappointment was Sarah's sixteen-year-old nephew, Winston. Having been given permission to attend the ceremony from Harrow, young Winston Churchill complained bitterly at being bundled back to school just as the fun was starting. This was nothing unusual. Winston's contacts with his aunt Sarah tended to be unfortunate.

Winston and Sarah did not get on well together. The ten years which separated them in age did not provide enough gap for them to ignore each other and their personalities were too positive to prevent them clashing. Sarah had a tendency to meddle in family affairs which Winston found difficult to stomach. As a schoolboy Winston was not highly regarded by his family and it was among his fault-finding elders that Sarah created the most mischief. Winston was constantly on the defensive: the state of their relationship could usually be gauged by whether he referred to his aunt as Sarah, Aunt Sarah or, with heavy sarcasm, Lady Sarah. A crisis was reached a couple of years after Sarah's marriage. At the time Winston had just completed his first year at Sandhurst and was trying to raise some extra cash by selling a pair of field-glasses. He advertised the glasses anonymously in *Exchange and Mart*. Somehow or other Sarah got wind of it and jumped to conclusions. Lord Randolph was away on his fateful world cruise and Sarah immediately assumed that Winston was trying to sell his father's property. Without making enquiries, she reported this to the Dowager Duchess of Marlborough as well as to other members of the family. Winston was justifiably furious. In an angry letter to his mother he proved that the glasses were his and roundly denounced Sarah as 'a cat'. He was even more emphatic when writing to his American aunt, Leonie Leslie, a month later. The incident, he claimed, was typical of 'Lady Sarah' and he doubted whether he would be 'a very dutiful nephew in future'. When old Sir Samuel Wilson died a year later, Winston was delighted with a rumour that his objectionable aunt had been by-passed in her father-in-law's will. He told his mother that he considered Sarah's income of £7,000 or £8,000 a year was ample; any more would make her unbearable.

But, family feuds apart, there can be no doubt that marriage suited Sarah. No longer a mere junior member of the 'Churchill lot' she was able to take her own place in society. Within no time it was reported that she was one of 'the smartest of young married women, having a knack of dressing always in good taste, and also having good looks'. Entering fully into her husband's love of the turf, she was thrilled when his horse Father O'Flynn won the Derby in the first year of their marriage —even if it did beat Lord Randolph's Ladas, upon which her brother had pinned great hopes. Partly in reparation, but mostly in admiration, the Wilsons named their first son, born a few months later, Randolph Gordon. When their second son, Alan Spencer, was born the following November, Lord Randolph was touring the far East; he had only three months to live.

Lord Randolph's death was the second blow suffered by his family within a few years. In 1892 Sarah's elder brother, the 8th Duke of Marlborough, had died at the age of forty-eight. With his death the Marlborough title passed to his son. To ensure both the succession and the family fortunes, the 9th Duke married, in 1895, Consuelo Vanderbilt, a rich American heiress. The newly married couple arrived in England some months after Lord Randolph's death. They were met at the station by a formidable contingent of the 'Churchill lot'—with Sarah well to the fore. At dinner that evening, it was Lady Sarah's sharp tongue that Consuelo found most frightening. When the conversation turned to the wedding, the bridegroom's mother complained that she had not been able to attend because her son had refused to pay her fare to America. 'Then,' says Consuelo, 'Sarah tittered and also regretted that she had not been present. "But," she added, "the Press did not spare us one detail," and I felt that the word 'vulgar' had been omitted but not its implications."' Consuelo never forgot that ill-considered remark. Years later when she came to write her memoirs she painted an acid picture of Sarah. 'Lady Sarah Wilson—a Churchill—was quite different,' she says. 'She told me to call her Sarah since she thought herself too young to be an aunt, and I felt an enmity I could not then account for. She seemed to me as hard as her polished appearance, and her prominent eyes, harsh and sarcastic laugh made me shudder... To me she was kind in an arrogant manner that made me grit my teeth.'

'Arrogant' was a word often applied to Sarah. It suited her. She had a blustering, bullying way that made people nervous. But this was more a matter of unthinking assertiveness than of snobbishness. Like many another overpowering personality, she was more than ready to respect those who stood up to her. Anyone who replied to her in kind (and Consuelo might well have pointed to Sarah's well-publicized wedding) soon found her willing to laugh at herself. She was hard but she was not frigid: there was nothing pompous about her. All her life she had to check her high spirits: the hoyden was never far behind that lady-like façade. Unnerving as it might be, Sarah's arrogance would help her out of many a tricky situation.

It was shortly after the arrival of the new Duke and Duchess that the Wilsons set off for South Africa. They had good reason to visit the country. Lord Randolph's expedition, for all the controversy surrounding it, had established firm links between the Churchills and the mining magnates of Johannesburg. As one of the original members of her brother's syndicate, Sarah had a financial and personal interest in South Africa. Without Lord Randolph's guidance, it was necessary for a member of the syndicate to obtain first-hand knowledge of the Transvaal situation. This was a matter of some urgency. For those in the know—and Lady Sarah Wilson was among them—it was obvious that momentous events were afoot in Johannesburg. It could not have been by chance that Lord Randolph's sister arrived in South Africa when she did.

*

The importance which Sarah attached to Lord Randolph's *Graphic* letters when writing to her mother from the Cape was, perhaps, a little exaggerated. Her description of the ferment in the Transvaal would also have struck the average citizen of Cape Town as a bit excessive. Lulled by the drowsy heat of a Cape summer, they would probably have dismissed her whole account as the usual alarmist nonsense of a newly arrived visitor. South Africans were too accustomed to impending upheavals to take each new development over-seriously.

The Transvaal was indeed seething with unrest; but then the Transvaal was always drifting from one crisis to another. A state of near revolution had existed there for some years; if things now seemed to be coming to a head they were no worse than they had been a few months earlier. Then President Kruger had created a dangerous situation by attempting to cut the merchants of Johannesburg off from the British colonies in the south. He had closed the river drifts (fords) into the Transvaal in an effort to make the mining community use the newly opened railway to Delagoa Bay in Portuguese East Africa. His action had produced a strong protest from the British Colonial Secretary and troopships bound for India had been diverted to the Cape. A showdown between Kruger and the Uitlanders had then seemed inevitable. The apparent *impasse* had been broken by Kruger's capitulation. He had opened the drifts and an uneasy peace had returned to South Africa. By the time Sarah arrived in December the 'drifts crisis' was over and, despite persistent rumblings from Johannesburg, most people were preparing for Christmas rather than for war. It was all part of the South African way of life.

If Sarah did not share the Cape's festive spirit, it was not because she was less hardened to the situation, nor was she misinformed. In fact, she was better informed than most people in Cape Town. Events in the Transvaal were about to take a dramatic turn and Sarah was one of the few people to know the direction in which they would be turning. Her letter to her mother hinted at things about which she could not write: things she had been told before she arrived at the Cape.

The s.s. *Tantallon Castle*, in which the Wilsons had sailed, had left Southampton at the end of November 1895. Apart from the fact that the ship was unusually crowded, there was nothing to distinguish the voyage from any other routine cruise of the Castle line. The long sultry days were given over to deck quoits and casual promenading; the evenings to gossip against a background of Strauss waltzes. For the majority of passengers, parading the decks in their newly unpacked cottons and tussore silks, shipboard life followed its usual monotonous course. If there was anything exceptional about the voyage it would not have been apparent to a casual observer.

But Sarah was no casual observer. She was very much involved with a group of first-class passengers who made her weeks at sea an unforgettable experience. Her shipboard companions included Lord Randolph's shy friend, Alfred Beit, and several other well-known South Africans. Sarah had known some of them before she left England; she quickly became acquainted with the rest. They proved to be stimulating company. For these seemingly staid financiers, with their high starched collars and waxed moustaches, had exciting things to discuss: they were returning to South Africa to play a part in one of the most audacious schemes ever concocted by the ambitious Cecil John Rhodes. Alfred Beit and his friends were, in fact, up to their necks in a devilish conspiracy. Their object was the overthrow of the Transvaal Government. Lady Sarah Wilson was soon drawn into the thick of it.

The plot of course centred on Johannesburg. The Transvaal situation had not changed much since Lord Randolph's visit four years earlier. Basically the position of the mining community was the same: it had merely been intensified by continuing frustration. The Uitlanders now outnumbered the Boers by almost six to one but they were still denied representation in the Volksraad. The unfair taxation had continued and so had the denial of their elementary rights as taxpayers; the only education provided for their children was instruction through the Dutch language. In August they had again petitioned Kruger and again their petition had been rejected. More than ever they were convinced that they could not expect a solution of their problems through constitutional reform. Their only hope lay in snatching the initiative from the obstinate old President: they must, almost in a literal sense, be in a position to hold a gun to his head. Their plot was aimed at putting them in just such a position.

In its rough outline it was as simple as it was bold. After years of threats and warnings, Johannesburg was to rise in armed rebellion. For months rifles and ammunition had been smuggled into the town among the goods and oil drums addressed to various Johannesburg merchants. However, for the rising to be successful it would have to be supported by more than an untrained citizen army. The Boers, despite their lack of numbers, were skilled marksmen and past-masters of guerrilla warfare. They would have to be met by a force sufficiently experienced to take advantage of a surprise attack. Such a force could only come from outside the Transvaal. What was equally important, it had to be assembled within striking distance of Johannesburg without arousing Boer suspicions. The solution had come through the railway which Cecil Rhodes was building to the north. Rhodes, who intended to use the Transvaal 'rebellion' to further his vision of 'painting Africa red', was not only the driving force behind the conspiracy but was in a position to make it feasible. The Chartered Company had managed to get the Colonial Office to cede a strip of the Bechuanaland Protectorate which ran along the western border of the Transvaal. It linked the Cape with what had once been Mashonaland and was now known as Rhodesia. Here, just north of the town of Mafeking, a detachment of the Company's police had been posted—ostensibly to guard the railway construction from hostile tribesmen. They were under the command of Rhodes's great friend, the administrator of the Company's lands, Dr Leander Starr Jameson. Altogether it was hoped to assemble here a well-equipped force of 1,500 men. As soon as the Johannesburg rising took place, the rebel leaders were to appeal to Jameson to come to their aid. The force would then invade the Transvaal, take over Johannesburg, and set up a provisional government. Kruger would then be forced to come in terms with the Uitlanders.

It was this knowledge which had prompted Sarah to write excitedly to her mother. How much she had known before she boarded the *Tantallon Castle* it is not possible to say. When she came to write about this visit to South Africa, many years later, she claimed that she had no inkling of the conspiracy until she was at sea. 'There is no such place for getting to know people well as on a sea voyage,' she wrote. 'Somehow the sea inspires confidence, and one knows that information cannot, anyway, be posted off by the same day's mail. So those who were helping to pull the strings of this ill-fated rebellion talked pretty freely of their hopes and fears during the long, dark tropical evenings.' But this seems far too facile an explanation. If it was not possible to post information by the same day's mail, there was plenty of time for the secret to leak out after the ship arrived at Cape Town. Only a long-trusted friend would have gained the confidence of the conspirators, and Alfred Beit, after all, had known the Churchill family for years. Sarah probably knew something of the intended rebellion when she booked her passage. Rumours that a rising was about to take place had been circulating London for some time (Rhodes's London solicitor had been twitted about his 'rebellion' by members of his club). Jameson's role in the affair was a much closer secret; it was most likely this aspect of the conspiracy that was revealed to Sarah on the *Tantallon Castle*.

Thrilled as she was by the cloak-and-dagger atmosphere, Sarah was by no means confident that the plot would be successful. Considering what was at stake, she thought the conspirators were strangely divided. They gave the impression of enthusiastic amateurs rather than of a body of single-minded, disciplined men. 'I must admit,' she confessed, 'it was the fiery-headed followers who talked the loudest—those who had nothing to lose and much to gain. The financiers, while directing and encouraging their zeal, seemed almost with the same hand to wish to put the brake on and damp their military ardour.' There was a definite difference of opinion over the question of how the rebellion should be inspired. Some hinted that the rising would receive the blessing of the Colonial Office and that the Union Jack should be the rallying standard. Others argued that this would alienate a considerable number of the non-British miners as well as outside opinion; the revolt, they claimed, was intended to right the Uitlanders' grievances and should not be turned into an Imperial crusade—the only flag that could be raised was that of the Transvaal republic.

But shortcomings and differences of opinion tended to be glossed over. Everyone was too excited to worry unduly. On the main score—that of bringing Kruger to book—they were all agreed; the settling of that score was more than enough to be going on with. The rising was expected to take place at the end of December and everyone was eager to play a part. Sarah, although she would only be an onlooker, was as keyed up as the rest. 'I was,' she declared, 'greatly excited at arriving in South Africa in such stirring times . . . all were so eloquent that by the time our voyage ended I felt as great a rebel against "Oom Paul" and his Government as any one of them.'

*

Shortly after they arrived in Cape Town, Sarah and Gordon were taken by Alfred Beit to meet Cecil Rhodes. It was an event to which Sarah had looked forward with immense interest. She had heard much about Rhodes from her brother. He was not only the most important Englishman in South Africa but the hub around which the forthcoming events would revolve. Everything she had heard about him appealed to her Churchillian taste for power politics.

At this time, Rhodes was busy making alterations to his house. When he had entertained Lord Randolph in 1891 he had merely been a tenant at The Grange. Since then he had bought the property, renamed it Groote Schuur, and employed a young architect, Herbert Baker, to restore it to its original architectural character. Building operations were much in evidence on the day that the Wilsons arrived. Driving along the sun-dappled avenue of Scotch firs, they rounded a bend and caught sight of the house they were to come to know so well. White-washed, low and rambling, with muscular gables and a thatched roof, it was an exact replica of those gracious homes established at the Cape by the early Dutch settlers. The right wing was still enmeshed in scaffolding and, as they drew closer, they noticed that workmen were busy putting in a new front door.

Their host, when he appeared, seemed as unprepared for their visit as was his house. As they stepped down from their carriage, Rhodes emerged from one of the unfinished rooms where he had been giving orders to the workmen. He was dressed in an old coat, a baggy pair of white flannels and a slouch hat. Sarah found him most impressive. His expression, she says, was a mixture of 'power, resolution and kindness'. Like many another, she was startled by the penetrating glance of his bright blue eyes: they seemed, she said, 'to read one through in an instant'. Rhodes—always on his guard when meeting a woman—appeared at first a trifle off-hand; but, with Sarah at her social best, this reserve soon broke down. As he conducted them over the house, pointing out various pieces of old Dutch furniture, his conversation became quite animated. He told them that he had bought the new front door for £200 from an old colonial mansion and that he intended every detail of the house to reflect the lives of the early Dutch settlers. This sense of period was so strong that he was even toying with the idea of having no electric light, or even oil lamps, and burning nothing but tallow candles to keep the illusion of age.

The tour over, Sarah and Gordon were taken to join some other guests sitting on one of the wide verandahs. Here Rhodes continued to enthuse about his plans for his estate. For Sarah, listening to Rhodes's high-pitched voice describing his private menagerie, the idea that she was in the presence of an arch-conspirator seemed absurd. He was more like an effervescent schoolboy than a statesman approaching the greatest test of his career. Fresh from the whisperings of the *Tantallon Castle*, Sarah must have felt as though she had exchanged a melodrama for a domestic comedy.

However, when the Wilsons lunched at Groote Schuur two days later they were again plunged into intrigue. In sharp contrast to their previous visit, the conversation was almost exclusively political. The problem of what was happening in Johannesburg was on everyone's mind. Rhodes kept himself aloof and for most of the meal he appeared to be preoccupied, although he did not neglect his duties as host. He did his best to make the Wilsons welcome and, on hearing they were about to leave for Kimberley, he pressed them to stay with him on their return. He then had second thoughts. 'My plans,' he explained, 'are a little unsettled.'

*

It was shortly after the Wilsons arrived in Kimberley that the first rumblings of revolt were heard. Sarah and Gordon were staying with J. B. Currey, a well-known Kimberley personality and father of Harry Currey, Rhodes's former private secretary. Although his son had now married and left Rhodes's employ, Currey was still closely connected with the De Beers mining organization; it was probably at the suggestion of Alfred Beit that he agreed to act as host to the Wilsons. Sarah is a little vague about the dates of her Kimberley visit, but it must have been on the evening of her arrival that her host arrived home with some startling news. Some women who had been preparing to leave Kimberley for the Transvaal had received telegrams telling them to delay their departure. This, says Sarah, 'was not so much a surprise to me as to the residents of Kimberley; to them it came as a bombshell.'

Tension mounted the following day when the newspapers published a manifesto issued by the Johannesburg Reform Committee, which set out the Uitlanders' grievances and called for a mass meeting on 6 January. Sarah must have found this puzzling. As far as she knew, the original plan had envisaged a rising that very day—28 December; with a meeting now called for 6 January, it was obvious that something had gone wrong.

The citizens of Kimberley, knowing nothing of the conspiracy and fully supporting the Uitlanders, greeted the manifesto with enthusiasm. For them it looked as if the Transvaal problem was about to be settled. After years of haggling, the gauntlet, as Sarah noted, had been 'thrown down with a vengeance'.

Two days of anxiety followed. Nearly everyone in Kimberley had a friend or relative in Johannesburg and there was no knowing how these English-speaking residents of the Transvaal would react. The problem of divided loyalties was an acute one and individuals would regard the crisis differently. The Boer Government also had claims on the younger men. J. B. Currey had two sons working on the Witwatersrand and he was afraid that, in the event of trouble, they would be commandeered to fight for the Transvaal. Sarah sympathized but was equally concerned on another score. 'One possibility I noticed was never entertained,' she says, '—that, if fighting occurred, the English community might get the worst of it.' Such an idea was laughed to scorn. The Boers, she was told, were lazy and unprepared. It would take them weeks to mobilize a force. So long was it since they had fought that their marksmanship was no longer what it had been. It was estimated that two hundred men 'ought to be able to take possession of Johannesburg and Kruger into the bargain'. This wild talk made Sarah uneasy. She was reminded of the over-confident young men in the *Tantallon Castle*. 'The thought flashed across my mind,' she says, 'that these possible foes were the sons of the men who had annihilated us at Majuba and Laing's Nek, and I wondered whether another black page was to be added to the country's history.'

The next news to reach the town broke like a thunderclap. On 30 December the citizens of Kimberley read with a mixture of incredulity and admiration that Dr Jameson and a contingent of the Chartered Company's police had invaded the Transvaal. For Kimberley the news had a special significance. Dr Jameson was known throughout the town. He had started his South African career in Kimberley as a humble general practitioner and had lived and worked there until he had gone to Mashonaland as Rhodes's agent. The idea of Dr Jim leading an invasion force was as startling as it was incomprehensible. When it was learned that nearly all the officers accompanying him held Imperial commissions, the first flush of enthusiasm gave way to bewilderment. 'One heard perfect strangers,' says Sarah, 'asking each other how these officers could justify their action of entering a friendly territory, armed to the teeth.'

For the next few days the town was in an uproar. While Sarah waited for news of the rising, the public clamoured outside the newspaper offices demanding action from their leading citizens. Many of the men offered to form a volunteer brigade to go to the assistance of Dr Jameson. Trains arrived at the station crammed with refugees; there were even two women carrying babies which had been born on their nightmare journey.

Then came the most stunning news of all. Dr Jameson and his men were reported to have been surrounded by a Boer force and taken prisoner. At first the town refused to believe it. Whatever they felt about the invasion they could not bring themselves to accept the fact that it had been turned into a fiasco. When a telegram was read out at the newspaper office denying Jameson's surrender, the huge crowd went wild 'and the town resounded with the refrain of "Rule, Britannia".'

But they were wrong. Johannesburg had not risen. Jameson had been captured and it was President Kruger who ruled as firmly as ever. Sarah's doubts had been justified.

CHAPTER SIX

The Aftermath

THE CAPTURE of Dr Jameson and his force was confirmed on Saturday, 4 January. The citizens of Kimberley rose to the occasion with an admirable, if misplaced, display of loyalty. Without waiting for further explanations they closed their ranks and rallied to their local hero. A petition—signed, it is said, 'by everybody in Kimberley'—was immediately despatched to the British High Commissioner: 'Your Excellency,' it read, 'should treat for the release of Dr Jameson and his comrades with full honours of war as of more importance than any other condition which the Government of the South African Republic is asked to grant.' They were no less decided when it came to identifying the villains of the piece. Everyone was convinced that the mining magnates of Johannesburg were responsible for the whole sorry business. 'Loud and deep were the execrations levelled at the Johannesburgers,' says Sarah, 'who, it was strenuously reiterated, had invited the Raiders to come to their succour and who, when the pinch came, never even left the town to go to their assistance.' But, as Sarah must have realized, it was not as simple as that.

At the last minute the conspiracy had gone haywire. The Uitlanders had discovered so many loose ends in their ill-spun plans that they had tied themselves in knots. Having set a provisional date for the rising, the Reform Committee had suddenly found themselves faced with more than they were equipped to handle. The rifles and ammunition smuggled into the town fell far short of that they had been led to expect; Jameson's force was nowhere near the 1,500 well-equipped men he had promised; the question of the flag was still undecided. . . . The telegraph wires between Johannesburg and Cape Town, between the Transvaal and Bechuanaland, buzzed with frantic muddled messages. Jameson became more and more impatient. Messengers were sent to explain the situation to him. It was no use. The impetuous doctor was in no mood for explanations: he suspected that the Johannesburgers were losing courage. On Sunday 29 December, after persuading one of the messengers to join his force, he sent his final telegram to the Reformers: 'I shall start without fail tomorrow night,' he announced.

The only hope of stopping him now rested with Rhodes. On that same Sunday the Reformers heard from Cape Town that a wire had been sent ordering Jameson to remain where he was. It gave them fresh hope; with Rhodes giving the orders the doctor would be forced to obey. But they reckoned without the jinx which was plaguing the whole affair. Rhodes's telegram—'On no account must you move. I most strongly object to such a course'—never reached Bechuanaland. There had been a delay in sending it owing to the Sunday closing hours of the telegraph office. By the time it was transmitted Jameson had cut the telegraph wires to Cape Town.

A combination of bad luck and bad organization led Jameson's force straight into the Boer ambush. Right up to the last minute Rhodes clung to the hope that his telegram had stopped the Raiders. When he heard that it had not, he was staggered. 'Old Jameson,' he told a visitor, 'has upset my apple-cart . . . I thought I had stopped him . . . Poor old Jameson. Twenty years we have been friends, and now he goes in to ruin me.' But he did not brood for long. There was a great deal to be done and he was not a man to wait on events. After resigning as Prime Minister of the Cape, he paid a lightning visit to Kimberley: he had to tie up his business concerns before leaving for England.

At Kimberley station he was met by the cheers of a huge crowd. He was, after all, almost a local boy himself. The demonstration touched him. 'In times of political adversity,' he told the crowd, 'people came to know who their friends were.'

Sarah and Gordon were not at the station. They had left for the Cape a day or so earlier. With the failure of the Raid, their plans were as confused as the general situation. Any hopes they may have had of joining the Reformers—victorious or otherwise—were completely dashed. The Transvaal was no place for visiting Englishmen, let alone Englishwomen. Harrowing accounts of the horde of refugees streaming into the Cape filled the papers: nobody in their right minds would dream of travelling the other way. Harry Lawson, a fellow guest at the Curreys, who was representing his father's newspaper, the London *Daily Telegraph* (and whose presence in Kimberley at this time was as significant as that of the Wilsons') had already run into difficulties trying to reach Johannesburg. He had managed to enter the Transvaal only by using a foreign name. For anyone as John Bull-like as Sarah, such a disguise would have been impossible: she could not have maintained it for long, even had she wanted to.

In any case, all their influential friends were at the Cape. Only by travelling south could they hope to keep in touch with events.

*

On arriving at Groote Schuur, they found Alfred Beit in charge. Of all the conspirators, the shy and secretive Beit seems to have taken the failure of the Raid most to heart. He appeared, says Sarah, 'quite crushed by the turn events had taken'. His concern was not for himself but for his friend and employee, Lionel Phillips, who, it had just been learned, had been arrested together with other leading members of the Reform Committee. In a way, this was the final irony of the whole bizarre adventure; as residents of the Transvaal, the Reformers were imprisoned under the very laws they had opposed for not granting them citizen rights. Unlike Jameson and his fellow Raiders, who were being shipped home to stand trial in England, they were now claimed by the Government which for years had done its best to ignore them.

Other than this, Beit could add little to what Sarah and Gordon already knew. Rhodes was at Kimberley and Sir Hercules Robinson, the British High Commissioner, had gone to Pretoria to confer with President Kruger. Cape Town, like the rest of South Africa, was left to speculate. The most puzzling aspect of the affair was Jameson's apparent disregard of Rhodes's final telegram. Nothing was known of the cut telegraph wires and the doctor's behaviour seemed inexplicable. Had he got the telegram or had it been intercepted by agents of the Transvaal? If he had got the telegram, why had he defied it? Everybody had his own theories and nobody felt quite safe.

In an attempt at British aplomb, Lady Robinson decided to hold a garden party in the grounds of the Governor's residence at Newlands. Sarah, together with Mrs Harry Lawson—who had accompanied the Wilsons from Kimberley—was invited to attend. It was a day of brilliant sunshine, the gardens looked lovely, and a military band played charming tunes under the enormous oaks; but the guests wandered about looking tense and miserable. 'It was,' says Sarah, 'rather a depressing entertainment.'

On 15 January it was learned that Sir Hercules Robinson had left Pretoria and that arrangements had been made to transport the Raiders to England That same morning Sarah heard privately that Rhodes was back in Cape Town and that he intended to leave on the evening mail-ship for England. Determined to see him before he left, she, Gordon and Mrs Harry Lawson went straight to Groote Schuur. They found the ex-Prime Minister in surprisingly good spirits. Unlike Beit, Rhodes had recovered from the first shock and was determined to salvage what he could. He was prepared to face any inquiry that might be instituted by the British authorities and to do what he could for the political prisoners. 'You see,' he told Sarah, 'I stand in so much stronger position than they do, in that I am not encumbered with wife and children; so I am resolved to strain every nerve on their behalf.'

For the time being he felt it best to keep out of the limelight. There had been no announcement of his departure in the press and in order to disguise his intentions he asked the Wilsons and Mrs Lawson to accompany him to the docks. According to Sarah the little party was meant to give the impression of making a tour of the harbour. It seems a most unlikely piece of subterfuge. For Rhodes to have set off on a sight-seeing tour at such a time would have awakened rather than lulled suspicion. As it happened, the only curiosity they aroused came from a P & O liner, the *Victoria*. This ship had been chartered as a troop carrier and, in accordance with Colonial Office instructions, had docked at Table Bay the day before on its way to Bombay. The lower decks and portholes were crowded with red-coated soldiers who, says Sarah, 'appeared to take a deep interest in our movements'.

Once aboard the mailship, Rhodes relaxed and became more talkative. Rather surprisingly he took Sarah into his confidence.

It is some indication of her authoritative personality that Rhodes, always supicious of feminine indiscretion, spoke so frankly to Sarah. Lacking the flirtatiousness, the excessive femininity, which so often unnerved Rhodes, Sarah's forthright, masculine turn of mind made it possible for him to treat her as a colleague. It was the beginning of what was to prove a life-long friendship. 'One lady Rhodes liked was Lady Sarah Wilson,' an employee at Groote Schuur was to recall, 'and that was because she was no fool. He used to talk politics to her like he did to Dr Jameson, and he always seemed at ease with her more than he did with most.' Now, pacing the deck and trying to keep his shrill voice under control, Rhodes confided to Sarah his fears for the future. As far as the political implications were concerned, his mind was more or less settled. He said that during the first six nights of the crisis he had been worried to death and had hardly slept. 'Now,' he went on, 'I have thought the whole matter out, I have decided what is best to be done, so I am all right again, and I do not consider at forty-three my career is ended.' He would no longer be Prime Minister of the Cape but, provided his Chartered Company was left intact, he felt he would survive. When Sarah told him that she had had a small bet with Harry Lawson that he would return as a dominant factor in South African politics within a year, Rhodes thought for a minute and then said: 'It will take ten years; better cancel your bet.'

They were still talking when the bell rang for visitors to leave the ship. Hurriedly Sarah wished him goodbye and good luck and scrambled down the gangway with Gordon and Mrs Lawson. Standing on the deck of the launch, the three of them watched the great ship pass into the night.

*

Sarah and Gordon had now been a month in South Africa. Their stay in the country could hardly be described as uneventful but they were beginning to feel rather restricted. After all, they had come out to visit South Africa and so far they had not got beyond the Cape Colony. The alarums and excursions of the Jameson Raid apart, they had not been particularly impressed by what they had seen. Kimberley, with its 'deadly respectability', had disappointed Sarah and now that Rhodes had left she found Cape Town pathetically dull. Whatever excitement and interest the country had to offer seemed to radiate from the Transvaal; the point of their visit would be missed if they did not see Johannesburg. Not only did Sarah have mining interests on the Witwatersrand, but Johannesburg had been the town that had most impressed Lord Randolph and the events of recent weeks added to its attractions. How to get there was the problem. The train journey to the northern Cape was long, uncomfortable and hazardous. Stories of the insulting manner in which visitors were searched at the Cape border—a proceeding which could entail endless delays—did little to encourage the Wilsons to retrace their steps. They had thought of sailing to Durban and approaching the Transvaal through Natal, but the *Roslin Castle*, on which they had booked a passage, had broken down and was already several days overdue.

This was the position when Sir Hercules Robinson proved, as Sarah put it, 'a friend in need'. One suspects that the unfortunate Sir Hercules (then a sick and worried man) had little option in the matter. Sarah was determined to get to the Transvaal and was not one to be balked by a faltering steamship. She would not have hesitated to demand assistance at the highest level and it would have taken a more robust man than the High Commissioner to withstand one of her frontal attacks. However it came about, no time was lost in getting the Wilsons on board a very exclusive liner sailing for Durban. The *Victoria*, the troopship they had noticed in the harbour when Rhodes left, was leaving for Durban on a highly confidential mission; Sarah and Gordon were among the few to know what that mission was. After swearing them to secrecy, Sir Hercules explained that the ship was due to pick up Dr Jameson and the other Raiders at Durban in order to take them to England. With feelings running high among all sections of the population, it was felt that the fewer people who knew about the Raiders' departure the more chance there would be of avoiding ugly demonstrations. The Admiral at Cape Town had given special permission for the Wilsons to sail in the *Victoria* as 'indulgence passengers'.

Sarah was delighted. She was not quite sure whether the curtain had just come down on a drama or a farce but, having said goodbye to the luckless producer, she was now anxious to catch a glimpse of the leading actors. There was also the thrill of being on board a troopship. As one of a small band of civilians, she was fascinated by the army at sea. From the morning parade of scarlet-coated soldiers lining the deck, until the evening meal accompanied by a briskly efficient military band, she was kept constantly entertained. The time, she says, passed too quickly.

The evening before they were due to arrive at Durban, Sarah was told to be dressed and ready to disembark at six the following morning. The ship was under orders to sail as soon as it had picked up its controversial passengers; its departure could not be delayed. However, waking at five o'clock, Sarah was horrified to find that the ship's engines had already stopped. She was even more alarmed, on looking out of the porthole, to discover that they were anchored outside Durban harbour and that a small, crowded lighter was bobbing its way towards them. Pulling on her clothes, she rushed to the deck to watch the lighter edge its way alongside. 'I shall never forget that striking and melancholy scene,' she wrote. 'The dull grey morning, of which the dawn had scarcely broken; the huge rollers of the leaden sea, which were lifting our mighty ship as if she had been a cockleshell; and the tiny steamer ... her deck crowded with sunburnt men, many of whose faces were familiar to us, and who were picturesquely attired, for the most part, in the same clothes they had worn on their ill-fated march—flannel shirts, khaki breeches, high boots and large felt hats of the Bechuanaland Border Police, which they were probably wearing for the last time.'

Her first panic had been unnecessary. Not until six o'clock was the order given for the prisoners to disembark. As Dr Jameson and his men came scrambling aboard, Sarah and Gordon rushed to have a word with the friends they recognized. They found them in good humour. One or two of the men resented the fact that they were now being held captive by their fellow countrymen and others were a little shamefaced ('like boys who expect a good scolding when they get home'), but for the most part they were inclined to treat the whole affair as a huge joke. The only cloud on their horizon was a slight anxiety as to what was in store for them. It was a question that was being pondered throughout South Africa; the Wilsons were as much in the dark as anyone.

Sarah gives no indication of her reaction to meeting Jameson for the first time. She could not have been impressed. Short, thin and balding, with a mousy moustache, the doctor hardly lived up to descriptions of him as either a hero or a desperado His best friends were forced to admit that Jameson was an insignificant-looking man. Only from an occasional glint in his alert, wide-set eyes was it possible to detect a hint of his adventurous nature. On being introduced to him, Sarah had only one question: had he or had he not received the telegram telling him not to start? Jameson shrugged. The same question had been fired at him continually for the past few days; he must have been heartily sick of it. 'I received so many messages from day to day,' he said wearily, 'now telling me to come, then to delay starting, that I thought it best to make up their minds for them, before the Boers had time to get together.'

And with this somewhat insouciant reply ringing in their ears, Sarah and Gordon were hurried on to the waiting lighter.

*

Insouciance, surprisingly enough, seemed to Sarah to be the spirit which permeated Johannesburg as well. Far from giving the impression of a recent storm centre, the town appeared quite unruffled by the events of the past two weeks. The Wilsons were shown about Johannesburg by Lord Randolph's former mining-expert, Henry C. Perkins, who, with his wife, had been living in South Africa for the past few years. Sarah was amazed at the unquenchable vitality of the place. Ever-moving crowds thronged the pavements; fashionably dressed women bowled along the streets in smart carriages; the shops, which a fortnight earlier had been barred and barricaded, looked gay and prosperous and everyone seemed more intent on building up their businesses than in bringing down the Government. 'For the first time in South Africa,' says Sarah, 'I saw life.'

The Raid had made no difference to Johannesburg's lavish hospitality. Invitations were pressed upon the Wilsons and, at the round of dinner parties to which they were entertained, the Raid was naturally the main talking point. Conversation tended to centre on what would have happened had Jameson reached the town. Nobody could agree. There were those who were convinced that the Boers would have cut off the water supply and starved the town out, while others were equally certain that the very name of Jameson would have carried the day. 'The more one heard of the whole affair,' sighed Sarah, 'the more it seemed to resemble a scene out of a comic opera.'

In Johannesburg Sarah and Gordon were guests at Clewer House, the home of Mr Abe Bailey, one of their fellow passengers aboard the *Tantallon Castle* and a close friend of the Churchill family. Lord Randolph had been entertained by Abe Bailey while he was in Johannesburg. When the Wilsons arrived, however, their host was not there to receive them. Like another of their shipboard acquaintances, Aubrey Woolls-Sampson, he had been arrested with the leading members of the Reform Committee and was now officially detained at Pretoria. Sarah and Gordon decided to visit him at the State gaol.

Once outside of Johannesburg, the unrest in the Transvaal became more apparent. It took a full three hours by train to cover the thirty-one miles to Pretoria. All along the line Sarah was conscious of the vigilance of the still suspicious Boer Government. White tarpaulin-covered wagons, drawn up to form a laager, could be seen from the train, and companies of mounted burgers, called from their farms to meet the crisis, were very much in evidence. 'Although the teeth of the enemy had been drawn for the present,' observed Sarah, 'the Boers were evidently determined to keep up a martial display.'

She says nothing of her meeting with Abe Bailey, but she did record the glimpse of another interesting personality. After she and Gordon had visited the prison, they were conducted round the town by a friendly Boer. There was not a great deal to see but they were suitably impressed by the caramel-coloured Volksraad building and by the imposing Government offices, both of which added a touch of elegance to the otherwise unpretentious main square. While they were dutifully gazing at these buildings, their guide became rather excited. He told them that they were in luck. The President was just about to leave his office on his way home for his midday meal. A few minutes later, the solemn old patriarch, flanked by four burgers, came shuffling down the steps and entered his carriage. Sarah, like her brother before her, was a little surprised at how, in appearance, Paul Kruger belied the reputation the Uitlanders had given him. 'We took a good look at this remarkable personage,' she says. 'Stout in figure, with a venerable white beard, in a somewhat worn frockcoat and rusty old black silk hat, President Kruger did not look the stern dictator of his little kingdom which in truth he was.' Once more she must have been aware of the gap between romance and reality. She had to remind herself that Kruger was 'a man of iron, like Bismarck'; but it was a fact difficult to accept. For all its swashbuckling overtones, the Jameson Raid had been sadly lacking in glamour. Not only did the hero look like a bank clerk, but the villain bore the unmistakable stamp of a heavy-gaited farmer.

That the affair could not be dismissed in comic-opera terms entirely was brought home to Sarah a few days later. To round off their Transvaal visit, the Wilsons went to see the place where Jameson had been captured. Here, at a shallow river ford haunted by vultures, they inspected the bullet-scarred koppies behind which the Boers had lain in ambush. The fight had been short and uninspired and had left little to excite interest. Only when they stumbled upon a trench filled with rocky boulders and covered with withered ferns was the pathos of the battlefield brought home to them.

It was the grave of the Chartered Company's dead.

*

They returned to England on the *Roslin Castle*—the ship which had let them down at Cape Town. Although the old liner had been pronounced seaworthy, she was still limping from the piston rod which had broken on her way out. The homeward voyage took longer than usual. It allowed them to unwind after their hectic South African holiday. They discovered that the captain of the *Roslin Castle* had commanded the ship which had brought Lord Randolph back from his Mashonaland expedition; a good deal of their time was spent playing whist with him and talking about Lord Randolph.

Sarah's verdict on South Africa was very different from that of her brother. In a diary which she kept at the time she recorded her impressions. They were far more tolerant than anything written in the notorious *Graphic* letters.

Among the guests whom the Wilsons met at the round of Johannesburg dinners were men who were willing to discuss the Transvaal situation with at least a degree of moderation. Listening to them Sarah had been struck by their conciliatory attitude. They had spoken of the Boers' bravery, of their simple, if unattractive, faith, and of their burning patriotism; qualities which, had they not been distorted by an illiberal disregard for others, would have earned them much wider respect. The praise, it is true, was not entirely free from prejudice. Even the most sympathetic trotted out the old imputations of laziness, slovenliness, backwardness and, with more justification, narrow-mindedness. But at least it helped her to see that the blame was not entirely one-sided.

'One could not forget,' she wrote, 'that the Transvaal was their country, ceded to them by the English nation. They left the Cape Colony years ago, to escape our laws, which they considered unjust. It is certain we should never have followed them into the Transvaal but for the sudden discovery of the gold industry; it is equally true they had not the power or wish to develop this for themselves, and yet without it they were a bankrupt nation.' If some of her views were debatable, they were certainly more comprehensive than those of Lord Randolph.

Had she not moved in such exclusive circles, Sarah's eyes might have been opened to more weaknesses in the Uitlanders' claims. In different company it would have been pointed out that, for all their pleas of oppression and injustice, the mining magnates were thriving. If Kruger claimed a share of their wealth, they were more than compensated by their own fortunes. A hard look at some of the men who were making the most noise would have revealed them to be in a state far removed from serfdom. Not only did they own large properties and live luxuriously, but among their number were some of the richest men in the world: men whose riches had been accumulated in the very country they claimed was penalizing them. To their claims of victimization, there were those who were ready to reply, somewhat tritely, that if the Uitlanders thought the Transvaal undemocratic they were perfectly free to leave. If they chose to remain it was simply because the flame of freedom tended to pale when set against the glitter of gold. The Uitlanders' desire to stay is understandable but it did not promote unbiased sympathy for their cause.

Nor can their protests that the Boers were supported by their labour be accepted without reference to their own dependence on the mine-workers whom they so blatantly exploited. The gold, which they claimed justified their demand for civil rights, was clawed out of the ground and brought to them on the backs of black workers whose underprivileged, under-paid and voiceless position they scarcely noticed. Indeed, it was Lord Randolph's passing reference to the plight of the Africans which had earned him the enmity of some of the Uitlanders. That this was due to the fact that it was the prevalent thinking of the age might well be true; but it gave a somewhat hollow ring to the high moral tone the Uitlanders were inclined to adopt.

There is much to be said also for the argument that, once given a voice in the administration of the Transvaal, the Uitlanders were in a position to take over the country. There would be nothing to stop them disrupting the Boers' chosen way of life and then leaving when it suited them to do so. It was a matter of hard politics as well as mystical belief that made Kruger stubborn: if he gave an inch, he knew his own days as head of State were numbered. But above all, the readiness of Cecil Rhodes—and possibly the British Colonial Office—to take advantage of the Uitlanders' grievances for ends far removed from the field of civil rights, clouded any clear-cut moral issues that might have existed. The extension of the Transvaal franchise was too closely connected with the extension of the British Empire to allow for a reasonable and just settlement.

If Sarah was not in a position to appreciate the full extent of the Uitlanders' equivocal arguments, there were plenty of others who were. Liberals in England and most Continental powers treated the Jameson Raid with contempt and suspicion. It was seen as a blustering attempt of a self-seeking group to overthrow a legally elected government. The British Colonial Office was thought to be more involved than anyone was prepared to admit. It brought Kruger a tremendous amount of sympathy. In doing so it helped create a further false assessment of the situation.

Whatever Kruger's virtues might have been—and he was, in many respects, a very virtuous man—he was ill-suited to the chivalrous role in which the world now cast him. His shifty handling of the Uitlander question, combined with his holier-than-thou attitude, made him as much to blame for the *impasse* as his opponents. The weight of right had been on his side; by temporising he forfeited his claim to it.

Both sides had been eager to snatch the best of all worlds and together they built up a desperate state of affairs. Tactically they were evenly matched. All the Jameson Raid had done was to confirm them in their false attitudes. It made reconciliation impossible. They were to continue juggling for position until they were forced into a decisive confrontation.

PART THREE

THE WAR

CHAPTER SEVEN

An Ambitious Young Man

WINSTON CHURCHILL was to claim that 'the beginning of these violent times in our country' could be dated from the Jameson Raid. He arrived at this conclusion in his maturity. At the time of the Raid he was twenty-one and regarded Dr Jameson's daring venture with all the enthusiasm of a young soldier on the threshold of his active career. The South Africa escapade was very much in tune with his own recent experiences.

When Jameson crossed the Transvaal border, young Churchill was able to follow reports of the event with a professional eye. A few weeks earlier he had been involved in an unorthodox military exploit himself. It had been in Cuba, where the inhabitants were engaged in a guerrilla war against their Spanish overlords. Churchill had little reason for being there, other than a youthful desire for action and the need to use up five months' army leave.

He had joined the 4th Hussars at the beginning of 1895. In October of that year, finding himself unable to afford to hunt during his winter leave, he had looked round for a suitably exciting alternative. More than anything, he was anxious to witness the army in action; to hear the whistle of bullets and to experience the thrill of a soldier's gamble with death. It was a tall order. The best the world could offer at that time was the Cuban revolution; so Cuba it had to be. With the help of his father's old Fourth Party colleague, Sir Henry Drummond-Wolff, then the British Ambassador at Madrid, he secured introductions to the Spanish military authorities and at the end of October, accompanied by a brother subaltern, set off for Cuba. As wars go, the Cuban campaign was a rather second-rate affair; it consisted largely of interminable marches through

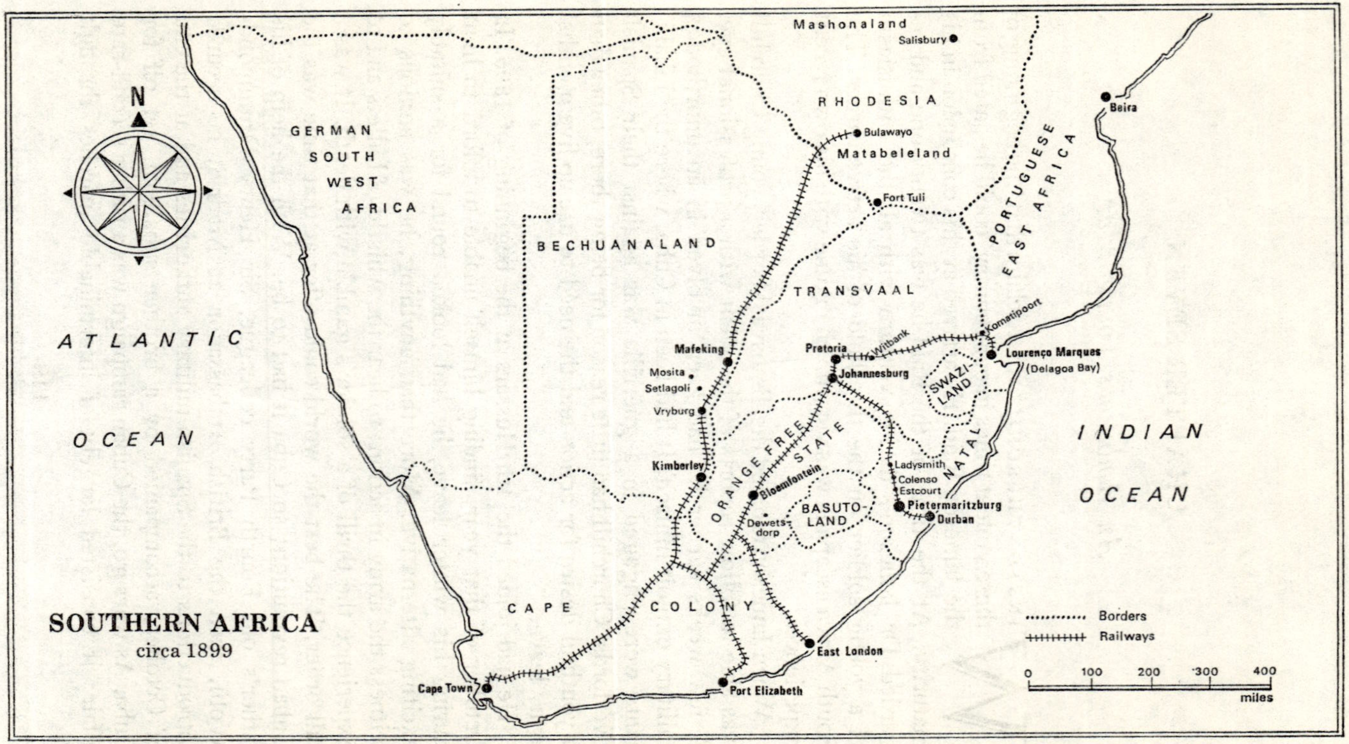
SOUTHERN AFRICA
circa 1899
N
ATLANTIC
OCEAN
INDIAN
OCEAN
GERMAN SOUTH WEST AFRICA
BECHUANALAND
RHODESIA
Mashonaland
Salisbury
Matabeleland
Bulawayo
Fort Tuli
TRANSVAAL
PORTUGUESE EAST AFRICA
Beira
Komatipoort
Lourenço Marques
(Delagoa Bay)
Witbank
Pretoria
Johannesburg
SWAZI-LAND
Mafeking
Mosita
Setlagoli
Vryburg
Kimberley
ORANGE FREE STATE
Bloemfontein
Dewetsdorp
BASUTO-LAND
NATAL
Ladysmith
Colenso
Estcourt
Pietermaritzburg
Durban
CAPE COLONY
Cape Town
Port Elizabeth
East London
Borders
Railways
0
100
200
300
400
miles

dense jungle in pursuit of an enemy who made their presence known only by occasional stray rifle shots. However, it brought its compensations. On his way to and from the Caribbean island, he called in at New York and glimpsed his mother's country; in Havana he was showered with courtesy and cigars; and on 30 November—his 21st birthday—a bullet whizzed close enough past his head for him to boast that he had, at last, been 'under fire'.

The Cuban adventure earned Churchill a courtesy decoration from the Spanish authorities and an ill-natured blast from the British and American press. 'Sensible people,' sniffed one English newspaper, 'will wonder what motive could possibly impel a British officer to mix himself up in a dispute with the merits of which he had absolutely nothing to do. Mr Churchill was supposed to have gone to the West Indies for a holiday. . . . Spending a holiday fighting other people's battles is rather extraordinary even for a Churchill.' This hostile attitude may have been due to professional jealousy. Lord Randolph's role as a special correspondent, four years earlier, had not been forgotten. To many a resentful newspaperman it must have looked as if Winston was about to follow in his father's journalistic footsteps. For, before leaving for Cuba, Churchill had arranged to send back an occasional letter to the *Daily Graphic*. His commission of five guineas a letter was a lot less than the spectacular fee paid to his father, but it did allow him to describe himself as a journalist. He wrote and illustrated five letters for the *Daily Graphic*. Unfortunately, by the time they were published, the war in Cuba had been overshadowed by Jameson's Raid. Not that this worried Churchill. He was heart and soul behind the Raiders. Although he recognized that they would have to be punished, he was loath to admit that they had done wrong. The only criticism he was prepared to make was that the conspirators had allowed the affair to go haywire. His first reaction to the widespread denunciation of Rhodes was curiously like that expressed by his aunt Sarah in South Africa. 'You know what Papa thought of him,' he wrote to his mother. 'I will wager that he will turn out to be a factor to be counted on.'

That not everyone regarded the Raid in the sporting spirit of the Churchills was brought home to him a few months later. His mother believed that the South African fiasco was nothing more than an awkward political issue which could be solved by social contact. She decided to treat it accordingly. She asked Sir John Willoughby—one of the Raiders whom Sarah had greeted on board the *Victoria*—to lunch with John Morley, a dedicated Liberal opponent of the Raid. The two men arrived for the meal before their hostess. It was left to Winston to perform the introductions. He did the best he could in a very awkward situation. John Morley responded with a stiff bow which Willoughby refused to acknowledge; the embarrassed Churchill struggled to keep up a semblance of conversation by talking to them separately. Even the tactful Lady Randolph, when she finally arrived, was unable to break the ice. The two guests started the meal by refusing to address each other and once they had taken up their positions nothing could make them budge. Many years later Churchill was able to recall the chilly atmosphere of this unfortunate luncheon: it was his first personal involvement in South African affairs.

*

Another three years were to pass before he set foot in South Africa. On 11 September 1896 he sailed with his regiment for India. He was stationed at Bangalore in the Madras Province of Southern India where, with two fellow subalterns, he lived in a palatial pink-and-white bungalow, the verandahs of which were wreathed in purple bougainvillaea. In the garden stood a hundred and fifty magnificent standard roses. It was a splendid life. At least, most young cavalry officers seemed to find it so. Waited on hand and foot, free from domestic cares and not overburdened with military duties, they were able to concentrate on the serious and all-absorbing business of polo-playing.

Nobody enjoyed this princely existence more than Winston Churchill. But for him the endless round of morning parades and evening polo, the triviliaties of Mess conversation and regimental rivalry were not quite enough. For six long hours every afternoon the heat of the Indian sun kept him indoors with nothing to do. He felt the need for mental stimulus; so he began to read. He read history, philosophy and economics: Gibbon and Macaulay, Plato and Schopenhauer, Malthus and Darwin. Boredom in India succeeded where Harrow had failed: for the first time he recognized the importance of an academic education.

His books were sent to him from England by his mother, but it was the memory of his father that spurred him on. The influence of Lord Randolph on his son's early career was profound. Theirs was a curious relationship. While Lord Randolph lived he was a remote, unapproachable and, more often than not, unsympathetic figure in the background of his son's life. Winston was more aware of his father as a public figure than as a parent. What contact there was between them tended to result in clashes of temperament, Lord Randolph forever criticizing his son's apparent lack of ability and Winston trying to defend himself. As a result Winston became resentful and unsure of himself. Deprived of the affection and reassurance which a boy expects from his father, he envied the children of lesser men. 'I would far rather have been apprenticed as a bricklayer's mate,' he was to write of his time at Harrow, 'or run errands as a messenger boy, or helped my father dress the front window of a grocer's shop. It would have been real; it would have been more natural; it would have taught me more; and I should have got to know my father, which would have been a joy to me.' His fear of being unable to match up to his father's brilliant reputation undoubtedly played an important part in his failure to distinguish himself at Harrow; feeling inadequate, he took refuge in rebelliousness. This only made matters worse. If there had been any hope of Lord Randolph warming towards his son, it was surely stifled by Winston's poor showing at school. Not until he had entered Sandhurst and, for a brief few months, was treated as an adult by his father, did there seem any likelihood of Winston winning the affection he craved. Even then it was never more than a remote possibility. 'If ever,' he wrote, 'I began to show the slightest idea of comradeship, he was offended; and when I once suggested that I might help his private secretary to write some of his letters, he froze me to stone.' In any case, Lord Randolph's death was soon to put an end to these tentative overtures. Winston was never able to draw close to the father he adored and, what was probably of greater importance, he was denied the opportunity of demonstrating his worth as a son. All this had a telling effect on his early career.

Many years later, recalling his father's death, he wrote: 'All my dreams of comradeship with him, of entering Parliament at his side and in his support, were ended. There remained for me only to pursue his aims and vindicate his memory.' The desire to perpetuate his father's name became the *leitmotiv* of his early career; never was it more in evidence than in the years immediately following Lord Randolph's death. 'I read industriously every word he had ever spoken,' he wrote, 'and learned by heart large portions of his speeches. I took my politics almost unquestioningly from him.' When he set out on his Cuban adventure, it was inevitable that he should have chosen the *Daily Graphic* as the medium for his reporting. In India it was his father's tastes and interests that inspired his reading. But these were merely manifestations of an obsession which appears to have had much deeper roots. As a child his father's off-hand treatment robbed him of his self-esteem; his efforts to model himself on Lord Randolph may well have been a subconscious striving to prove himself not only a worthy son but, in most respects, his father's equal. This in no way detracted from his genuine devotion to Lord Randolph's memory; his was an imitative, rather than a hostile, rivalry. It was as if he wanted it to be said, not that he was Lord Randolph Churchill's son, but that Lord Randolph Churchill had been his father.

To do this he first had to emerge as a personality in his own right; to draw attention to himself as a Churchill, so that anything he might say about his father would make an impact and be taken seriously. For a young man who had shown little promise at school or as an army cadet, this was no small undertaking. Opportunities for him to make his mark were not readily available. Whatever he did would have to be spectacular. Much would depend upon his ability to convert an initial enthusiasm into a sustained sense of purpose: an ability which had been far from conspicuous at Harrow and Sandhurst. He set about his self-imposed task with an intensity which, in time, was to earn him abuse as a 'self-advertiser' and a 'medal-seeker'; but once started he never wavered. The transformation of Churchill the feckless student into Churchill the ambitious, assertive young man can be dated to 1895. It was the year he was gazetted to the 4th Hussars. Of equal, if not of greater, significance, it was the year his father died.

Ten months after Lord Randolph's death, Winston was in Cuba dodging his first bullet and sending back reports to the *Daily Graphic*. When this failed to bring him the glory he sought, he looked about for other likely trouble-spots. His regiment was under orders for India; a posting far too routine for his requirements. He was determined to bring himself to public notice before he was buried in an outpost of Empire. The island of Crete was seething with unrest and he applied to the *Daily Chronicle* to be sent there as a Special Correspondent. His application was refused and he turned his attention to Africa. General Kitchener was about to embark on an expedition up the Nile and Winston started to pull family strings in an attempt to have himself seconded to the expeditionary force. He was unsuccessful but he remained hopeful. Within weeks he was applying, with his mother's backing, to join Sir Frederick Carrington's force in Rhodesia where a serious Matabele uprising (foreseen by his father) was threatening the Chartered Company's territories. His failure this time caused him to despair. 'The future is to me utterly unattractive,' he wrote to his mother. 'I look upon going to India . . . as useless and unprofitable exile . . . a few months in South Africa would earn me the S.A. medal and in all probability the [Chartered] company's Star. Thence hotfoot to Egypt—to return with two more decorations in a year or two—and beat my sword into an iron despatch box. Both are within the bounds of possibility and yet here I am out of both. . . . It is useless to preach the gospel of patience to me. Others as young are making the running and what chance have I of ever catching up? . . .'

But it was no use. India it had to be; India with its military drill, polo-playing and long afternoons of study—all very well in its way, but far from the paths of glory. Then, when an opportunity to prove himself in India did present itself, he was not there. In the summer of 1897 a revolt of the Pathan tribesmen on the North West Frontier offered a splendid chance for adventure, but Winston was in England on his first leave. As it happened, Sir Bindon Blood, the general commanding the frontier force, had once promised him the chance of active service and so, when he read of the revolt in an English newspaper, he promptly sent a cable reminding Sir Bindon of this promise and set off for India. He was too late to join the frontier force as a staff officer but, at Sir Bindon Blood's suggestion, he made his way to the front as a war-correspondent. He was commissioned to cover the campaign by an Indian newspaper, *The Pioneer*, and his mother persuaded the *Daily Telegraph* of London to accept his reports at £5 a column. He did not confine himself to newspaper reporting. Attached to a Sikh regiment, he borrowed a rifle and entered into the thick of the fighting. He found it sufficiently dangerous to be enjoyable. Indeed, his initiative in a particularly tight corner earned him a mention in despatches: a Brigadier-General saw fit to draw official attention to 'the courage and resolution of Lieutenant W. L. S. Churchill, 4th Hussars, the correspondent of the *Pioneer* newspaper with the force, who made himself useful at a critical moment.' His mother wrote and told him of the citation and he was overjoyed. Not only was he anxious to gain a reputation for personal courage but, as he was quick to recognize, it was the sort of distinction that would further his political ambitions. It was a slight compensation for the disappointment he had experienced when he learned that his reports to the *Daily Telegraph* had been published as 'from a young officer' instead of under his own name.

Denied public credit for his newspaper letters, he embarked on a more ambitious literary venture. On returning to Bangalore, he put aside the novel he had recently started to write and set about writing an account of the frontier campaign. He regarded the publication of this book, *The Story of the Malakand Field Force*, as the most significant event in his life up to that time and hoped to gauge his standing in the world by the way it was received. He was not disappointed. Within nine months of publication some 8,500 copies of the book were in circulation which, considering the limited appeal of the subject and the poor job his uncle, Moreton Frewen, made of revising the proofs, was extremely encouraging. At last, it seemed, a section of the public was beginning to take notice of young Winston S. Churchill.

It was a good start but, in itself, it was not enough. He realized this before the book was in print. However *The Story of the Malakand Field Force* fared, he would have to follow it up with a further display of initiative. Hardly had he finished the book before he was preparing for another adventure. Once again his hopes were pinned on the North West Frontier. An expeditionary force was still campaigning there and he hoped to join it. At first he was unsuccessful but in March 1893, taking advantage of the few days' leave remaining to him after a polo tournament, he made an unorthodox dash for the Afghan border. Arriving at Peshawar, where the expeditionary force was headquartered, he was able, with the help of a new friend, Captain Aylmer Haldane, to get himself appointed as an extra orderly on the personal staff of the Commander-in-Chief. This appointment, together with some useful advice he was able to give his superiors on the subject of newspaper controversy, won him the confidence of the senior officers who, he says, treated him as if he were 'quite grown-up'. Unfortunately, this was the only benefit he could claim from his second frontier experience. The expected campaign failed to materialize and once more he found himself surveying the trouble-spots of the world in his relentless quest for action.

Actually, it was not so much a search as an intensification of his earlier efforts. The war he was looking for was already in progress and now, more than ever, he was determined to play a part in it: somehow or other he intended to join Sir Herbert Kitchener's force in Africa.

*

By the early summer of 1898, Kitchener's Expeditionary Force had reached the confluence of the Nile and the Atbara in the Sudan. In April of that year Kitchener had put to rout a strong Arab force at the Battle of Atbara and he was now poised to strike at the dervish stronghold at Omdurman, some 200 miles to the south.

It was towards the end of 1896 that Kitchener had started his slow advance up the Nile, building a railway as he went. He was then the Sirdar of the Egyptian Army; ruthlessly ambitious and set upon consolidating his growing reputation by reconquering the Sudan and avenging the death of Gordon at Khartoum twelve years earlier. Omdurman lay close to Khartoum. The progress of the expeditionary force had been hampered by a series of calamities: a cholera epidemic in the army, an unprecedented outbreak of storms which washed away a twelve-mile stretch of the newly built railway, an explosion which burst the cylinder of a gun-boat that had been designed to attack the dervish forts along the Nile. Kitchener was brought to the point of tears but the advance continued. By July 1897 the Sudan military railway extended across 103 miles of the Nubian desert; in that same month Kitchener's forces stormed and captured the strategically important village of Abu Hamed. The following month the town of Berber (surprisingly evacuated by the enemy) was occupied. The next important engagement took place eight months later. Kitchener, whose Egyptian army had been reinforced by British units, attacked and defeated the Emir Mahmoud in his encampment at the Atbara river on Good Friday, 8 April 1898. After the Battle of Atbara, Kitchener placed his army in summer quarters to await the seasonal rise in the level of the Nile in August when the advance to Omdurman was expected to take place. Further reinforcements were being sent from Britain for this last push, and competition among young British officers to be included in the brigades leaving for the Sudan was keen. Although far removed from the excitement, Lieutenant Winston Churchill was leaving no strings unpulled in his attempts to be in at the kill.

He had been trying to get to Egypt for many months. When his first request to join Kitchener had been turned down in 1896, he had not given up hope. On arriving in India he had begun to bombard his mother with letters pleading with her to make every effort to get him a posting with the Egyptian army. In January 1898, when the first detachments of British troops had been sent to the Sudan, he had returned to the attack with renewed vigour. 'You must work Egypt for me,' he told Lady Randolph. 'I have written to Lady Jeune to ask Sir Evelyn Wood (he could do it in a minute). Also to Bimbash Stewart to write to Kitchener. . . Now I beg you—have no scruples but worry right and left and take no refusal.' His mother did her best. So did his father's old friend, Lady Jeune. Feelers were put out in all directions but nothing was forthcoming. Kitchener's answers were evasive. Then, in July 1898, the Sirdar sent a firm refusal. He was prepared to accept two other officers recommended to him but he had no room for Lieutenant Churchill. Writing many years later, Churchill was inclined to attribute Kitchener's hostility to his own unfortunate reputation as a pushing, publicity-seeking young officer; it is equally probable that the Sirdar, having come up the hard way, was jealous and suspicious of the aristocratic influence being exerted on Churchill's behalf. Whatever the reason, the decision appeared to be final.

Churchill had just arrived back in England on his second leave from India when Sir Evelyn Wood, the Adjutant-General of the

Forces, informed Lady Randolph that Kitchener had declined to consider his application. It was then the beginning of July. The general advance of the army in the Sudan was due to take place in a month's time. It looked very much as if that advance would take place without Lieutenant Winston Churchill: at least, that is how it would have looked to a less determined young man. But, as he himself admits, Churchill was not wanting in perseverance. What is more, he was not lacking in powerful friends. He had, in fact, just acquired an extremely influential admirer. Shortly after his arrival in London, he had been sent for by the Prime Minister who had complimented him on the publication of *The Story of the Malakand Field Force*. Although Lord Salisbury's political association with the Churchill family had been far from fortunate, he appears to have been sufficiently impressed by Winston's book to forget past differences. At the close of the interview he had remarked on the likeness between Winston and Lord Randolph and added: 'If there is anything at any time that I can do which would be of assistance to you, pray do not fail to let me know.' His offer was quickly taken up. On hearing of Kitchener's refusal, Churchill wrote asking the Prime Minister to intervene. Salisbury, while making no promises, agreed to do what he could and a wire was duly despatched to Cairo. Still Kitchener refused to yield. However, this time his negative reply proved ineffective. By the time it arrived Churchill had adopted new tactics. Acting on a hint from Lady Jeune, he let Sir Evelyn Wood know that his application was now supported by the Prime Minister. This did the trick. Wood, already incensed by Kitchener's high-handed attitude towards the War Office, welcomed the opportunity to overrule the Sirdar. Within two days Churchill had secured his posting to the Sudan. An order from the War Office informed him that he had been attached to the 21st Lancers as a supernumerary lieutenant and that he was to proceed to Egypt at his own expense, on the understanding that, should he be killed or wounded, there would be no claim on British Army funds. It was good enough. Without waiting to hear whether his application for extended leave from his own regiment had been granted, he set off for Egypt.

He arrived at Cairo on 2 August, just in time to join 'A' squadron of the 21st Lancers before it started for the front. After the rush, tear and uncertainty of his short London leave, the long slow journey up the Nile proved a pleasant means of relaxation: relaxation made all the more enjoyable by the knowledge that he had reached Egypt without being recalled by the Indian Army authorities. 'It is a vy strange transformation scene that the last 8 days have worked,' he wrote to his mother from Luxor. 'When I think of the London streets—dinners, balls, etc and then look at the khaki soldiers—the great lumbering barges full of horses—the muddy river and behind and beyond the palm trees and the sails of the Dahabiahs.' It was the Egypt he had been dreaming of for months.

He occupied his spare time by writing the first of a series of letters which he had contracted to send to his friend Oliver Borthwick of the *Morning Post*. He was to be paid £15 a column. These letters, which were sent to the newspaper via his mother, were intended to be published anonymously and made to appear as if they had been written by a young British officer to 'a friend'. However, they contained sufficient clues for the anonymous officer to be identified; by leaving them open to speculation, Churchill hoped they would bring him wider publicity. Unfortunately, the gimmick misfired when Borthwick decided to publish them not as private letters but as straight reports. This, in Churchill's opinion, destroyed both their novelty and their elegance. But this was a matter for future concern. In the meantime he had to contend with the business of defeating the dervish hordes.

Since the beginning of July, Kitchener had been moving his army forward to Wad Hamed, sixty miles north of Omdurman. Churchill reached this concentrated force of the Anglo-Egyptian army on the eve of its final advance. The march along the west bank of the Nile began on 24 August. Covering the front of the advance, the cavalry fanned out to ensure against an attack on the desert flank. It was an unnerving operation. 'Those of us who, like my troop, composed the advance patrols,' wrote Churchill, 'expected as we filtered through the thorn scrub to find enemies behind every bush, and we strained our ears and eyes and awaited at every instant the first clatter of musketry.' But there was no attack. The more sceptical began to doubt whether a dervish army existed. Rumour had it that the enemy had fled and that it might be necessary to pursue them as far as the Equator. Then, early in the morning of 1 September, rumour gave way to reality; mirage-like patches on the blurred horizon solidified into the domes and minarets of Omdurman. As the morning brightened, a long dark smear in front of the town—which, at first glance, had looked like a forest of thorn bushes—rippled into life and was seen to be a swiftly advancing dervish host. Churchill was among those who witnessed the awe-inspiring transformation. 'While we watched, amazed at the wonder of the sight,' he reported, 'the whole face of the slope became black with swarming savages . . . between the masses horsemen galloped continually; before them many patrols dotted the plain; above them waved hundreds of banners, and the sun, glinting on many thousand spear-points, spread a sparkling cloud.'

He was not left to survey the scene for long. News of the advance had to be taken to Kitchener; Lieutenant Churchill was chosen as messenger. After taking stock of the situation, he rode back six miles to meet the oncoming army. His chief concern appears to have been, not so much the imminent battle, but the terrifying prospect of coming face to face with the Sirdar whose authority he had so blatantly defied. Upon sighting Kitchener's marching columns, he paused to rest his horse and to take in the impressive spectacle: the infantry battalions stretching back along the bank of the Nile, a conglomeration of steamers and sailing boats supporting them from the river and the combined Egyptian cavalry and Camel Corps protecting the desert flank. 'The sight,' he says, 'was truly magnificent.'

Kitchener was at the centre of the infantry mass. Riding alone, a few yards ahead of his headquarters staff, he was flanked by two standard bearers carrying the Union Jack and the Egyptian flag. Churchill approached at an angle, circled and drew his horse alongside. He saluted and gave his message. Kitchener listened impassively. Then he asked: 'How long do you think I've got?' The question was totally unexpected but Churchill gave his answer in a flash; he estimated that, at the present rate of progress, an engagement could be expected in an hour, perhaps an hour and a half. Kitchener replied with a curt nod and the brief exchange was closed. Churchill was left wondering whether he had in fact been recognized: but by that time it had ceased to matter.

As the Sirdar rode on, Churchill tried to calculate how

accurate had been his guess about the expected engagement. He decided that he had not been far out. As it happened his estimate was not put to the test. For some reason the dervish advance came to an unexpected halt. Kitchener, taking advantage of the respite, was able to allow his men a night's rest.

The attack came at dawn. Kitchener's force had reassembled well before daybreak. They were fully prepared when the distant murmur of dervish war-cries rose to a roar and the Arabs came swarming over the rise which separated the two armies. As soon as they were within range, Kitchener's field artillery opened fire, wreaking fearful havoc amid the fanatically advancing horde. For almost two hours the yelling dervishes hurled themselves with suicidal determination at the massed guns: none of them succeeding in approaching within 300 yards of the Anglo-Egyptian position. The long-awaited battle was turned into a near massacre. Such was the superiority of Kitchener's mechanized army that, by the time the Moslem survivors withdrew, they left over 2,000 dead littering the desert.

Churchill played no part in this initial action. At five o'clock that morning the 21st Lancers had been ordered to reconnoitre the surrounding hills. Churchill, at the head of his patrol, had watched the futile dervish attack from a ridge overlooking the battlefield. Apart from a few token revolver shots at some fleeing horsemen, he had been obliged to assume the role of a passive—but by no means unexcited—spectator. 'Talk of Fun!' he remembered thirty years later. 'Where will you beat this! On horseback, at daybreak, within shot of an advancing army, seeing everything, and corresponding direct with Headquarters.' The cavalry withdrew before the dervish attack was repulsed. On an order from his squadron-leader, Churchill retired from his ridge and took up a position in the infantry lines. However, there was still no active part for him to play.

Not until later that morning did he get his chance. Kitchener, starting his advance towards Omdurman, ordered the cavalry to clear the ground. It was hoped that this mounted force would cut off the Moslem host from the city and thus prevent street fighting. This clearing action appeared, at first, to be a simple routine operation. The plain separating them from Omdurman offered no opportunity for one of those well-rehearsed charges that had been such a feature of their cavalry training. This was a distinct disappointment: the prospect of a spectacular charge had excited the cavalry officers from the time they had arrived in Egypt. Now it looked as if the enemy had been vanquished by the artillery and that the cavalry had been reduced to the role of scouts. But the longed-for opportunity presented itself quite unexpectedly. A body of dervishes, concealed in a dried-up watercourse which ran across the plain, opened fire. The action bugle sounded. Sixteen troops of Lancers wheeled into line and, without waiting to estimate the strength of the enemy, charged headlong at the gully. It was a bold but foolish decision.

Three hundred horsemen were launched at three thousand determined warriors, lined up twelve deep to receive them. The cavalry—riding knee to knee, with levelled lances—plunged into the gully and were engulfed in a mêlée, far removed from the textbooks tactics of Aldershot. Everything was dust-dimmed confusion. Churchill, armed with an automatic Mauser pistol and riding a grey Arab pony, hurtled into the gully, oblivious of everything but 'the great grey mass gleaming with steel'. Two dervishes appeared in his path and, as he rode between them, they both opened fire. He careered on across the gully, firing wildly at swordsmen who rushed his pony, and then discovered he had been separated from his troop. Some forty or fifty yards away, on the fringe of a huddled enemy mass, two or three riflemen knelt and aimed their rifles at him. For the first time he felt afraid. Realizing how vulnerable he was, he crouched over his saddle and galloped hard after his troop. He found them close by. Together with three other troops of the squadron, they had already faced about and were beginning to re-form. Suddenly, from out of nowhere, a solitary dervish appeared brandishing a spear. The troopers turned on him with their lances, but he managed to dart between them and, although badly wounded, staggered towards Churchill at whom he levelled his spear. Churchill shot him dead at less than a yard. He was amazed to find how easy it was to kill a man. Not that he had time to think about it. The bullet had been the last in his magazine and he was too busy putting in a new cartridge clip to philosophize. Then he turned to his second sergeant and asked if he had enjoyed himself. 'Well,' said the sergeant, 'I don't exactly say I enjoyed it, sir; but I think I'll get more used to it next time.' Everybody laughed. The famous charge of the 21st Lancers was over.

The charge had been described as a 'magnificent folly'. It was also a costly one. It was responsible for a high proportion of the British casualties that day—five officers and sixty-five men killed and wounded and 120 horses lost within the space of three minutes—and it had little or no effect on the outcome of the battle. In a letter to his mother, two days later, Churchill claimed he had shot five men 'for certain and two doubtful'; but when writing to a friend he changes his estimate to three killed for sure and two doubtful. Perhaps it is indicative of the confusion that he should be more certain of the doubtful than he was of the definite.

Kitchener occupied Khartoum and, within a week of the battle of Omdurman, the 21st Lancers started for home. Churchill went with them. He was back in England by the beginning of October. Upon his return to London, he began to think seriously about his future. Four years in the army had brought him some rewards but he was far from solvent. His family's fortunes had always been shaky; the one chance of repairing them—Lord Randolph's South African investment—had disappeared when the mining shares had been sold to pay his father's debts. His mother had enough to live on but he was anxious not to be a burden on her. As he saw it, there was no alternative but for him to leave the army and devote himself to journalism and the writing of books. The letters he had written to the *Daily Telegraph* from India had earned him five times as much as he was paid by the army; his more recent letters to the *Morning Post* had provided an additional £300. This, together with what he could make from his books—he was already planning *The River War*, his account of the Sudan campaign—would keep him in pocket money. It would also allow him to concentrate on the political career which, as Lord Randolph's son and champion, was still his ultimate ambition. So he planned his career: first he would return briefly to India to play in the important inter-regimental polo tournament; then he would send in his papers, come back to England, write his book and seize the first opportunity for entering Parliament.

Before leaving for India, at the end of November, he was allowed to address Conservative gatherings at Rotherhithe, Dover and Southsea. The drift of his speeches left no doubt as to his political philosophy. 'To keep our Empire we must have a free people,' he told the Southsea Conservative Association, 'an educated and well-fed people. That is why we are in favour of social reform. This is why we long for Old Age Pensions and the like. The Radicals—I do not mean Radical Imperialists like Lord Rosebery—for Radical Imperialist is, if you tell the truth, only Tory Democrat spelled another way—the Radicals (I mean those of Mr Morley's school) would have no Empire at all. We would have one and make all share the glory. *"Imperium et Libertas"* is the motto of the Primrose League, and it may also be the motto of Progressive Toryism. You have two duties to perform—the support of the Empire abroad and the support of liberty at home.' It was Lord Randolph all over again.

Churchill went to India and left his regiment in a blaze of glory. Shortly before the long-awaited polo tournament, he fell downstairs, sprained both ankles and dislocated his right shoulder. Despite this, he went on to the field (with his upper right arm strapped to his side) and, in the final match, scored at least two of the winning goals which gained the 4th Hussars the tournament victory. At his farewell regimental dinner his fellow officers paid him the rare compliment of drinking his health. It was a fitting finale to his not uneventful army career; as a civilian such popularity would be harder to come by.

He had already begun to prepare for his new life. On his way out to India he had started work on *The River War*; he was still busy with it on his homeward journey. Originally he had intended the book to be a simple account of the Omdurman campaign, based on his letters to the *Morning Post*; but, almost unwittingly, it grew into a history of Kitchener's three-year war. Not everything he had to say about the Sirdar was complimentary. It entailed a great deal of reading and research and on his way back to England he stopped for two weeks in Cairo where he submitted the bulky manuscript to Lord Cromer, whose criticism he found invaluable. He was well rewarded for his pains: *The River War* proved another best-seller and, in the opinion of many, it was the best book he ever wrote. However, much was to happen before it was published.

He arrived back in London at the end of April 1899 and found himself much in demand. An election was due within the next eighteen months and—such was his newly acquired reputation as a soldier-correspondent—various Conservative Constituency

Associations were eager to adopt him as a prospective candidate. Among those seeking his services was a Mr Robert Ascroft, the Conservative member for Oldham, who, as the representative of a two-member constituency, suggested that they fight the seat together. It was arranged that Churchill should address a meeting at Oldham, to introduce him to the constituency. But before this meeting took place, Mr Ascroft unexpectedly died. Nevertheless, Churchill's nomination, backed by the Conservative Central Office, went ahead and he found himself prematurely plunged into a widely publicized by-election. His running mate for this largely industrial Lancashire constituency was a local trade unionist whose concept of Tory Democracy verged upon what Churchill described as 'Tory Socialism'. It was a tough fight. Churchill threw himself into the public debates with such zest that he developed a sore throat. This worried him but he did not allow it to discourage him: having won a polo tournament with an injured shoulder, he saw no reason why he should not win an election with an inflamed tonsil. But politics were not polo and, despite his efforts, he and his partner were beaten by their Liberal opponents. The Oldham seat had been held for the Tories by the popularity of Mr Ascroft, who was known locally as 'The Workers' Friend'; Churchill, for all his push and drive, was unable to match the appeal of a local celebrity. Bright as was his star in influential Conservative circles, his public image still lacked his father's sparkle. If there was a lesson to be learnt from the Oldham by-election, it was surely to push on with his campaign of 'self-advertisment'; only thus could he hope to equal Lord Randolph's vote-catching reputation. Some might scorn, but it was essential that he keep himself before the public's notice.

As it happened, he did not have long to wait for his next opening. Three months after the Oldham contest, war was declared in South Africa. He was a soldier turned journalist. Here surely was a chance for him to shine.

*

All that summer war between Great Britain and the Transvaal republic had been in the offing. Tension, in fact, had been building up for the past three years. The Jameson Raid had destroyed any hopes of a peaceful agreement between President

Kruger and the Uitlanders. Churchill had been quick to recognize this. Within a year of the Raid, he had written a private memorandum entitled 'Our Account with the Boers'; in it he had predicted that only a direct confrontation between the British and Transvaal Governments could settle the Uitlander problem. This, as he readily acknowledged, meant war; but it was a war which, in his opinion, was inescapable if national honour and the rights of British subjects were to be upheld. He was not alone in his views. A great many Englishmen felt the same. When, in 1897, Sir Alfred Milner was appointed High Commissioner and Governor of the Cape, it was hoped that his cool handling of the situation would make Kruger see reason—that the Uitlanders' rights would be secured by diplomacy. And for a while it looked indeed as if this might happen. Shortly after his arrival in South Africa, Milner expressed his conviction that the Transvaal problem would be solved by the internal opposition of the Boers to the Kruger régime. All that was needed was patience. This hope was short lived. In the Transvaal elections of 1898, Kruger was returned to office with more than twice the number of combined votes cast for his two opponents. Milner's attitude underwent an abrupt change. 'There is no way out of the political troubles of S. Africa,' he wrote to Joseph Chamberlain, the British Colonial Secretary, a few days after the election results were announced, 'except reform in the Transvaal or war.' From then on he was to see to it that the possibility of reform became less and less likely so that 'the case for intervention' was, as he put it, 'overwhelming'. Things came to a head in June 1899. At a conference in Bloemfontein, the capital of the Orange Free State, Milner and Kruger met for what appeared to be an eleventh-hour attempt to settle their differences. There was little hope of a settlement and they both knew it. Milner arrived at the conference—which lasted from 31 May to 5 June—determined to force the issue. When he demanded prompt and wholesale reform of the franchise, Kruger cried: 'It is our country you want!' Kruger's own attempts to bargain were imperiously rejected and, as was expected, the conference ended in a stalemate. As the Boers amassed arms in the Transvaal, British troopships were again despatched to the Cape. If history was repeating itself it was doing so in a much more determined fashion.

At the beginning of September, when the South African

crisis had reached a new height, Alfred Harmsworth, of the recently established *Daily Mail*, telegraphed Churchill asking him to act as the paper's war-correspondent. However, Churchill, conscious of his previous obligations, promptly offered his services to his friend Oliver Borthwick of the *Morning Post*. He was now in a position to dictate conditions. He informed Borthwick that he wanted £1,000 for four months, plus £200 a month for any longer period, as well as his expenses and the copyright of his work. His offer and the conditions were immediately accepted. The terms of his contract are said to have been the most generous ever ceded to a war correspondent up to this time. Like his father, Winston Churchill was determined to make the most of his South African venture.

On 9 October 1899 the British Agent in Pretoria was handed an ultimatum from the Transvaal Government. It demanded that all points of difference between the two countries should be referred to arbitration. In the meantime British troops should instantly be withdrawn from the borders of the Transvaal and all reinforcements which had arrived in South Africa since 1 June 1899 should be removed within a period of time to be agreed upon. Those troops then on the high seas should not be landed in any part of South Africa. The British were given forty-eight hours in which to reply. The ultimatum reached England early the following morning. When it was shown to Joseph Chamberlain he declared: 'They have done it!' That evening the British Government cabled a formal rejection. On 11 October Britain was at war with the Transvaal and her sister republic, the Orange Free State.

Three days later Winston Churchill boarded the R.M.S. *Dunottar Castle* at Southampton. Accompanying him as a soldier-valet was Thomas Walden, his father's manservant, who had travelled to Mashonaland with Lord Randolph in 1891; and in the hold was a sizeable crate of wines and whisky which—unlike his father's well-stocked expedition—seems to have been the only provision he made for facing the rigours of the South African veld. He also carried several letters of introduction. Some of these had been given to him by Alfred Beit and were intended to introduce him to various mining magnates and politicians at the Cape. Joseph Chamberlain had supplied him with a personal note to Sir Alfred Milner. 'I am sending a line to anticipate a probable visit from Winston Churchill, the son of Lord Randolph Churchill...' Chamberlain wrote. 'He is a very clever young fellow with many of his father's qualifications. He has the reputation of being bumptious, but I have not found him so, and time will no doubt get rid of the defect if he has it...'

A wildly cheering crowd was at the dock to see the *Dunottar Castle* off. They were cheering, not Churchill, but Sir Redvers Buller who was sailing for the Cape to take command of the British forces in South Africa. Already rumours were being spread of great battles and terrible disasters and the one fear of everybody on board was that the war would be over before they reached the Cape. No one dreaded this more than Churchill; in fact, the combination of rough weather and the frustration of being cut off from all news made the first part of the voyage almost unbearable. He filled the long boring days as best he could: studying Sir Redvers Buller and his officers and getting to know the other war correspondents. One of these correspondents, J. B. Atkins, was to remember his first impressions of the restless Churchill on board the *Dunottar Castle*. 'He was,' says Atkins, 'slim, slightly reddish-haired, lively, frequently plunging along the deck "with neck out-thrust", as Browning fancied Napoleon... When the prospects of a career like that of his father, Lord Randolph, excited him, then such a gleam shot from him that he was almost transfigured. I had not encountered this sort of ambition, unabashed, frankly egotistical, communicating its excitement, and extorting sympathy... he had acquired no reverence for his seniors as such, and talked to them as though they were his own age, or younger... He stood alone and confident, and his natural power to be himself had yielded to no man.'

Once the ship left Madeira the weather improved. But blue skies and a calm sea did little to soothe the apprehensive army officers. They were all convinced that the 'amateur' Boer commandos, consisting of burgers called up from their farms, could never match the skill of British professional soldiers. The lesson of Majuba Hill was conveniently ignored. Anyway, the situation was entirely different. The troops now in South Africa were better equipped to meet an emergency. If the Boers invaded Natal this time they would be met by General Penn Symons who commanded an infantry brigade, a regiment of cavalry and two batteries of artillery. In the circumstances the war could not possibly last more than a few weeks. Sir Redvers Buller was seen at times to be looking very gloomy. Churchill, although not so confident of the outcome, was equally gloomy. His depression alternated between thoughts of the Boers occupying Cape Town and the British capturing Pretoria: in either event there was a possibility of peace.

Then, two days before they arrived at the Cape, their fears looked like being realized. A tramp steamer sailing from South Africa was sighted and, on the insistance of some of the younger passengers, the *Dunottar Castle* signalled to it to change course so they might obtain news from 'the land of knowledge'. It was alarming news. When the tramp came within a hundred yards, they were able to read a message scrawled on a blackboard: BOERS DEFEATED. THREE BATTLES: PENN SYMONS KILLED. The gloom on the *Dunottar Castle* deepened. If battles serious enough to claim the life of a British general had been fought, the Boers must have exhausted their meagre resources. The war was as good as over. Only Redvers Buller was able to summon a semblance of optimism: there might, he thought, be enough Boers left to put up a fight outside Pretoria.

There was a noisy welcome waiting for them at Cape Town. Crowds had stood in the rain all morning to cheer Sir Redvers Buller. Churchill, however, saw little of these loyal demonstrations. In Cape Town he managed to find time to present Joseph Chamberlain's letter to Sir Alfred Milner, who informed him that not only was the war against the Transvaal still very much in progress but there was a likelihood of rebellion breaking out in the Cape. As Lord Randolph had predicted, the Cape Afrikaners felt strongly about their kinsmen in the north.

Sir Redvers Buller was proceeding to Natal on the *Dunottar Castle*. But Churchill, anxious to reach the front before the Commander-in-Chief, decided to make a dash across country in order to arrive at Ladysmith in Natal in the shortest possible time. On the evening that the *Dunottar Castle* docked he, accompanied by his valet, J. B. Atkins and another war correspondent, boarded a train for East London in the eastern Cape. The train journey lasted four days and, upon reaching East London, they were able to wangle a passage on a small coasting vessel sailing for Durban. The short sea voyage was extremely rough. 'You were not concerned', wrote J. B. Atkins, 'in the simple calculation whether or not you were a good sailor, it was rather a question whether you had a good enough head to sit on the shoulder of a spinning peg-top without reeling from giddiness.' However, they reached Durban well ahead of the *Dunottar Castle* and, after estimating that it would take Sir Redvers Buller several days to assemble his stores, decided to complete their journey by rail. The train took them as far as Natal's capital, Pietermaritzburg, where, in order to continue their dash to the front, they were obliged to hire 'a special train for Ladysmith'. It turned out to be an unnecessary expense. Several miles short of Ladysmith they were brought to an abrupt halt. At the little village of Estcourt they learnt that the Boers had beaten them to it: the line was cut and Ladysmith was besieged.

There was nothing for it but to await the arrival of Sir Redvers Buller. With the main body of the Natal force shut up in Ladysmith, there could be no hope of relieving the town until the Commander-in-Chief arrived with reinforcements. Churchill and Atkins decided to make the best of it. 'We pitched our tents in the railway yard at Estcourt,' reports Atkins. 'We had found a good cook and we had some good wine. We entertained friends every evening, to our pleasure and professional advantage and, we believed, to their satisfaction.'

Among the various war correspondents now gathered at Estcourt, Winston Churchill was by no means the most inconspicuous. Although he was younger and less experienced than most of them, the reputation he had gained in India and Egypt—together with the terms he had obtained from the *Morning Post*—singled him out for special distinction. He had been in South Africa for a matter of days only, but already he had succeeded in attracting attention. In Cape Town a pro-Boer paper, striving to emphasize the capitalist influence behind the war, used him as an example of the fortunes that were being made from the conflict. 'During the present campaign,' it reported, 'war correspondents are receiving a higher rate of remuneration than was ever paid in any previous campaign. Not only are they being paid a big salary, but in some cases a handsome amount is given them for their literary work. . . . Thus, in one case, that of Mr Winston Churchill of the *Morning Post*, the sum of £800 is paid him for his letters alone, whilst all his out-of-pocket expenses in South Africa, as well as a salary which is nearer £3,000 than £1,000.' Despite the obvious exaggeration, the report is some indication of his growing notoriety. If he was not being watched as closely as Lord Randolph, his journalistic activities were undoubtedly of interest to friends and foes alike.

For all that, he still appears to have been somewhat unsure of himself. Journalism and South Africa awoke memories of his father and for some—himself not least—the shadow of Lord Randolph still loomed large. J. B. Atkins was later to record a significant conversation between Churchill and himself at Estcourt. 'He showed me some articles already published in the *Morning Post* and two in manuscript,' says Atkins, 'and invited my opinion. He was gratified by the wide interest which his work had already aroused. When I read his articles, he said, "Now what do you think of them? Is the interest due to any merit in me or is it only because I am Randolph's son?" ' Atkins told him that he thought the articles were good but that he doubted whether they would have aroused the same interest if he had written them. 'A fair verdict,' replied Churchill. 'But how long will my father's memory help me?'

Assertive, bombastic and self-reliant as he appeared to some, it seems that behind his bold front there was still something of the neglected, troubled schoolboy who had vainly sought to win his father's respect. It was, perhaps, only natural that during these first days in South Africa he was particularly conscious of Lord Randolph's lingering image. This was the country which had witnessed his father's last spectacular venture. The widely publicized expedition to Mashonaland had taken place only eight years earlier; when Winston was at Harrow and of an age to be sensitive to the contrast between his own shortcomings and his father's celebrity. To equal, if not to outshine, Lord Randolph's South African adventures he would need to assert himself as never before. The challenge was formidable but with a full-scale war in progress the ground was at least fertile. It was a matter of recognizing the right opportunity and seizing it.

The same thought must have occurred to another member of his family. Winston was not the only Churchill in South Africa intent on making his mark.

CHAPTER EIGHT

Lady in Waiting

SARAH had reached there before her nephew. She had, in fact, been in southern Africa for over four months by the time war was declared. It was her second visit to the country and it was to prove far more eventful than the first.

In the three years that had elapsed since the Jameson Raid, Sarah and Gordon had seen a great deal of their South African friends. The leaders of the Reform Committee, whom they had visited at the Pretoria gaol, had (after four of them had been sentenced to death and then reprieved) eventually been granted their freedom by President Kruger. With the Jameson fiasco behind them, they had resumed their influential positions in London society. For these were the years when the fabric of London's social life was threaded with the bright gold of Johannesburg's *nouveaux riches*. 'The Nineties,' says a historian of the period, 'were the high and palmy days of the great Randlords . . . Johannesburg seemed nearer to London than any English town.' With gold fever running high, Lady Sarah Wilson's intimate experience of South African affairs had given her a special priority among the lion-hunting hostesses of Mayfair.

The most sought after lion was, of course, Cecil Rhodes. Despite his pessimism when Sarah had bid him goodbye at Cape Town, he had managed to survive the Jameson Raid. He had been helped by the courage he had displayed in settling the serious Matabele uprising that had followed close on the heels of the Raid. This had done much to re-establish him in the eyes of the world. When, in 1897, he had returned to England to face the official inquiry into the Jameson Raid, he had been given something like a hero's welcome. 'I found all the busmen smiling at me when I came to London,' he said; 'so I knew it was all right.' From then on his position with the English was secure; not even the loudly voiced suspicion that he and Joseph Chamberlain had rigged the ludicrous Jameson Raid Inquiry could shake his countrymen's confidence in him.

Of all his English friends, few were more loyal than Sarah. She entertained him whenever he came to England and earned the unusual distinction of being one of the few women whom the misogynistic Rhodes trusted. Their friendship ensured not only Sarah's loyalty but her continued interest in South Africa.

These years had also seen the development of her friendship with Dr Jameson: the friendship which evolved from that embarrassing meeting on board the *Victoria*. At his trial in London, Jameson had been sentenced to fifteen months' imprisonment, but, after serving four months, his ill-health prompted the Home Secretary to order his release. Since then he had come to know the Wilsons well. It was in Jameson's company that Sarah and Gordon had sailed for South Africa at the beginning of May 1899. Leaving their small sons, Randolph and Alan, with Gordon's mother and taking with them Sarah's German maid, Metelka, they set off to spend two months in Rhodesia.

Rhodesia gave them their first taste of life in the African veld. After landing at Cape Town, they travelled with Dr Jameson direct to Bulawayo. For the next five weeks they were the guests of Major Heaney—a red-headed, red-bearded American who had been a member of Rhodes's pioneer force. Bulawayo—a little red-brick and corrugated iron town—merely served as their base. Most of their time was taken up with excursions in the veld; inspecting the mines of which Major Heaney was managing director. Sarah responded to the rough camp life with gusto. Travelling by pony and mule wagon, sleeping in tents, straining to catch a glimpse of the elusive lions which they heard roaring at night, she found it far more exciting than the tame life of South African cities.

But civilization could not be entirely ignored. Remote as they were, the rumblings from the south reached them. They had been in Rhodesia only a matter of a few days when news of the abortive Bloemfontein Conference came through and the war-scare that had been building up for months took on an added intensity. Once again they found themselves on the edge of a South African maelstrom.

It was a cable from Cecil Rhodes inviting them to stay at

Groote Schuur that finally decided them to return to Cape Town. They arrived at the Cape early in July. Rhodes returned from England a few days later. Removed, for once, from the immediate crisis, he drove to Groote Schuur along a route decked with flags. That evening the Wilsons attended a monster meeting at Cape Town's Drill Hall to welcome him back. As he mounted the platform, says Sarah, 'the cheering went on for ten minutes, and was again and again renewed, till the enthusiasm brought a lump to many throats, and certainly affected the central figure of the evening.' Like London, Cape Town—or, at least, a large section of it—had forgiven its ex-Prime Minister.

Cecil Rhodes's return to South Africa on this occasion was to prove memorable for reasons other than his tumultuous welcome. He had been accompanied on his voyage from England by the Russian-born adventuress, Princess Catherine Radziwill. From now on the Princess was to be a frequent visitor to Groote Schuur. Not only was she to pursue Rhodes with an obsessive determination but her unscrupulous interference in his political life was to culminate in a titanic clash of wills which, in the opinion of many, hastened Rhodes's death. All this was to happen after Sarah had left the Cape, but already she appears to have taken the Princess's measure. Unlike young Winston Churchill, who had met Catherine Radziwill at an English country house in 1894 and found her 'charming . . . somewhat eccentric and afflicted with second sight,' Sarah was not at all amused by Rhodes's new friend. The way in which she snubbed Princess Radziwill at Groote Schuur was later repaid by some scathing public comments from the Princess. When some were accusing Sarah of using her Churchill influence to draw attention to her activities in South Africa, Catherine Radziwill was quick to add her own spiteful remarks.

The enmity between the two women was no doubt sparked off by their rivalry for Rhodes's attention. Sarah's motives in trying to monopolize Rhodes were entirely innocent; for that reason she was more successful. At every turn she scored off the Princess. She met Rhodes at breakfast every morning, often went with him for his morning rides and spent almost every evening teaching him to play bridge. She also went with him to the sittings he was giving to the portraitist P. Tennyson Cole.

For this the artist was extremely grateful. 'Lady Sarah struck me,' says Cole, 'as pugnacious, provocative and outspoken, although as entertaining a lady as one could meet. The resilience of her conversation had a distinct charm for Rhodes, and so it was that I counted myself lucky on finding she had been invited to "sit and watch" while this great but erratic genius sat for me.... Her presence, I felt, would render Rhodes "safe" while I painted him, for an hour or two at least. Beguiled by her conversational shafts, he would be unlikely to rise and leave abruptly in the middle of the sitting, as he had done so often when sitting for other artists.'

The weeks following Rhodes's return to South Africa were tense. The ex-Prime Minister, pottering about Groote Schuur re-arranging his blue Delft china, was certain that the crisis would be overcome and war averted. 'Nothing will make Kruger fire a shot,' he declared. Others were not so sure. At Government House, Sarah was introduced to Sir Alfred Milner: she found him 'a man of intense strength of mind and purpose.' Just how strong his purpose was had become only too apparent. Contingents of British troops were now arriving at the Cape; it was obvious that Sir Alfred intended to have his war.

On 25 July a troopship bringing a sprightly forty-two-year-old officer on his third appointment in South Africa docked at Table Bay. Colonel Robert Stephenson Smyth Baden-Powell had arrived at Cape Town with instructions from the British War Office to raise two regiments of mounted infantry which, in the event of war, would defend the Rhodesia and Bechuanaland frontiers. Apart from his instructions and a small staff of officers, Colonel Baden-Powell came with little else. During the short time he was at the Cape he attempted to raise men and money. On both counts he was frustrated by the Cape authorities. He was told that he could not recruit men in the Cape for fear of alarming the Dutch. There was no money for a war which, officially at least, was by no means certain. Furthermore he was forbidden to station men at Mafeking, in Bechuanaland, because of its close association with the Jameson Raid.

Undeterred, Baden-Powell instructed his chief-of-staff, Major Lord Edward Cecil (son of the British Prime Minister, Lord Salisbury) to remain at the Cape and use his influence to raise money and supplies and then left for Bulawayo where he intended

Portrait of Lady Sarah Wilson as a war correspondent in South Africa

The wrecked armoured train at Chieveley, Natal. From a photograph taken the day after the derailment.

Star, Johannesburg; Barnett Collection

to raise his troops. Although he had been unable to enlist men at the Cape, he had succeeded in obtaining an aide-de-camp. The affable Captain Gordon Wilson was now appointed to Baden-Powell's staff.

In August Sarah and Gordon once again left Cape Town for Bulawayo.

*

Bulawayo was not the best place in which to wait for a war. It was a friendly, easy-going little town but it offered visitors few distractions. Its menfolk retained something of the early pioneer spirit and were more or less content with their unsophisticated existence; but their wives battled to keep boredom at bay. They surrounded themselves with reminders of the great world they had left and flung themselves into a variety of amateur entertainments. Sarah was roped into a committee of the town's leading ladies who were organizing a 'Café Chantant' which then mysteriously changed its character and developed into a 'Geisha Tea'. But it took more than 'thirty well-known ladies' in correct Japanese costume and 'three well-known ladies' singing 'Three Little Maids from School' to offset the disquietening news that was being telegraphed to Sarah from Cape Town.

When Gordon was in town the time passed pleasantly enough. During the day Sarah was able to watch the officers drilling their new recruits and in the evening Baden-Powell's staff would join them for a hand of bridge. They were even able to continue their excursions in the veld. But such activities were exceptional. More often than not Gordon was away on duty. Baden-Powell, obeying the letter if not the spirit of the Cape prohibitions, had established a second recruiting base at Ramatlhabama, a few miles north of Mafeking. His officers, dressed in civilian clothes—their luggage marked with a plain Esq.—were already a common sight at Mafeking station. Both he and his staff spent much of their time dashing backwards and forwards between Bulawayo and Bechuanaland. During Gordon's absences, Sarah was left to occupy herself 'learning how to bandage by experiments on the lanky arms and legs of a little black boy'. They were experiments which were later to prove extremely useful.

The last hopes of peace disappeared at the end of September.

Kruger ordered his burgers to mobilize. Men from towns in the Western Transvaal formed commandos and massed on the border of the northern Cape. At last Baden-Powell was given permission to move an armed guard into Mafeking. 'But,' he observed breezily, 'as the strength of that guard was not stipulated I moved the whole regiment into the place without delay.' However, he did not move his entire force into the town. His orders, given verbally, had been to defend the Rhodesian frontier. He therefore detailed Colonel Herbert Plumer, with a regiment raised in Bulawayo, to provide a mobile patrol centred on Fort Tuli.

With war imminent and Gordon ordered to Mafeking, Sarah decided that the time had come for her to leave. Preparations were made for her to return to the Cape, from where she would sail for England. The ladies of Bulawayo thought she was mad to attempt a journey through South Africa at such a time. They told her as much. The train, they said, 'might be stuck up, fired on and the like'. This made no difference to Sarah. She had no intention of sitting out the war in Bulawayo.

'Lady Sarah Wilson arrives, I believe, one day this week,' wrote a guest at Groote Schuur on 2 October. But she did not arrive. She got no further south than Mafeking.

*

In the language of the Baralongs, a local African tribe, Mafeking means 'a place of stones'. This description was inspired by the unusual outcrop of rocks on the banks of the near-by Molopo river; it could have applied equally well to the town itself. It was an ugly little place—'a mere tin-roofed village' Conan Doyle called it—situated some ten miles from the western border of the Transvaal. Planned round a large dusty market square, its unpaved streets stretched scarcely half a mile in any direction. Until Rhodes had carried his railway on to Bulawayo, Mafeking had acted as a rail-head; its workshops, sidings and engine-house still retained a busy importance in the life of the town. It boasted a chemist, a barber, a public library, a bank and a small printing works; and its general stores provided a wide variety of goods. Its three hotels, although not luxurious, were— as Lord Randolph had testified after staying in one—efficiently run and their saloon bars lent a hint of raffishness to what was otherwise a staid community. Recently, the addition of the Victoria Hospital, with forty beds, had given a much needed fillip to the town's scanty medical services. But for all its facilities, it bore the unmistakable stamp of a South African dorp. Architecturally it was featureless. With the exception of the newly built Catholic convent, its mud brick houses, fronted by wooden stoeps and roofed with corrugated iron, were all single storied. It was dust-blown, stark and relieved only by the ragged pepper trees lining its streets. In summer it could be intolerably hot.

As soon as Baden-Powell had officially entered the town, he set about preparing for a probable siege. He wanted to accomplish as much as possible before war was actually declared. All the able-bodied men were enrolled in a Town Guard. A chain of outposts was established, trenches were dug and defence works started. Stock was taken of the town's supplies and arrangements were made for those women wishing to leave Mafeking for the Cape.

When Sarah arrived the siege preparations were in full swing. 'I little thought,' she wrote home, 'when we left England in May last for a two-months trip to South Africa that in four months' time I should be in a partly beleaguered town . . . yet this is the case.' Her journey from Bulawayo had, despite all warnings, been uneventful. About fifty miles outside Mafeking a white-painted covered truck had been attached to the train and from under its hood a dozen troopers had kept watch. Somewhat to Sarah's disappointment the precautions had proved unnecessary. 'Though all day in close proximity to the Transvaal frontier,' she complained, 'not a vestige of a Boer did we see.' However, she found the atmosphere of Mafeking charged with expectancy. The Town Guard was drilling on the Market Square, houses were being sandbagged, an armoured train puffed aggressively into the station, war correspondents from London newspapers had begun to arrive and Baden-Powell and his staff seemed to be everywhere at once. The streets were alive with the sound of marching feet and the chatter of gossips. With an attack expected at any moment, rumours of the Boers' approach buzzed as incessantly as the swarm of locusts that plagued the town. 'On arriving here,' wrote Sarah, 'we found the inhabitants fairly scared, and on Sunday morning just as I was going to church, the landlady met me with a grave face, and solemnly assured me 5,000 Boers were in laager on the border and were to attack the town on Tuesday. I thought we had left rumour behind us and being, so to speak, on the spot, we should know the truth and nothing but the truth. This however is a fallacy.' The rumours were repeated with such conviction that they resulted in the constant ringing of alarm bells calling out the town militia. At night, rockets fired into the air would send the bemused population scurrying to their posts. The night alarms became so frequent that most people took to sleeping in their clothes. 'I must admit,' said Sarah, 'that these nocturnal incidents were somewhat unpleasant.'

Yet, despite sleepless nights, she was enjoying the crisis enormously. 'We were, indeed,' she says, 'as jolly as the proverbial sandboys during those few days in Mafeking before the war commenced.' For the short time that she expected to be in Mafeking—before continuing to the Cape—she and Gordon had taken a small cottage in the town. For their meals they went to Dixon's Hotel; the same hotel that her brother had stayed in on his way back from Mashonaland. Sarah found the food 'weird' but the conversation of the army officers was stimulating. They were all anxious for the fighting to begin and never stopped talking of their plans for outwitting the Boers. There were several of Sarah's London friends attached to Baden-Powell's staff—including her cousin by marriage, Captain Charles Fitzclarence—and in no time she felt very much at home. 'In spite of wars and rumours of wars,' she reported, 'we eat, drink and have our joke, even play a game of bridge after dinner, although sometimes this is apt to be abruptly broken in upon by one of the party being mysteriously "wanted" outside.' Listening to the officers, she felt a twinge of regret at the thought of leaving before the real fun began. She bought a white pony called 'Dop' from a Johannesburg polo-player and spent her mornings and evenings riding round the outskirts of Mafeking inspecting the fortifications. It all added to the feeling of suspense and urgency.

Her enjoyment was marred only by the fact that there was no real part for her to play in the siege preparations. To overcome this sense of frustration, she decided to send a description of the town to a London newspaper. Why she chose the *Daily Mail* is not certain: the paper already had a correspondent in Mafeking. However, her article was received with enthusiasm. The *Daily Mail*, having recently failed to persuade Winston Churchill to act as a correspondent, was only too pleased to accept Sarah's services. Her report, giving a colourful account of Mafeking 'from a woman's point of view', created a 'great sensation'. She was immediately enrolled as a Special War Correspondent and became—as the *Mail* was quick to point out—'the only woman acting as such for any paper in South Africa'.

There was plenty to report. Siege preparations were now at their height and tension was mounting rapidly. To the fear of war was added the fear of traitors. Boer agents were said to be infiltrating into Mafeking, spreading discontent among the already suspect 'Dutch' element of the town. Spies were reported everywhere. On 7 October, Lord Edward Cecil, Baden-Powell's second-in-command, issued a threatening, if somewhat naïve, notice. 'There are in town today nine known spies,' it announced. 'They are hearby warned to leave before 12 noon tomorrow or they will be apprehended.' On the same day a more alarming notice, signed by Baden-Powell, was posted outside Dixon's Hotel. It aimed to prepare the citizens of Mafeking 'for eventualities'. Forces of armed Boers were now massed on the Natal and Bechuanaland borders, it stated. It was possible that the town might be shelled. Every effort would be made to provide shelter for women and children, but it could be arranged for them to leave for a place of safety. Those women and children wishing to leave should inform the stationmaster. 'The men would, of course, remain to defend Mafeking.'

Baden-Powell was trying to clear the town of unnecessary liabilities. He would have quite enough on his hands without adding to his responsibilities. When Dr Jameson arrived unexpectedly, hoping to play a part in the siege, he had been sent packing 'with more haste than courtesy'. With memories of the Raid still fresh, the little doctor would have been a particularly offensive red rag to the Boers. Baden-Powell had told him bluntly that if he meant to stay it would take a battery of artillery to defend the town: he must go and go quickly.

Sarah was aware that she was equally unwelcome; but still she could not make up her mind to quit. 'Colonel Baden-Powell did not look on my presence with great favour,' she said, 'neither did he order me to leave.' Her original enthusiasm was now backed with a 'sort of presentiment' that she might be needed. 'Partly from a wish to be useful, as I have lately been attending lectures on "First Aid to the Wounded," ' she wrote, 'and partly, I suppose, from a love of excitement, I have elected to remain here.' Another officer's wife, Mrs Godley—a sportswoman after Sarah's own heart—had followed her into the town and the two of them determined to stick it out. Their stand was hailed by the pressmen. 'There is no rush to take advantage of the railway facilities to places of safety,' one of them reported, '[and] many of the bolder spirits, led by Lady Sarah Wilson, flatly refuse to leave and have banded themselves as Red Cross nurses.' But Baden-Powell had other ideas.

*

On 8 October, Mafeking received details of the ultimatum which Kruger was about to serve on Britain, demanding the withdrawal of troops from the Transvaal borders. Baden-Powell redoubled his efforts. The ultimatum gave him his deadline. He knew, as did everyone, that there was little chance of its conditions being observed. 'Every effort is being made to press forward the work of constructing the defences,' wrote Angus Hamilton of *The Times* on 9 October, 'and everyone appears willing to assist. The aspect of the town is gradually changing, and in the little time that is left to us we hope to ensconce ourselves behind something of an impregnable defence.'

For her part, Sarah moved to the house of Mr Benjamin Weil, a well-known Mafeking merchant. The house was in the centre of the town, not far from the railway station. It was considered fairly safe and she hoped to turn part of it into a hospital. There was no longer any question of her returning to the Cape. It was extremely doubtful whether another train would leave for the south and even if it did there was a chance that the Boers would tear up the lines.

But she would not be staying in Mafeking. With the ultimatum running out, Baden-Powell took action. He sent a staff officer to call on Sarah with an urgent message. It had been learnt on trustworthy authority that a large Boer force was likely to arrive at Mafeking the following day. It was thought that they would rush the town and the garrison would have to fight its way out. Sarah was instructed to leave for a place of safety immediately.

Much as she resented it, there was no question of her disobeying the order. As a soldier's wife she was conscious of her duty. She had been about to go to bed when the officer arrived; now she changed into travelling clothes. 'I shall never forget that night,' she declared: 'it was cold and gusty after a hot day, with frequent clouds obscuring the moon, as we walked round to Major Goold Adams' house to secure a Cape cart and some Government mules, in order that I might depart at dawn.' At first it was suggested that she should make for a mission station some seventy miles away in the Kalahari desert. (A reporter actually wrote to his paper saying that she had been escorted out of Mafeking by a missionary.) But this plan was quickly abandoned. The mission station was extremely isolated and it was thought that provisions would run short. Instead she was told to head for Setlagole. Here, forty-six miles from Mafeking, there was a lonely trading store which acted as an hotel. Not only would she be provided for but, as it was on the main road to Kimberley, she would be on the direct route of any relieving column arriving from the Cape.

Her preparations did not take long. She and her maid, Metelka, quickly packed two small hand bags which were strapped on to the Cape cart. The cart, drawn by six mules, was to be driven by a Cape coloured man, and a Zulu servant, Wilhelm (whom Sarah mistakenly called Vellum), was to ride behind them on Sarah's pony. Unlike her other servants, this Zulu—who had once been employed by Dr Jameson—was to remain at Sarah's side throughout the hectic days ahead. 'Beneath his dusky skin beat a heart of gold,' said Sarah, 'and to him I could safely have confided countless treasures.'

The preparations complete, they sat down to wait for the dawn. It was not possible to sleep. As the night wore on the wind strengthened and howled mournfully round the house. Shortly before daybreak they got ready to leave. With Baden-Powell's warning of the coming attack ringing in her ears, Sarah struggled to keep calm as she said her farewells. Convinced that the men would sell their lives dearly, she was certain that she would not see many of them again. After a last hug from Gordon, she climbed on to the cart beside Metelka. The coloured driver flicked his whip and the little party trundled forward. They drove through the dawn-dark streets, bumped across the railway lines and headed for the open veld.

At about the same time, another party set out in the opposite direction. Mrs Godley had also been given marching orders and was making for Bulawayo. 'Both wished to remain handy,' said Major Godley, 'for the few weeks during which, if it took place at all, it was expected that the siege would last.'

*

'So that afternoon our burgers crossed the border near Mafeking,' wrote Alida Badenhorst from a little town just within the Transvaal, 'they tore up the railway line and destroyed the telegraph wires . . . next morning we heard a deep booming. We could not think what it was, only our hearts beat with anxiety. Soon the tidings reached us: war had broken out.'

That same morning Sarah, too, listened to the distant booming of guns. In her little white-washed bedroom at the Setlagole store, she stood transfixed as she counted each dull thud. She counted five—then came a pause. Within seconds the guns started up again. Altogether, she estimated, twenty shots were fired. Although the bombardment was by no means as heavy as Sarah imagined, these were the opening shots of the Anglo-Boer War.

The silence which followed was intensified by the almost unreal tranquillity of the empty landscape. The sky was cloudless; a faint early-morning glow blurred the horizon. Sarah stood numbed. She was used to cannon fire—to salutes on ceremonial occasions, to the gun displays on field days of Gordon's regiment—but this was different. This was war. Each shot had been aimed at human beings: more than likely at the very men to whom she had said goodbye the previous day. Realization of this, she says, sent a shiver down her back 'akin to that produced by icy water'.

Pulling herself together, she quickly closed the door and started to dress. There was a great deal to be done. Setlagole had not proved the haven she had been promised. The whole of the previous day, in fact, had been disastrous. From the time they had left Mafeking in the chilly half-light, they had been at the mercy of the desolate veld. As the sun had risen, so had the wind. The dust and sand had whipped at the cart with a stinging, blinding intensity. About twelve miles outside Mafeking they had stopped for breakfast at the farm of a sympathetic Boer and had then pressed on. By the afternoon the wind had become a hurricane; the sun was scorching. 'I have never experienced such a miserable drive,' wrote Sarah, 'and I almost began to understand the feelings of people who commit suicide.' Towards sunset, after jolting across the rocky, dried-up bed of a river, they had come in sight of the Setlagole store. Sarah's first glimpse of this dingy grey house, surrounded by a wooden trellised stoep, was to become one of her most vivid memories. 'The troop of donkeys grazing close to the front door, the fowls and turkeys in a rough pen at the side, the dilapidated stables a stone's throw off, the group of idlers—white men and black— sitting or standing round the door of the adjoining store. . . and the setting sun tinging all with gold,' she recalled. 'I who had left scenes of strife, excitement, and the impending horrors of an invested town, looked with amazement on this calm and peaceful landscape.'

This first impression was deceptive. After being welcomed by Mr and Mrs Fraser, the loyal old Scots couple who kept the store, she received a visit from the sergeant of the local Mounted Police. He told her that African runners had reported several hundred Boers encamped some ten miles away. It was said that they were lying in wait for an armoured train that was expected at Mafeking that night. The sergeant, who was something of an alarmist, thought it more than likely that after ambushing the train they would come to Setlagole to loot the store. He advised Sarah to leave the area as soon as possible. He even suggested that she continue her journey that very night.

The news threw Sarah into a quandary. Characteristically, she was not so concerned about her possible fate at the hands of the Boer marauders as she was about the ignominy of a British officer's wife being captured by the enemy. Having left Mafeking where she might have been some use, she had no intention of becoming a prisoner-of-war. 'I was fully determined,' she said, 'that . . . I would run no risks of capture or impertinence from the burghers, who would also certainly commandeer our cart, pony and mules.' On the other hand, both she and her servants were worn out from their journey and the mules would certainly be in no condition to start another trek. Her mind was made up for her by the coloured driver. Boers or no Boers, he flatly refused to move that night. There was nothing for it but to accept the risk and wait until morning.

The night seemed endless. Once again, in spite of her exhaustion, she was unable to sleep. Lying with the curtains open, she watched the moon go down and listened apprehensively to the occasional barking of the farm dogs. At about four o'clock the faithful Wilhelm appeared at the window. He wanted to know whether he should inspan the mules. As everything was still quiet, she told him to wait until the sergeant arrived. She got up to look at the weather about an hour later: it was then that the firing began.

The gun-shots brought the local Africans hurrying to the house. Huddled in their blankets against the cold morning air, they joined the handful of Europeans gathered outside the store. By the time Sarah had dressed, the farmyard was alive with noisy groups, all staring in the direction of the firing. Shortly afterwards an African horseman arrived with news that the Boers had derailed an armoured train. His message, accompanied by a great many gesticulations, was muddled and inconclusive; it was not clear in which direction the train had been travelling or whether there were any casualties. He could only repeat that the train had 'fallen down' and that he had left when the big guns had opened up.

Sarah, who had to rely upon an interpreter to understand what was being said, found the news alarming. If the Boers had captured the train then they could be expected at Setlagole at any moment. She must leave immediately. The police sergeant had left the previous night for the Boer encampment; but she dare not wait for his return. Instead, she instructed Wilhelm to remain at the store and gather such further news as he could before joining her that night. Then, as soon as the driver had harnessed the mules, she and Metelka climbed on to the cart for their second day in the veld.

They had been instructed to make for Mosita, twenty-five miles west of Setlagole. This was a small African village well off the beaten track. The solitary European house there was occupied by a Mr Keeley who, in times of peace, acted as the local magistrate. Sarah was assured that she would be made welcome and kept well out of harm's way.

The journey was accomplished in comparative comfort. The vicious wind of the day before had dropped and the parched, stony countryside gave way to fine open grassland. There was not a house in sight. Only the driver swearing at the mules, or the curious chuckle of the large African pheasants starting up from the long grass, disturbed the serenity of the veld. During their four-hour drive, the only signs of human habitation were two Africans driving a herd of cattle towards Mosita.

Their arrival at the little mud-hut village created great excitement. Visitors to Mosita were few and far between and the the driver was forced into a long pantomime of the recent fighting ('imitating even the noise of the big gun') before the enthusiastic crowd of Africans allowed them to pass on to the house. A mile or so further along the road, they skirted a huge dam and drove up to the Keeley farm. Here, their reception was by no means as cheerful.

When Sarah marched in and boldly announced that she had come to beg a few nights' lodgings, she discovered that Mr Keeley was away at Mafeking where he had been detained to help in the defence of the town. His wife, a worried-looking woman of Sarah's age, had not only been left with five children but was expecting a sixth. With the family having always been staunchly pro-British, Mrs Keeley was afraid of possible reprisals on the part of the local Boers: except for a young brother, she was entirely without male protection. 'At last,' declared Sarah, 'I had found someone who was to be pitied more than myself.'

*

It was the endless days without news that made life at Mosita so tedious. With the railway lines torn up, the telegraph wires cut and no newspapers, the household was completely isolated. They were left to the mercy of local rumours and odd scraps of information brought to them by African runners. For anything more definite they could only wait, wonder and hope.

At long last news of a sort did arrive. One evening, as they took up their vigil on the stoep after supper, a rider cantered up with a batch of letters from Mafeking. They had been smuggled out of the town by Sarah's colleague on the *Daily Mail*, Mr Hellawell, who was on his way south to send off some cables. One of the letters was from Gordon. From it they learnt of the unsuccessful attempts which the Boers had made on the town shortly after Sarah's departure. There were also details of Mafeking's first bombardment; during which the widely aimed shells had proved singularly ineffective. Gordon, who imagined Sarah to be at Setlagole, had ended his letter by assuring her that the Boers had been told of her presence at the store and had been asked to leave her unmolested.

Although the news was inconclusive, it did much towards heartening the household. It inspired Sarah with the idea of playing a more definite part in the war. If news could be smuggled out of Mafeking, it could also be smuggled in. The information she had gathered at Mosita was extremely scrappy but, for what it was worth, she was determined to pass it on to the invested town. After selecting a loyal African, named Boaz, to act as her messenger, she wrote a short note and folded it into a used cartridge case. Then, having carefully explained the importance of his errand to the messenger, she sent him hurrying towards Mafeking.

For Boaz, who was paid at the rate of £3 each way, this first successful run was the beginning of a lucrative, if risky, career. During the next few weeks he was to be constantly employed in carrying despatches to and from the town. It was a service which was to prove of no small importance. Not only did Sarah keep the garrison in touch with local rumours but, according to Angus Hamilton, she 'acted as the chief medium by which Baden-Powell managed to get his despatches through to the Government in Cape Town'. Within a short time Mosita became a recognized clearing centre for despatches. 'Sometimes they got through, sometimes not,' said Baden-Powell, 'so she took care that her messages had a cheerful tone lest the Boers should think we were weakening.' Major Dennison, who was operating from Kuruman in the Kalahari desert, says that his despatches 'were handed by the natives to Lady Sarah Wilson . . . by whose kind aid the letters were sent on by her trusted boy to their destination.' She deserved, he says, 'great credit for the service she rendered our corps while outside Mafeking.' Unfortunately, this same service was to land her in serious trouble.

Once the excitement created by the arrival of the letters had died down, the household was again thrown back upon the boredom of Mosita; the interminable days of waiting and the uncertainty of conflicting rumours. Even the despatches which they relayed were vague and often contradictory. But, at least, they were not the only ones to suffer. The local Boers, as they were soon to discover, were as much in the dark as themselves.

Since the outbreak of war, the Boers living near Mosita had kept up a wary relationship with Mrs Keeley. Many of the men had slipped over the border to join their compatriots, but their wives and daughters continued to call at the magistrate's house. The Keeleys, despite their political sympathies, were widely respected. If Mr Keeley was recognized as an officer of the law, his wife was equally esteemed for her knowledge of medicine. Her home-cures and elementary dosings were acclaimed throughout the neighbourhood. But although the women who now called upon her expressed great sympathy for 'her troubles', they made no secret of their interest in what was going on in the house. The presence of the strange Englishwoman mystified them. However, it was not until a large party arrived one morning after breakfast that Sarah discovered just how suspect she had become.

They drove up to the house in a large rickety cart. After solemnly seating themselves in the dining room, they announced that they had come to spend the day. Mrs Keeley, who was used to such visits, quickly whispered to Sarah that the only thing to do was to supply them with food and leave them alone. When Sarah came in for her luncheon they were still sitting silently in the dining room and, much to her surprise, raised no objections when Mrs Keeley ushered them on to the stoep so that she could lay the table. They finally left at five o'clock that afternoon. Mrs Keeley sighed with relief. The reason for their visit, she explained, was to find out whether Sarah was a man in disguise. A Transvaal paper had reported that Mafeking was in the hands of the Boers and the rumour had spread that the sole survivor of the garrison had escaped in woman's clothes. Only when Mrs Keeley's young brother had shown them the cart and mules with which Sarah had arrived had the visitors accepted that she was a woman.

Apart from a visit from an English farmer, who told them that the nearest town, Vryburg, had fallen to the enemy without so much as a shot being fired, they had little definite news until the unexpected arrival of Mr Keeley. He had been allowed to leave Mafeking to look after his family and farm. The news he brought was not reassuring. The Boers, he told them, were now drawing closer to Mafeking and, although the town was not completely surrounded, he had had to ride for his life to escape. The garrison was still in high spirits and were proposing to solve the problem of the now regular bombardments by digging underground shelters. There were rumours that the Boers intended to step up the shelling with a new siege gun capable of firing a 94lb shell.

Depressing as was his news, Mr Keeley's presence gave the women new confidence. He did not rule out the possibility of an attack on the farm but he felt he had sufficient influence with his neighbours to keep them quiet. After days of uncertainty it was comforting to off-load some of their responsibilities on to a man's shoulders.

When the next scare came, however, Mr Keeley was away visiting a neighbouring farmer. One evening, just as they were going to bed, Metelka happened to look out of the window to see a tall figure step out from the shadow of a clump of fir trees. Their first thought was that it was a marauding Boer but, as the man crossed the yard in the bright moonlight, they recognized him as the police sergeant from Setlagole. Once again the sergeant was the harbinger of alarming news. Setlagole, he told them, was swarming with Boers and he and his men had had to evacuate their barracks. He had come hotfoot to warn them to drive all the cattle off the farm and prepare themselves for the Boers' arrival. 'This information,' said Sarah stoutly, 'did not conduce to a peaceful night, but anyway, it gave one something to think about besides Mafeking.' Mrs Keeley immediately arranged for the cattle to be dispersed and Sarah buried her jewel-case and despatch box in the garden. They then went to bed.

The Boers did not arrive that night and there was no sign of them the following morning. All through the long hot day they waited nervously, wondering what to expect when the commando arrived. Mrs Keeley was quite certain that they would not be molested and was rather relieved that her husband was not there: she felt quite sure that he would have been arrested.

Rather ingenuously, they decided that their best plan would be to offer the burgers coffee and trust that they would not be too angry at finding the cattle gone. But they need not have worried. When the sun set that evening they were still alone. 'The stars came out one by one,' says Sarah, 'the goats and kids came wandering back to the homestead with loud bleatings; and presently everything seemed to sleep—everything except our strained nerves and aching eyes, which had looked all day for the Boers, and above all for news, and had looked in vain.'

Although the Boer commando failed to materialize, the household was alarmed some days later by the sight of an approaching horseman. Mrs Keeley, her nerves at breaking point, immediately assumed that this unkempt, slouch-hatted figure, wrapped in a long cloak, was the long-expected Boer who had come to arrest her husband. Telling Sarah to keep out of the way, she sent her brother to find out what the man wanted. Once more their fears proved groundless. The horseman was merely Mr Hellaway—the Mafeking correspondent of the *Daily Mail*—who, having ridden south and sent off his cables, was on his way back to the besieged town. Much as Sarah admired his dash, she could not help feeling that his excessive zeal was imprudent. She did not appreciate that war correspondents would take considerable risks for a good story.

CHAPTER NINE

'Everyone is talking about Mr Churchill'

THE CHANCES of obtaining a good story at Estcourt seemed somewhat slim to Winston Churchill during his first few days there. He sent reports to the *Morning Post* describing the village and giving details of its military strength but, short of a surprise attack by the enemy, it appeared unlikely that he would see any action until General Buller arrived with reinforcements. Indeed, it was rumoured that Estcourt would soon be evacuated. Frantic efforts were being made to strengthen Pietermaritzburg (the capital of Natal) some seventy-six miles further back and, although Estcourt was now regarded as 'The Front', the possibility of it becoming a base for full-scale operations was open to doubt. Much depended on the arrival of Buller. 'Meanwhile,' complained Churchill, 'we wait, not without anxiety or impatience.'

In order to break the monotony, some of the war correspondents took to accompanying the reconnaisance patrols that daily scouted the district. Churchill was quick to make the most of such opportunities. A couple of days after his arrival, he travelled in the village's much depised armoured train along what remained of the railway line to the north. The precise nature of the train's daily expeditions was a matter of mystery to most of Estcourt's inhabitants. It lacked the mobility of the cavalry patrols and its noisy progress rendered it useless as far as spotting any unsuspecting Boers was concerned. Moreover, the fact that it was confined to the railway line made it particularly vulnerable to attack. For, despite the impressive-looking steel plating which encased the trucks, it needed only an obstruction on the line to place it at the mercy of the enemy. The soldiers regarded it as a 'death-trap' and dreaded the occasions when they were called upon to man the trucks. 'Day after day,' one of them remembered, 'the armoured train . . . used to press forth unattended beyond the line of outposts, heralding, by agonized gasps and puffs, and clouds of smoke and steam, its advent to the far-sighted, long-hearing Boer. Daily, too, did it return in safety to the siding whence it had sallied forth at daybreak on its fruitless mission. How relieved the occupants looked when they climbed over its plated sides and congratulated themselves that their turn to form the freight of this moribund engine of war would not come round again for at least some days!' However, a trip on the train was one of the few diversions that Estcourt had to offer and Churchill was not one to pass up a new experience. The journey proved as useless as the train's previous reconnoitring efforts. They travelled as far as the forlorn and deserted village of Colenso, inspected the rails that had been torn up beyond the village and then beat a hasty retreat. Apart from the train's strange appearance frightening one bewildered African and the vague rumours that were collected from local tribesmen, they had achieved nothing. The train 'puffed and trundled home again', says Leo Amery, who was acting as correspondent for *The Times*, 'having secured information which one mounted scout could have gained more fully and at less risk.'

The following day Churchill was again engaged in reconnaissance. This time he accompanied a cavalry patrol. The sound of gun-fire had been heard coming from the direction of Ladysmith and the troops were sent out to investigate. Churchill rode to a flat-topped hill to the north-west of Estcourt, hoping to get a glimpse of the besieged town but found his view obscured by a further range of hills. After being given a meagre meal by one of the few farmers who had remained in the district, he returned home convinced of Estcourt's vulnerability. 'The garrison is utterly insufficient to resist the Boers,' he wrote; 'the position wholly indefensible. If the enemy attack, the troops must fall fall back on Pietermaritzburg, if for no other reason because they are the only force available for the defence of the strong lines now being formed around the chief town. There are so few cavalry outside Ladysmith that the Boers could raid in all directions.'

This view was shared by most of the newspapermen. Leo Amery was one of the few correspondents to express doubts about the strength of the Boer commandos in Natal. His views, he says, made him 'very unpopular both with soldiers and correspondents'. Churchill had known Amery as a schoolboy at Harrow. Soon after his arrival at the school he had made the mistake of pushing Amery (a sixth-former) into a swimming-pool, but this unfortunate accident had long since been forgotten and Amery was now sharing a tent with Churchill and Atkins. He was one of the many acquaintances that Churchill had met at Estcourt. Another was a friend from his North West Frontier days: the six-foot, fiercely moustached Captain Aylmer Haldane. Haldane, after being wounded in one of the early battles of the war, was now temporarily attached to the Royal Dublin Fusiliers until he could rejoin his battalion of the Gordon Highlanders in Ladysmith. Like Churchill, Captain Haldane had little faith in the Estcourt command.

On 14 November, eight days after Churchill's arrival, Estcourt faced its first real crisis. Advance Boer patrols were sighted and it was rumoured that the village was to be speedily evacuated. Tents were dismantled and the troops were ordered to stand to their arms. Nothing was certain. Churchill, like the rest of the correspondents, hung about the command office hoping to pick up a few scraps of information. While he was waiting there, Aylmer Haldane came out and told him that he had been ordered to take out the armoured train the following morning to support the cavalry reconnaissances. As Churchill had already been out in the train and knew the country, Haldane invited him to join the expedition. Haldane was later to condemn this assigment as 'the height of folly' and, at first, Churchill appears to have shared his view. He was not at all keen to go. However, he eventually agreed and it was arranged that they should meet at the station the following morning.

That evening, according to Leo Amery, Colonel Long, the officer commanding at Estcourt, dined with the war correspondents and Churchill did his best to persuade him not to evacuate the village. Atkins also remembered this dinner. 'The talk was all about the policy of retirement,' he says. 'While we ate and drank the clanging of guns being loaded into a train was an incessant accompaniment. With an unblushing assurance, which I partly envied and partly deprecated, Winston impressed upon his senior that Joubert was probably too cautious to advance yet; that he would continue to enjoy the pleasing security of the Tugela until more of his commandos could join him; that it would be a pity, and a blunder, to point the way to Maritzburg, and so on.' Shortly after Cononel Long had left the clanging outside ceased; then it began again. It was obvious that the train was now being unloaded. 'We smiled at each other,' says Atkins. 'Winston said, "I did that!" but gracefully added, "We did that." Whether his claim was correct I do not expect ever to know. Long may have received some news that gave him his desired pretext.'

Persuasive as Churchill undoubtedly was, his mounting enthusiasm failed to move his tent-mates. At dawn he woke both Amery and Atkins and tried to talk them into accompanying him on the armoured train. They both firmly declined. It was pouring with rain and Amery used this as an excuse for staying in bed. Atkins was more definite. He said that he was being paid to follow the war from the British side and saw no reason why he should risk landing himself in an enemy camp. 'That is perfectly true,' agreed Churchill. 'I can see no fault in your reasoning. But I have a feeling, a sort of intuition, that if I go something will come of it. It's illogical, I know.' With that he disappeared through the tent flap, headed for the station.

*

The armoured train was composed of five trucks, an engine and tender. It was designed on a similar pattern to that of most armoured trains then in use. The sides of the trucks were covered with steel plating and one of them, at least, was fitted with loopholes through which the soldiers travelling in it could fire. The engine and tender occupied a central position: pushing two trucks and pulling three. The front truck, in which Churchill and Haldane travelled, carried an ancient muzzle-loading gun, manned by four naval ratings. This was followed by an armoured truck, the engine and tender, two more armoured trucks and a wagon which contained breakdown equipment. There were 120 soldiers in the armoured trucks, as well as a small civilian gang of platelayers. In theory it was a travelling fortress, equipped to deal with any contingency.

It steamed out of Estcourt sometime after five o'clock on the morning of 15 November. About an hour later it reached Frere station. Here it was met by eight men of the Natal Mounted

Police who told Haldane that their advance patrols were reconnoitring the area further along the line. So far there had been no signs of the enemy and all seemed quiet. After a short stop at Frere, the train continued on another five miles to the next station, Chievely, which, the previous night, had been occupied by the Boers. From now on they could expect trouble. It did not take long for the risks they were courting to become apparent. As they steamed into Chievely station, Churchill sighted a column of mounted Boers riding towards the railway at their rear and, at the same time, a row of black spots lining a hill beyond the station showed that if they proceeded any further north they would run into a sizeable commando. A telegraphic message from Estcourt confirmed their fears. Haldane was instructed to return to Frere station and remain in observation: a Boer patrol and three wagons were reported to be moving south on the west side of the railway: it was essential that he safeguard his retreat. More than ever Haldane regretted his ill-advised mission. 'I do not wish to lay blame on anyone but myself,' he was to say, 'but had I been alone and not had my impetuous young friend Churchill with me, who in many things was prompted by Danton's motto, "de l'audace et encore de l'audace et toujours de l'audace", I might have thought twice before throwing myself into the lion's jaws by going almost to the Tugela. But I was carried away by his ardour and departed from an attitude of prudence.'

However, there was nothing for it now but to obey orders. The train was immediately put into reverse. The gun-carriage, in which Haldane and Churchill were travelling, was now being pulled in the rear and the engine was pushing two armoured trucks and the breakdown wagon. They clattered on for almost two miles before they sighted the enemy. Churchill had climbed on to a box to get a better view and he was one of the first to spot the Boers on the crest of a hill which commanded the railway line ahead: through his field glasses he was also able to see that the so-called wagons accompanying the patrol were mounted guns. The guns opened fire as soon as the train was within range. Churchill quickly clambered down from his box and the engine driver put on full steam. Shells exploded overhead and rifle bullets spattered the sides of the trucks as the train careered round a curve in the line and picked up extra speed as it ran down a steep gradient. The thought occurred to Churchill that they were running into a trap; as he turned to suggest this to Haldane a tremendous jolt threw him from his feet against the side of the truck. The engine had been brought to a juddering halt and the rear trucks had cannoned into it.

As soon as he was able to scramble to his feet, Churchill again mounted his box and peered over the side of the truck. He was unable to stay there long enough to get a clear view. Men were streaming down from the hill behind them and rifle bullets whistled about his head and 'splattered on the steel plates like a hailstorm'. He ducked down and went into a quick consultation with Haldane. It was agreed that the naval gun should be brought into action while Churchill went to the front of the train to investigate. By this time the guns on top of the hill had changed their position and were again pounding away; rifle fire was peppering the train from three sides. Jumping into this storm of shell and shot, Churchill darted along the line trying to assess the damage. He found that the engine and tender—like the two rear trucks—were still on the metals, but the three front trucks had been thrown from the tracks after crashing into boulders placed on the rails. The leading breakdown wagon had somersaulted and lay upside down—completely free of the line—and the two armoured trucks were jammed together: one standing upright and the other wedged on its side, half on and half off the rails. As he was running past the engine, a shell burst overhead, raining shrapnel in all directions and causing the engine driver to leap from the cab and dash for shelter beneath the overturned truck. Churchill chased after him. It was obvious that the only hope of escape lay in the possibility of the engine butting the obstructing truck from the rails and this could only be done if the driver remained at his post. To get him to return was not easy. His face had been cut by a shell splinter; he was dazed and angry. Churchill pleaded with him. He explained that no one was hit twice on the same day and appealed to the man's sense of gallantry. 'Buck up a bit,' he said, 'I will stick to you.' Finally the man agreed. Pulling himself together, he wiped the blood from his face and climbed back into the cab.

Now Churchill faced the challenge of clearing the rails under heavy bombardment. As far as he could see the line was undamaged. If the engine could push the overturned truck from the rails it might be possible for the entire force to escape in the rear armoured trucks. He ran back to tell Haldane this. Haldane agreed to the plan and said he would keep the enemy 'hotly engaged meanwhile'. The next hour was critical. There was no sign of the breakdown gang. Some had been killed when their truck overturned; the rest had fled. Their tools were scattered across the veld. Everything depended on the engine.

First the engine was uncoupled from the rear trucks. Then began the precarious business of pulling and pushing the wreckage. Backwards and forwards the engine shunted, its wheels skidding under the strain and its boiler threatened by the rifle fire. Churchill called for volunteers among the soldiers to assist in the operation. He wanted twenty men, but only nine—led by Captain Wylie of the Durban Light Infantry—volunteered to expose themselves to the incessant cross-fire. Churchill ran up and down the line rapping out orders to the men and the engine driver. Faced with a situation that called for resolute leadership, he was in his element. His calm was phenomenal. There can be no doubt about it. Everyone who witnessed the incident paid tribute to his cool courage. Without him all would have been lost.

As it was, the success of the operation fell short of his expectations. Once the forward line had been cleared an attempt was made to couple the engine to the rear trucks. It failed. A shell had shattered the coupling and a corner of the overturned truck now lay between the engine and the undamaged trucks. There was nothing for it but to make the most of what had been achieved. As many of the wounded as possible were crowded on to the engine and tender—some of the men clinging to the cowcatcher in the front. One of the last to be hauled aboard was Captain Wylie who, in the final stage of the operation, had been shot in the hip. Churchill himself was unintentionally caught on the engine as it steamed away. He remained wedged among the wounded men until they reached Frere station. Then, forcing his way out of the cab, jumped on to the lines and started to run back to the scene of action.

In the meantime, Captain Haldane was fighting a desperate rearguard defence. As soon as he had given orders for the engine to leave, Haldane withdrew his men from the trucks, intending to retreat to some houses 800 yards distant. Unfortunately, the men, attempting to seek cover, became scattered and, much to Haldane's disgust, two of them started to wave white handkerchiefs. The Boers stopped firing and rode up to the retreating soldiers who were now completely confused and obeyed the demands for surrender. Haldane, together with his second-in-command, Lieutenant Frankland, and fifty men, was promptly taken prisoner.

Unaware of this, Churchill came panting along the line. He reached a shallow cutting and saw two civilians advancing towards him. At first he thought they were platelayers; then he realized they were Boers. He turned to run back and the men opened fire. The cutting, with its six-foot banks, made a deadly corridor. With bullets whizzing within inches of his head, Churchill realized he must get into the open. He flung himself against one of the banks. Bullets sucked into the earth beside him. He scrambled up the bank, ducked through a wire fence and crouched in a small hollow, trying to regain his breath. His hand had been grazed by a bullet.

Fifty yards away he saw a platelayer's hut. Two hundred yards away was a rock-strewn river course. He decided to make for the river. As he jumped up, a horseman came riding towards him, shaking his rifle and shouting to him to stop. Churchill's hand flew to his belt. He had set out that morning armed with a Mauser pistol but now discovered that he was no longer armed. The pistol had been left on the train. The Boer had him covered. He had no alternative but to give up gracefully. Ducking under the wire fence that separated them, he walked over to his captor.

It had started to rain. As Churchill trudged along beside the Boer's horse, he remembered the two clips of Mauser bullets that he had in his pocket. War correspondents had no right to be armed. He slipped his hand into his pocket and silently dropped one of the clips to the ground. He was about to drop the second clip when the Boer saw him and demanded to know what he had in his hand. Churchill showed him. The man took one look at the clip and threw it away.

*

The identity of the man who captured Churchill has been the subject of considerable speculation. Many years later, a South African journalist, trying to get at the truth, found himself faced with a mass of conflicting evidence. 'In an idle moment,' he says, 'I counted the number of men who claimed at one time or another to have had a hand in the capture. The figures showed that no fewer than 43 had led, pushed or otherwise propelled the young war correspondent into captivity.' Most of the claims are suspect. The evidence offered rarely fits the circumstances of the capture. One widely accepted version, for example, says that after Churchill had been taken prisoner, he and his captors were joined by three other Boers. These men are supposed to have taken Churchill to a stable, where he spent his first night in captivity. The men quarrelled about what they should do with him. One wanted to shoot him as a spy, but another opposed this and appointed himself Churchill's guardian. As a result of this quarrel, it is said, a feud sprang up between the two men concerned, extended to their families and persisted until quite recently. But Churchill's own account shows that he was immediately taken to join the other prisoners. He makes no mention of the three Boers. Moreover, both he and Haldane state quite clearly that their first night of captivity was spent at Colenso station. Yet this and other stories continue to be believed.

For Churchill the mystery was solved three years after the war. At a private luncheon he was introduced to General Louis Botha. Both were then well-known men. They spoke about the war and Churchill described his capture. 'Botha listened in silence,' says Churchill; 'then he said, "Don't you recognize me? I was that man. It was I who took you prisoner. I, myself," and his bright eyes twinkled with pleasure.' The idea of this reunion between the famous prisoner and his famous captor was romantic. It appealed to Churchill. He remained convinced that he had been captured by Botha personally until the end of his life. But this seems extremely doubtful. As has since been pointed out, when Botha met Churchill after the war his command of English was poor. He probably did not make himself clear. It seems likely that he was referring to the fact that he was in command of the troops that captured Churchill and not that he was the lone horseman who brought Churchill in. This is the theory held by those who have investigated the matter; it seems the most likely explanation.

Churchill's captor was probably Veld-Kornet Oosthuizen,

who was killed during the war. A telegram sent to Pretoria from Colenso by the redoubtable Boer scout, Danie Theron, two weeks after Churchill was taken prisoner, seems fairly conclusive. After explaining the part played by Churchill in freeing the engine, Theron says: 'He also refused to stand still until Veld-Kornet Oosthuizen warned him to surrender. He surrendered only when he aimed his gun at him.' This telegram was not published until long after Churchill had written his own account, but it fits the details he gives.

Whatever the truth about Churchill's capture, there can be little doubt what happened him to afterwards. Both he and Haldane have left detailed accounts of their journey from Natal to Pretoria. After Churchill had joined the other prisoners, they were marched along the muddy road towards Colenso. It was drizzling and they were soon soaked to the skin. Even so, Churchill was not unduly depressed. According to Haldane, he took comfort in the thought that although he was temporarily deprived of his post as war correspondent his recent exploit would undoubtedly help his political career. He had been the 'star turn' of the armoured train incident and this would not pass unnoticed. However, he promised to see that Haldane got his fair share of praise.

The Boers were very good to them. They were told that they need not walk fast and one of the guards, noticing that Churchill was hatless, threw a soldier's cap to him. 'So they were not cruel men, these enemy,' remarked Churchill. 'That was a great surprise to me, for I had read much of the literature of this land of lies, and fully expected every hardship and indignity.' There were further surprises in store. Once they had passed the enemy guns, they were led over the crest of a hill into the camp of a large commando. Some 300 men had attacked the train but here, within calling distance, was a force of between 3,000 and 4,000. 'It was plain to me now,' says Haldane, 'that we were in the thick of a strong force which was on its way southwards.' It said little for the reconnaisance of the British scouts.

Once they were in the camp they were made to line up outside a make-shift tent. Churchill was quick to explain that he was a newspaper correspondent and asked to be taken to see General Joubert, whom he presumed was inside the tent. His request was refused but his papers were taken for examination. The prisoners immediately became the centre of attention. 'A crowd of rough-looking, and for the most part bearded, fellows soon gathered round us,' says Haldane, 'and while Churchill's case was under the consideration of the commandant-general, a running fire of questions on various matters connected with the struggle which we had so recently begun was maintained.' When it was learned that Lord Randolph Churchill's son was among the prisoners, the burgers became very excited. They gathered round Churchill, pointing at him and repeating his name: undoubtedly many of them must have heard of his father.

There was little hope of Churchill being released. Not only had he played a conspicuous part in defending the armoured train but he had now had the opportunity of assessing the size and strength of the commando. It would have been extremely foolish of the Boers to have set him free at this stage. Nevertheless he continued to protest his civilian status. When, after standing in the drizzling rain for some time, the prisoners were ordered to continue their march, Churchill tackled the leader of the mounted escort. He said that if he was not to be taken to see General Joubert, his papers should be returned to him. The only response he got was a sharp order to march.

For six hours they marched: tramping across the rain-sodden veld and squelching along slippery mud tracks. By the time they reached Colenso they were worn out. They had not eaten since leaving Estcourt that morning and were weakened, not only by the day's exertions, but by hunger. Night was falling as they marched into the village where they were immediately herded into a corrugated iron goods-shed next to the station. 'Here,' says Churchill, 'we flung ourselves down exhausted, and what with the shame, the disappointment, the excitement of the morning, the misery of the present, and physical weakness, it seemed that love of life was gone.'

Two fires were lit outside the shed. The prisoners were allowed to gather round them to dry their clothes and to cook the strips of meat they were given from a newly slaughtered ox. Rain was still falling and a strong wind blowing, but the meat—cut into small pieces and toasted on sticks—brought some relief. While they were eating, a party of Boers stationed in Colenso came over to inspect them. Among the party were two English-speaking brothers who tackled Churchill on the rights and wrongs of the war. The argument did not last long; by the time they parted they had become so friendly that one of the brothers took off a blanket he was wearing and gave it to Churchill.

Returning to their temporary prison, the soldiers did their best to make themselves comfortable. 'Selecting a corner apart from the men,' says Haldane, 'we made a bed by spreading on the concrete floor the contents of some compressed forage bales. Burying ourselves in the short dry hay, we huddled close together, endeavouring thereby to retain such warmth as still remained in our weary limbs.' Neither Churchill nor Haldane could sleep. They lay listening to the Boers singing their evening psalms. 'Ah, but it was worse than shells to hear,' Churchill told a friend. 'It struck the fear of God into me. What sort of men are these we are fighting? They have the better cause—and the cause is everything—at least, I mean to them it is the better cause.' Haldane was less generous. He dismissed the hymn singing as hypocritical. Lying on his straw bed and gazing at the skylight in the roof, he vaguely contemplated an escape; but he was too tired to do anything about it. He resigned himself to a sleepless night; punctuated by the snores of his men and the incessant patter of rain on the iron roof.

There was a slight consolation in the knowledge that news of their capture had been sent to England. On arriving at Colenso they had been met by two Boer newspapermen who had promised to 'telegraph to England at the earliest opportunity the fact that we were alive'. This news, however, was known long befor any such cables were sent.

*

After Churchill had left the tent in Escourt that morning, Atkins and Amery had returned to sleep. They were awakened a couple of hours later by the sound of gunfire. Leaping out of bed, they began to run and walk to the scene of action. About two miles outside of Estcourt they met the engine of the armoured train. 'Men stood on the footplates of the engine,' says Atkins, 'sat on the cow-catcher in front, and hung on to the sides of the tender; and when we ran to the track they waved their arms and pointed backwards and threw up their hands again, like men who would signalize something horrible.' The two correspondents hurried along the line in the pouring rain until they met twelve men of the Dublin Fusiliers. The soldiers were full of praise for Churchill. They told the reporters how he had walked calmly among the bullets saying, 'Keep cool, men,' and 'This will be interesting for my paper.' Leaving the soldiers, the two men pushed on until they came within sight of the abandoned trucks. According to Amery, they reached the wreckage just in time to get 'a distinct glimpse of the main body of Boers and their prisoners disappearing over the skyline'.

The story of the attack and Churchill's conduct was well known by the time the correspondents returned to Estcourt. The courage shown by the *Morning Post*'s correspondent was the talk of the town. A group of railwaymen, who had escaped in the engine, insisted that the part played by Churchill should be officially recognized. They approached the local railway inspector and got him to write a letter of appreciation to the General Manager of Railways. 'Sir,' ran the letter. 'The railwaymen who accompanied the armoured train this morning ask me to convey to you their admiration of the coolness and pluck displayed by Mr Winston Churchill, war correspondent, who accompanied the train and to whose efforts, backed up by driver Wagner, is due the fact that the armoured engine and tender were brought successfully out after being hampered by derailed trucks in front, and was able to bring the wounded in here. The whole of our men are loud in their praises of Mr Churchill, who, I regret to say, has been taken prisoner. I respectfully ask you to convey their admiration to that brave man.' No less unstinting in his praise was the wounded Captain Wylie. 'Capt. Wylie, who is doing well,' it was reported, 'describes Mr Winston Churchill's conduct in the most enthusiastic terms as that of as brave a man as could be found. It was on Mr Churchill's initiative that Capt. Wylie and a number of his men worked to get the trucks blocking the line out of the way. . . .' These spontaneous tributes, coming immediately after the action, effectively refute later insinuations that Churchill's heroism had been magnified by his friends.

Speculation in Estcourt as to Churchill's fate was of particular interest to his valet, Thomas Walden. As soon as it was known that he was a prisoner and alive, Walden cabled Lady Randolph. The following day, the valet travelled to Pietermaritzburg with

Charles Wagner, the engine driver, who gave him details of the derailment, which he immediately passed on to Churchill's mother. His letter was later published in the *Morning Post*. 'I am sorry to say Mr Churchill is a prisoner, but I am almost certain he is not wounded,' he wrote. I came down to Maritzburg yesterday to bring all his kit until Mr Winston gets free... Every officer in Estcourt thinks Mr C. and the engine-driver will get the V.C. ... How the engine escaped being blown up I don't know; it was a total wreck. The engine, with Mr C. on it, got back to Frere station safe, and then Mr C. would get off and go back to look after Captain Haldane. Mr C. left his field glasses and revolver on the engine, and the driver says he had lost his hat. It was a frightful morning too. It had been raining for about twenty-four hours, and it rained in torrents all day, so he must have been very wet; he had a good mackintosh on though. The driver says he was as cool as anything and worked like a nigger, and how he escaped he doesn't know, as about fifty shells hit the engine. Everyone in Maritzburg is talking about Mr Churchill...'

Soon, not only Maritzburg, but all England was talking about Mr Churchill. His daring, his audacity and the fact that he was a Churchill lent a touch of glamour to what was proving a dismal campaign. The popular press played up the armoured train incident for all it was worth. Several papers repeated the suggestion that Churchill be awarded the Victoria Cross. At last he had achieved the fame he sought. Not only was he Lord Randolph's son but he was a hero in his own right.

Unfortunately he was in no position to enjoy this acclaim. Indeed, the excessive publicity was to prove an embarrassment. 'Mr Winston Churchill is a prisoner with the Boers, and is understood to have been wounded in the hand,' stated one report. 'The exact nature of the wound is not known, but there are strong hopes that no serious harm has happened to him... The position of a war correspondent who takes an active part in a fight is technically peculiar.'

*

From Colenso the prisoners were marched to a camp just beyond Ladysmith. As they by-passed the besieged town they heard the sound of gunfire and caught a glimpse of the balloon that had been hoisted by the British garrison. 'Those are our blokes,' said one of the soldiers. 'We ain't all finished yet.' Churchill, looking in the direction of the town, could only envy its inhabitants. 'Beleaguered Ladysmith, with its shells, its flies, its fever, and its filth seemed a glorious paradise to me,' he remarked.

They marched on: slithered down rocky slopes, forded waist high through the Klip River and came in sight of a Boer encampment. Here they were to spend their second night. Once again they were exhausted. Arriving at the camp they threw themselves on to the ground in the shade of some stunted oaks. They were soon surrounded by a crowd of burgers who began to question them on the conduct of the war. Churchill was too tired to answer. He lay stretched out beneath a bush, oblivious to all that was going on.

Only when the camp commandant arrived with tea and bully beef and invited the officers to his tent did Churchill begin to revive. Several of the Boers followed them into the tent and the inevitable argument started once more. What was the war about? Who was behind it? Why were they fighting? Churchill parried the questions as best he could. He said that the Boers were trying to drive the British from South Africa and that the British had no intention of going. This produced heated denials. That was not the reason for the war. The war had been engineered by the capitalists of Johannesburg: Rhodes, Beit and Chamberlain wanted to divide the wealth of South Africa between them. This was the line taken repeatedly by the Boers. Churchill's replies were equally predictable. He argued patiently—with an attempt at reason and not in the highhanded manner of Lord Randolph—but the points he made were far from original. It was useless to tell the Boers that the gold mines were owned by shareholders—many of whom were French and German—and that while an extension of the Transvaal franchise might produce a more efficient government it would not affect the ownership of the mines. The Boers had heard all this before; they were not impressed. Like President Kruger at the Bloemfontein Conference, their cry was: 'You are trying to take our country from us.' And so they went on arguing in circles. Two nephews of General Joubert arrived and joined in. 'Churchill, needless to say, afforded all the greatest source of interest,' says Haldane. 'With much ability, coupled with quick repartee, he defended the justice of the war; but it struck me that these plain-spoken, ignorant farmers, who based their arguments on the capitalists and Mr Chamberlain . . . somewhat shook his faith, and certainly gained his sympathy.' Haldane himself began to waver, but he later put this down to his ignorance of the issues at stake. 'A few months have made it clear to me,' he said, 'how insidiously the country Boer has been taught to believe those specious arguments which are everywhere on the tip of his tongue.'

The camp commandant eventually put an end to the wrangling. It began to grow dark and he directed the prisoners to some tents in a corner of the camp. The officers were provided with a special tent; Churchill had to decide whether to join them or share with the men. He chose the officers and later regretted it.

The generous way the prisoners were treated at this camp was remarkable. The camp commandant was more like a host than a gaoler. Even the sceptical Haldane was impressed by him. 'I have the most vivid and lasting recollection,' he says, 'of the attention and kindness which this old Dutch farmer lavished upon us. Throughout the journey to the Boer metropolis we met with nothing but the greatest consideration; but this old commander not only gave us of the best he could—and at that time the Boer commissariat arrangements were in their infancy—but insisted on lending us some of his blankets, provided us with candles, and with his own hands brought us coffee on the following morning.' They were closely guarded but, so well were they treated, they felt it would smack of ingratitude even to contemplate an escape.

At daybreak they were on the march again. This time their destination was the Moddersspruit railway station: a stop on the line which connected Natal with the Transvaal. According to one of their escorts, the prisoners arrived at the station in the pouring rain and Churchill was shut up in the ticket office until a train arrived. But both Churchill and Haldane say that the train was waiting for them and they boarded it immediately: the officers in a first-class carriage and the men in covered trucks. Food was provided for them and again they became the centre for a large crowd of Boers. Among the men who peered in the windows of the train was a doctor who, noticing that Churchill's hand was bandaged, offered to look at his wound. The cut was not bad but, having been neglected for two days, it had begun to fester. The doctor hurried away and returned with hot water and fresh bandages: again Churchill had reason to feel grateful to his enemies.

Not until the journey had started did his new-found sympathy for his captors begin to wane. As usual he was soon caught up in a friendly argument with two of the Boer guards. Both these men, according to Haldane, had taken part in the armoured train fight; one of them had actually placed the boulders on the line. However, military tactics were not responsible for the sour note of this discussion. The trouble arose from the difference between British and Boer concepts of freedom.

'We want to be left alone,' said one of the Boers. 'We are free, you are not free.' Churchill asked him what he meant. 'Well,' he said, 'is it right that a dirty Kaffir should walk on the pavement—without a pass too? That is what they do in your British Colonies. Brother! Equal! Ugh! Free! Not a bit! We know how to treat Kaffirs.' Here, Churchill felt, was the fundamental cause of the Boer's dislike of British rule. Not past conflicts, not Majuba or the Jameson Raid, but the difference in attitude towards the African was at the root of the enmity between the two white races. 'British government is associated in the Boer farmer's mind,' he said, 'with violent social revolution. Black is to be proclaimed the same as white. The servant is to be raised against the master; the Kaffir is to be declared the brother of the European, to be constituted his legal equal, to be armed with political rights.' To these men, for all their simple and kindly ways, such a thought was anathema. '*We* know how to treat Kaffirs in *this* country,' the Boer continued. 'Fancy letting the black filth walk on the pavement!' It put an end to the friendly discussion. 'After that,' says Churchill, 'no more argument: but a gulf widening every moment.'

Haldane appears to have taken no part in the argument. He was busy talking to a new acquaintance. At Modderspruit Churchill and the two officers had been joined by a new prisoner. He was introduced to them as a lieutenant of the Natal Carbineers who had been captured outside of Ladysmith; but, as he was quick to inform Haldane, he was Sergeant-Major Brockie of

The Staatsmodelskool, Pretoria, where Winston Churchill was imprisoned

John G. Howard,
nager of the Transvaal
Delagoa Bay
llieries where Churchill
hidden after his escape
m Pretoria

(l. to r.) General Snyman and General Botha, the Boar officers commanding the force which besieged Mafeking

the Imperial Light Horse and had assumed a false rank to avoid being sent to the Pretoria gaol. 'He knew,' says Haldane, 'that such would be his fate should it transpire to what corps he actually belonged, for the members of the Imperial Light Horse are held in particular aversion by the Boers. The reason is not far to seek. The majority of those serving in this corps . . . are residents of Johannesburg, and many had taken a prominent part in the Jameson Raid, some having actually served on the Reform Committee.' The officers regarded Brockie as an important acquisition. Not only did he speak the language of the Boers but he knew several African dialects as well. In an attempted escape his services would be invaluable. For most of the journey, Haldane and Brockie were huddled together—joined occasionally by Churchill—formulating plans for a break-out once they arrived at Pretoria.

At every stop the prisoners were treated with a mixture of curiosity and kindness by the local Boers. On arriving at Germiston in the Transvaal, the usual crowd of burgers surrounded the train and passed cigars through the carriage windows. A Special Mines Police Commandant, Mr Ferrand, pushed his way through the crowd and asked Churchill if he was an American.

'Half and half,' replied Churchill.

'I am also some such sort of American,' said Ferrand. 'We are brothers perhaps?'

But Churchill was not to be drawn. He 'looked slyly at my uniform,' says Ferrand, 'and said, "Yes, but we are enemies." I asked him if he were well treated by the Boers. "Splendidly," he answered. "The Boers," he said, with emphasis, "will fight to the last." The train was just starting when the guards forbade further conversation.'

A large party of burgers and journalists was waiting for them at the Pretoria station. They arrived there in the middle of a sunny day. After the train had pulled up at a siding, the prisoners were assembled on the platform to face a battery of clicking cameras. Prisoners-of-war were still a novelty at the Boer capital and Churchill was immediately conscious of the hostility of the crowd. 'Now for the first time since my capture I hated the enemy,' he said. 'The simple valiant burghers at the front, fighting bravely as they had been told "for their farms", claimed respect, if not sympathy. But here in Pretoria I seemed to smell corruption in the air.' They were kept standing on the platform for about twenty minutes. Then, to Haldane's dismay, Brockie was led away by two plain-clothes policemen and Churchill was ordered to join the men. When Haldane protested that Churchill was not only a war correspondent but the son of a lord, he was quickly put in his place. 'We know and care nothing for your lords and ladies here,' he was told. The two officers were then put in the charge of a strong police escort and led away. They had only gone a few yards, however, when Haldane spotted another Boer official and tackled him about Churchill's position. This time he was more successful; a few minutes later Churchill was brought to join the officers.

The men were marched to the racecourse on the outskirts of the town, but Churchill and the officers—each flanked by three armed policemen—were led through the back streets to the Staatsmodelskool. Arriving at this makeshift prison—a long, single-storied, red-brick building fronted by iron railings—they noticed that the verandah was crowded with bearded men in khaki uniforms. Haldane recognized several acquaintances. 'They looked up as we arrived,' says Churchill. 'The iron gate was opened, and passing in we joined sixty British officers "held by the enemy"; and the iron gate was then shut again.'

CHAPTER TEN

Betrayed by a Pigeon

SHORTLY after Winston Churchill arrived at Pretoria, his family name was again making the headlines of the British press. 'Anxieties crowd upon the Spencer Churchill family at the present time,' announced the *Daily Mail*, 'for in addition to the distress in which they are plunged over Mr Winston Churchill's fate, they are uncertain as to the welfare of Lady Sarah Wilson, although a news-agency reported the other day that she was safe at Setlagole. It was well known that she left Mafeking with her maid, riding out across the veldt for at least 200 [*sic*] miles—a sensational feat at any time for two women to accomplish, but in the midst of a war a most remarkable exploit. Since this ride was achieved Lady Sarah's sisters have heard from her that she is safe, but they are now anxiously awaiting a cable from herself confirming the report of the news-agency.' Claiming Sarah as 'Our Own War Correspondent', the *Mail* did its best to match her 'daring feat' with the heroism of her nephew: even suggesting that she had undertaken her ride from Mafeking in 'her capacity as war correspondent'. Other newspapers, while full of admiration, were not so overwhelmed at Sarah's fortitude. It was 'all very well for Lady Sarah, who doubtless was accustomed to violent exercise,' remarked one of them, 'but we commiserate with her poor maid.'

Had Sarah known of these reports she would have been astonished. At the time these reports were sent from South Africa, her life was far removed from that of a popular heroine.

*

Life at Mosita was completely uneventful.

One morning, as Mr Keeley was busily beating off a swarm of locusts that had descended on his vegetable patch, Sarah joined him to find out what he was doing. He told her and asked her to take over while he lit his pipe. Seizing the switch, she made a determined attack on the pests. Many years later, this incident was to be recalled as her one and only attempt to help with the running of things during these trying weeks.

In fairness, there had been nothing in Sarah's background to make her realize that her help might be necessary. Surrounded all her life by servants, it would never have occurred to her to offer assistance. She was certainly not lazy, but she was incapable of bringing her active, keenly political mind down to a domestic level. Ironically, if she had only shouldered some of the household burdens, she would have made life less irritating, not only for the Keeleys, but for herself. She longed for some sort of action. The endless days of waiting were beginning to shred her nerves.

At last she could stand it no longer. With her husband and fellow countrymen besieged a few miles away it seemed ridiculous to be idling away her time at Mosita. She was still keeping Boaz busy as a despatch runner, but the information she was sending to Mafeking was trivial and unreliable. It was hardly worth the risk or the expense involved. In any case, she was now running short of money with which to pay the messenger. She decided that the time had come to take action herself.

The news that the neighbouring town of Vryburg was occupied by the Boers had tantalized her from the time of first hearing it. With the enemy practically on the doorstep, it should be possible to obtain some worthwhile information. However, this was not a task which could be left to African runners. They were not in a position to unearth military details and there was no point in paying out money for more vague rumours. She would have to go herself. It was not a mission that could be approached lightly. If she were discovered she would most certainly be taken prisoner. First it was necessary to test the vigilance of the enemy.

Living on a near-by farm was a family of Boers who had taken a lively interest in her association with the Keeleys. The son of the house was captivated by her white pony, Dop. Now, hearing that the boy was about to take some cattle into Vryburg, Sarah offered him the loan of the pony. The youngster was delighted. He had no hesitation in offering to act as her messenger. She gave him some letters to post for the English mail and a short note to the English magistrate asking for newspapers and reliable information. She also gave him a cheque to cash at the Vryburg bank. If he managed to get away with such blatant trafficking with the British, she felt it would be worth risking a visit herself.

The boy returned a few days later. Sarah was staggered at how well her plan had worked. Not only had he succeeded in cashing her cheque but, he told her, the bank had been only too pleased to get rid of the gold in exchange for an order on a London bank. He had contacted the magistrate and Sarah was amused to see that the reply he had brought was in an official envelope with the bold 'On H.M. Service' neatly crossed through. He had been unable to post her letters, however. The post office would only recognize Transvaal stamps and she had used those of the Cape Colony: the fact that the letters had been addressed to England had apparently roused no curiosity.

The youngster was full of depressing stories. Rumours of Boer victories were current in the town and the magistrate's letter was pessimistic. Nevertheless, the fact remained that discipline at Vryburg was obviously slack. Sarah felt she could pay her visit.

If the Keeleys had any objection to her plans, they knew her well enough by now not to oppose them. It was arranged that young Arthur Coleman, Mrs Keeley's brother, should drive her into Vryburg in a trap with a pair of ponies. Word was spread locally that she had toothache and was going to the dentist. Sarah could hardly wait to get under way. 'I was much excited at the prospect of visiting the Boer headquarters in that part of the country', she says, 'and seeing with my own eyes the Transvaal flag flying in the town of a British colony. Therefore I thought nothing of undertaking a sixty-miles drive in broiling heat and along a villainous road.'

The first day's travelling went well. The road was deserted and the farmhouses they passed were mostly empty. Towards sunset they arrived at a wayside store and were given a night's lodging by a friendly Jewish trader. They were about five miles outside Vryburg the following morning before they saw signs of the Boer occupation. A party of horsemen appeared on the brow of a hill and seemed to be riding towards them. They began to prepare their excuses but, after a casual glance in their direction, the men circled and galloped away.

Vryburg had once been described to Sarah as a town that had gone for a walk and got lost. Seeing it for the first time, she could understand why. Situated in a slight hollow, its neatly planned streets led straight into the veld and the railway by-passed it completely. There seemed no reason for it to be there. From a distance, the only point of interest, as far as Sarah could see, was the Boer laager on the outskirts.

As they drove down the main street, their attention was caught by the heavily guarded Court House. Armed men were passing in and out of the building, sentries patrolled the streets and more were crowded round a notice pinned to a tree. Through the surrounding trees they could see the boldly striped *Vierkleur*, the Transvaal flag, fluttering from the roof. There could be no doubt that they were in enemy territory.

Arriving at the Central Hotel, Sarah marched in and announced herself. The English-speaking manager looked at her aghast. He hurried her to a room, advised her to stay there and said that on no account must she mention her name. The newly appointed Landrost (magistrate) had arrived that same day and was already making his presence felt. It was rumoured that strict regulations concerning the arrival and departure of visitors were about to be enforced. The chances of her being able to leave Vryburg seemed remote.

For the next few days she was obliged to remain in the hotel. Only once did she venture out. After the armoured train had been derailed near Mafeking, some of the wounded British soldiers had been brought to the Vryburg hospital; Sarah paid them a secret visit. This somewhat risky excursion satisfied her curiosity. From then on she decided that it would be wiser to remain out of sight. Most of the day was spent sitting at the window of her room watching the mounted burgers patrolling the town. It was not a sight which impressed her. 'When you have seen one you have seen them all,' she wrote disparagingly. 'I never could have imagined so many men absolutely alike: all had straggling beards, old felt hats, shabby clothes, and some evil-looking countenances. Most of those I saw were men from forty to fifty years of age, but there were also a few sickly looking youths, who certainly did not look bold warriors.'

Her main concern of course was to get back to Mosita. As the hotel manager had feared, the new Landrost was proving far more efficient than his predecessor. An order had been put out that no one was to leave Vryburg. Those travelling on business could only do so on a special pass issued by the Landrost's office. Armed sentries were posted on all roads, and vehicles and their passengers were liable to be searched. The hotel manager did his best to dissuade Sarah from attempting to leave. He was quite sure she would not obtain a pass and to smuggle her past the sentries would be too risky.

But Sarah was not to be put off. She decided to bluff it out. Arthur Coleman, who spoke the Boers' language, was sent to the Landrost's office to apply for a pass. He told the officials that he was a young Boer who had come into town with his sister to buy provisions and that they now wanted to return to their farm. After a nerve-racking wait and some 'pointed questions' the pass was eventually issued. They could hardly believe their luck and decided to leave at daybreak.

They were up before the sun rose. The hotel manager lent Sarah a shabby ulster which all but enveloped her; she covered her face with a heavy veil and wound a woollen shawl round her sailor hat—it was the best she could do in the way of a disguise. With Sarah sitting slumped forward beside him, Coleman drove the cart to the outskirts of the town. Here they were stopped by sentries. Sarah, numb with apprehension, climbed down from the cart and stood some distance off while Coleman went to show the pass. To excuse her apparent shyness and muffled appearance, the youngster explained that she was suffering from toothache and had a swollen face. The formalities took some minutes—'the longest,' says Sarah, 'I have ever experienced.' But at last Coleman returned and they bundled back into the cart and headed for the open road.

They covered the sixty miles to Mosita in one day.

*

The next few days were an anti-climax. Vryburg, for all its excitements, had provided little significant information. The hotel manager had passed on some news of the early fighting in Natal (though not of the part played by Winston Churchill) which Sarah had mistakenly found encouraging; but, once this information had been sent to Mafeking, she found herself back where she had started.

For the first time she became overwhelmingly depressed. She even took to arguing with Mr Keeley about the necessity for the war. In her opinion, all that the fighting had done was to sow further distrust among the already hard-pressed farming community. To droughts, locust plagues and cattle disease was now added internecine warfare. Sarah, for all her Englishness, was refreshingly free of the unquestioning jingoism of so many of her compatriots. She was no longer sure of the rightness of the Uitlander cause. 'It seemed to me then,' she argued, 'we were not justified in letting loose such a millstream of wretchedness and destruction, and that the alleged wrongs of a large white population—who, in spite of everything, seemed to prosper and grow rich apace—scarcely justified the sufferings of thousands of innocent individuals.'

To Sarah's depression was added the uncertainty of her own position. The rumours started by her arrival at Mosita had now grown out of all proportion. The local Boers found her presence at the lonely farm house extremely suspect. She was told that she was believed to be Baden-Powell's wife in hiding or, alternatively, 'a grand-daughter of Queen Victoria, sent specially out by Her Majesty to inform her of the proceedings of her rebellious subjects.' Whichever version was accepted, it had become plain that her days at Mosita were numbered. Should a Boer patrol arrive in the neighbourhood, she would undoubtedly be sought out.

She decided that her best plan was to return to Setlagole. There was nowhere else for her to go. The road south to Kimberley was blocked; to the west lay the formidable Kalahari; to the east the Transvaal. The Boers had been informed that she was at the store, and it was at least one stage nearer Mafeking to which, despite everything, she still hoped to return. Once her mind was made up, she lost no time in acting upon her decision. 'With many grateful thanks to the Keeleys,' she says, 'I rode off one morning with Vellum [Wilhelm] in attendance... We thought it prudent to make sure there were no Boers about before bringing the Government mules and cart. Therefore I arranged for my maid to follow in this vehicle if she heard nothing to the contrary within twenty-four hours.' She felt a pang of regret at leaving the little homestead. To the Keeleys' credit, they had successfully stifled their well-warranted irritation and made her feel that she was not only welcome but part of the family. In her rather off-hand way she had become fond of them. 'The kindness of the Keeleys,' she was to write, 'is a bright spot in my recollections of those dark weeks.'

She found the atmosphere at Setlagole much livelier. This was due mainly to the vociferous jingoism of Mr and Mrs Fraser, the owners of the store. Unlike the more down-to-earth Keeleys, the Frasers exercised no discretion in proclaiming their loyalty to Queen and Empire; their outspoken patriotism had already attracted the attention of passing Boer patrols. With the store situated on the main road between Mafeking and Vryburg—the one occupied by the British, the other by the Boers—hardly a day passed without bringing some frightening rumour or threat.

But for all that, the news that reached Setlagole was no more reliable than the rumours that filtered through to Mosita. Just how unreliable it was became apparent to Sarah the day after she arrived. That morning some Africans rushed into the store with what appeared to be well-authenticated news of a British victory just outside Vryburg. They also reported that the railway line was being repaired and that the staff of a near-by station had returned to work. Things seemed to be returning to normal and the optimistic prophecies of peace by Christmas looked like being realized.

Yet, despite the jubilation of the Frasers, Sarah remained sceptical. She decided to investigate the railway story for herself. Saddling up Dop, she rode to the station. She found the place locked and barred. Only when she strode over to the stationmaster's house did she discover the source of the rumours. There, seated on the rickety stoep, she found the stationmaster engrossed in *Nicholas Nickleby*. He told her that he was the only member of the staff who had returned and he was there only because it was his home: he knew nothing about the line being repaired. 'Vague native rumours. . .' wrote Sarah, 'are of all known means of conveying news quite the most irritating, as well as the most astonishing, one can imagine; the vivid imagination of the intelligent black, combined with a retentive memory and his imperfect knowledge of the white man's language, defying every possibility of arriving at the true version of any occurrence.'

However, her visit to the station had roused her curiosity. With so many rumours centred on the possibility of re-opening railway communication with Mafeking, she was anxious to discover the extent to which the line had been disrupted. Although she had heard the gunfire which had derailed the armoured train and had visited some of the survivors in the Vryburg hospital, she had been unable to discover just how bad the damage was. A detailed report on the capsized trucks would, she felt, be invaluable to any plan for relieving Mafeking.

Once again she faced the problem of obtaining a reliable report, and once again she decided to undertake the mission herself. The Frasers were not enthusiastic and she received no encouragement from the English-speaking farmers who congregated at the store. She was told that the railway line was being watched and that particular interest was being paid to the area in which the train had been derailed: any attempt to approach the wreckage would invite capture.

Not until a correspondent from Reuter's, a Mr J. E. Pearson, arrived at the store was she able to persuade anyone that the risk was worth taking. The saddle-sore reporter was on his way to Mafeking from Cape Town and had stopped at Setlagole to give his horse a few days' rest. Pearson seemed the ideal person to accompany her; for, not only could he carry a report to Baden-Powell, but he had the added advantage of possessing a camera. The opportunity was too good to miss.

Taking an African guide with them, they set off after an early lunch the following Sunday. 'There was not much fear of meeting any Boers,' says Sarah, 'as the latter were always engaged that day in psalm-singing and devotions.' Galloping across the flat tawny veld, they were seen only by groups of Africans who stared at them in astonishment. A woman on horseback was a rare sight in that sparsely populated country and the spectacle of Sarah charging hell-for-leather past their huts created a sensation among the tribesmen. At every kraal they were greeted with shouts and their guide was bombarded with questions. Sarah found this reassuring. 'As long as you were accompanied by a native,' she says, 'you were always sure of information concerning the whereabouts of the

Boers; but to these latter they would lie with stupid, solemn faces.'

Arriving at the railway line, they left their horses at a Baralong village and proceeded on foot to the wrecked train. The countryside was barren and exposed; only a few scattered rocks afforded any semblance of cover. It was behind these rocks that the Boers had waited to ambush the train. The crumpled wreckage, shimmering in the heat, was a depressing sight. The pilot coach was embedded in the dust, the bullet-riddled engine—with its battered armoured truck—was still on the rails, and the rear carriage was upended in a near-by culvert. Leaving her companion busy with his camera, Sarah scrambled about the trucks trying to assess the damage. Unlike her nephew in Natal, she was able to carry out her inspection undisturbed: in fact the eerie silence made her decidedly edgy. 'All the time,' she says, 'I gave cursory glances right and left, to make sure no Boers were prowling about, and I should not have been surprised to have seen an unkempt head bob up and ask our business. But all remained silent as the grave.' The only sound came from a swarm of locusts massed beneath the engine.

It was too quiet for comfort. Sarah could not get away from the place fast enough. As soon as she had seen all there was to see, she hurried over to Pearson, badgered him into putting away his camera and hustled him back to their horses. Not until they arrived back at Setlagole did she feel free to draw breath.

The expedition reawakened her spying instincts. She had at last accomplished something worth while. Her report—backed up by the photographs—was far more substantial than the rumours she had passed on from Mosita. Now that she was beginning to find her feet in the country the possibilities for espionage seemed limitless. But to be a successful spy it was neccessary to establish regular contact with Mafeking. This had never been easy and now she no longer had Boaz at her disposal it would be more difficult. Local Africans were not eager to act as runners. There had been too many messengers caught to make the trip to Mafeking an attractive proposition. Any African caught working for the British could expect little mercy. 'Several of the native runners were shot in cold blood by the Boers, many of whom take a delight in putting natives up in the road and coolly shooting them down,' said Major Dennison, one of

Sarah's contacts. 'The shedding of native blood is not counted as murder by many of them; on the contrary, they talk and laugh over the deed, describing the fear and agony of the poor sufferer with jeers and laughter. All are not thus; too many, nevertheless, can be charged.' That volunteers to enter Mafeking were becoming fewer by the week is hardly surprising.

Sarah found a solution to her problem a few days later. J. E. Pearson, having completed his hazardous ride in and out of Mafeking, stopped at Setlagole on his way back. He reported that all was well in the town, although the inhabitants were now living mostly underground because of the constant shelling. Knowing Sarah's plans, he had brought back a basket of carrier pigeons. He assured her that by using these birds she would be able to 'communicate swiftly and safely with the garrison'. Sarah was delighted; but she was a little dubious about managing the pigeons. To demonstrate how easy this was, Pearson suggested that they send one of the birds on a trial flight. With Sarah's help, he wrote a note to Baden-Powell outlining the situation at Setlagole and passing on one of the bizarre rumours that Sarah had received: a camel corps was reported to be 'skirting the Kalahari' in an attempt to communicate with the beleaguered garrison. Pearson ended the note by giving details of the local farms (including the Keeleys) and added: 'Lady Sarah Wilson is here doing good work as an intelligence officer.' After selecting a pigeon, the reporter clipped his note to the bird's leg and set it loose. With a flutter of white wings, the pigeon soared into the air, hovered for a second, and then—to Sarah's alarm—began to circle wildly as if at a loss to know in which direction it should fly. Pearson was unperturbed. He 'assured me,' says Sarah, 'this was their usual habit, and that this particular bird knew its business, having taken several prizes; so, as it eventually disappeared, I thought no more of it.'

But this, unfortunately, was not to be one of the bird's prize-winning flights. Although headed in the right direction, it never reached Mafeking. It came down in the Boer laager, settled on the roof of the commanding officer's house and was promptly shot by an observant Veld-Kornet. A Transvaal newspaper reporting the incident said: 'A carrier pigeon hovering around Mafeking was shot by a burgher yesterday.... One of Lieut. Jooste's men left immediately for Pretoria with the despatch. The contents are still secret here.' They were not to remain secret for long.

*

The Boers arrived at Setlagole store two days later. Early that morning a party of armed burgers had left the laager near Mafeking and by midday were seen to be approaching Setlagole.

Sarah, who had spent the morning at the back of the house, had no inkling of the Boers' approach until she came in for luncheon. She then learned of their expected arrival in an almost farcical manner. Strolling unsuspectingly into the dining room, she saw two of her fellow guests on their knees in the far corner. One of them—a short, stocky American relative of Mrs Fraser's —was trying to prise up the floorboards with an axe. He was being watched by a tall, heavily built Englishman who had taken refuge at the store after his own trading station had been sacked by the Boers. Hurrying across to them, Sarah found that they were trying to widen the trapdoor of a small underground food cellar. 'We are going to hide, Lady Sarah,' explained the little American. 'The Boers are on the premises.' Sarah, alarmed but ever practical, immediately pointed out that they would never fit into such a small space and that even if they did they would most likely suffocate. This rather obvious piece of advice stopped them short. Jumping up they began to look for another hiding place.

The sound of men and horses outside was now unmistakable. The two men became quite desperate. The shorter one, still shouldering his axe, rushed about the room repeating that he was a free-born American and refused to fight for the Boers, until eventually—spying the only possible hiding place—he dived beneath a velvet cloth covering the grand piano. When his head popped out again, he looked so terrified that Sarah could not contain herself: she collapsed on a sofa hooting with laughter.

The thought of the Boers quickly brought her back to earth. She took charge of the situation. Ordering the little American to his feet, she gave both men a brisk lecture. If the house were searched, she said, they were bound to be discovered and no gentleman, be he English or American, could allow himself to be dragged from under a piano. They must face up to their position calmly. Never one to mince words, she told the smaller man bluntly that he was far too puny for a Boer commando; there was no fear of his services being commandeered. She then advised his companion—whose fate was more uncertain—to lie on the sofa and feign illness. 'And I really believe,' she says, 'anxiety and worry had so preyed on him that he was as ill as he looked.'

Determined not to be flustered, Sarah sat down to eat her lunch. A few minutes later Mrs Fraser came panting in to report what was happening. Some thirty or forty Boers 'armed to the teeth' had invaded the store and demanded food. After helping themselves to several tins of salmon and sardines, they had been provided with coffee and were now seated in the yard devouring their ill-gotten meal. By peering through the green Venetian blinds, Sarah was able to catch her first glimpse of the enemy in action: she was no more impressed than she had been at Vryburg. Sprawled in the shade behind the store, the bearded burgers, dressed in an odd assortment of civilian clothes, with cartridge belts slung across their shoulders, seemed too motley a force to be challenging the British Army. She was fascinated by the way they ate the sardines out of the tin and finished by drinking the oil; she was even more intrigued to learn that, whenever possible, they preferred to mix the oil with golden syrup. Officers some of them might be but, in her eyes, they were certainly not gentlemen.

For the rest of the afternoon she paced the darkened room while one of her jittery companions kept watch at the window. The stifling heat, the curtained gloom and the tense atmosphere contrasted sharply with the boisterous behaviour of the men outside. Their meal finished, the Boers again crowded into the store and Mrs Fraser came flying back to report that they were now helping themselves to clothes and cigarettes. She was convinced that the farm was about to be ransacked. But—to everyone's surprise—the Boers made no attempt to search the house: they contented themselves with some desultory shooting at a row of bottles, set up at the end of the yard.

The reason behind their visit only became known after a few of them had helped themselves to some bottles of cheap brandy at the back of the store. In a fit of drunkenness, the leader of the party, a man named Dietrich, suddenly turned on old Mr Fraser and demanded to know the whereabouts of the newspaper reporter who had written to Baden-Powell. He was also interested in the Englishwoman mentioned in the note. Mr Fraser pretended not to understand what he was talking about. This produced another outburst. With God's help, the man explained, the Boers had captured a carrier pigeon headed for Mafeking and they were now waiting for a senior officer to arrive before rounding up all the people mentioned in the note that had been found on the bird. They had already sent for a former owner of the store, Mr Lamb, who was expected to help them in their search.

Alarming as this news was, there was nothing that could be done about it. Not only would it have been dangerous for Sarah to leave the surrounded store but, even had she managed to escape, there was nowhere for her to go. Mr Keeley had been one of those mentioned in the note so there could be no question of her returning to Mosita. Indeed, the thought of the trouble in store for the Keeleys worried Sarah more than her own fate. To have taken refuge with any of the other English farmers in the neighbourhood would only worsen the damage already done.

Just as the sun was setting that evening, they heard someone joking in English with the Boers outside. Hopefully they rushed to the window and, peering into the gathering dusk, they were able to make out the figure of a man riding up to the store with the drunken Dietrich. The Frasers recognized him as Mr Lamb. His arrival did much to ease the tension. As a trader who had lived in the district for some years, Mr Lamb knew most of the Boers well. Within no time he had persuaded them to put away their guns and settle down for the night in the outhouses and stables. As soon as the Boers had dispersed, Sarah and her companions came out on to the stoep and sat breathing in the cool night air. Mr Lamb joined them. There was, he assured them, no cause for alarm; when the Veld-Kornet arrived the following morning he would see to it that they were not molested. Sarah was amazed at the way in which the camaraderie of these neighbouring farmers had survived the outbreak of war: it was, she later pointed out, 'a curious illustration of a phase of this war'. Unfortunately it was a phase which did not last long.

The alarms of the day were not entirely over, however. While they were sitting on the stoep, talking and laughing over the somewhat haphazard invasion, their conversation was rudely interrupted. 'I suddenly looked up,' says Sarah, 'and round the corner of the verandah saw the unsteady form of a typical Boer—slouch hat, bandolier and rifle complete—staggering towards us, truly a weird apparition. The rising moon on the rifle barrel made it glitter like silver. I confess I disappeared round the corner to my room with more haste than dignity.' Her misplaced panic is a good indication of the state of her nerves. The sinister apparition turned out to be nothing more fearsome than the befuddled Dietrich who, in an upsurge of *bonhomie*, had come to assure them they had nothing to fear and could rest in peace. He was led back to bed by the tactful Mr Lamb.

A cloud of white dust on the road from Mafeking the following morning announced the arrival of Veld-Kornet De Koker. The coming of this bombastic, middle-aged man quickly put an end to the optimism of the night before. He was immediately recognized by the Frasers as a local Boer who had recently been convicted of sheep stealing. Hardly had he arrived than he gave orders for a full-scale search. Sarah immediately sprang into action and, after hustling the timid lodgers into position, had the satisfaction of seeing her ruse work. When the search party came crashing into the dining-room they wasted little time on the occupants; 'giving a passing glance at the sick man lying with closed eyes and treating his diminutive friend with ill-concealed contempt.' For the rest of the day the Boer officers shut themselves up in the living-room, sending out from time to time for refreshments. When they finally emerged, the household was assembled and Dietrich read out a proclamation. 'This country now being part of the Transvaal,' he announced, 'the residents must within seven days leave their homes or enrol as burgers.' With mixed feelings—the Frasers indignant, their lodgers petrified—the occupants of the store signed the blank piece of paper thrust before them: their only consolation being that no mention had been made of fighting for the Boers.

In Sarah's case the conditions did not apply. She was to be made a prisoner.

Replying to her flood of protests, De Koker informed her that as she was a foreigner she must remain under arrest until such times as she could produce 'satisfactory credentials' for being in the territory. The Veld-Kornet then ordered his men to saddle up. He said that they were leaving for Mosita and would return the following day. Three sentries were left to watch Sarah; she was dismayed to find that one of them was her *bête noire*, Dietrich.

De Koker and his party returned at dusk the following evening. With them they brought Mr Keeley as a prisoner: after weeks of anxiety Mrs Keeley's worst fears had been realized and Sarah was distressed to think that she was largely responsible. Seething with indignation, she again tackled De Koker about her own position. She was a woman and a non-combatant, she argued; what grounds had he for treating her as a prisoner-of-war? The Veld-Kornet was polite but firm. He said that a report of her case was being sent to Pretoria and, until further orders were received, she must remain at the store; three men would be left to guard her and she was 'on no account to leave the precincts of the farm'.

Sarah considered this worse than being carted off to the Boer laager. To be confined to Setlagole was bad enough; to be left there in the charge of the uncouth Dietrich was unthinkable. She decided to appeal to a higher authority. As the Boers prepared to leave the following morning, she scribbled a note to the Boer Commandant and gave it to one of Mr Keeley's escort to deliver. In the note she asked permission to pass through the enemy lines and join her husband in Mafeking. Mr Keeley was not hopeful. He told her that the Boers had been watching her closely and were aware of her moves since she had left Mafeking: they even knew of her trips to Vryburg and the armoured train wreckage. To make matters worse, the Boer laager was now under the command of a General Snyman, a bigoted man who was unpopular even among his own troops. There was little hope of her softening Snyman's heart. The men rode off leaving Sarah cursing the ineptitude of carrier pigeons.

Early the following morning, Veld-Kornet De Koker returned. He had discovered Sarah's note and had come to offer her a pass to the Boer laager. He assured her that General Snyman was always polite to ladies and offered to escort her personally to the laager. The Frasers were very suspicious of the Veld-Kornet's change of heart and warned Sarah not to go with him. She thought it wise to take their advice. It took her some time to persuade De Koker to accept her refusal of his offer; eventually, however, he agreed to leave the pass with her and said that if she decided to take advantage of it she must be sure to call at his farm, which was on the way to the laager.

That same evening Mr Keeley arrived back at the store. Having been friendly with General Snyman before the war, he had managed to convince the Boer Commandant that he offered no threat to the Boer forces and, after being solemnly warned to remain neutral, he had been allowed to return to his family. Now, on his way back to Mosita, he had called in to deliver an answer to Sarah's note. The letter had been handed to him as he was leaving the Boer laager. Its contents came as no surprise. Sarah was informed that the pass she had requested could not be granted. She was to remain where she was under the surveillance of the Transvaal burgers. This attempt at politeness did nothing to soothe the indignant Sarah. 'It was,' she remarked tartly, 'exactly the surveillance of one of his said burghers that I wished to avoid.'

CHAPTER ELEVEN

Over the Garden Wall

WINSTON CHURCHILL was singled out for special attention by the reporters who met the prisoners at Pretoria station. He was the only one mentioned by name in the reports in the Transvaal papers the following day. One expressed surprise at his 'very youthful appearance'; another declared that it was only necessary to get a glimpse of his 'mug' to see what a rogue he was. Both emphasized the fact that he was Lord Randolph Churchill's son.

The day after the prisoners arrived at the Staatsmodelskool, newsmen from *De Volksstem* and *The Standard and Diggers' News* were allowed to visit them. Churchill seized the opportunity to protest his non-combatant status. 'Mr Winston Churchill,' reported *The Standard and Diggers' News*, 'declares that at the time of his capture near Estcourt, he was only armed with a reporter's notebook and pencil. He was busy recording impressions of armoured train warfare and its effects on modern formations, when the ironclad on wheels was derailed and hurled him and fifty-six others into space. He was hopelessly involved with Jack Tars, regulars and volunteers in the mêlée and was slightly wounded in the hand. The Government is considering representations made on his behalf and it is believed that his enforced detention is only temporary.' The representations that were being made appear to have originated entirely from the prisoner himself. On the day he was interviewed, he wrote a letter to Louis de Souza, the Transvaal's Secretary of State for War. He asked to be returned to the British lines and pointed out that he was an unarmed war correspondent when he was captured, that he had presented his credentials to General Joubert immediately and that his identity had been clearly established. He also tactfully acknowledged the kindness he had received on his journey from Natal. At the same time he wrote to his mother asking her to work for his release and discreetly hinting at the line she should take.

There was little hope of his argument succeeding. His father's reputation among the Boers and the publicity given to his heroism during the armoured train fight were against him. The reports of his protests to the Transvaal newspapers appeared at the same time as the Natal press was singing his praises. This, as far as General Joubert was concerned, settled the matter. 'I understand,' he wired Pretoria, 'that the son of Lord Churchill maintains that he is only a newspaper correspondent and therefore wants the privilege of being released. From a [Natal] newspaper it appears entirely otherwise and it is for this reason that I urge you that he must be guarded and watched as dangerous for our war; otherwise he can still do us a lot of harm. In a word, he must not be released during the war. It is through his active part that *one section* of the armoured train got away.'

President Kruger, when first he heard that Churchill had been captured, said that 'they might as well let him go as one man could do no harm'. But as the prisoners had then been on their way to Pretoria, it had not been possible to act on the President's suggestion; now it was too late. On receipt of Joubert's telegram, the President changed his mind. When Churchill's application came before him it was refused. 'The Government will act accordingly,' noted F. W. Reitz, the State Secretary, at the bottom of Joubert's telegram. This, of course, did not stop Churchill. He continued to demand his release both in writing and in the interviews he had with Boer officials. His arguments were as varied as they were ingenious. He pointed out that his detention would bring the Boers into bad odour with the world press; that it would be thought he was being held as a hostage. He promised that if he were released he would observe his non-combatant status, or even withdraw from South Africa, and that his newspaper would pay any expenses incurred by the Transvaal Government in keeping him captive. He got Haldane to support his claim to be a non-combatant and, at one stage, tried to take advantage of a contemplated exchange of prisoners. But it was no use. Always he was frustrated by the publicity he had so assiduously courted.

The Boers' suspicions of him were reinforced by a rumour that he had been armed when taken prisoner. How this rumour started it is not possible to say. Perhaps it was because of the cartridge clips he had been discovered trying to get rid of; or because he was known to have started out from Estcourt with a Mauser pistol; or simply because of his reputation for daring. Whatever the reason, the rumour has persisted to the present day. Deneys Reitz, the son of the Transvaal State Secretary, was one of the many Boers to add colour to the rumour. At the time of Churchill imprisonment Reitz, then a boy of seventeen, was spending a few days in Pretoria on leave from the Boer forces in Natal. In his well-known book, *Commando*, he says that he accompanied his father on a visit to one of the prisoners at the Staatsmodelskool. 'His name was Winston Churchill, a son of Lord Randolph Churchill, of whom I had often heard,' he writes. 'He said that he was not a combatant but a war-correspondent, and asked to be released on that account. My father, however, replied that he was carrying a Mauser pistol when taken, and so must remain where he was. Winston Churchill said that all war-correspondents in the Soudan had carried weapons for self-protection, and the comparison annoyed my father, who told him that the Boers were not in the habit of killing non-combatants.' But, it would seem, Reitz either misunderstood or mistakenly remembered this conversation: for, even had he been armed, it is most unlikely that Churchill would have admitted as much after so many denials. There seems, in fact, to be no truth in the rumour. The story has only ever been told as hearsay and there is no mention of a Mauser pistol, or any other type of weapon, in official Boer reports. Moreover, in his letter to Lady Randolph, Churchill's valet—writing two days after the event—states quite clearly that the Mauser pistol was left on the engine of the armoured train.

If a pistol had been taken from Churchill it would undoubtedly have been produced during the protracted negotiations with the Boer authorities. It was not. The correspondence between the prisoner and his gaolers shuttled back and forth and, as in the endless discussions on the rights and wrongs of the war, the arguments tended to go round in circles. Meanwhile, Churchill was forced to endure the boredom of imprisonment. 'The days I passed at Pretoria,' he was to write, 'were the most monotonous and among the most miserable of my life.' His experiences at the Staatsmodelskool gave him a life-long sympathy for prisoners of all types.

*

The captive British officers were treated extremely well. Apart from the inevitable tedium, they had little cause for complaint. Churchill admitted this freely. Throughout his captivity he had nothing but praise for his gaolers.

The Staatsmodelskool had been opened shortly before the war and, as its name implies, was intended to function as an exemplary educational institution. With the influx of a great many prisoners during the early months of the war, it had been commandeered as a prison. Some of the classrooms had been turned into dormitories, one served as a dining-room, and a lecture hall and the gymnasium were used for recreation. In the playground at the back of the building there were tents for soldier servants and the police guard. The prisoners had free run of the school and, in the hot weather, were allowed to sleep on the outside verandahs. Upon arrival Churchill, Haldane and Frankland were put in a room with Lieutenant Gallwey and the following morning they were joined by Sergeant-Major Brockie who, still assuming the role of an officer, had persuaded the Boers that he was entitled to the privileges of the Staatsmodelskool. There was plenty of room in the dormitory and the officers were reasonably comfortable; Churchill, however, appears to have preferred sleeping in the corridor or on one of the verandahs.

A month before Churchill's arrival, a Commandant Opperman had been appointed chief officer at the Staatsmodelskool. Churchill has described Opperman as an honest, patriotic Boer, too fat for fighting. Others were not so generous. Haldane maintains that Opperman was 'not exactly the pattern of every virtue' while the Rev. Adrian Hofmeyr—an Afrikaner parson, arrested by the Boers on suspicion of being a 'Rhodes man'—found him to be both stupid and objectionable. 'He is,' says Hofmeyr, 'a short, thickset man, generally very curt and uncourteous, and a terrible hater of the English. He shows his lack of intelligence and commonsense by believing that if the country is conquered by us he will be shot and his wife degraded to the rank of a servant. He consequently talks of shooting himself and her before it comes to that.' The second-in-command, Dr J. W. B. Gunning, was more likeable. A Hollander who had lived in the Transvaal since 1896, Dr Gunning was more interested in the Zoological Garden he was forming in Pretoria than in his duties at the Staatsmodelskool. His enthusiasm for the zoo, in fact, had landed him in trouble before the war. Anxious to increase his stock of animals, he had rashly accepted the gift of a lion named Fanny from Cecil Rhodes. The presentation of this symbolic animal from the British arch-Imperialist had been seen as an insult by the Boers and Dr Gunning had been severely reprimanded. He confessed to Churchill that President Kruger had spoken to him 'most harshly' and ordered him to return Fanny immediately. Dr Gunning was very popular with the prisoners and, says Haldane, 'did all that he could to make our confined existence as bearable as possible'.

Two other members of the prison management board visited the school regularly. One of these was the portly Veld-Kornet Malan—the man who had rescued Churchill from being sent with the troopers to the racecourse. This was the only service he performed for Churchill; the two of them appear to have taken an instant dislike to each other. Churchill was to remember Malan as 'a foul and objectionable brute. His personal courage was better suited to insulting prisoners in Pretoria than to fighting the enemy at the front.' The other visitor was the genial Louis de Souza, Transvaal Secretary of State for War and a great favourite with Churchill. It was through the medium of Mr de Souza that Churchill carried on his negotiations with the Boer authorities; negotiations made all the more pleasant by the fact that 'the Secretary of State for War, a kind-hearted Portuguese, would smuggle in a bottle of whisky hidden in his tail-coat pocket or amid a basket of fruit.' Understandably many members of the Boer administration regarded Louis de Souza with suspicion.

Apart from bottles of whisky smuggled in by the Secretary of State for War, the prisoners were able to obtain whatever luxury goods they wanted. Their official daily ration of $\frac{1}{2}$ lb of tinned or fresh beef, bread, tea and potatoes was sufficient but dull; to add some variety, the officers set up a mess committee which undertook to feed them at a reasonable rate. Goods were obtained from a local dealer, Mr Boshof. According to Haldane, those who wanted to could buy 'almost anything but firearms'.

When Churchill and his friends arrived no alcoholic liquor was allowed but representations were made to President Kruger and, after some soul searching, the prisoners were permitted to buy bottled beer. Perhaps the most surprising concession applied to clothing. Upon arrival each officer was issued with a civilian suit. These suits were a hideous mustard colour and, as Haldane says, 'quite unsuitable for passing through Pretoria unnoticed'. Churchill's group, still eagerly discussing escape plans, quickly recognized the advantage of wearing civilian clothes; by pretending that the suits issued to them were too large they were able to obtain less conspicuous clothing, Churchill's being a dark tweed suit. Their request for felt hats, however, was considered excessive: it was pointed out that pith helmets were available and these were adequate for keeping the sun off their heads.

The prison administration was far from efficient. Most of the guards were middle-aged burgers, too old to be sent to the front. Occasionally detectives watched the men exercising in the yard but this did not prevent them communicating with the outside. A constant stream of curious citizens paraded up and down in front of the Staatsmodelskool and the officers came to know some of them extremely well. At one time messages were sent to and received from a near-by house and the dealer from whom they bought their supplies even hinted that passports could be obtained at a price. The model school was by no means a model prison.

But, despite the leniency, life at the Staatsmodelskool was both boring and frustrating. Chess, whist, patience, books from the Government Library and various forms of exercise were not sufficient to compensate for loss of freedom. Most of the officers were regular army men who had come to South Africa eager for action: to be shut up in Pretoria so early in the war was galling. 'Our daily routine reminded one of school,' says Haldane, 'without work or common task to fill the hours which dragged by.' The news in the Pretoria and Johannesburg papers did not help matters. The Transvaal press was naturally pro-Boer and the most widely read newssheet—a special edition of *De Volksstem*, in Dutch and English—was blatantly propagandist. True, things were not going well with the British forces, but the bold headlines of *De Volksstem*, reporting mythical Boer victories and British cowardice, were excessively depressing. Churchill considered these reports to be 'probably the most astounding tissue of lies ever presented to the public under the name of a newspaper'. There was nothing to counterbalance these newspapers and the prisoners were subjected to all the doubts of the partially informed.

Churchill felt his captivity more than most. The visitors he was allowed brought him no comfort. On 23 November he complained bitterly to a Reuter's correspondent that, although he had no complaints about his treatment, he found his confinement 'close and severe'. A day or two later he was visited by the American Consul in Pretoria—a visit organized by his mother through Mr Bourke Cockran, an American Senator and family friend—and was surprised to find how little sympathy there was for Britain in the United States. This determined him to undertake a lecture tour of America if and when he regained his freedom. But the chances of his being released seemed as remote as ever and it was his inability to make plans for the future that sickened him most. Not only was there scant hope of his lecturing America but he was missing so many other opportunities. Writing to the Prince of Wales on his twenty-fifth birthday, 30 November, in the hope of obtaining some recognition for the gallantry of the driver of the armoured train, he expressed regret at being prevented from writing a general account of the war: arrangements had been made with a publisher for such a book but it now seemed as if it would be impossible for him to write it. It added extra bitterness to the humiliation of being captured. By now, of course, he was only too aware of the sensation created by his exploits in the armoured train fight. It was the sort of splash he had hoped for; but it looked like being wasted. Other names were making the headlines. Soon he would be forgotten. He was in no position to help the floundering British cause or his own career.

Throughout his life Churchill was subjected to recurring bouts of acute depression—or the 'Black Dog' as he called them—and he invariably sought release through action. Such a mood afflicted him now; he did not have far to look to find a remedy. Plans for escaping were the topic of endless secret discussions. He began to take an active interest in them.

*

The first plan in which Churchill was involved was formulated about a week after his arrival. It was not so much a plan as a collective day-dream. For days the younger officers were kept busy working out the details.

The idea of a mass breakout appears to have originated from one of their outside contacts, a Pretoria telegraphist named Patterson. Mr Patterson sent word that if the officers rose against their gaolers he could provide assistance. It was an exciting thought which was immediately taken up by some of the bolder spirits. After several sessions of deep discussion—in which Churchill played a prominent part—a breathtaking scheme was evolved. In theory it seemed foolproof.

There were approximately seventy British prisoners at the Staatsmodelskool; sixty officers and ten soldier servants. They were guarded by forty middle-aged Boers. Ten sentries patrolled the building in four-hour shifts, while twenty occupied themselves in the guard tent in the playground: ten who were officially off-duty usually went into town. This gave the prisoners thirty armed Boers to contend with. At night most of the men in the guard tent were asleep. Investigations showed that the sleeping men were in the habit of stacking their rifles and bandoliers on racks inside the tent. It was therefore decided that a couple of officers should distract the sentry guarding the tent while others entered through a slit in the canvas at the back and seized the guns. Once this had been done they would be in a position to tackle the armed sentries patrolling the building. The fact that the wires controlling the entire lighting system passed through one of the dormitories meant that the prison could be plunged into darkness at any given moment and this, it was hoped, would create sufficient confusion to enable them to take the sentries by surprise. This was to be stage one.

The take-over was not to end at the Staatsmodelskool. On the racecourse, a mile and a half away, were some two thousand troopers. These men were not receiving the luxurious treatment given to the officers and were known to be dissatisfied and restless. Once the Staatsmodelskool had been captured word could be passed to them to rise and the officers would come to their assistance by attacking the racecourse from the rear. Success at the racecourse would mean that a considerable British force could be armed within the Boer capital. Further opposition was discounted. It was known that the Pretoria town guard consisted of no more than five hundred burgers—mostly Government clerks and men unfit for the front—who would be no match for a large contingent of trained soldiers. 'Suppose this thing had happened,' mused Churchill. 'Suppose the Boer armies woke up to find their capital was in the hands of the masses of prisoners-of-war whom they had so incautiously accumulated there without adequate garrison! . . . If we got Pretoria we could hold it for months. And what a feat of arms! President Kruger and his Government would be prisoners in our hands. . . . Perhaps with these cards in our hands we could negotiate an honourable peace, and end the struggle by a friendly and fair arrangement which would save armies marching and fighting. It was a great dream.' And a dream it had to remain; wars are not ended so easily. When the senior officers heard of the plan, they threw cold water on it and the plotters lost heart. Some of them were loath to abandon the scheme entirely and it was a topic for discussion long after Churchill had left the Staatsmodelskool, but—like the Union Jack stitched together for the great day—it never really got off the ground.

Churchill had reached desperation point when this plan was rejected; this, probably more than anything else, decided him to join in an alternative scheme.

On Monday 1 December, Haldane and Brockie came to a definite decision to break out on their own. Their escape plan was so simple that its greatest danger lay in its obviousness. On the dark side of the playground there was a circular lavatory standing in front of a six-foot corrugated iron fence. The entrance to this lavatory faced the fence. By ducking into the lavatory it was possible to remain hidden until the time was opportune to scale the fence. The garden on the other side of the fence belonged to a house which was thought to be empty; so, once over the fence, there would be little difficulty in reaching the street. The greatest risk, of course, was the possibility of being spotted by one of the sentries patrolling this side of the playground: once astride the fence a would-be escapee would be plainly visible. Success depended as much on luck as on timing.

Having made their decision, Haldane and Brockie began accumulating food and planning a route out of the Transvaal. A week later all was ready. Then, on 7 December, they experienced a slight set-back. Two of the soldier servants—Troopers Cahill and Bridges—usurped their plan and escaped. However, it soon became clear that the soldiers had not been missed and the officers considered it was still safe to make their own escape. On that same day Churchill hinted that he would like to go with them but Haldane was not keen. One of the many advantages of Commandant Opperman's inefficient administration was that the prisoners did not have to answer a roll call; this meant that it would be possible for an escapee to be missing for days before his absence was detected. Troopers Cahill and Bridges had demonstrated how true this was and Haldane and Brockie were hoping to have the same luck. However, if Churchill went with them they could hardly hope that their escape would pass unnoticed. For Winston Churchill was far and away the most conspicuous prisoner in the Staatsmodelskool; everything he did attracted attention. Not only was he visited by the Secretary of State for War, the American Consul and innumerable newspaper reporters, but he was on display to anyone who took the slightest interest in him. Lord Randolph's son had become one of the sights of Pretoria. His absence would be detected immediately. Well aware of this, Haldane was not very receptive to his hints.

But Churchill was not easily put off. Two days later he again tackled Haldane. 'Up to this time Churchill had some hopes of release,' says Haldane, 'but on the 9th December he told me they were dissipated, and knowing that Sergeant-Major Brockie and I intended to escape, he suggested coming with us.' Haldane was in an awkward position. Brockie was very much opposed to the inclusion of a third person in their plan but, on the other hand, Haldane felt under obligation to Churchill for the risks he had taken on the armoured train. According to his own account, he told Churchill of Brockie's objections and left him to decide what to do. Churchill, however, claims it was openly agreed that the three of them should go together.

Whatever the truth, the escape plan was definitely modified to include Churchill. It was agreed that as Churchill was not as fit as the others—he was still suffering from the shoulder he had dislocated at polo—he and Haldane should attempt the fence together so that Haldane could give him a leg up. Once they were over the fence Brockie would follow. From then on Haldane would take command.

They decided to make an attempt on 11 December. The dinner hour, which started at 7 o'clock, was considered the best time because the sentries were usually more relaxed while the officers were eating. The afternoon was spent in an agony of suspense. Churchill was to claim that he had not experienced such uncertain terror since his schooldays and it appears, from an entry in Haldane's diary, that he caused the other two much anxiety by talking openly about the intended escape. He undoubtedly had good reason to feel nervous. Any prisoner caught attempting an escape would be at the mercy of the trigger-happy sentries; once astride the fence even the most inexperienced marksman could not miss them.

Shortly before the dinner bell rang, Haldane and Churchill crossed to the lavatory. They were accompanied by several officers who were in on the secret. It was hoped that these officers, by returning to the main building separately and at intervals, would give the sentry the impression that the lavatory was empty and that he might then feel free to move from his post. But it did not work out like that. The officers left, the sentry remained firmly in position and, eventually, Haldane and Churchill were forced to abandon the plan. However the experience was not entirely wasted. While waiting, they had noticed that by 7.45 the moon illuminated the area. This cut their time for manoeuvring to a minimum.

The following day they received news of the British defeats at Stormberg and Maggersfontein: defeats so decisive that even *De Volksstem* did not need to exaggerate them. This made them more determined than ever to escape. A second attempt was planned for that evening.

It started very much as before. At seven o'clock Churchill, Haldane and a group of officers again crossed the yard and entered the lavatory; again the officers left and the sentry showed no signs of moving and again Churchill and Haldane decided to postpone their escape. On returning to the main building this time, however, they were met by Brockie who had been waiting on the verandah and who now accused them of being afraid. This annoyed Haldane; he told Brockie to go and judge the situation for himself. Brockie crossed the yard and disappeared into the lavatory. Churchill and Haldane waited for a while, then Churchill decided to go and see what was happening. He met

Brockie coming out of the lavatory; they passed and Brockie muttered something which Churchill did not hear. Both were conscious that the sentry was within earshot.

Once inside the lavatory, Churchill was able to watch the sentries through a crack in the metal wall. By this time he had become rather impatient and was probably smarting from Brockie's taunt of being afraid. Determined to break the deadlock, he appears to have been eager to demonstrate his initiative by giving the other two a lead. But, at first, his chance to do so seemed as remote as ever. The sentries stood stolidly at their posts. Half an hour passed. Still the sentries stood. Then, one of them strolled over to his companion and began to talk: they had their backs to Churchill. It was too good an opportunity to miss. Standing on a ledge, he gripped the top of the fence and pulled himself up. Twice he faltered; the third time he managed to get astride the fence. This was the danger spot. To his dismay he found that his waistcoat had got caught on some jagged iron work. 'I had to pause for an appreciable moment to extricate myself,' he says. 'In this position I had one parting glimpse of the sentries still talking with their backs turned fifteen yards away. One of them was lighting his cigarette, and I remember the glow on the inside of his hands as a distinct impression which my mind recorded. Then I lowered myself into the adjoining garden and crouched among the shrubs. I was free!'

But he was not free: not yet. In fact he soon realized he was in a very precarious position. The first shock came with the realization that the neighbouring house was not only occupied but extremely lively. The windows were brightly lit and he could see figures moving about inside; a man came into the garden, passed close, and then joined another man smoking a cigar on the verandah. Shortly afterwards a dog chased a cat through the bushes and crashed into him. It was all very nerve-shattering, but he dared not move. He was honour bound to wait for Haldane and Brockie. After a while, he heard an officer enter the lavatory on the other side of the fence and tapped to attract attention. When the officer replied he told him to find Haldane and tell him that he had climbed the fence and was waiting for the others to join him.

Meanwhile, Haldane and Brockie had gone to the dining-room to snatch a quick meal. When they came out Haldane went to the dormitory and, finding Churchill was not there, examined his bed. He was somewhat surprised to find that the hat Churchill had borrowed from the Rev. Hofmeyr was not in its usual place under the pillow. (Though, since Churchill must have had the hat with him all the evening, Haldane's surprise is difficult to understand.) Then someone arrived and reported that Churchill was on the other side of the fence; this was confirmed a little later by the officer to whom Churchill had spoken. It was not possible for Haldane and Brockie to go to the fence immediately as the sentry was now back at his post but, as soon as they heard he had moved again, they crossed the yard with some other officers. By this time Haldane appears to have grown desperate, for he took a wild chance by pulling himself on to the roof of the lavatory. But the moon was high and he was immediately spotted; a sentry levelled his rifle and ordered him down. At that moment a relief patrol arrived to relieve the guard and the corporal in charge rushed across to the lavatory, seized the first officer he could lay hands on and rushed him to the Commandant's office.

This was only one of a series of suspicious incidents that had occurred near the fence that evening. At the subsequent inquiry into Churchill's escape, one of the sentries was to report that, at ten minutes to eight, he had seen Lieutenant Grimshaw and two others near the fence and that, when Grimshaw had attempted to peer over the fence, he had shouted: 'Go back, you b———!' And Captain Lonsdale, of the Royal Dublin Fusiliers, was to admit that he had looked over the fence and seen Churchill crouching in the garden. Yet, despite this whirl of activity in the vicinity of the prison's most obvious loophole, it did not occur to the guards to examine the fence. What is still more incredible, even after one officer had been whisked off to the Commandant's office, Haldane was still able to get close enough to the fence to hold a whispered conversation with Churchill. The sentries, however, were sufficiently alert to prevent Haldane making any further attempt that evening. He told Churchill this when he spoke to him. Churchill, perhaps only too aware of his lack of local languages, asked whether Brockie could get out. Haldane said there was no chance of this but offered to throw a compass and some chocolate over the fence (thereby making it quite clear that he agreed to Churchill going on alone). But Churchill, fearing that these objects would make a noise when they fell into the garden, declined the offer. They then said goodbye and, according to Churchill, Haldane wished him good luck.

He was certainly in need of all the luck he could get. His first concern was to get out of the garden. This, he decided, could best be accomplished by a bold move. Putting on the Rev. Hofmeyr's hat, he walked into the middle of the garden, continued on past the lighted windows and then strolled out of the gate. A sentry stood on the pavement five yards away. Not daring to hesitate, Churchill turned his face in the opposite direction and, desperately restraining an impulse to break into a run, walked on.

He walked a hundred yards without being challenged; then the truth dawned: 'I was,' he realized, 'at large in Pretoria.'

*

When discussing likely escape routes in the Staatsmodelskool, the prisoners had come to the conclusion that there were really only two. They could either make for Mafeking, the nearest British garrison; or they could head east in the hope of crossing the Transvaal border into Portuguese East Africa. The Mafeking route was favoured by those anxious to rejoin a British force as soon as possible; but, as it entailed crossing the Transvaal on foot and then penetrating the enemy lines, it was less attractive to others. The alternative route through Portuguese East Africa offered distinct advantages. A railway line connected Delagoa Bay with Pretoria and, if a train could be boarded, it might be possible to remain concealed until the train had crossed the border and thus effect a much speedier escape. Once having reached Lourenço Marques—the town at Delagoa Bay—it would be a simple matter to board a ship sailing to the British colonies in the south. The chief drawback to this route was that the railway provided the most obvious means of leaving the Transvaal and was consequently closely guarded. All trains travelling to Portuguese East Africa were bound to be searched as soon as it was known that a prisoner had escaped.

Strolling through the Pretoria streets, nonchalantly humming, Churchill now had to consider the alternatives as something more than a diverting discussion for the officers' mess. He was still very much on his guard and it was not until he reached a

Petrus Viljoen (blindfolded) preparing to leave Mafeking in exchange for Lady Sarah Wilson

£25.—.—

*(vijf en twintig pond stg.)
belooning uitgeloofd door
de Sub-Commissie van Wijk V
voor den Specialen Constabel
dezer wijk, die den ontvluchte
Krijgsgevangene
        Churchill.
levend of dood te dezer kantore
aflevert.—*

            *Namens de Sub-Comm.
                    Wijk V*
            LODK de HAAS
                    /Sec

Notice offering a reward of £25 for the capture of Winston Churchill, dead or alive, after his escape from Pretoria

Africana Museum, Johannesburg

Translation

£25

(Twenty-five Pounds stg.) REWARD is offered by the Sub-Commission of the fifth division, on behalf of the Special Constable of the said division, to anyone who brings the escaped prisoner of war

CHURCHILL,

dead or alive to this office.

For the Sub-Commission of the fifth division.
        (Signed) LODK de HAAS, Sec.

1899

Winston Churchill at the Durban dockside after his escape from Pretoria

South African Library

bridge away from the centre of the town that he was able to give the matter serious thought. Sitting on the bridge he pondered his chances. Haldane and Brockie had worked out an escape route but they had purposely kept the details from him. Moreover, they were to have brought a map, compass and emergency rations with them. Having refused the compass and having only four bars of chocolate in his pocket, Churchill's chances were now minimal. For although he had £75 in cash, his inability to speak the languages of the country made the buying of food a risky business. Any thought of a long cross-country walk—either east or west—was therefore out of the question. Somehow or other he had to find the Delagoa Bay railway.

Using the stars to guide him, he walked in a southerly direction. He had gone only half a mile when he came to a railway. It seemed to run northwards. Hopefully he walked along the line, making short detours at likely danger spots. At last he saw the lights of a station ahead. He left the line and hid in a ditch a short way from the platform. He reckoned that if a train came it would have to slow up at this point and that would give him a chance of boarding it. Apart from a whimsical vision of bribing 'some fat first-class passenger' he had little idea of how he would conduct himself once he was on the train. He waited some time and began to grow impatient. Eventually, a distant whistle and the rattle of coaches told him that a train was coming. As the engine passed him he saw the driver silhouetted against the glow of the furnace. 'Then,' he says, 'I hurled myself on the trucks, clutched at something, missed, clutched again, missed again, grasped some sort of hand-hold, was swung off my feet—my toes bumping on the line, and then with a struggle seated myself on the coupling of the fifth truck from the front of the train.' When he pulled himself into the truck, he discovered that he was on a goods train which was taking empty coal sacks back to a colliery. He buried himself beneath the sacks, not knowing where he was headed or if he had been seen.

He fell asleep and woke up with a feeling of panic. It was still dark. The train was rattling on. He realized that if he waited for it to stop he would be discovered when the sacks were unloaded. He decided that he must leave the train before daybreak, hide himself, and catch another train the following night. Lowering himself on to the couplings, he grasped an iron handle at the back of the truck and jumped. The train was travelling at a fair speed and he was hurled into a ditch. But he was unhurt. When he pulled himself together he set off in search of a stream. He was terribly thirsty.

*

By following a gully he found a pool of water and drank his fill. Daybreak came and he was relieved to see that the railway ran towards the rising sun. For a while he tried to rest beneath some trees; but it became too hot and the ominous presence of a vulture made him feel uneasy. He stood up, looked across a valley, and saw the tin roofs of a small town in the distance. Occasionally some figures moved about the valley but nobody came near him. He turned his attention to the railway, planning the next stage of his journey. He decided to find a steep curved gradient, where the train would be forced to slow down and where he could board a truck while it was on the bend, out of sight of the guard's van. A few trains passed along the line; he felt sure there would be more during the night.

As soon as it was dark he hurried to the railway line. Selecting a suitable spot, he sat behind a bush and waited. No train came. He waited until after midnight and could stand the suspense no longer. Impatient to be on his way, he again started along the line: this time he did not get far.

The moon was bright and he found every bridge was patrolled by sentries. Village stations appeared at intervals and he was continually forced to creep along the ground, or make wide detours. At one station he was seized by the idea of boarding a stationary truck in a siding, in hopes that the train would move the following day. But first it was necessary to ascertain the direction in which it was travelling: he might find himself back in Pretoria. Creeping along the deserted platform, he edged himself between two trains in the siding but his investigations were disturbed by the sound of laughter which made him retreat into the grass and head for the open veld.

Miserably he made his way until bright lights on the horizon showed that he was nearing a big town. He thought it might be Witbank or Middelburg; whichever it was it would not be safe. To his left he saw fires burning. They looked like the fires of an African kraal. There was a hope that Africans might prove friendly to a man escaping from the Boers. It was the only hope he had, so he started towards them. He had walked several miles before he realized that the fires were not kraal fires but the furnaces of a coal mine. The nearer he got the more clearly he was able to make out the outlines of slack-heaps and mining apparatus. He was too dispirited to turn back. He was tired, he was hungry, and there seemed no point in continuing his futile wandering. There was just a chance that the miners might prove friendly. At the Staatsmodelskool there had been talk of Englishmen who had been allowed to remain in the Transvaal to keep the mines working. That he had stumbled upon one of these English communities seemed highly improbable; but he could not do otherwise than take the risk.

The nearest building was a single-storeyed stone house. 'The garden of this house was tidy and looked like an Englishman's,' says Haldane who visited it later. No such patriotic assessment comforted Churchill; when he banged on the front door he was understandably nervous. But luck—or what his mother called his 'Star'—was with him. The voice that answered his knock spoke Dutch but when the door opened a tall thin man, with a melancholy moustache, addressed him in English. He had no alibi ready. He had not thought that far. On the spur of the moment he made up an improbable story about being a burger who had fallen from a train while on his way to join his commando. The man obviously did not believe him; nevertheless he asked him in. Once inside Churchill saw it was hopeless to keep up a pretence and blurted out the truth. 'Thank God you have come here!' said his host after locking the door. 'It is the only house for twenty miles where you would not have been handed over. But we are all British here, and we will see you through.'

The man was Mr John Howard, manager of the Transvaal and Delagoa Bay Collieries. British-born Mr Howard had lived in the Transvaal for some years and was believed, mistakenly, by the Boers to be a naturalized burger of the South African Republic. He considered himself lucky at not having been called out to fight in a Boer commando; but he was on parole to observe a strict neutrality and ran the risk of being shot for treason should it be discovered he had aided an escaped British prisoner. The risk was a real one. The hue and cry that had followed Churchill's escape had already reached this neighbourhood; that very afternoon a local Veld-Kornet had made enquiries at the mine. Hearing this, Churchill immediately offered to leave, but Howard brushed aside his offer. Something could be arranged, he said, but it would be necessary to move carefully. Besides himself and his secretary, there was a Lancashire engineer and two Scottish miners employed at the colliery. These men were in the same position as Howard but he thought he could rely on them. The real danger lay in the two Boer maids who were then sleeping in the house and in the chance that the African labourers employed on the mine might talk.

After sitting Churchill down with a leg of cold mutton and a bottle of whisky, Mr Howard went off to devise a plan. He returned an hour later. 'It's all right,' he said. 'I've seen the men, and they are all for it. We must put you down the pit tonight and there you will have to stay till we can see how to get you out of the country.' One slight difficulty remained. This was the problem of provisions. The maids kept a careful eye on the food; already Howard was worried by the thought of having to explain away the mutton eaten by Churchill. However, he assured his guest that they would try to make him as comfortable as possible.

At dawn the two men crept out of the house and hurried across the yard to the pit-head. Here Howard introduced Churchill to Mr Dan Dewsnap, the mining engineer from Oldham—the constituency that Churchill had contested. 'Dewsnap,' says his grandson, 'shook Churchill's hand and said in a broad Lancashire voice: "When you go to Oldham again, lad, they'll all vote for you. Good luck!"' The two Scottish miners, Joe McKenna and John McHenry, were waiting at the bottom of the shaft with a mattress, a bundle of blankets and a chamber pot. Churchill followed them along the dark winding tunnels until they reached a small recess. The mattress and blankets were laid out and Mr Howard produced some candles, whisky and a box of cigars. Then, instructing Churchill to remain quietly where he was, the four men left. 'Viewed from the velvety darkness of the pit,' Churchill recalled, 'life seemed bathed in a rosy light. After the perplexity and even despair through which I had passed I counted upon freedom as certain . . . In this comfortable mood, and speeded by intense fatigue, I soon slept the sleep of the weary— but the triumphant.'

It was strange to find freedom at the bottom of a coal mine. But he had much to console him. Whatever happened now, he would not be forgotten. Once again his name was attracting attention; he did not need Mr Dewsnap's assurance to know that his political future was secure. The country that had witnessed the crumbling of his father's hopes had provided him with the kudos he was seeking. He had good reason to feel triumphant.

The timing of his escape from Pretoria is not without interest. He was not the only Churchill to gain a questionable freedom that week. Five days before he scaled the fence of the Staatsmodelskool his aunt Sarah had crossed the enemy lines. Indeed there might have been some slight connection between the two events. For his offer to accompany Haldane and Brockie was made the day after the Transvaal papers had announced that Lady Sarah Wilson had been released from close confinement and allowed to join her husband in beleaguered Mafeking.

CHAPTER TWELVE

Swopped for a Horse Thief

FROM THE moment that she had received General Snyman's order to remain at Setlagole, Sarah had begun looking for an excuse to disobey it. She had no intention of sitting out the war in an isolated, tin-roofed store, watched by the bibulous Dietrich and with no distraction other than gossip from occasional travellers along the dusty main road. More than ever she was determined to return to Mafeking. She had greatly resented being turned out of the town by Baden-Powell; now that her expulsion had been confirmed by the enemy she was doubly incensed. Seeking an excuse to defy both British and Boer commanders, it was not long before she came up with one.

The disruption of the railway service had affected the entire district. Food supplies had been cut off and provisions were fast running out. On the day that Mrs Fraser announced that there was only enough meal to last a week, Sarah decided she had good reason for moving on. 'As every mouth to feed was a consideration,' she says, 'I determined to see if I could personally induce the Boer General to pass me into Mafeking.' She still had the pass issued by Veld-Kornet De Koker and this, she felt, would enable her to shake off her guards and ride to the Boer laager; once there she had no doubt that she could bluff her way into Mafeking. In her opinion, her case was convincing. Not only was food becoming scarce at Setlagole, but she had heard that a Mrs Delpoort, a 'Dutchwoman' in Mafeking, was anxious to return to the Transvaal. Sarah, pleading that she was a burden on the Frasers, intended to offer herself in exchange for Mrs Delpoort. It would be simply pig-headed of Snyman to refuse.

Her concern about the food shortage did not prevent her from saddling the Frasers with her maid. 'I did not wish,' she explained, 'to expose her to any hardships in the laager.' With

Metelka she left her pony, Dop. Before leaving, she took the precaution of sending a runner ahead to warn Baden-Powell that she was on her way. Then, with Wilhelm driving the mule cart and an extra African servant riding behind, she set off along the treacherous Mafeking road.

The thought of invading the enemy camp was exhilarating. As the hooded cart trundled along, Sarah's customary aplomb blossomed into a jaunty optimism. Neither the oppressive heat nor the choking dust could stifle her high spirits. This was far and away her most exciting trip. Whatever happened at the end of it, she would at least have put an end to her boring isolation. Whether she was kept a prisoner at the Boer laager or allowed to enter Mafeking, she would have reached the battlefield. The thought that what she was doing might prove dangerous does not appear to have entered her head.

Her optimism, as far as the Boers were concerned, is understandable. There had been little in her experience to make her fear the enemy. Rough-hewn as many of the burgers were, they had treated her with the utmost respect: even the objectionable Dietrich had proved more exasperating than insolent. She had no reason to think that she would be badly treated by the senior Boer officers. But the light-hearted way in which she viewed her return to Mafeking is somewhat surprising. Apart from Baden-Powell's objections, the prospect of living in the invested town was hardly inviting. However scanty her information, it should have been sufficient to make her think twice before volunteering to take up residence in Mafeking. The town had been constantly bombarded from the time that the Boers had installed their Creusot siege gun; although reports of the actual damage done varied, it was well known that the inhabitants were forced to spend most of their days in underground shelters. There had been no signs of the Boers abandoning the siege and the possibility of relief seemed remote. If food was short at Setlagole, Mafeking—where no supplies at all could get through—was in a worse position. Well aware of all this, Sarah nevertheless approached the town with all the elation of a pilgrim headed for Mecca.

They rested the mules twice on the forty-six-mile journey. The second halt was made at the house of Veld-Kornet De Koker. Sarah's pass took her only so far; she needed another to proceed to the Boer laager. Driving up to the Veld-Kornet's house, Sarah was surprised at the activity in the yard: horses were tethered outside the front door, armed men were hurrying in and out and everything was 'a great stir and bustle'. As the mule cart creaked to a halt, the Veld-Kornet came hurrying across the yard. After handing Sarah down, he escorted her to the house where the entire family—the women in faded print dresses, the men puffing long-stemmed pipes—had gathered to welcome her. It was Sarah's first experience of a *platteland* home; she found it quite bewildering. One by one the unsmiling members of the household were ceremoniously introduced to her. '[They] do not shake hands,' she remarked; 'they simply extend a wooden member, which you clasp, and the greeting is over.' Having pumped her way along a line of women and children, she found she had to repeat the performance with the men and guests. The solemn business was made all the more unnerving by being carried out in complete silence.

The introductions over, the entire party crowded into the tiny living-room. Here, seated in a circle, they started an animated conversation. Sarah sat with a fixed smile, understanding nothing. Occasionally one of the men would nod affably, or one of the women would give her a fleeting smile, but the only direct attention she attracted was from the wide-eyed children hiding behind their mother's skirts. After a while she was presented with coffee in a cracked cup. By gamely dissociating it from the remains of breakfast which littered the table, she managed to gulp it down. She offered the men some cigarettes. 'They were enchanted,' she says, 'laid aside their pipes, and conversed with more animation than ever; but it was only occasionally that I caught a word I could understand.' The sentence *'twee duisend Engelsmanne dood'* (two thousand Englishmen dead) was being repeated with distressing frequency.

There was nothing for Sarah to do but sit gazing idly about the shabby, overcrowded room. She was surprised to find it had a mud floor but decided that this was just as well 'as they all spat on it in intervals of talk, and emptied on to it the remains of whatever they were drinking.' She was further embarrassed by the arrival of an African servant with a basin of water. 'She proceeded,' says the astonished Sarah, 'to plentifully sprinkle the floor, utterly disregarding our dresses and feet. Seeing all the women tuck their feet under their knees, I followed their example, until this improvised water-cart had finished.' It was all a far cry from the domestic arrangements at Blenheim Palace.

After four or five more women had edged their way into the stuffy little room, Sarah decided that she had had enough. By no means certain that she would be allowed to leave, she brazened the matter out. Rising firmly to her feet, she nodded and smiled her way to the door and called for Wilhelm to inspan the mules. She was followed into the yard by the entire company who fell into line for an unsmiling handshaking farewell. This final ceremony over, she was handed a pass to the laager and drove off with a bemused sigh of relief.

At about four that afternoon she crested a slight rise in the flat plain and caught a glimpse of Mafeking: its corrugated-iron roofs shining tantalizingly in the heat-hazed distance. She drove on for two miles. The countryside seemed deserted; the mud huts of the Baralong *stad* on the outskirts of Mafeking were invitingly close. She was seized by an impulse to make a dash for it. By whipping the mules, she estimated they could be half way to the town before the Boers realized and Baden-Powell would surely send out a party to cover them the rest of the way. But the two Africans would not hear of it. 'They resolutely declined to attempt it,' she complained, 'as they feared being shot, and they assured me that many Boer sharpshooters lay hidden in the scrub.'

She was soon to realize how true this was. Having reluctantly turned the cart towards the Boer laager, she drove into a hidden outpost. A Boer officer—every bit as startled as she—ordered her down from the cart and told she would have to remain there until dark. He pointed out that she was on a road well within the range of the Mafeking guns; she might be shot at by her own people. She had no alternative but to obey his orders.

Sitting beside her cart, she listened glumly to the sounds of war. Desultory bursts of gun-fire echoed from the town, punctuated now and again by the reverberating boom of the Boer cannon. All around her the grizzled burgers sat silently puffing their pipes. Over an hour passed before the officer ordered a party to saddle up and escort her to the laager. Flanked by a bodyguard of some eighteen to twenty burgers, their rifles gleaming dully in the setting sun, she went jolting on the last stage of her journey.

An enormous force of armed men came swarming out of the laager as they approached. The cart was quickly surrounded. At last her invasion was being taken seriously. After stumbling somewhat unheroically upon the outpost, Sarah now had the satisfaction of riding into the enemy camp surrounded by a large commando. It was a fitting reception for a Churchill.

When the news of her arrival reached Mafeking it created a stir. Sarah was one of the few contacts that the town had with the outside world; her activities had been followed with great interest. Her unexpected arrival at the enemy headquarters was soon made known. 'When Lady Sarah arrived within a short distance of the Boer laager,' it was reported, 'for some inexplicable purpose General Snyman . . . turned out three hundred Boers, armed for battle, who at once proceeded successfully to capture a solitary woman.'

*

General Snyman had established his headquarters in a deserted farm house. Unlike his predecessor, General Cronjé, he had resigned himself to a lengthy siege and forsaken the traditional ox-wagon for something more permanent. When Sarah's cart drew up in front of the whitewashed house, it was immediately hemmed in by a crowd of jostling burgers. These men, accustomed to thinking of women strictly in terms of hearth and home, were completely mystified by Sarah's bold invasion. Shouting and nudging each other, they pressed forward to get a better look at this defiant Englishwoman.

Their boisterous curiosity was open to misinterpretation. For the first time Sarah's courage failed her. Much as she would have loved to have marched into the General's office, she was nervous about pushing through what looked like a menacing crowd. She did the next best thing. Determined not to show her fear, she demanded, in a loud clear voice, that General Snyman be informed of her arrival. One of the men at the back of the crowd disappeared into the house. Sarah, flanked by her two apprehensive servants, sat gazing impassively over the heads of the gaping burgers. After an 'interminable wait', Snyman's secretary came squeezing through the crowd and, much to Sarah's relief, addressed her in English. The General, he said, would see her immediately. Squaring her shoulders, Sarah climbed down from the cart and prepared to follow the man as he elbowed his way back to the house. Only then did she realize how groundless her fears had been. As she stepped forward, the men parted rather sheepishly to allow her a clear passage. They were, she was forced to admit, 'very civil, nearly all of them taking off their hats as I passed through them'.

Inside the house she was conducted along a gloomy passage and ushered into a low dark room. Seated on a bench in the corner, two old men watched her approach. One of these, a gaunt-faced, steely-eyed burger with a long white beard, was the unpopular General Snyman and one glance was enough to confirm all Sarah had heard about him: if he was not exactly the 'psalm-singing, sanctimonious, murderer of women and children' that the inhabitants of Mafeking believed him to be, he was clearly a man to be taken seriously. His ruddy-faced companion, Commandant Botha, was more amiable ('a good sportsman', said the British), but on this occasion he looked almost as formidable as his chief. 'I was struck at once,' says Sarah, who was motioned to a chair opposite them, 'by the anything but affable expressions on their countenances.'

The interview started off badly. Having made up her mind to face the General with stiff-backed dignity, Sarah was thrown off her guard by being given a bowl of coffee which she had to balance awkwardly with both hands. She felt that this put her at a distinct disadvantage. However, she refused to be cowed. Speaking through an interpreter she outlined her position. She had come to the laager, she said, at the suggestion of Veld-Kornet De Koker. She had no relations in South Africa, except her husband in Mafeking. She had been forced to leave Setlagole because of the food shortage. She was now prepared to ask Colonel Baden-Powell to exchange her for Mrs Delpoort who, she believed, was anxious to leave Mafeking. She would like General Snyman's permission to apply for the exchange.

The two men listened in silence. When she had finished Snyman rapped out his reply. Her request was turned down. Without a word of explanation or a second's hesitation, she was told that the exchange was not possible. She could hardly believe her ears. Having been assured by De Koker of the General's chivalrous attitude, she was staggered by his lack of courtesy. It had never occurred to her that her request would be dismissed in such an off-handed fashion. Looking at Snyman's grim, implacable face, she realized how sadly she had misjudged the situation. 'Then it occurred to me,' she says, 'that this old gentleman meant to keep me a prisoner-of-war, and my heart sank into my shoes.' The prospect filled her with horror. To be placed under arrest was a thousand times worse than being confined to Setlagole. In desperation she pleaded for a respite. Would Snyman at least consider her case before taking further action? To her surprise the General agreed. Meanwhile, however, she had to remain a prisoner at the laager. The secretary was ordered to take her to the field hospital.

Still dazed, Sarah was led back through the staring crowd to her cart. The hospital was about half a mile from Snyman's headquarters. Arriving there she was shown into a tiny room where she was told she could sleep. It was sparsely furnished, reeked of disinfectant and the walls and windows were riddled with bullet holes. There was no bed; only a broken-down sofa. In the middle of the room there was a long table. The combination of the smell, the table and a dilapidated wash-stand made it obvious that it was an operating room. She did not relish the thought of being confined there, but by that time she was past caring. She suddenly felt desperately tired.

However, the secretary had not yet finished with her. He told her that before she could be left alone all her luggage would have to be searched. He took away her bags and called in two nurses to search her dressing case. Despite her exhaustion, Sarah was amused at the way the nurses conducted their search. 'They did [it] most unwillingly,' she says, 'remarking to me that they had not contemplated searching people's luggage as part of their already onerous duties.' But this did not prevent them from carrying out their instructions to the letter. When they had finished with the dressing case, Sarah was made to undress while they searched her clothes. Meanwhile, the men outside were poring over her papers and correspondence. They found nothing. Sarah had wisely destroyed all evidence of her despatch-running before leaving Setlagole.

The search had just been completed when a messenger arrived from General Snyman. Thinking over her request he had decided to agree to an exchange. He was not prepared to accept Mrs Delpoort in her place, however. Only if Baden-Powell would agree to release a certain Petrus Viljoen would he allow her to return to Mafeking. When Sarah heard that Petrus Viljoen was a convicted horse thief, who had been in the Mafeking gaol since before the war, she was outraged. How dared they think of exchanging a woman for a criminal? The suggestion was disgraceful. She would not dream of asking Colonel Baden-Powell to do such a thing. It was highly irregular. The British authorities would never entertain such a request. . . .

Calming down, she asked permission to write to her husband. This was agreed to and the secretary sent for paper and ink. Making it quite clear that she would only mention the proposed exchange as an impossible condition she scrawled a quick note.

December 2nd 1899.

My dear Gordon,
I am at the laager. General Synman will not give me a pass unless Colonel Baden-Powell will exchange me for a Mr Petrus Viljoen. I am sure this is impossible so I do not ask him formally. I am in a great fix, as they have little meal left at Setlagole or the surrounding places. I am very kindly looked after here.'

There was nothing more she could say or do. When the secretary had gone she settled down for the night on the lumpy sofa. She now held out little hope of returning to Mafeking.

In fact, her plight was more serious than she appears to have imagined. Not only was there little chance of her returning to Mafeking but, unless Baden-Powell agreed to Snyman's terms, there was a strong possibility that she would remain a prisoner until the war ended. Snyman's harsh attitude had been assumed with a definite purpose. The trip Sarah had made to Vryburg, the ride to the armoured train and the note found on the carrier pigeon had made the Boer General extremely suspicious. This is made clear from a telegram he sent to Pretoria. 'What shall I now do with Lady Sarah Wilson?' he wired. 'Please answer speedily. In my opinion she is an important spy.'

*

Gordon received Sarah's note the following morning. He took it straight to Baden-Powell. They both agreed with Sarah; the idea of exchanging her for a horse thief was unthinkable. In a very formal letter (written as much for the Boers as for Sarah) Gordon informed her that 'Colonel Baden-Powell finds it impossible to hand over Petrus Viljoen' as he was a convicted criminal. 'I fail to see in what way it can benefit your captors to keep you prisoner,' he ended indignantly. 'Luckily for them, it is not the custom of the English to make prisoners-of-war of women.'

Baden-Powell took much the same line. 'Lady Sarah Wilson wrote saying that she had arrived in Snyman's laager,' he noted in his diary, 'but that he would not pass her unless Viljoen were released from prison here. This man has been fined £100 for inciting natives to rise, and was doing 6 months for theft; both crimes committed just before the war began.

'I replied that women were not usually considered prisoners-of-war; and I could not send a criminal in exchange for Lady Sarah—as he was a civil prisoner—not prisoner-of-war. Pointed out that Linchere's men had on 25th ult. taken some Boer women and children and my officers had at once returned them to their laager.' He then sent a telegram to Sir Alfred Milner in Cape Town asking for instructions.

Neither Gordon's nor Baden-Powell's reply had any effect on Snyman. Two days later they were still waiting for an answer. Baden-Powell again wrote to the Boer General and at the same time sent a cheery letter to Sarah. Gallantly he overlooked her disobedience and took the entire blame for her predicament upon himself. 'I had hoped to save you the unpleasantness of the siege,' he apologized.

Confident that Snyman would eventually give in, he sent for Mrs Delpoort to prepare her for the exchange. To his annoyance she blandly announced that she had changed her mind. On talking the matter over, she said, she had decided that it would be unwise to leave the shelter of the town. Nothing Baden-Powell or his officers could say would make her alter her decision. This *volte-face* came as a shock. When the news leaked out the entire town became involved in a search for a substitute. Gordon offered a reward to any woman who would take Mrs Delpoort's place. Only two women responded. One of them turned the offer down as she considered the price was not high enough; the other backed out at the last minute because 'she had too many children to leave behind'. Perhaps the most bizarre suggestion was that which came from Thomasina Cowan, the sister of one of Baden-Powell's officers. 'In a mad moment I wrote to Mr Graepon, who is a galloper to the Colonel,' she noted in her diary. 'I told him to ascertain if a substitute was still wanted and if so, he knew a lady who would offer herself *pro-temps*, for two weeks as a substitute, but if not required would rather not disclose her name.... The motive that I had in view was not money certainly, but just to give her a holiday. Had I been in her place, I should have been thankful if anyone had offered to give me freedom even for a week.'

Baden-Powell was intrigued to know who this whimsical creature was but did not think the Boers would be interested in her offer. Then Mrs Delpoort again changed her mind. 'Wrote to Genl Snyman asking for a reply to my letter,' noted Baden-Powell, 'saying that Mrs Delpoort was now willing to be exchanged for Lady Sarah Wilson.' But it was to no purpose. 'Snyman replying to my letter,' continued Baden-Powell, 'says he will not take anyone in exchange for Lady Sarah Wilson except Petrus Viljoen.'

The Boer General seems to have been playing a crafty game of his own. He had already wired to Pretoria saying he had refused the proposed exchange. Moreover he made no mention of an exchange of women but said that Baden-Powell was offering 'a certain Jeffrey Delpoort'. 'I have rejected this proposal,' Snyman informed his superiors, 'because on a former occasion when I requested the release of Jeffrey Delpoort, Baden-Powell refused to consider it.' None of this fits the details given in Baden-Powell's diary; nor is there any mention of 'Jeffrey Delpoort' in independent accounts kept at the time. Petrus Viljoen was the grandson of a well-known Boer Commandant and the telegrams sent to Pretoria make it clear that, from the moment Sarah arrived, Snyman had decided to use her to secure the horse thief's release.

Consternation in Mafeking was almost equalled by the concern shown for Sarah in London. The story was immediately taken up by the popular press. The telegrams they published from South Africa were as contradictory as they were misinformed. General Joubert, the Boer military leader, was said to be bargaining for a suitable exchange. President Kruger was reported to have personally ordered Sarah's release. Sir Alfred Milner was credited with having wired to the Colonial Office for instructions. The *Daily Mail*, prouder of its intrepid correspondent than ever, was quick to compare Sarah with her nephew. 'Will it be,' it pondered hopefully, 'that Lady Sarah will have to go to Pretoria to join her nephew, Mr Winston Churchill, and thus form the nucleus of a pleasant family circle on the Pretoria racecourse [*sic*]? We shall soon know.'

Despite the concern, there were those who were confident of Sarah's ability to stand up to her captors. When the news first reached England, Lady Randolph Churchill was spending the week-end at Windsor Castle. 'The Queen,' she wrote, 'was full of enquiries about my sister-in-law, Lady Sarah Wilson, who was then reported to be a prisoner in the Boers' hands. "They will not hurt her," she said with a charming smile.'

*

During the day Sarah was allowed to wander about the hospital. Far from being kept prisoner in the operating-room, she was rather alarmed to find there was no lock on the door. At night she barricaded herself in by pushing the wash-stand against the door as a precaution against the sentries on the stoep. These guards, she was assured, were not there to watch her but to protect the hospital. Any doubts she may have had on this score were dispelled when she complained to one of the nurses that the men's talk and pipe fumes made it impossible for her to sleep. Much to her amusement, the nurse returned to say that the men had been insulted by her complaints and, as the guard duty was voluntary, they had threatened to withdraw their protection. 'We both laughed,' says Sarah, 'and agreed it would not matter much if this calamity occurred.'

Nevertheless, she discovered that the hospital marked the limit of her freedom. Only by talking to the patients and their visitors was she able to find out what was going on in the camp. The nurses—many of whom were German girls—were far too busy and suspicious of her to be very forthcoming; Sarah became tired of their endless complaints and they resented the extra work she made for them. Sarah took a particular dislike to a harassed, overworked woman doctor. The idea of a professional woman outraged her sense of propriety; she was still very much her mother's daughter. The 'lady doctor', she claimed, was 'the first of her species I had ever come across... she looked singularly out of place, which I remarked to several people, partly from the irritation I felt on hearing her addressed as "Doctor". No doubt these remarks were repeated to her, and this accounted for her black looks.'

If the hospital staff was short with her, she had no real cause to complain about her treatment. True, her room was hot and stuffy at night and swarming with flies during the day but these conditions prevailed throughout the laager. She was wakened with a cup of coffee and her meals were laid out in her room. The food was good and plentiful; one day only was she left without meat. 'The other days,' she says, 'they gave me eggs, very good beef, splendid potatoes, and bread in any quantity. Besides this I was able to buy delicious fruit, both figs and apricots.'

She was a source of endless fascination to the burgers. Those who had to visit the hospital for treatment would make a special detour in order to pass her window; if they happened to catch sight of her they would raise their hats in embarrassed salutes. Even those who came over from the laager for the sole purpose of gazing at 'the captured *rara avis*, an Englishwoman', always did so at a respectful distance. Their interest sometimes took unexpected turns. For instance, she was surprised to hear of the reputation her pony, Dop, had acquired among the Boers: he was said to be 'not a horse, but lightning'. When it was learned that she had not brought Dop with her, a party of burgers rode to Setlagole to recover the pony. They returned empty handed. Sarah later heard that Metelka had stoutly refused to part with the animal; insisting that he had been given to her in lieu of wages. Standing firmly on her rights as a German subject, she threatened to write to the Kaiser if any attempt was made to remove the pony.

The burgers were respectful but not sympathetic towards Sarah. Most of them resented her intrusion and fully supported Snyman in his refusal to allow her into Mafeking. As the Boer commando system rested on a rough-and-ready type of democracy, this lack of sympathy did little to bolster Sarah's flagging spirits. There was some depressing talk about her being sent to

Zeerust, a small town in the western Transvaal. She was even further depressed when she received Gordon's note confirming that the exchange for Petrus Viljoen was not possible.

Determined not to give in, she bombarded Snyman with imperious protest notes. She also roundly attacked the General's messengers. The young man who brought her the news of Mrs Delpoort's original defection was harangued unmercifully. She demanded to know what they intended doing with her. She had no intention, she said, of being detained in her wretched quarters indefinitely. If no exchange could be arranged then she insisted on being allowed to return to Setlagole. The unfortunate messenger tried vainly to placate her. When he timidly suggested that she might be sent to Pretoria where she would find 'pleasant ladies' society' she was left speechless with anger. 'Seeing my look of angry surprise,' she says, 'he hastily added that he only wished he had a house of his own to place at my disposal.' Changing her tactics, she adopted the rather unconvincing pose of a helpelss female. Blithely ignoring the fact that she had been careering about the veld for weeks, she pointed out that it would be extremely improper for an Englishwoman to travel alone in the Transvaal. The young man's assurance that she would be provided with an escort came a little too pat for her liking. 'These words were quite enough to denote the way the wind was blowing,' she says, 'I would not for an instant admit they had the right to detain me or send me any place against my will.' She made this quite clear to the messenger. Then, learning that there was to be a meeting of the Boer commanders the following morning, she sent him hurrying back to Snyman with a demand that the suggested exchange for another woman be given full consideration. She was determined, she says, 'to leave them in no peace till they gave me a definite reply'.

But when the reply came it was as evasive as ever. Sealed in an enormous envelope, it informed her that Snyman had wired to Pretoria and could do nothing until he received an answer. Once again she was left kicking her heels.

The suspense was made all the more nerve-racking by the closeness of the Boer guns. On the third day of her captivity there was a violent thunderstorm. Rain deluged the camp and the laager was reported to be 'simply one pool of water'. That evening the guns thudded more ferociously than ever. As water trickled through the roof and spattered the floor of the operating-room, Sarah held herself tense at the sound of each explosion. She realized that the Boers were taking advantage of the fact that the Mafeking trenches were flooded and unoccupied. 'It was trying on the nerves,' she says, 'to sit and listen to the six or seven guns all belching forth their missiles of death on the gallant little town.'

As the days passed without word from Pretoria, Sarah began to grow desperate. She thought seriously of escaping and making her way to Mafeking on foot. To slip past the sentries during the night would be easy. Then it would only be a matter of dodging the Boer outposts and crossing the veld. As there was little night shelling there was nothing to fear from the long-range guns. She was held back only by the thought that she would not be able to warn the town of her approach; the danger of being fired at from Mafeking seemed far greater than that of being detected by Boer sentries.

It was while she was pondering this problem that an Englishman arrived at the hospital. Hearing an English voice outside her room one afternoon, she went on to the stoep to investigate. The newcomer, after staring at her for some time, came across and introduced himself. His name was Spencer Drake and he told Sarah that he had met Lord Randolph when he had visited the Transvaal. Upon Sarah expressing surprise at finding an Englishman in the laager, he was quick to excuse his loyalty to the 'Queen's enemies'. His family (who claimed descent from Sir Francis Drake) had been settled in South Africa for some years and he had become a Transvaal burger. 'I owe everything I possess to the South African Republic,' he said, 'and of course I fight for its cause; besides which, we colonials were very badly treated and thrown over by the English Government in 1881, and since then I have ceased to think of England as my country.'

This was Sarah's first experience of the bitterness with which the English-speaking population of the Transvaal had reacted to Britain's capitulation after Majuba. If Britain had deserted them, they argued perversely, then they had no option but to desert Britain. It was a movement which, starting slowly in these early years, was to gather momentum during the next half-century. The sad thing was that the majority of defectors did so, not on the liberal principle of assisting the wronged Boers, not because they opposed Imperialism: it was rather that they considered Britain to be losing her colonial ambitions. All too often they were to cling to their Imperial sentiments long after a new age had dismissed such sentiments as anachronistic and pernicious. If Mr Drake was a new species to Sarah, he undoubtedly represented the inception of a peculiarly South African *ancien régime*.

Not wishing to annoy her new friend, Sarah changed the subject. She asked Mr Drake what his status was in the laager. He told her that he was Snyman's adjutant and that he had been away from the camp on business. Learning that Sarah was at the hospital, he had come to ask whether he could be of service. This was too good an opportunity to miss. Sarah immediately launched forth on a series of complaints, ending by pointing out that she had not even a bed to sleep upon. Drake was left in no doubt as to what she thought of Snyman and the Pretoria authorities. Rather shamefaced, he admitted that the General was not easy to handle, but he promised to do what he could. Sarah felt much better after he had left; so much so that, when Snyman's secretary arrived a little later, she backed up her latest protests with a few more blasts. 'I requested this young man,' she says, 'to tell the General that I could see that they were taking a cowardly advantage of me because I was a woman and that they would never have detained a man under similar circumstances.' That this was strange reasoning does not seem to have worried her: by that time she was more concerned with her nuisance value than her logic. 'In fact,' she went on, 'I was on every occasion so importunate that I am quite sure the General's Staff only prayed for the moment that I should depart.'

How right she was. There can be no doubt that her harrying tactics were beginning to take effect. General Snyman might have been a bogyman to the inhabitants of Mafeking and a downright terror to his subordinates, but he had met his match in Sarah Wilson. Although he had not seen her since that first interview, the messages conveyed to him had made him decidedly uneasy. There is more than a hint of panic in the telegram he sent to Pretoria that afternoon. 'Please, please send me at once your decision concerning Lady Sarah Wilson,' he wired. 'She is most unwilling to stay here any longer.'

The pleas of both Sarah and Snyman were answered the

following morning. At six o'clock, Spencer Drake knocked on her door and told her to be ready to leave in half an hour; Colonel Baden-Powell had agreed to exchange her for Petrus Viljoen. As Sarah hurried into her clothes there can be little doubt that she congratulated both herself and Mr Drake. In truth, their efforts had only been incidental to her release. Much against his will, Baden-Powell had felt compelled to accept Snyman's terms. '. . . altho. Lady Sarah Wilson is being well treated by the Boers just now,' he noted in his diary, 'there is a very grave risk to her should they suffer—as they most probably will shortly do—a reverse, and have to retreat hurriedly and they might at any time of difficulty use her as a hostage. It is therefore desirable to get her now at any price. After consultation therefore with the Resdt. Commr. I have concluded to agree to exchange Viljoen for her under protest on condition that he does not take up arms against the British.'

Not everyone was happy about the exchange. There was much resentment against Viljoen in Mafeking; some doubted the wisdom of allowing him to rejoin the Boers. 'We should have liked to have kept the gentleman where he was,' grumbled one inhabitant, 'as he tried to get the Kaffirs to rise against us shortly before the war.' There were others who felt that the horse thief's knowledge of Mafeking would prove invaluable to the enemy. And, to make matters still more complicated, Viljoen was extremely reluctant to leave. Baden-Powell found himself in the unexpected position of having to order a convict to accept his release.

It is said that it was Lord Edward Cecil who finally tipped the scales in Sarah's favour. The idea of leaving an Englishwoman in enemy hands, he told Baden-Powell, was unforgivable. If support were needed for accepting Snyman's dubious bargain, he was willing to take the responsibility. Coming as it did from the Prime Minister's son, it was an offer which Baden-Powell felt bound to recognize. But he was still determined not to let the Boers think that they were getting the best of the bargain. If they were insisting on a horse thief, then Mafeking was happy to welcome back its valuable spy. He was prepared to negotiate Lady Sarah Wilson's release 'in recognition of the service which she has rendered as an intermediary in carrying despatches between Mafeking and the south'. As the Boers knew all about

Sarah's activities anyway, it was felt that such a statement would not prejudice her position. With honour duly satisfied, it was agreed that a truce would be observed until eight o'clock the following morning so that the exchange could take place.

'A common prisoner for a titled lady,' enthused a local bank clerk, 'not a bad exchange.'

The Boers were equally delighted. Snyman had evidently convinced his superiors of the importance of getting Viljoen back and had been instructed to make every effort to bring this about. Once he had Baden-Powell's agreement, he lost no time in informing Pretoria. He emphasized the need for immediate action. A reply came from President Kruger's office: 'I am of course agreeable for Viljoen to be exchanged and thus request you to act without delay.' With everyone so anxious that Sarah should be set free, it is not surprising that the British press was fond of comparing her to her bullying ancestress and namesake, Sarah Jennings, first Duchess of Marlborough.

'As may be imagined,' wrote Sarah, 'I could hardly believe my good fortune, and lost no time scrambling into my clothes while the cart was being inspanned.' Whether it was her haste or whether (as was later claimed) the Boers confiscated some of her cases, is not clear, but she certainly left the hospital minus several items of clothing. Some weeks later, when General Cronjé's wife was leaving to join her husband in exile on St Helena, it was noticed that she carried over her arm 'a smart dress "commandeered" from Lady Sarah Wilson's belongings with the name of its Bond Street maker showing.' This dress was to become the subject of an incredible amount of semi-humorous and—considering Mrs Cronjé's plight—often unkind comment. Typical is the observation of a fashionable columnist: 'It speaks volumes for Mrs Cronjé that, with an exceedingly limited wardrobe at her command, she had the discrimination to select this much-talked-of dress. Coming from New Bond Street it is a pretty safe conjecture that it would be of first-rate composition. Mrs Cronjé may yet become the nucleus of a fashionable circle at St Helena.'

Clothes, however, were the least of Sarah's concerns as she prepared to leave the laager. What did worry her was the stubbornness of her mules. With the precious minutes of the truce running out, they refused to be caught. Sarah was afraid that any delay would give Snyman time for second thoughts; if the exchange had to be put off until the following morning he might think up new conditions. It was with a sigh of relief that she at last saw the mules harnessed to her cart. Then, escorted by some artillery officers, she drove to Snyman's headquarters. Making her way through the crowd of burgers outside the house, she went in to say goodbye to the Boer General. The meeting was formal and polite. Snyman asked her some pointless questions and she, having heard that his eyes were inflamed, enquired after his sight. 'Then he rose and held out his hand, which I could not ignore,' she says, 'and without further delay we were off.'

At the same time as Sarah was leaving the Boer laager, Petrus Viljoen, the horse thief, was leaving Mafeking. A small crowd gathered outside the buildings of Dixon and Company watched him being put into an open cart. 'He, I fancy,' noted an observer sourly, 'will look fatter and in better condidion than his friends outside, and did not appear over-keen to join them.' Lieutenant Moncrief climbed on to the cart and, once Viljoen had been blindfolded, the vehicle, with its white flag fluttering, went trundling out of town.

A faint drift of dust on the far horizon was the crowd's first indication of Lady Sarah Wilson's approach. From this dust emerged a white tented cart, drawn by four mules and accompanied by outriders. In the open veld, halfway between the laager and the town, the approaching Sarah and the departing Viljoen met. She was delighted, she says smugly, to see that her counterpart seemed dejected and anything but pleased to be handed over to his friends. The exchange formally made, Moncrief swopped vehicles, and the little cart came rattling across the stony ground towards Mafeking.

Sarah was given an extraordinarily enthusiastic welcome. That the ovation was as much for what she represented to the besieged garrison as for whom she was was neither here nor there. The normally silent trenches came alive as the men flung their hats in the air and raised cheer upon cheer. From the first redoubt sprang Gordon, Baden-Powell and Lord Edward Cecil. Waving their arms they came running up to greet her. As she entered the town, men and women pressed about her cart, shouting her name and reaching up to shake her hand.

In the middle of this surging river of excited people her cart went bobbing though the Market Square towards her old quarters at Mr Weil's house. She entered with the cries of her wellwishers still ringing in her ears.

The enemy had not forgotten her either. Hardly had she disappeared from view before 'Creaky'—the Boer's great siege gun—sent what she called 'a parting shot'. It had a sobering effect on the excited Sarah. That day there were three men killed and eight wounded in Mafeking.

CHAPTER THIRTEEN

'Churchill, dead or alive . . .'

EARLY ON the morning of 13 December, a soldier servant arrived at Winston Churchill's room in the Staatsmodelskool and placed a cup of coffee on the chair beside Churchill's bed. He was closely watched by Haldane and the other officers. It was the day after Churchill's escape; his friends, anxious to give him as long a start as possible, were doing their best to prevent his absence from being discovered. The previous night they had rigged a dummy figure in his bed which had such a lifelike appearance that the soldier servant spoke to it and, getting no reply, deposited the coffee and left the room suspecting nothing.

But the deception could not be kept up long. By some oversight, Churchill had arranged for a haircut at eight o'clock that morning. The barber, a little Hollander who visited the prison twice a week, arrived on time accompanied as always by one of the police guards. Haldane and the others tried to get rid of him by saying that Churchill had changed his mind, but he refused to be put off. The Rev. Adrian Hofmeyr, who was in on the secret, has left an amusing account of the uproar that followed. 'Sorely afraid of losing his sixpenny fee,' says Hofmeyr, 'the little man ran up and down the building, interrogating everyone he met. Some gave him no answer, just looked him up and down, the little there was of him; others referred him to the most unlikely corners; a third said, "In his bath". And so outside the bathroom barber and bobby took up a strong position, holding it against all comers for fully half an hour. Then it struck the little man that perhaps they had been guarding an empty bath, so he knocked gently and apologetically. No answer. A louder, rather self-assertive knock then. Still no answer. And so a loud, peremptory, taking-no-refusal knock came, but yet no answer.

Bobby then ventured to turn the knob and open the door inch by inch, peeping in gingerly. Is the man perhaps dead? Has he cut his throat? What ghastly sight am I doomed to see? He opens the door a little more. There is no one. It is a little room about 8 feet by 3 feet. Yet he examines carefully. Under the bath? No. Behind the door? No. Under the chairs? No. He gets wild and excited. He examines sponges and towels. Under these, perhaps? No. Where, then? Bath and water, soap and towels are there, but where the bather? Consternation is now changed into panic.'

The policeman went running to fetch Dr Gunning, the assistant commandant. Gunning arrived, questioned every officer in sight, but got no further than the barber and policeman. Asked when they had last seen Churchill, the officers looked blank and muttered vaguely: 'Last night.' At 9.30 Commandant Opperman came on duty and ordered a roll call. It became evident that Churchill was indeed missing and Opperman got into 'a great stew'. To the amusement of the officers—who knew Churchill had climbed the fence during the dinner hour—the Commandant paced up and down declaring that he had seen Churchill on the verandah at ten-thirty the previous evening. Later he changed his story; he told newspaper reporters that he distinctly remembered Churchill sitting on the verandah, smoking, as late as eleven o'clock.

However, nothing could disguise the fact that the Staatsmodelskool's most important prisoner had escaped. The security force was informed and several 'big bugs' descended on the school. No one was more incensed than Churchill's old enemy, Veld-Kornet Malan. Blustering into the Rev. Hofmeyr's room, he demanded to know when the parson had last seen Churchill. 'Of course my answer, too, was "Last night",' says Hofmeyr. 'The big man then said to the two trembling gaolers: "Well you must produce Churchill; if not General Joubert will hang you!" He looked daggers at them and they shook.' A thorough search was made but all it produced was a letter, found on Churchill's bed, addressed to Louis de Souza. In this letter Churchill explained that he had decided to escape and hinted that he was being helped by friends outside. He thanked the Boer authorities for their kindness and promised to publish a full and fair account of his experiences as soon as he reached the British lines. More it was not possible to discover. To a man, the officers refused to give any relevant information. Their loyalty is doubly commendable because, according to Haldane, feeling against Churchill was running high in the prison. Brockie was particularly angry at having his plan usurped and his own chances spoiled. Later it was claimed that many of the officers were displeased with Churchill for breaking out and seemingly leaving Haldane and Brockie in the lurch. In his book, *Twice Captured*, Lord Rosslyn said: 'There was a general impression that Churchill had behaved in an unfair way to the other fellows—taking their plan of escape and leaving them behind him. At any rate he seems to have followed the plan of *"sauve qui peut"* instead of *"shoulder to shoulder"*.' This accusation plagued Churchill for many years. When he first read it he contemplated suing Rosslyn for libel. Certainly it seems an unfair interpretation of his impulsive action in escaping when a likely chance arose; the fact that he waited so long after climbing the fence makes it abundantly clear that he had not contemplated leaving without his friends. Once over the wall it would have been madness to climb back. However, his action was open to misinterpretation and in the confined atmosphere of the Staatsmodelskool suspicion was bound to be exaggerated. But it should be noted that Haldane's remark about the ill-feeling towards Churchill is not borne out by Hofmeyr. Far from resenting the escape, Hofmeyr says: 'For us the whole thing was a grand pantomime—a screaming farce.'

Neither farce nor friction was apparent to the Boers. Their only concern was to track Churchill down. His hint that he had been helped by outside friends was acted upon immediately. Search warrants were issued and homes were ransacked. 'The popular impression is,' reported a local paper, 'that Mr Churchill is in hiding in Pretoria and that he is being succoured by English sympathizers.' Many an English-speaking resident of Pretoria was to recall the sudden invasion of his house by heavy-footed, determined policemen. Some suffered more than others. One unfortunate young woman, who had been seen smiling at the prisoners, was reported to have been hauled before a magistrate and fined £25 on suspicion. And Hofmeyr claims that a hospital nurse from the Cape, who was suspected of supplying Churchill with one of her uniforms, was put over the border. Even Dr Gunning, the assistant commandant, came under suspicion. As a Hollander married to an Englishwoman, Gunning was thought to have been too lenient towards the prisoners and his house was searched. This unwarranted treatment of Gunning was not without a touch of farce: for the amiable doctor was responsible for supplying the prisoners with library books and, according to the indignant *Volksstem*, the last book issued to Churchill was John Stuart Mill's *On Liberty*. This must have looked incriminating indeed.

Descriptions of Churchill were circulated throughout the Transvaal. He was said to be 'about 5' 8" or 9", blond with a light thin moustache, walks with a slight stoop, cannot speak any Dutch, during long conversations he occasionally makes a rattling noise in his throat.' Later an old photograph of Churchill was issued with a poster which offered £25 for 'CHURCHILL, dead or alive. . .' The description which accompanied this poster was a little more accurate. He was said to be twenty-five, with red brown hair and 'speaks through his nose, cannot pronounce the letter "S" '. It was not long before rumours of his whereabouts and means of escape were circulating Pretoria. At first it was said that 'the bold escape was made in lady's clothes' and that there was little chance of his crossing the border 'as all arrangements were speedily made to frustrate his efforts'. This was followed by a report that he had been 'recaptured in a Transvaal policeman's clothes on the Delagoa line at Komati Poort'. Shortly afterwards it was announced that 'Mr Winston Churchill . . . has been recaptured at Waterval Boven'. This last report was not as absurd as it appears. A young soldier, looking very like Churchill, was captured in the eastern Transvaal and taken to Pretoria. The dismay on the face of the official who received the captive at Pretoria station only added to the hilarity of the situation. Similar stories poured in from all over South Africa.

The rumours brought little solace to the angry Boer policemen. Poor Commandant Opperman was beside himself with rage. His first reaction had been to lay the blame squarely on the shoulders of his guards. After telling newspaper reporters that he had seen Churchill on the verandah, he wrote to Louis de Souza in an attempt to exonerate himself. He said that Churchill had been acting strangely for some days, walking about dreamily and keeping away from the other prisoners; the only way he could have evaded the guards was by bribing them. But he was unable to make this charge stick. At an official enquiry, held later that day, it was shown that the blame lay not so much with individual guards but with faulty administration. Not only was there no roll call, but on that evening the normal sentry patrol was reduced to eight men; the guard who should have been on duty at the corner where Churchill ducked out did not take up his post until 8 p.m. To make matters worse, it was also revealed that the two private soldiers who had escaped two days before had later been recaptured without the guards reporting their absence. It said little for the confidence that Opperman inspired or for the control he exercised. The Commandant was fully aware of the slur on his efficiency. 'Our uncourteous gaoler,' says Hofmeyr, 'now became, if possible, more uncourteous still and more morose. He no longer shaved, seldom brushed hair or clothes—in fact, he looked as fierce as the famous "Wild Man of the West".'

The most unfortunate result, as far as the prisoners were concerned, was an immediate tightening up of the administration. Some of the more inefficient guards were sent to the front, extra sentries were posted in the adjoining garden, roll calls took place twice a day, the beer ration was stopped, newspapers forbidden and hospital visits, walking in the yard at night and sleeping on the verandahs prohibited. 'For a time,' says Haldane, 'we were subjected to many petty annoyances, which displayed to fine advantage the narrow-minded and malicious nature which actuated our warders.' Even worse was the fact that Churchill's impulsive action had seemingly reduced the possibility of further escapes to nil. The same repercussions would undoubtedly have followed had Haldane and Brockie gone with him, but this was small comfort to the officers. They resented being outdone by a newspaper reporter.

Perhaps the most devastating irony of the entire affair was that, as it turned out, Churchill's escape was unnecessary. For the following day, Louis de Souza told Haldane that he had received a telegram from General Joubert authorizing Churchill's unconditional release. This was the final result of those long and tedious negotiations. In his telegram Joubert said that he was prepared to recognize Churchill as a non-combatant, despite reports to the contrary in the British press. 'Seeing that a parole was promised him and that he suggested leaving Africa to return to Europe where he would report and speak only of his experiences. . .' Joubert concluded, 'then I have no further objections to his being set free, without our accepting somebody else in exchange.' Only on one score did the Boer commander have doubts. '*Zal hy de waarheid gaan vertellen?*' he added in a postscript, '*Hy zal ook wel een aardje naar zijn vader bebben.*' Which can be freely translated: 'Will he tell the truth? He might well be a chip off the old block.' The ghost of Lord Randolph still loomed large in South Africa.

General Joubert's telegram arriving a day too late was to cause Churchill endless trouble. It seems likely that it was the source of the repeated calumnies hurled at him by political opponents. For many years it was impossible for him to fight an election without being accused of having broken his parole in Pretoria. He instituted several legal actions to refute this slander but it persisted; it can still be found in print to this day. There seems not a word of truth in it. In all the documents released by the Boers, there is no mention of Churchill breaking his parole. The nearest reference to it is Joubert's 'a parole was *promised* him'. But obviously this was only a promise. His fellow prisoners were adamant in their denials of his having broken faith with his captors. Haldane, who disagreed with Churchill on some points concerning their imprisonment, was fully prepared to support him in nailing this lie; as well as another pernicious rumour to the effect that the Boers had deliberately allowed Churchill to escape. Hofmeyr dismissed the suggestion with contempt. 'The idea!' he scoffed. 'A man gives parole, and yet he is guarded by men armed to the teeth!'

The origin of the rumour is not difficult to trace. It appears to have been started by Churchill's *bête-noir*, Veld-Kornet Malan, who had probably been given a garbled version of Joubert's telegram. At least, this is the impression gained from Hofmeyr's account. Describing the way the prison was searched he says: 'Right airily the officials informed us that "Of course he can't escape; he will be caught soon enough, and then put in prison, and very likely all the officers too." The big, blustering Field-cornet went so far as to say, "Churchill is a blackguard; he gave his parole, and that is the way he keeps his English word of honour." Well, Churchill was not the blackguard. Somebody else was—a baffled official who takes refuge in lies ... with some of these officials anything will do for a figleaf. Public opinion, they knew, would point to them for remissness, and therefore any cowardly lie would do for subterfuge.' Once this sort of rumour was started, it was bound to catch on.

The Transvaal papers made no reference to a parole. They were too busy alternating between threats and enticements to lure Churchill from his hiding place which, they suspected, was in Pretoria. On 'good authority' *De Volksstem* promised that 'if captured he will be leniently treated, and after it is discovered who assisted him he will probably be released'. This, of course, was quite the wrong line to take with Churchill, even had he been able to read the paper. *The Standard and Diggers' News* spoke to him in a language he understood. After describing him as 'the melodramatic descendant of the great Marlborough' it went on to say: 'There is really nothing to be gained by Mr Churchill from this latest journalistic exploit save "copy". Though he successfully eluded the vigilance of the Model School guard any attempt to return to the British Forces must be rendered abortive by the strict passport system now in force and though every credit should be given to the enterprising young gentleman for his latest newspaper exploit, it will be some considerable time before his glowing narrative of "How he escaped from Pretoria" can reach his friends.'

*

Winston Churchill was mercifully unaware of all these false and malicious reports. Life at the bottom of the mine was bad enough as it was. He soon discovered that his underground hideout was infested with rats: white rats with pink eyes. Fortunately he was quick to realize that they were more afraid of him that he was of them; all the same, they proved a confounded nuisance. When he woke from his first sleep he reached for a candle but was unable to find it. He lay in the darkness for some hours before Mr Howard arrived with a lantern and explained that he should have put the candle under his mattress while asleep as it had most certainly been eaten by the rats.

Howard brought him some food—including a cooked chicken obtained from the local doctor—several books and a half-a-dozen more candles. The mine manager was still somewhat worried about food. It was difficult getting anything past his maids and he was not helped by the fact that news of Churchill's escape was now well known locally. Once more Churchill offered to leave and make his own way to the frontier. But Howard would not hear of it. He said he was sure some plan could be devised to get him out of the country.

When Howard left, Churchill again settled down to sleep. This time he tucked the candles under his pillow. When he woke he was immediately conscious of the rats and realised they had been attempting to get at the candles. He struck a match and there was a great scurrying. This went on all the time. 'The three days I passed in the mine,' he wrote, 'were not among the most pleasant which my memory re-illuminates. The patter of little feet and a perceptible sense of stir and scurry were continuous.'

He had another unwanted visitor whom he does not mention. According to Mr Howard, one of the African mine-workers was attracted by the smell of a cigar which Churchill was smoking. 'When the native got a whiff,' says Howard, 'he trailed it down . . . but as soon as he saw Mr Churchill he bolted and told the other boys that there was a spook in that part of the mine. For a long time afterwards we could not get any of the boys to move in that vicinity at all.'

However, such distractions were few and far between. For the most part Churchill was left to the company of his four-footed friends. The monotony began to tell on his nerves. Years later he was to insist that his children learn long poems by heart in case they should find themselves in a situation where they would have to provide their own mental stimulus: his daughter Sarah considered this to be a legacy of the days he endured at the Transvaal and Delagoa Bay Collieries. Howard and others did their best to keep him entertained. On his third day he was taken on a tour of the mine by the mine-captain, Joe McKenna, and was surprised to catch a glimpse of sunlight up a disused shaft and to learn that the mine was only two hundred feet deep. But the excursion did little to offset the hours of loneliness and inactivity. 'Mr Churchill remained underground for two or three days,' says Howard, 'when I noticed he was becoming very nervy, this being probably due to his solitary confinement.' It was decided that he should be allowed a breath of fresh air. On the evening of 15 December he was brought to the surface for a

Lady Sarah Wilson at the entrance to her bomb-proof shelter in Mafeking

Interior of her shelter

Lady Sarah Wilson in her self-designed 'Mafeking outfit'

stroll on the veld; the following day—advised by Dr Gillespie, the local English-speaking doctor, who was in on the secret—he shifted his quarters to a storeroom at the back of Howard's house.

The room was filled with packing cases and bags of grain, among which Churchill could hide, and special signals were agreed upon to prevent him opening the door to strangers. The food problem was overcome with the help of two sympathetic women at a near-by boarding house. This meant there were now nine people involved in the conspiracy: Howard and his secretary, John Adams, Joe McKenna and John McHenry and Dan Dewsnap, Dr Gillespie and the two women. To avoid suspicion, they spoke of Churchill among themselves as 'Dr Bentick'. Before long the group had acquired a tenth, somewhat uncertain member. 'As the office boy was sweeping the stoep one morning,' says Howard, 'he either let his broom fall or placed it against the door of the room in which Mr Churchill was concealed. The noise which the broom made was evidently interpreted by Mr Churchill as a signal, and, thinking that one of us wanted to see him, he unlocked the door and found himself face to face with a native, much to their mutual surprise. The boy rushed off at once and informed someone in authority that there was a stranger in the room. Immediately we heard of the discovery we bound the boy to secrecy, promising him a new suit of clothes, which he received in due course.'

Obviously this precarious state of affairs could not be prolonged indefinitely. The hue and cry that had followed Churchill's escape had died down, the authorities seemed more certain than ever that he was hiding in Pretoria; but the local Boers had by no means abandoned the search. With two Africans having stumbled upon him during the few days he had been at the mine, it would not be long before the secret was out. Once the mineworkers began to talk, further investigations could be expected. The conspirators held several meetings to decide what to do. Mr Howard thought of calling in Charles Burnham, a local storekeeper. Burnham (whom Churchill mistakenly refers to as Burgener) regularly sent goods to Delagoa Bay and there was a possibility that he could provide the means for Churchill to cross the frontier. When sounded out by John Adams, the storekeeper proved only too willing to assist.

There is some doubt as to who devised the escape plan eventually adopted. Howard says it was his idea, Burnham claims that he thought of it. 'I was present at meetings held in the sitting room of the mine office,' says Burnham, 'at which we discussed the question of devising means to get Churchill out of the country. Those meetings were attended by Mr Howard, Mr Adams, Dan Dewsnap, the engineer, and myself, and on one of those occasions it occurred to me that, as I had a number of bales of wool to consign to Lourenço Marques, we could smuggle Churchill away in them.' Whoever was responsible, it was, of course, the most obvious thing to do. There were seven trucks at the local railway siding and Burnham had enough wool to fill six. By spreading the load it was possible to provide a hiding place for Churchill. Burnham and Adams undertook to rearrange the bales and by 18 December they were able to report that all was ready.

Churchill spent his last afternoon at the mine office trying to concentrate on Robert Louis Stevenson's *Kidnapped*. Reading was not easy. Once he was startled by the sound of gunfire and sprang to the conclusion that the police had arrived and engaged the conspirators in battle. There was nothing he could do. He was under strict instructions to remain hidden. After an agonizing wait, he heard laughter and realized all was well. Later, Mr Howard arrived grinning broadly. He said that the local Veld-Kornet had called to report that the escaped prisoner from the Staatsmodelskool had been recaptured at Waterval Boven. 'I didn't want him messing about,' Howard went on, 'so I challenged him to a rifle match with bottles. He won two pounds off me and has gone away delighted.'

Just after two o'clock the following morning Churchill crawled into his hiding place on the goods truck. He squeezed his way along a tunnel in the wool bales until he reached a space wide enough to allow him to sit up. After a wait of three or four hours, the truck was coupled to an engine and the long journey to Delagoa Bay began. By this time there was sufficient light coming through cracks in the side of the truck for Churchill to examine his new hide-out. He found it well stocked. Not only had his friends supplied him with a revolver, two roast chickens, cold meat, bread, a melon and three bottles of cold tea, but, according to Mr Howard, there was also a little whisky.

One item only was missing. 'Smokes were taboo,' says Howard, 'for the scent of a cigar or tobacco might lead to his discovery.'

The journey to the coast was expected to take sixteen hours; he had enough provisions to allow for unexpected delays. Shut up amid the bales of wool, he was as cut off from the world as he had been at the bottom of the mine. Once the train was under way, he crawled back along the entrance tunnel and squinted through a chink in the side of the truck, but he was unable to see much. Earlier he had learnt by heart the names of the stations along the line to the frontier and was thus able to keep a vague check on the train's progress. But this was entirely guesswork; for the most part he was conscious only of the rattle of the truck, an occasional series of jolts as it was shunted into a siding and the constant fear of a search.

He tried desperately to keep awake but was not always successful and this made it difficult to gauge the distance travelled. Only by conjuring up visions of the triumph which would undoubtedly accompany his return to freedom was he able to stave off the frightening thought that a zealous railway official might take it upon himself to examine the truck; once the tarpaulin was removed there was little chance of his escaping detection. That this did not, in fact, happen was due largely to the efforts of Charles Burnham.

At the last minute it had been decided that Burnham should travel on the train as a passenger. It was as well that he did. The trucks were taken from the mine to the nearest station, Witbank, by the colliery engine. Here they were shunted into a siding and Burnham was told that it would not be possible for them to leave that day. Luckily it was a week before Christmas and under the pretence of handing out Christmas boxes Burnham was able to bribe the officials to link the trucks on the next train passing through. From Witbank Burnham travelled in the guard's van; with the help of a bottle of whisky he was able to win over the guard. At Waterval Onder, however, the trucks were detached, and the guard, who was then leaving the train, held out little hope of persuading his relief to take them on further unless another bottle of whisky was forthcoming. Burnham went off to buy the whisky at a local hotel and took advantage of the wait to snatch a quick meal. 'While dining at the hotel,' he says, 'the subject of conversation was curiously enough in regard to

Churchill's escape from Pretoria. The proprietor of the hotel, a foreigner, I believe, remarked with some show of assurance during the conversation, "Oh, yes, Churchill passed here two days ago, dressed as a Roman Catholic Priest." The circulation of a rumour like that I regarded as distinctly advantageous to my plan.' The bottle of whisky proved even more helpful. When the next train arrived, Burnham had little difficulty in getting his trucks taken on.

A far more serious threat materialized the following morning when the train arrived at Kaapmuiden, the last stop before the border. The station was occupied by a Boer commando. When Burnham made his way along the platform to look at the trucks, he was alarmed to find an armed burger leaning against the one in which Churchill was hidden. Not knowing what else to do, he went up to the man and asked where he could get a cup of coffee. 'He surveyed me as if I were an awful "mug",' says Burnham, 'as the coffee stall was staring me in the face. "Why there it is," he said and when I remarked "All right, Oom," and invited him to join me in a cup of coffee, so as to get him away from the truck, he accepted with pleasure.' Burnham was able to keep the man talking until the train left; he was relieved to find that the rest of the commando paid no attention to the trucks.

At the Transvaal frontier post, Komatipoort, Burnham says that he was able to persuade the customs officer to allow the trucks through; but upon reaching Ressano Garcia, on the Portuguese side, he was less successful. The Portuguese officials refused to allow the trucks to continue with the passenger train and insisted that they remain in a siding until a goods train arrived the following morning. When Burnham found that the Portuguese would not accept his bribe, he contrived 'with as much secrecy as I could in the circumstances observe, to approach the Churchill truck and explain the situation to the fugitive.' He then left on the passenger train for Lourenço Marques.

Churchill makes no mention of this whispered conversation. He was convinced that he waited that night on the Transvaal side of the border. On several occasions, he says, he heard people walking past talking Dutch. But he was in no position to judge and may well have mistaken the language. When the train moved off the following morning, however, he was quick to realize he had left the Transvaal. 'As we rumbled and banged along,' he says, 'I pushed my head out of the tarpaulin and sang and shouted and crowed at the top of my voice. Indeed, I was so carried away by thankfulness and delight that I fired my revolver two or three times in the air as a *feu de joie*. None of these follies led to any evil result.'

Burnham was waiting for the trucks when they arrived at Lourenço Marques that afternoon. No sooner had the train stopped, he says, than Churchill, 'black as a sweep', sprang out and followed him to the British Consulate. It was well after four o'clock when they arrived at the Consulate and they had some difficulty in persuading the secretary to let them in. On being told that he would have to return at nine the next morning, Churchill kicked up such a fuss that the Consul himself came hurrying to the door. It took some time to convince the officials that Churchill was not a soot-begrimed stoker from one of the ships in the harbour, but once his identity had been established he was welcomed with open arms. 'From that moment,' he says, 'every resource of hospitality and welcome was at my disposal. A hot bath, clean clothing, an excellent dinner, means of telegraphing—all I could want.'

He read through the newspaper files and sent off several telegrams. Although he gives no details of these telegrams, two of them are not without interest. One was to the Boer Government, cheekily announcing his safe arrival at Delagoa Bay. The other evidently resulted from his reading the Transvaal papers. It was addressed to the editor of *The Standard and Diggers' News* in Johannesburg: 'Am now writing "How I escaped from the Boers," ' it read; 'but regret cannot for obvious reasons disclose many interesting details. Shall be happy to give you any you may require when next I visit Pretoria, probably third week in March.'

The newspaper published this telegram two days later: on another page of the same issue there was a notice appealing for volunteers to guard the military prisoners.

*

Lourenço Marques was a hive of intrigue. As the only neutral port in southern Africa it attracted agents, informers and spies from both sides; most of the misleading rumours spread concerning the progress of the war originated from this Portuguese town. At the time of Churchill's arrival, Boer sympathizers tended to preponderate. For, not only was Lourenço Marques the Transvaal's only outlet to the sea, but the large numbers of European volunteers who had rallied to the Boer cause invariably made their way to the Transvaal via Delagoa Bay. Knowing this, the British Consul was none too easy about harbouring such a well-known fugitive: he feared that a determined attempt might be made to recapture his guest and send him back to Pretoria. His fear increased when, later that evening, a suspicious looking crowd gathered outside the Consulate. These men, however, turned out to be a band of patriotic Englishmen who, as soon as they heard of Churchill's arrival, had formed themselves into an armed guard to meet any contemplated attack on the Consulate.

They did not have to protect Churchill for long. As luck would have it, the weekly steamer to Durban was in the harbour, due to sail the following morning. 'It might almost be said,' remarked Churchill, 'it ran in connection with my train.' Flanked by his self-appointed bodyguard, Churchill marched down to the docks at ten o'clock that night and boarded the s.s. *Induna*. His departure was observed by a Boer agent who immediately reported to Pretoria.

' "Marlbrook" in a Coal Truck,' sneered *The Standard and Diggers' News*, when it became known how Churchill had arrived at Lourenço Marques. And, in a leading article, it answered his offer to send details of his escape. 'Mr Churchill is a very young man who has his way to make in the world, and we would, from our maturer experience, venture to suggest that it would be advisable to bear in mind the old adages "A still tongue makes a wise head" "Least said soonest mended." And to demonstrate to our journalistic fledgling the true appreciation of his particular desire we would recommend that he alter the title of his lucubration to "How I was allowed to escape from the Boers"... Scene Pretoria War Office: 9 a.m. Mr Churchill reported missing; orders of arrest issued to police authorities. 11 a.m. Receipt of official letter by morning's mail from Commandant-General Joubert dated Volksrust, December 13th, 1899, ordering release of Mr Churchill as non-combatant. Orders to police not to execute arrest.' Considering that *The Standard and Dig-*

gers' News had faithfully reported the hue and cry—the false alarms and false arrests, the 'dead or alive' poster and the rest—that had followed Churchill's escape, it is astonishing that this particular canard should have gained currency: but it did. The story that the Boers had deliberately allowed him to escape, like the accusation that he had broken parole, was to pursue Churchill throughout his life. It is only necessary to know the origins of such stories to assess their validity.

The s.s. *Induna* left Lourenço Marques early on the morning of Friday, 22 December and arrived at Durban at four o'clock the following afternoon. Churchill had plenty to keep him occupied during the voyage. The newspaper files that he had devoured at the British Consulate had contained more than news about his exploits. They had not made cheerful reading. For he discovered that his escape had coincided with a series of unpredecented reverses for the British troops. This was the notorious 'Black Week' of the Anglo-Boer war: the defeats at Stormberg and Maggersfontein (which had spurred Churchill and his companions in their determination to escape) had been followed by an equally disastrous battle in Natal, when General Buller, in an attempt to relieve Ladysmith, had been brought to a humiliating halt at Colenso by a Boer force commanded by Louis Botha. The total British casualties in these three battles was estimated in the region of 3,000. Morale was at its lowest ebb. Churchill was determined to do something towards boosting it. His days at sea were spent composing a stirring cable for the *Morning Post*.

He had continued to write to his paper while at the Staatsmodelskool. Some of his reports were generously forwarded by the Transvaal authorities; others were suppressed and were discovered many years later among documents kept by Louis de Souza. These reports, in any case, were extremely circumspect; only now was he able to give his feelings full rein. He was concerned with talk, current on both sides, of a negotiated peace. 'Although the Boers are confident that they will drive the British into the sea,' he wrote, 'they want to return to their farms, and complain bitterly of the hardships in the field. They therefore talk of compromise. . . .' Such talk, he felt, should not be listened to. If the British opened negotiations after their crushing defeats they would be negotiating from weakness: it would be Majuba all over again. His attitude was—as it continued to be in similar situations throughout his life—victory first, concessions later. It was necessary to assess the enemy's strength and deal with it accordingly. 'We must face the facts,' his cable concluded. 'The individual Boer, mounted, in a suitable country, is worth three or four regular soldiers. The power of modern rifles is so tremendous that frontal attacks must often be repulsed. The extraordinary mobility of the enemy protects his flanks. The only way of treating them is either to get men equal in character and intelligence as riflemen, or, failing the individual, huge masses of troops.... We should show no hurry, but we should collect masses of troops. It would be much cheaper in the end to send more than is necessary. There is plenty of work here for a quarter of a million men, and South Africa is well worth the cost in blood and money. Are the gentleman of England all fox-hunting? Why not an English Light Horse? For the sake of our manhood, our devoted Colonists, and our dead soldiers, we must persevere with the war.' A later generation would find much that was familiar in the tone and intent of this cable.

But would he be listened to? Was his standing such as to make what he said appear important? These thoughts must have occurred to him. He knew he had made a splash and was considered a hero. But how great a splash; how great a hero? He was soon to find out.

On Saturday 23 December, the *Natal Mercury* announced that Churchill was expected at Durban that day on the *Induna*. There was no mention of an official reception; it was by no means certain what time the *Induna* would dock. This vagueness did not deter the citizens of Durban. By 1 o'clock that afternoon, a considerable crowd had gathered at the docks, and flags and bunting had begun to decorate the ships in the harbour. By the time the *Induna* steamed in—shortly before 4 o'clock—there were well over a thousand people waiting at the quayside. Somewhat to the crowd's disappointment the *Induna* did not make for the passenger jetty, but swung round outside two other ships moored at the main wharf. 'Over the two vessels the crowd rushed in a hurry scurry,' it was reported, 'and, swarming on every portion of the *Inchanga*, waited to lionize the one passenger—the only passenger so far as they were concerned—which the Rennie liner had brought from the Portuguese port...

As the *Induna* came nearer, the object of quest was descried on the captain's bridge, his round boyish face shaded by a large-brimmed hat. The instant he was recognized, a rousing cheer went up ... Mr Churchill bowed his acknowledgment ... The cheering was continuous and enthusiastic, and amid it all could be heard voices shouting "Well done, sir." '

When the *Induna* finally docked, some of the crowd sprang on to the deck without waiting for the gangway to be lowered. Churchill was seized, lifted shoulder high and paraded round the deck. 'I was nearly torn to pieces by enthusiastic kindness,' he said. After shaking hands with various officials, he was carried to the main wharf by the crowd. Here he stood on a box and made a short fighting speech. 'When I see around me such a crowd as this,' he said, 'such determination and such enthusiasm, I am satisfied that, no matter what the difficulties, no matter what the dangers, and what the force they might bring against us, we shall be successful in the end. ...' His voice was drowned by cheering; someone at the back of the crowd sobbed: 'God bless you, my boy.' Struggling to make himself heard, he went on: 'Because our cause is a just and right one, because we strike for equal rights for every white man in South Africa and because we are representing the forces of civilization and progress, in the end we must bear down these reactionary Republics that menace our peace, and, when this war is over, and the British arms shall be victorious, you will see in this country the beginning of a new era, when peace and prosperity shall reign, so that the Cape may be in fact as well as in name a Cape of Good Hope.'

He was photographed at the end of his speech—clutching his hat and smiling, almost diffidently—as the cheers of the crowd broke about him.

Once more he was seized, dumped into a ricksha, together with a Reuter's correspondent and the editor of the *Natal Mercury*. 'And away the crowd travelled,' wrote an astonished witness, 'the vehicle all the time being besieged by men desirous of shaking hands with Mr Churchill, and having a few words with him. "This is sincere, sir," shouted one. "It is, indeed," replied Mr Churchill; "I never thought of anything like this. This is a British community." ' At times the press was so great that the ricksha almost capsized. A Union Jack on poles headed the procession and the crowd bellowed 'Rule, Britannia' and 'Soldiers of the Queen' as they marched. Churchill was in his element. 'His heart evidently pulsated with those of the people doing him honour,' remarked one of the crowd. 'I was struck by his coolness through it all. Most men would have felt embarrassed, but all through he was level-headed, shaking hands with everyone, quietly answering every remark made to him. "This is good." "This is kind," he frequently ejaculated.' Only one sour note marred the proceeding. The story that he had broken his parole had already begun to circulate; someone in the crowd taxed him with it. 'No, it is not true,' he yelled back. 'I was in exactly the same position as all the other prisoners.'

By the time the Town Hall was reached, the crowd had almost trebled. Once again the cry went up for Churchill to address them. 'Nothing would content them but a speech,' he says, 'which after a becoming reluctance I was induced to deliver.' Standing on a small cart which had been drawn up outside the Town Hall, he waved to the crowd for silence, but his voice was lost in the cheering, followed by another blast of 'Rule, Britannia'. Eventually he was able to make himself heard and embarked on the second rallying speech of his life. He expressed his gratitude for his reception and went on: 'This is not the time for a long speech. We have got outside the region of words: we have got to the region of action. We are now in the region of war, and in this war we have not yet arrived at the half-way house. But with the determination of a great Empire, surrounded by Colonies of unprecedented loyalty, we shall carry our policy to a successful conclusion, and under the old Union Jack there will be an era of peace, purity, liberty, equality, and good government in South Africa. I thank you once again for your great kindness. I am sure I feel within myself a personal measure of that gratitude which every Englishman who loves his country must feel towards the loyal and devoted Colonists of Natal.'

He was rescued from the cheering crowd by the Town Commandant, Captain Scott, who took him to his office and handed him a bundle of congratulatory telegrams. The crowd was waiting for him when he reappeared and he had to pose for more photographs. He told them that his one desire was to return to the front as soon as possible. At this, the ricksha—now draped with Union Jacks—was pushed forward and, climbing into it, he was dragged to the railway station, trundled along the platform and deposited in the carriage of the 5.40 train to Pietermaritzburg. 'The platform was simply packed with people,' it was reported. 'The railway officials gave the signal, the engine whistled, and away went the train, while the crowd cheered and waved handkerchiefs, ladies being as enthusiastic as the men.'

That night, at the invitation of the Governor of Natal, Sir Walter Hely-Hutchinson, he slept at Government House in Pietermaritzburg. The following day was Christmas Eve and he celebrated it with a group of army friends: his quarters being the platelayer's hut which stood within a hundred yards of the spot where he had been captured some six weeks earlier.

*

There could no longer be any doubt about it: he was not only free, he was famous. His escape, both in its execution and its timing, had captured the imagination of the world. It was the one bright spot in an otherwise dismal campaign, and the press—not only in England but throughout the English-speaking world—played it up for all, or rather more, than it was worth. In the space of a few days he had established himself as a personality to be reckoned with. His cable to the *Morning Post*, calling for massive reinforcements, became the subject of earnest leading articles. Even in America, where pro-Boer feelings ran high, his courage, his daring and his breathtaking audacity evoked widespread admiration. The telegrams handed to him at Durban proved to be only the first trickle of a flood of congratulatory messages that poured in from every corner of the world. An English governess in Roumania wrote to tell him of her tearful pride; from Central Russia an exiled resident of Oldham promised him an extra vote in the next election; another man sent his praises in the form of a poem which he hoped would be set to music; an American suggested that a second Jameson Raid into the Transvaal should be led by Churchill so that the rising among the prisoners at Pretoria should become a reality, and a man from Manchester announced that he was naming his new-born son Cecil Winston. By jumping over the fence of the Staatsmodelskool, he had done more than free himself from the Boers: he had escaped, once and for all, from the oppressive shadow of his father. From now on, as Esme Wingfield-Stratford has remarked, 'Winston Churchill was established as one of those people about whom everybody talked, joked, or disputed, and at the mention of whose name people got violently excited. He was definitely, and permanently Winston.'

Not all the publicity was favourable. From the moment he was captured, political opponents had done their best to minimize his achievements. The old taunts of 'self-advertiser' and 'sensation-seeker' had been trotted out, and one Radical newspaper had gone so far as to say that the part he had played in defending the armoured train entitled the Boers to 'order his execution'. Now that he was free this type of criticism grew both in volume and intensity. Nor was it confined to political opponents. The Duke of Manchester, who was touring America, was no less scornful than the Radical press. 'I don't see why he should have so much fuss made over him,' he told a reporter in Philadelphia; 'he's only done his duty.'

But the greatest sceptic was undoubtedly Commandant Opperman of the Staatsmodelskool. 'Our poor gaoler could not, and would not, believe that the escape was a *fait accompli*,' says Hofmeyr. 'Long after Churchill had . . . addressed the public in Durban and Maritzburg he said to me, "I don't believe that he has escaped from Pretoria. Some of the accursed English are hiding him here somewhere.'"

CHAPTER FOURTEEN

Shut up in Mafeking

THE DAY after Sarah's return to Mafeking, she was publicly welcomed by the town's newspaper. 'We are sure we represent the whole of Mafeking,' announced the *Mafeking Mail*, 'when we offer the most hearty congratulations to Capt. Wilson and Lady Sarah Wilson on her ladyship's safe arrival in our tight little garrison, after her experiences with the Boers.' A few days later, the editor used Sarah's captivity to illustrate what he considered to be the Boers' lack of humanity. 'To capture a lady and keep her in discomfort and what would have become absolute peril when our force advances,' he wrote, '... does not apparently strike them as incongruous with their late arrogation of equality amongst civilized powers.' Baden-Powell, in his letter to Snyman acknowledging Sarah's arrival, was every bit as indignant. 'In treating this lady as a prisoner of war,' he thundered, 'as well as in various other acts, you have, in the present campaign, altered the usual conditions of war. This is a very serious matter; and I do not know whether it has the sanction of General Joubert or not, but I warn you of the consequences ... [it] may shortly be very serious to your own people, and you yourself will be to blame for everything that may happen.'

There was a double intent behind these fulminations. Not only were they meant to admonish the Boers, but they were designed to bolster the morale of the town. The siege had by that time lasted fifty days. They had been eventful, often exciting, days but they had led to frayed nerves and short tempers. The daily shelling, the food rationing, the fading hopes of relief and the recent flooding of the trenches, had all encouraged the growing despondency. To counteract this, Baden-Powell seized every opportunity for a display of confidence. His slight, jaunty figure was to be seen everywhere. His jokes and puns—which now appear laboured and unfunny—eased even inveterate complainers out of their sulks. Swinging his cane and whistling operatic arias, he seemed assured and tireless. 'Colonel Baden-Powell,' wrote Sarah, 'has inspired all ranks with confidence; while never sparing himself, and seeming scarcely ever to take any rest, he has made the timid feel they can repose with confidence, and the pugnacious that no opportunity will be lost to strike when the occasion offers.'

In Sarah he gained a valuable ally. 'She was a most remarkable woman,' he was to say, 'and the influence she had on the morale of the defenders was immense.' Arriving fresh from the enemy camp, she lost no time in spreading her opinion that the Boers were on the point of surrender. They were, she assured war correspondents who flocked to interview her, heartily sick of the war and cynical about Snyman's leadership. Baden-Powell was so much impressed by Sarah's reports of dissatisfaction in the Boer laager that he immediately addressed a letter to the 'Burghers of the South African Republic at present under arms near Mafeking,' advising them to lay down their arms and return to their farms. This letter brought a sharp retort from Snyman, who accused Baden-Powell of adopting childish and underhand methods.

Once Sarah had settled in, her first concern was to arrange a bomb-proof shelter for herself. Helped by a group of army officers, she set about constructing a dug-out in front of Mr Weil's house. Some eight feet deep, it was roofed with a double set of steel rails, covered first by sheets of corrugated iron and then by a huge tarpaulin to keep out the rain. On top of this was piled nine feet of solid earth, while row upon row of sandbags were stacked at the entrance to guard against shell splinters and stray bullets. The inside chamber was reached by twelve wooden steps, panelled in white-painted wood and, reported Sarah, 'much resembles the cabin of a yacht'. To add a touch of patriotic colour she hung one wall with a huge Union Jack. The shelter was, as she says, 'a triumph in its line' and to inaugurate it she gave an underground dinner for six guests.

Within a few days of its completion, it was put to a severe test. A shell exploded at the entrance; filling the cellar with dust and killing a linesman who was fixing telegraph wires connecting Sarah with Baden-Powell's headquarters. On another occasion it stood up to a direct hit by one of Creaky's shells: the explosion blasted the front of Weil's house but left the shelter unshaken. 'It is, I think,' claimed the proud Sarah, 'the only shelter in the town on top of which a 94lb shell actually exploded —without even making the glasses jingle, or disturbing war trophies on the walls.'

The shelter quickly became one of the wonders of Mafeking. Photographs of the interior were smuggled out of the town and published in London magazines. Sarah was photographed and sketched beside it in a variety of poses and costumes: standing at the entrance in a simple cotton dress, mounting the steps wearing a Dutch *kappie* and seated on top of the sandbags in a rakishly tilted boater. Its fame even spread to the Transvaal, and the Boer papers, while reporting Winston Churchill's escape, were able to report that his aunt was living in a luxurious shelter of her own making.

Sarah had to adjust herself to the town's routine. During the first two months of the siege, life in Mafeking had taken on a definite pattern; it was a pattern which newcomers recognized more by example than by instruction. Baden-Powell's instructions, in fact, had been kept to a minimum and were confined to elementary safety measures. For example, the shell warnings consisted merely of bells ringing from the look-out posts (Sarah was privileged in being notified by telephone); once the warning had been sounded everyone was expected to take cover; after that the townspeople were left to their own devices. The number of hours spent in the dug-outs depended on the Boers' energy and the weather, but they were invariably periods of unrelieved boredom.

During these early days, Sarah was able to while away her time listening to the town gossips. Stories of near-misses and lucky escapes were legion. The day after Sarah arrived, a trooper had been standing in some stables singing 'Down among the dead men' to his seated companions when a shell exploded; the trooper was killed instantly but his companions were practically unscathed. Another shell landed on Mr Weil's store, leaving the staff uninjured but carrying an account book from the counter and depositing it on a near-by roof. A splinter from the shell that exploded on Sarah's dugout had flown into a house opposite, destroying a sewing maching at which a girl had been working three minutes earlier. Another splinter from the same shell had taken a canary and its cage and dropped them in the next street. . . . The behaviour of animals under fire provided another fund of stories. There was the post-office monkey who would scuttle from his perch when the shell warning sounded and hide under a biscuit tin; the Resident Commissioner's dog would leave her dinner and dive into a dugout at the sound of the alarm; other dogs would gaily chase the flying shrapnel. . . .

For all this, Sarah was under no illusions about the seriousness of the bombardments. The jauntiness with which she had entered Mafeking did not last for long. 'The siege of Mafeking is no joke . . .' she wrote to England. 'Death is ever present with us, a stern reality. Do we but cross the street we cannot tell whether we shall not be suddenly struck down from an unexpected quarter or maimed for life, and this in spite of prudence and precautions. For in a siege of this duration one cannot live an entirely underground existence; business and duties must be gone through with, although it sometimes staggers me to see how unconcernedly men walk about the streets whistling and joking in the intervals of shelling, to note the clang, clang of the blacksmith's anvil, close to my bomb-proof, before even the noise of the explosion has died away—and to watch the happy unconcern of the black boys, whose lively chatter is wholly undisturbed by these terrible missiles. While the damage done is marvellously little—owing to the wide streets—most houses show signs of shelling.'

Like the rest of the town, Sarah looked forward to the interval of peace that came with nightfall. She considered the half hour between sunset and moonrise to be the most pleasant of the day. Herds of mules would be driven along the dusty streets to be watered; cattle and goats would return from the veld. The townsfolk would sit on the steps or on the sandbags of their shelters, chatting and fanning themselves in the cool evening breeze. Some bolder spirits—women shopping, men on duty—would hurry through the streets, keeping close to the sides of the houses. Then, when the sun had set, the last hour's bombardment would commence, the thunder of the guns made all the more terrifying by the echoing darkness.

Sunday was a day of peace. By a bizarre mating of Christianity with war, the Boers had refused to fight on the Sabbath. Their demand for a Sunday truce had been accepted somewhat warily by the beleaguered town. 'I suppose,' suggested one smug patriot, 'we are the only two nations who would observe it.' However, Mafeking was quick to take advantage of this singular situation. Dressed in their Sunday clothes, people would saunter about the town, meeting friends, entertaining at afternoon teas and relaxing, as one of them put it, 'with the knowledge that one might walk anywhere without being killed at any moment and carried to the cemetery sewn up in a sheet on a truck a few hours later.'

On her first Sunday, Sarah was up and on a pony by 6 a.m. She and Gordon rode out to inspect the defences of the town with a group of army officers. After breakfast she attended morning service at the spruce little Anglican church which, except for a few splintered rafters, had thus far escaped the shelling. The hospital, which Sarah visited immediately afterwards, had not been so lucky. Together with the Catholic convent next door, it had attracted more than its share of shells. This was due largely to the prominence of the convent; as the only two-storeyed building in Mafeking it provided a natural target for the Boer gunners. From the very beginning of the bombardment, all buildings in the vicinity of the convent had been subjected to unremitting shelling. Sarah was conducted over the hospital by the youthful-looking matron, Miss Hill. This young woman, with her handful of nurses, had won the admiration of the entire town. In an inadequate, overcrowded hospital, with a minimum of medical supplies, they had created an oasis of cool efficiency amid the horrors of the siege. Their treatment of badly maimed patients was harassed by the incessant bombardment. Shortly after Sarah visited the hospital, a shell landed in a ward where a serious operation was taking place; by some miracle none of the patients was injured, but a woman who had previously been wounded by a Mauser bullet died of fright.

In the afternoon Sarah was able to witness a brighter side of siege life. At a gymkhana on the Recreation Ground, she mingled with a holiday crowd cheering on competitors in sporting events: tilting-at-the-ring, lemon cutting and tug-of-war. Baden-Powell, in evening dress and a comic hat, was enjoying himself immensely. Flourishing a long ring-master's whip, he jollied along competitors, joked with spectators and served tea to all and sundry from a travelling wagon. Dinner at Dixon's Hotel that evening was no less gay. Food was surprisingly plentiful: fresh tomatoes, young cabbages, beef and eggs, 'even', says Sarah, 'the stocks of Schweppes soda-water appearing inexhaustible'. Seated at table, surrounded by old friends, she felt as if no time at all had elapsed since she had left the town two months earlier.

And within a few weeks of her return, it was to seem as though she had never known a different way of life.

*

The inhabitants of Mafeking were beginning to think of Christmas. To some it looked like being a bleak affair. Sarah's impression of abundance was by no means shared by everyone. 'Provisions are getting short,' noted one. 'All luxuries are eaten up, so no Christmas, except for a plain one, even to the pudding. Eggs cost 5/- per dozen, butter and beastly tinned Danish stuff... smelling ten yards off goes at the price of 6/- per lb. Cow's milk very scarce.'

But Sarah welcomed the approaching season as an excellent time in which to make herself useful. Many of the poorer women were housed in a laager on the outskirts of the town and, when visiting them, Sarah had been touched by the pale, hungry-looking children who were forced to spend their days in underground shelters. Christmas, she decided, would provide an opportunity for organizing a children's treat. With a committee of energetic women, she explored the town's resources. Old toys were unearthed and renovated, lengths of ribbon, bunting and coloured paper were draped, bunched and twisted to decorate the Masonic Hall. Mr Ben Weil was approached to donate provisions and a Christmas tree; an army of women set to work baking cakes, puddings and mince pies. Officers of the Protectorate Regiment were roped in to provide transport to and from the women's laager, while Captain Cowan and the officers of the Bechuanaland Rifles agreed to form a band for carol singing. Even Captain Cowan's capricious sister, Thomasina—the young lady who had whimsically offered herself in temporary exchange for Sarah—was badgered into assisting at what she called 'Lady Sarah Wilson's Bean Feast'. This was something of a triumph for Sarah, whose popularity among the officers was greatly resented by Thomasina—the one-time darling of the officers' mess. 'Lady Sarah Wilson was flirting about usually with three men in her wake carrying candles (I mean cameras,' Thomasina noted in her diary shortly after Sarah's arrival. 'We were in the officers' tent and the best thing *we* had was a cup of tea.'

Christmas Day fell on a Monday. It was by no means certain that the Boers would observe a truce (their own festival usually being held on New Year's Day), so Mafeking decided to celebrate a day earlier. On Wednesday, 20 December, a notice appeared in the *Mafeking Mail* inviting children between the ages of three and thirteen to a party to be held the following Sunday between 4 p.m. and 6 p.m.

Over two hundred and fifty children turned up. They were brought from the laager, shrieking, cheering and waving Union Jacks, in gaily decorated brakes driven by Baden-Powell's officers. A prize had been offered for the fastest run and was won, to everyone's delight, by popular Captain Ronald Vernon. The entire town turned out to welcome the youngsters. Baden-Powell, the Mayor, the nurses, the nuns, all joined in singing carols, serving tea and pulling home-made crackers. The high-spot came when each child marched solemnly up to the sparkling Christmas tree to receive a gift from Sarah.

In spite of gloomy predictions, the traditional Christmas on the following day was a huge success. The Boers observed the truce and most people in Mafeking sat down to a hearty Christmas dinner. Sarah and Gordon entertained Baden-Powell, Ben Weil and seven officers to luncheon. 'By a strange and fortunate chance,' says Sarah, 'a turkey had been overlooked by Mr Weil when the Government commandeered all livestock and foodstuffs at the commencement of the siege, and, in spite of the grilling heat, we completed our Christmas dinner by a real English plum-pudding.' In a photograph taken after the meal, only Sarah—stiff-backed in a wicker chair, wearing a wide-brimmed felt hat—seems suitably dressed. The men, in an assortment of cloth caps, collarless shirts and waistcoats, appear to have abandoned themselves to the heat and the plum-pudding. 'We had,' says one of them, 'a great feast.' For some, however, this Christmas dinner was to be their last.

On the previous evening, as Sarah had walked home from the children's party, she had been accompanied by Ronald Vernon. This lively officer, whose high spirits had made him the hero of the day, had been in an expansive mood. Taking Sarah by the arm, he had talked excitedly about his squadron's eagerness for action. Then he had told her, in strict confidence, about a plan to attack a Boer gun emplacement to the north of the town. The sortie was to be made at Game Tree Hill. It was scheduled for the early hours of Boxing Day.

Christmas night was cool and clear. As the sun rose, the sleeping town was wakened by the distant rappings of Maxims and the faint crackle of rifle-fire. Sarah was up immediately. She telephoned headquarters to ask if Baden-Powell and his staff were there. She was told that they had left at 2.30. The assault on Game Tree Hill had begun.

From the roof of Weil's house there was a clear view of the little hill, surmounted by its solitary tree. As soon as the firing had started, Weil's cockney manservant had climbed on to the roof to watch the fighting; every so often he would hurry down to describe the action to Sarah. His reports were not encouraging. Soon it became obvious that something had gone seriously wrong. The British armoured train had come to a halt in front of the Boer position and there were no signs of the men who should have been storming the fort. Reinforcements were being brought up from behind the enemy lines. Sarah, torn by anxiety, paced up and down. Gordon was among the attacking force, as were most of her friends. 'Are you scared, lady?' asked the little cockney. She was too preoccupied to answer.

For two agonizing hours the firing continued; then it petered out. Weil's servant came down to report that the British were retreating and that ambulances could be seen on the field. The Boers were still entrenched on the hill.

As the men straggled back the dismal story unfolded. A combination of bad scouting, ambiguous information and security leakages had led them into a hopeless position. The Boers had been fully prepared for what should have been a surprise attack. The armoured train, which should have covered the enemy from behind, had been brought to a halt by the tearing up of the line. The Boer fort, which had been described as little more than a dugout, had been protected by an 8-ft. wall of sandbags. The force holding it had been strengthened during the night. After a few valiant charges, the British had been ordered to withdraw. Hopelessly outnumbered and exposed to the enemy's guarded fire, they had not stood a chance.

At ten o'clock the armoured train returned to the station opposite Sarah's dugout. It had brought back the dead and wounded. Out of a force of a hundred men, the casualties numbered almost fifty; twenty-four men and officers killed, between twenty and thirty wounded. It was a serious loss for the tiny garrison. Among the dead was Sarah's friend, Captain Ronald Vernon. Having been twice wounded, he had continued to lead his men until, on reaching the enemy trench, he was killed by a third bullet. His squadron—C Squadron—had suffered the most severe losses.

As the slow stream of limping men and covered stretchers left the station, Sarah was numbed by the contrast to the light-heartedness of the day before. 'I could hardly realize in particular the death of Captain Vernon,' she said, 'who had been but a few hours before so full of health, spirit and confidence.'

But she spent little time brooding. There was much to be done. Hearing of the chaos at the hospital, she offered her services to Miss Hill. She was given the task of clearing the wards of convalescents, to make room for the wounded. It was decided to house these patients in the Railway Institute near the station, and Sarah, with a trained nurse, Miss Crauford, and four other women, set to work to prepare the hall for their reception. There were no beds, no crockery, no cooking utensils and no food. Once again Mr Weil, that 'universal provider', came to the rescue. From his inexhaustible store he managed to provide all that was needed. Everything arrived at once—the equipment, the food and the hospital wagons bringing the patients. Confusion was at its height when Creaky thundered forth. The shell soared over the approaching ambulance and landed about a hundred yards from the improvised hospital. The workers and patients took the explosion in their stride. By working non-stop, they managed to get the place in order by sunset. Arrangements were made for Miss Crauford to attend every day and the four women to take a day's duty in turn; Sarah was to be there at all times to supervise the running of the place.

Running back to her quarters that evening, Sarah was stopped short by the sound of bugles repeating the Last Post. 'In the still atmosphere of a calm and beautiful evening,' she says, 'I knew the last farewells were being said to the brave men who had gone to their last rest.'

*

'Of course Mafeking's losses on that Black Boxing Day were infinitesimal compared to those attending the terrible struggles going on in other parts of the country,' Sarah was to write; 'but, then, it must be remembered that not only was our garrison a very small one, but also that, when people are shut up together for months in a beleaguered town—a handful of Englishmen and women surrounded by enemies, with even spies in their midst—the feeling of comradeship and friendship is tremendously strengthened. Every individual was universally known, and therefore all the town felt they had lost their own friends, and mourned them as such.'

Yet, grievous as was the outcome, it did nothing to disspirit the defenders. If anything, the courage shown by the troops strengthened their resolve to hold on. Of more concern was the increased activity of the besieging force. If Mafeking did not regard Game Tree Hill as a defeat, Snyman was not allowed to claim it as a victory. Having assured Pretoria that the town was throroughly demoralized, the unexpected spirit shown by Baden-Powell's force had earned him a sharp rebuke. He was urged to intensify the bombardment. As the old year drew to a close, a war correspondent noted: 'The authorities in Pretoria had sent to the commandant of the Boer forces investing us a New Year's gift of three wagon-loads of ammunition. A new gun was also despatched to them, and its position being constantly shifted, its fire has since played upon every quarter of the town.'

New Year's Day, which had been confidently expected as a day of truce, saw the opening of this new offensive. The marksmanship of the Boers seemed to improve, and rumour had it that this was because of the expert advice of Petrus Viljoen. Sarah refused to credit this. She was always to maintain that the Boers had wanted Viljoen for some past offence. All the same it must have been something of a relief to hear, shortly afterwards, that the horse-thief had been killed in battle.

Sarah experienced the full weight of the increased bombardment. Between her bomb-proof shelter and the Railway Institute, where she now worked every day, there was a foundry which manufactured primitive shells. The enemy knew of this factory and kept it under constant fire. Sarah was forced to run the gauntlet of bursting shrapnel and rifle fire whenever she went on duty. 'I had some very exciting walks to and fro,' she remarks modestly, 'very often alone, but sometimes accompanied by some chance visitor.' On reaching the convalescent home she was by no means free from danger. The area surrounding the railway station was a favourite target with the Boer gunners. On 16 January, for example, no less than thirty-four shells were placed in or about the Railway Institute. Rather characteristically, Sarah says little about the hazards of these days, but others have testified to her bravery. 'She ran some considerable risks,' said Baden-Powell. '. . . Once she had just finished moving some men out of a tea room into the recreation room when a shell arrived and carried away the whole place where they had just left.' 'Lady Sarah,' says another account, 'regarded the explosions with an equanimity hardly outdone by the onlookers at Crystal Palace fireworks.'

In January Sarah's difficulties multiplied. Miss Crauford, now recognized as one the town's most efficient nurses, was asked to take charge of a hospital in the woman's laager. This left Sarah in sole charge of the Railway Institute. Then, two weeks later, Gordon was added to the invalids in her care: having survived the Game Tree Hill assault, he suddenly collapsed under a sharp attack of peritonitis. There was no room at the hospital and it was decided that he should recuperate in Sarah's dugout. The strain of nursing him, attending the convalescents and sleeping in the dank shelter were too much even for the hardy Sarah. Just as Gordon began to mend, she caught a chill which was aggravated by a sore throat and mild attacks of fever. 'I managed, however, to go about as usual,' she says, 'but one afternoon, when I was feeling wretchedly ill, our hospital attendant came rushing in to say that a shell had almost demolished the convalescent home, and that, in fact, only the walls were standing. The patients mercifully escaped, owing to them all being in the bomb-proof, but they had to be moved in a great hurry, and were accommodated at the convent. For weeks past this building had not been shot at, and it was therefore considered a safe place for them, as it was hoped the Boer gunner had learned to respect the hospital, its near neighbour.'

Within a few days both she and Gordon were ordered to join the patients in the convent. The continuing heavy rains made the stifling shelters extremely unhealthy. Fever and dysentery had spread through the town; an outbreak of typhoid in the women's laager had caused great alarm. The doctors insisted that Sarah and Gordon remove themselves above ground. With Gordon still too weak to walk, they were driven through heavy shelling to the bomb-scarred convent. Here, at the end of a corridor on the upper floor, they were given two small rooms which, they were assured, were safe from shelling.

The nuns, who had been forced to abandon the convent during the earlier bombardments, were in constant attendance. Although they were a teaching order they had devoted themselves to nursing from the beginning of the siege. With the extra convalescents on the lower floor, they now had their hands full. Nevertheless, they found time to make the Wilsons comfortable. Sarah, a staunch Protestant, was full of admiration for these 'kind, excellent ladies who have been unceasing in their efforts to assist the over-taxed nursing staff of the hospital'. Over half a century later, two bright-eyed elderly nuns, who had been novices during the siege, remembered Sarah with affection. 'She was,' declared one of them, 'a lady in every sense of the word. I have never met anyone so easily pleased as Lady Sarah Wilson. She went out of her way to avoid giving us any unnecessary work.'

But the convent proved a disturbed haven. Baden-Powell had taken advantage of its deserted upper storey to post look-outs in the empty rooms. From her quarters at the end of the corridor, Sarah could hear the men shouting to each other as they watched the Boer gunner through a telescope. On her first night, having just crawled thankfully into bed, she was suddenly brought to her feet by the sound of heavy boots clattering along the wooden passage. A voice shouted: 'The gun is pointed at the convent!' Then Creaky belched forth. The shell went soaring over the building and buried itself in a cloud of dust close to a herd of cattle half a mile away. It was not, as Sarah says, 'a very reassuring experience on my first night above ground.'

She came to dread the setting of the sun. 'There was something very eerie in the long nights,' she says, 'for after the sudden fall of darkness no lights were allowed for fear of drawing fire. Occasionally the intense quiet would be broken by a volley from the enemy . . . lasting for ten minutes, and then dropping to single shots fired at intervals. Unable to sleep from pain, I would creep down the pitch-dark corridor, and peep out, through a jagged hole marking the entry of a shell—on the mysterious moon-lit veld—until at length would come the blessed daylight.'

But it was in the early evening that she had her narrowest escape. January 26 was a day of vicious shelling. It started early in the morning when a shell all but demolished Bradley's Hotel. Late that afternoon, as Sarah and Gordon were about to sit down to their evening meal, Major Goold-Adams paid them an unexpected visit. The three of them were chatting when Creaky opened up. Within seconds there was a terrifying din above their heads and the wall against which they were sitting caved in. 'I was aware that masses of falling brick and masonry were pushing me our of my chair,' says Sarah, '. . . . that all was darkness and suffocating dust. I remember distinctly that after my head had been hit twice by something hard and heavy, putting up my hands, clasped to shelter it, and then I recollect my relief to find the bricks had ceased to fall. My next thought was for my companions, and the moments seemed years before the voice of first one, and then another came out of the darkness —"All right! How are you?" . . . the feeling of relief I shall never forget.'

A rescue party quickly appeared and dragged them out. Dazed, covered with brick dust, they were led downstairs. Sarah had been cut on the head and the two men bruised. When their room was examined the following day, it was found that some two tons of bricks and mortar had fallen into a space no more than five feet square. Against the legs of Sarah's chair, they discovered two enormous pieces of shell, each weighing fifteen pounds. Only by the fact that their chairs had been against the wall and not drawn up to the supper table had their lives been saved.

Not surprisingly, Sarah left the convent that evening. Back in her bomb-proof shelter she slept more soundly than she had done for many a night past.

If nothing else, their days at the convent had restored both Sarah and Gordon to health. By the time they returned to the shelter they were both on their feet and it was not long before Sarah was as active as ever.

In addition to her other duties, she was now a regular correspondent for the *Daily Mail*. Her forebodings about the reckless Mr Hellawell, the *Mail*'s official correspondent, had proved all too justified. Riding south from Mafeking in the middle of December, he had been surrounded and taken prisoner. Although he managed to escape in the darkness, he had been discovered at Vryburg and eventually sent to Pretoria. The editor of the *Daily Mail* had then wired Sarah, asking her to share the duties of correspondent with Mr Whales, editor of the *Mafeking Mail*. Her lively despatches were later described as 'one of the sensations of the war'. Unlike the reports of other correspondents, hers were free from complicated military detail and graphically reflected the views of Mafeking's civilian population. They were also surprisingly professional. In one of her early despatches she forcefully depicted the apprehension, resignation and defiance that prevailed during the early months of 1900.

'No doubt,' she wrote, 'books without end will be written about this siege—I have already heard of ten or twelve would-be authors—and of the military and political aspects, which will probably prove of the utmost importance, I have no wish to discourse; but I think it may interest friends at home to hear how a handful of Englishmen and Englishwomen have passed the last three months in this little town on the bare veld, closely invested by a force which at first outnumbered the besieged by about ten to one. . . . The burghers' advance trenches have been but a mile from the fringe of this little town, and it was rather a shock to me to see their white tents gleaming in the sun at this unpleasantly near locality. Walking abroad is, in consequence, anything but a joy, as some days and nearly always in the evening, the Mauser bullets whistle through the streets and the Market Square, ringing sharply on the corrugated iron roofs, and this, apart from the incessant shelling. . . Everyone is now more or less resigned to an indefinite prolongation of the siege. We have food and provisions in plenty, and have ceased to believe the many fairy tales of approaching army corps, brought in by sanguine natives, and look for assistance, which is no doubt more required elsewhere. . . . As to our soldiers, they may no doubt think they would like more fighting, though it seems to me there has been enough here to satisfy most people—they may grumble at being cooped up in this little town—but when the history of this war comes to be written, people who should know are of the opinion that Mafeking will be found to have played no small part in the huge task of holding South Africa.'

Reports were sent out of Mafeking with remarkable frequency throughout the siege, but the task of carrying them was not undertaken lightly. Messengers were not always easy to find. One of the notable aspects of Sarah's reporting was her ability to get her despatches forwarded. 'During the whole course of the siege,' states a contemporary history of the war, 'Lady Sarah often managed to get her messages through when it was out of the power of other correspondents to do so, and her descriptions of life in the besieged town were full of brightness and point.'

Nor was her correspondence entirely one way. She received almost as many letters and telegrams as she sent. Indeed, some of the information smuggled into Mafeking hardly seems worth the risks involved. In the middle of February, for example, Sarah received a letter from Cecil Rhodes, who was similarly shut up in the besieged town of Kimberley. Rhodes's letter had to pass through the enemy lines outside Kimberley as well as those surrounding Mafeking. 'Just a line to say I often think of you,' he wrote. 'We play bridge every evening. I wonder do you, it takes your mind off hospitals, burials and shells. . .'

A more encouraging telegram which reached Mafeking in February was addressed to Baden-Powell. It arrived at the end of the month and was Queen Victoria's personal message congratulating the garrison on its stand. Coming as it did, direct from the Queen and not through one of her ministers, it was a source of pride to the entire town. Even more important, it made the defenders realize the significant part they were thought to be playing in the war: much to their surprise, they found that they were considered heroes. 'I really think,' says Sarah, 'that no one except a shipwrecked mariner, cast away on a desert island, and suddenly perceiving a friendly sail, could have followed our feelings of delight on the occasion. We walked about thinking we must be dreaming.'

But perhaps the most comforting message for Sarah that

month was the one which came from her sister-in-law, Lady Randolph Churchill. In a telegram sent from Cape Town, Lady Randolph was able to give Sarah news that she had been longing to receive. 'Very grateful; your wire first direct news of family received,' Sarah telegraphed back. 'We receive scanty news. Please wire again. Congratulate you on Winston's plucky escape.'

By the time Sarah's reply reached her, Lady Randolph had left Cape Town. She was travelling on a hospital ship and had just arrived in Durban.

CHAPTER FIFTEEN

Churchills in the Maine

LADY RANDOLPH had heard of her son's successful escape from the Boers the day before she sailed from England. On 15 December the editor of the *Morning Post* had telephoned her to say that Winston had broken out of the Staatsmodelskool and eight days later, 23 December, she received the news of his safe arrival at Lourenço Marques.

When the telephone rang on this second occasion she was busy making final arrangements for her voyage to South Africa. Picking up the receiver, she was mystified to know what the call from the *Morning Post* was about. 'All I could hear,' she says, 'was "Hurrah! Hurrah!" repeated by different voices, as one after another seized the instrument in their kind wish to congratulate me.' The news could not have been more timely. Worry about her son had added considerably to the anxieties of her departure. Never a good organizer, she had been in a state of despair over the hitches that had arisen as the time approached for her to leave. Now, despite petty irritations, she could sail for the Cape with a reasonably light heart.

The voyage had been planned some two months earlier. At the outbreak of war, she had been approached by an American woman, Mrs Blow, to help in a scheme for sending a hospital ship to South Africa. Mrs Blow had lived for some years in South Africa and was anxious to involve her fellow Americans in the war effort: inevitably she had picked upon Jennie Churchill, probably the best-known American woman in London, to assist her. The idea had not, at first, appealed to Lady Randolph. She had recently started an ambitious literary magazine, *The Anglo-Saxon Review*, and, being fully occupied with this, she had been inclined to regard the hospital-ship project as impracticable. However, on talking it over with an army friend, she had decided to give it more serious consideration. Her emotional links with the war in South Africa might also have influenced her. For, not only had her son been sent to cover the fighting by the *Morning Post*, but he had been followed a few days later by George Cornwallis-West, a twenty-five-year-old Guards officer whose periodic proposals of marriage the widowed Lady Randolph was beginning to find difficult to ignore. Whatever sparked it off, once her enthusiasm has been aroused it was wholehearted.

Lady Randolph Churchill, at forty-five, was still a beautiful and spirited woman. It was to her dark good looks and vital personality, as much as her title, that she owed the social prominence which she continued to enjoy after Lord Randolph's death. She could thus bring, not only talent and enthusiasm to the hospital-ship project, but a great many influential contacts. At the first committee meeting, held at her home on 25 October to launch a fund-raising campaign, she was elected chairman. Among the American-born women at this meeting, her family was well represented: her two sisters, Clara and Leonie, her niece by marriage, the young Duchess of Marlborough, and her sister-in-law, Lily, Duchess of Marlborough, were all elected to the executive. A resolution was passed to the effect that, while regretting the necessity for war, the American women in London would endeavour to raise 'a fund for the relief of the sick and wounded soldiers and refugees in South Africa'. The money was to come from Americans in England as well as in the United States. 'It is proposed to despatch immediately,' the resolution went on, 'a suitable hospital ship, fully equipped with medical stores and provisions, to accommodate 200 people, with a staff of four doctors, five nurses, and forty non-commissioned officers and orderlies.' The target aimed at was £30,000.

The ship was provided by Mr Bernard N. Baker, President of the Atlantic Transport Company, who had placed a similar ship at the disposal of the United States Government during the Spanish-American war of 1898. It was a small trans-Atlantic steamer, conveniently named *Maine* after the United States battleship that had mysteriously exploded in Havana harbour and thus sparked off America's war with Spain. 'Remember the *Maine*' was still an emotive slogan in America; the women adopted it for their fund-raising campaign. Even so, it was not easy to interest Americans in sending a hospital ship to South Africa. 'It would be useless to deny...' wrote Lady Randolph, 'that the war was viewed with disfavour by my countrymen. They had a fellow-feeling for the Boer, fighting, as they thought, for his independence.' She met with several rebuffs from American business friends and her request to President McKinley for an American flag was politely turned down. Nevertheless, by a series of well-organized concerts, matinées and other entertainments, the women were quickly able to raise the money needed. On 19 November, after a highly successful concert at Claridge's Hotel—attended by Lady Randolph's friend, the Prince of Wales—it was announced that 'the Fund now stands at £20,000. Within a month this had been increased to well over £40,000.

At a widely publicized launching ceremony, the Duke of Connaught presented the *Maine* with a Union Jack from Queen Victoria, and Lady Randolph, disregarding the piratical implications of sailing under two flags, took it upon herself to hoist the Stars and Stripes. The Sunday before sailing the public was allowed to inspect the ship. Loading arrangements were extremely disorganized and the invasion of some 10,000 sightseers in one day considerably added to the confusion. 'Perhaps the most comfortable part of the ship,' remarked a visitor, 'is given over to Lady Randolph Churchill, whose cabin is decorated in a manner suggestive of a lady's boudoir, rich in the luxuries of silken hangings and cushions.' To match her elegant quarters, Lady Randolph had designed an equally *chic* uniform for herself: a crisp white jacket and skirt, embroidered blouse and a starched white cap. She gave the impression of calm efficiency but, as she was the first to admit, this outward show was extremely deceptive. Management was not her strong point. Hardly a day passed without some crisis or other. A climax was reached when, shortly before the ship sailed, three of the male orderlies walked off in protest at having to act as waiters for the medical officers. It is hardly surprising that her sister, who went to see her off, reported her as looking tired and depressed.

The first few days at sea did little to cheer her. They ran straight into a terrifying gale which lasted unremittingly for six days. 'I never realized before how one can suffer by colour,' she wrote. 'The green of my attractive little cabin which I had thought so reposeful became a source of acute suffering, and I have to find a quiet, neutral-tinted cushion on which to rest my eyes. The sound of the waves breaking on deck with the report of cannon balls brought to my mind our mission, and I thought, as I rolled in sleepless wretchedness, if we go to the bottom, at least we shall be counted as victims of the war.' After leaving Las Palmas, the weather improved and for the next seventeen days they were kept fully occupied in restoring the ship to order. To the chaos created by the over-loading of stores was added the damage done by the storm. At times it seemed as if they would never be in a fit state to receive patients. 'In the hurry of departure,' she lamented, 'many things were forgotten and many put anywhere to be out of the way. We had very little time before us to appear ship-shape. . . It seems to me a ship goes through the same troubles as a dirty child—as soon as its unwilling face is washed and it is dressed up for the day, either the elements or its own antics make it dirty again and the process has to be repeated.'

The arrival of the *Maine* in Cape Town was somewhat overshadowed by the fact that it followed in the wake of a far more important ship. After the disasters of 'Black Week,' Lord Roberts had been appointed to supersede Sir Redvers Buller as Commander-in-chief in South Africa. Roberts and his Chief of Staff, Lord Kitchener (now a peer and the idol of the British public after his successes in Egypt) had sailed for South Africa in the *Dunottar Castle*, which had left England at the same time as the *Maine* but had reached Cape Town almost two weeks earlier. The arrival of these two distinguished officers had given new heart to the floundering British cause: they were still in Cape Town and were the centre of much attention when the *Maine* docked on 22 January.

Lady Randolph was greatly impressed on arriving at the 'seat of war'. Cape Town's bay was crowded with transport ships disembarking troops, the docks bustled with activity and the streets were full of khaki-clad soldiers. It seemed, she said, 'indeed the real thing'. This sense of purpose was not so apparent at Government House, where she was entertained to dinner by Sir Alfred Milner. As had been the case when Winston Churchill had called on the Governor of the Cape, Milner was plagued with doubts about loyalty in Cape Town and tended to see spies everywhere. 'I was struck by the melancholy

Lady Randolph Churchill and the wounded John Churchill on board the hospital ship 'Maine' at Durban

South African Library

A little-known photograph of Winston Churchill as an officer
of the South African Light Horse

Cape Argus

oppressing everyone,' wrote Lady Randolph. 'The absence of news that day was making all anxious.'

The *Maine* was instructed to proceed to Durban as soon as it had refuelled. The coaling operations took two days and during that time Lady Randolph and her staff were invited to a reception given at the Mount Nelson Hotel by a committee of American ladies. 'It was very pleasant,' noted Lady Randolph, 'eating strawberries and walking about the pretty garden.' The day before the ship sailed Lord Roberts and Lord Kitchener sent word that they wanted to inspect the hospital arrangements. By that time some sort of order had been imposed below decks; after a tour of the wards, mess rooms, dispensary and operating room, the Commander-in-Chief was able to signify his approval. 'All we wanted,' said Lady Randolph, 'were the beds filled with wounded, to prove our efficiency.'

The inordinate time it had taken the *Maine* to reach South Africa was not without its compensations. It enabled Lady Randolph to be joined in Cape Town by her younger son, Jack. Like most young Englishmen, the nineteen-year-old Jack Churchill had long been seeking an opportunity to join the army in South Africa. After the depressing news of 'Black Week' he, together with thousands of others, had enlisted in the Yeomanry but there had seemed little chance of his seeing active service until his brother Winston, shortly after arriving back in Natal, wangled him a commission in the South African Light Horse. Upon learning that this post was waiting for him, he had wired Winston to let him know he was on his way; then, sporting a wide-brimmed hat and hung about with rifles and revolvers, he had caught the next ship to Cape Town. He had left Southampton on 6 January—two weeks after his mother—but had arrived at the Cape in time to beg a lift to Durban in the *Maine*.

Accompanied by Jack and expecting soon to be reunited with Winston, Lady Randolph had good reason to be pleased that she had come to South Africa. Only one small cloud threatened her domestic horizon. At Las Palmas she had learned that her young admirer, George Cornwallis-West, had left South Africa. Having spent some three weeks at the front, Lieutenant Cornwallis-West had suffered sun-stroke and, failing to recover after ten days in hospital, he had been invalided home.

The s.s. *Pannonia* in which he had returned to England must have passed the *Maine* somewhere at sea.

The voyage to Durban was rough. Once again the staff of the *Maine* battled to keep on their feet in a hailstorm which, at times, appeared to bring the ship to a stop. There was such a heavy swell when they reached Durban that they were told it would not be possible for them to enter harbour until the following morning. This proved too much for young Jack Churchill. Anxious for news, he and one of the ship's officers set off for shore in a small steam launch. 'Luckily,' says Lady Randolph, 'they were hailed by a tug, with a midshipman on board . . . who was the bearer of a message to me from Captain Percy Scott, to the effect that my son Winston was in Durban, having come on two days' leave from Frere to meet me.'

When they landed the following day, Lady Randolph decided to take advantage of the short wait before her patients arrived to snatch a few days' rest. She had an invitation to stay with the Governor of Natal, Sir Walter Hely-Hutchinson, and Winston had arranged for the necessary passes which would allow her to travel up-country. That evening, accompanied by her chief assistant, Miss Warrender, and her two sons, she left for Pietermaritzburg. She spent two days at Government House: it gave her time to relax and to catch up with Winston's news. He had a great deal to tell her.

*

Two days before the *Maine* had arrived at Cape Town it had sighted a small steamer sailing in the opposite direction. Following the by then established custom, the *Maine* had signalled for news. 'Buller crossed the Tugela,' was the reply. 'Ladysmith rumoured relieved. Continued fighting.' It had not been very satisfactory and, on reaching Cape Town, they had found that most people there were almost as vague as to what was happening in Natal. As Lady Randolph had noted, it was the absence of definite news that had added to Sir Alfred Milner's depression. All that was certain was that, contrary to Lord Roberts's specific orders, General Buller had embarked upon a new campaign to relieve Ladysmith. Arriving at Durban, Lady Randolph had rejoiced at being in the 'active zone' and confidently expected some reassurance from the men on the spot. But, as she quickly discovered, the news was as uncertain in Natal as it had been in the Cape. The midshipman who had reported that Winston was in Durban was extremely pessimistic. 'There was,' he told them, 'no fresh news or change in the military situation . . . Ladysmith had neither fallen nor was relieved. The enemy's big guns were firing with the same monotonous regularity, and we were adding steadily to the list of our reverses.' Winston, however, was able to provide a more detailed explanation. He had been very much involved in the recent fighting; as a war correspondent he had been well placed to observe the muddled campaign that had started shortly after his return to Natal.

No one had been more anxious to meet Churchill after his escape than Sir Redvers Buller. The General greatly admired his daring. 'He really is a fine fellow . . .' Buller wrote to Lady Londonderry, 'I wish he was leading irregular troops instead of writing for a rotten paper.' This wish was soon realized. After examining Churchill on conditions in the Transvaal, the General asked if there was anything the authorities could do for him. Needless to say, Churchill had a request ready. He asked for a commission in one of the irregular corps that were being formed. The idea of a war correspondent doubling as an army officer was highly unorthodox but, after some humming and hawing, Buller agreed to his serving under Colonel Byng in the South African Light Horse. 'You will have to do as much as you can for both jobs,' he said. 'But you will get no pay for ours.'

Churchill was thrilled. The Boers had insisted upon treating him as a combatant and now, once again, he was one. The officers in the South African Light Horse wore a large slouch hat, decorated with a coloured plume; they were known as the 'Cockyollybirds'. Both the uniform and the nickname pleased Churchill. Being back in the army—even on a temporary basis— provided him with the fillip he needed. The strain of his days in hiding had evidently played havoc with his nerves. J. B. Atkins, who met him on his return to Natal, describes him as looking pale and haggard.

He responded eagerly to the challenge of relieving Ladysmith, although he was fully aware of the difficulties. The time he had spent in the Transvaal had given him a healthy respect for the enemy. In his despatches to the *Morning Post* he was full of praise for the strategy of the Boers in Natal and he made no secret of his admiration when discussing the war with his colleagues. 'I know,' reported J. B. Atkins, 'he sits in my tent with a new and lively conviction of the Boer military genius.' However, what Churchill did not bargain for was the ineptitude of his own commanders.

After his disastrous defeat at Colenso in December, Sir Redvers Buller was eventually forced to abandon the idea of crossing the Tugela at that point. The river was the main obstacle to his approach on Ladysmith. He decided to overcome it by directing his reinforced columns some 25 miles upstream, hoping to outflank Louis Botha's commandos. On 11 January, a cavalry brigade went ahead and seized some heights on the near side of the river, overlooking fordable drifts. Churchill went with them. It was nearly dark when they climbed the heights; not until the following morning were they able to take stock of their position. For his part, Churchill did not find the outlook reassuring. The river was indeed fordable but beyond it a range of hills barred the approach to Ladysmith; the hills gave the Boers an excellent defensive position. Churchill estimated that a frontal attack would cost at least 3,000 men. However, like the others, he consoled himself with the thought that the Commander-in-Chief had a few extra tricks up his sleeve.

But Buller hardly had a plan, let alone extra tricks. In a situation calling for a swift, mobile force, his main concern seemed to be for the baggage accompanying the forward troops. 'The vast amount of baggage this army takes with it on the march,' wrote Churchill, 'hampers its movements and utterly precludes all possibility of surprising the enemy ... roads are crowded, drifts are blocked, marching troops are delayed, and all rapidity of movement is out of the question. Meanwhile, the enemy completes the fortification of his positions, and the cost of capturing them rises. It is poor economy to let a soldier live well for three days at the price of killing him on the fourth.' Buller thought otherwise. Four valuable days were lost in bringing up unnecessary supplies.

A crossing of the Tugela was made on 17 January. It was a slow business. Sir Charles Warren, the eccentric Lieutenant-General in charge of the operation, was as baggage-conscious as Buller and insisted upon bridges being built to get his wagons across. One way and another the enemy was given plenty of time to prepare. The following evening Churchill took part in a skirmish in which some twenty-odd Boer prisoners were taken. The sight of these captives filled him with elation: it seemed to compensate for some of the men he had left behind at the Staatsmodelskool. This sense of triumph did not last long. At the sight of the Boer dead—a grey-haired Veld-Kornet, clutching a letter from his wife, lying next to a seventeen-year-old boy, shot through the heart—he was overcome with remorse. 'Ah, horrible war,' he concluded his letter to the *Morning Post*, 'amazing medley of the glorious and the squalid, the pitiful and the sublime, if modern men of light and leading saw your face closer, simple folk would see it hardly ever.'

The first attempt to storm the heights was made on 20 January. Warren ordered an attack on a hill to the left of the range, under cover of an artillery bombardment. Churchill was among those who reached the crest of the hill, only to discover that it levelled to a 'table-top', upon which the Boers were securely entrenched. After four hours spent trying to advance—with a loss of 300 men—the attack was called off. In a second unsuccessful attempt on the hill the following morning the British lost a further 170 men. The part played by Buller in these assaults was that of critic rather than commander. He was full of advice but reluctant to give orders. When Warren suggested a prolonged bombardment before another attack was launched, he flew into a rage and threatened to withdraw the army across the Tugela. Eventually a compromise was reached: a new attack would be made further to the right—at Spion Kop, a gently domed, rock-strewn hill which rose some 1,400 feet above the river. 'Spion Kop . . .' reported J. B. Atkins, 'was the key of the position, and the key that would open the door of Ladysmith. Patrols had reported that there were only a few Boers on it. Therefore Sir Charles Warren presented his scheme for capturing it, and it was accepted by Sir Redvers Buller.'

On the night of Tuesday, 23 January, an assault party, commanded by General Woodgate, climbed the slopes of Spion Kop in the drizzling rain. Reaching what appeared to be the top, they stumbled upon a Boer picket which they charged and put to flight. Having no other means of communication, they gave three loud cheers to signal that they were in possession of the summit.

They then started digging defence works. At daybreak, a thick mist prevented them from ascertaining their position but, at seven o'clock, it lifted sufficiently for Woodgate to realize that he had not occupied the true summit. The crest of the hill lay a hundred yards ahead of them. Not until the sun broke the mist, about an hour later, and the Boers opened fire on three sides did he appreciate how badly he had misjudged his position. Far from taking possession of the hill, his force was entrenched in the centre of the plateau; it was too late now to dig a second trench at the crest of the hill. They had to try and hold the crest as best they could. Meanwhile the Boers—alerted by the fleeing picket—had clambered up the far slope unopposed. Thus began one of the most extraordinary battles of the war.

At about ten o'clock General Woodgate was mortally wounded; for a long time uncertainty as to who was in command added to the general confusion. The Boers continued to press in; the British struggled desperately to retain their precarious foothold. From below, Warren sent up reinforcements with orders not to surrender, but made no attempt at a diversionary attack which might have relieved the pressure on Spion Kop. Buller, with an army of 30,000 at his disposal, did little more than bluster from the other side of the Tugela. As the dead piled up on the summit, and the wounded cried desperately for water, those forced to watch from the foot of the hill were filled with horror. 'I saw it from below,' says J. B. Atkins. 'I shall always have it in my memory—that acre of massacre, that complete shambles, at the top of a rich green gully with cool granite walls . . . which reached up the western side of the mountain.'

Churchill could not bear to stand idly by. During the afternoon he rode about trying to find a vantage point from which to observe the action. What he did see sickened him. At about four o'clock, he and a fellow officer rode to Warren's headquarters to find out what was happening. The first person they saw was Captain Levita, Warren's despatch officer. Churchill rushed across to him. 'For God's sake, Levita, don't let this be a second Majuba,' he panted. Levita said they were doing all they could and that he was very busy: if Churchill had any suggestions he should make them to Sir Charles Warren. Churchill did not need a second bidding. A short way from where Levita was working, Warren was pacing up and down; Churchill darted across to him and started a long harangue. But Sir Charles was in no mood to be lectured. 'Who is this man?' he shouted. 'Take him away. Put him under arrest.' In an attempt to pacify Churchill, Levita asked him to act as a messenger. Word had to be sent to the summit to tell Colonel Thorneycroft that he was now in charge; several messengers had already been sent, but Levita was not sure whether they had got through. Churchill was asked to confirm Thorneycroft's command.

Leaving their horses, Churchill and his companion began to climb the hill. They were met by a stream of wounded straggling down to the hospital tents at the foot. Arriving at the crest, they tried to crawl forward but the concentrated firing of the enemy drove them back (a bullet cut the plume on Churchill's hat). Colonel Thorneycroft already knew of his appointment and they were told that he had had to prevent his men from showing the white flag. The massacre so appalled the two men that they went tearing down the hill to report the situation.

Warren had only the vaguest idea of what was happening on Spion Kop. He had received very few messages from the summit and had made little effort to find out for himself. This time he listened glumly to what Churchill had to say. Even then he did not appear to appreciate the gravity of what he was told. However, a staff officer informed Churchill that they intended sending fresh troops up that night, who would dig in and hold the position the following day. He asked Churchill to return and tell Colonel Thorneycroft this. Churchill asked for written authority. He was given a hastily scrawled note. 'The General Officer Commanding Force,' it read, 'would be glad to have your views of the situation and measures to be adopted, by Lt. Winston Churchill, who takes this note.'

It was pitch dark when Churchill pushed his way through the never-ending stream of wounded for a second time. He found Thorneycroft sitting dejectedly on the ground at the top of the hill. By this time the firing had almost ceased: only occasionally could the crack of rifles be heard. Churchill handed over his note and gave his message. Thorneycroft listened with understandable cynicism. The promise of reinforcements was meaningless: what he needed was an assurance that Warren was working to a general plan. He had already ordered his men to retire; he saw no reason for calling the retirement off. Churchill offered to return to the base for further instructions. But it was no use. Thorneycroft had made up his mind. 'Better six good battalions safely off the hill tonight,' he said, 'than a bloody mop-up in the morning.' With Churchill at his side, he joined the long files of men stumbling down the hillside. Nearing the bottom, they met a column of men armed with picks and shovels. The officer in charge said he had a message from Sir Charles Warren. Thorneycroft asked Churchill to read it to him. The message was brief. Thorneycroft was informed that 400 sappers were on the way and Warren urged him to entrench and hold on. Waving his walking stick, Thorneycroft ordered the relieving troops to about face and join the withdrawal. At the bottom of the hill they reported to Sir Charles Warren.

But none of them was aware of the crowning humiliation. The Boers had also been taxed beyond endurance. As Thorneycroft retreated, the Boers, convinced that they had failed to dislodge the British, scrambled down the other side of the hill. Deneys Reitz, the young man who had earlier visited Churchill at the Staatsmodelskool, was among the last to leave. 'We descended the hill,' he says, 'by the way in which we had climbed up nearly 16 hours before, our feet striking at times the dead bodies in our path. When we reached the bottom most of the horses were gone, the men who had retired having taken their mounts and ridden away.'

Except for the mass of dead and wounded, the rock-strewn summit of Spion Kop was deserted. Not until a Boer patrol discovered this astonishing fact an hour or so later was Louis Botha able to rally his dispirited force and claim his hard-earned victory.

Nothing became the British generals so much as their going. 'Sir Charles Warren made his retirement memorable for speed and orderliness,' reported J. B. Atkins. 'The last group was crossing the river early on Friday morning when a Boer shell plumped into the river. It was a signal of success, but Sir Redvers Buller, who stood by, would have watched anything else in the world with the same impassivity. We had lost 1,500 odd men in a week's fighting.' The Boers, with a force a fraction the size of Buller's, were able to claim victory at the cost of 300 men.

This was the sorry tale that Churchill had to tell his mother.

He had left the Tugela as soon as the retreat had been completed. For this reason he had to return immediately. Young Jack Churchill went with him. 'It was hard,' says Lady Randolph, 'to say goodbye to the two boys.'

*

Two weeks after the disastrous battle of Spion Kop, Sir Redvers Buller made his third attempt on the hills beyond the Tugula. He blamed the earlier failures on Warren and confidently announced that he now had 'the key to Ladysmith'—a gap in the hills further to the right. An elaborate plan of attack was agreed to and operations commenced on 5 February. But hardly had the assault begun, than the General started to lose heart. For three days he vacillated and then, on 8 February, ordered another general retirement.

The Churchill brothers had watched the fighting from the near side of the river. Their cavalry contingent had been ordered forward but had not been called into action. It must have been a bitter disappointment for Jack Churchill—who had celebrated his twentieth birthday the day before the attack began—that his first experience as an active soldier should have been that of a spectator to disaster. However, his time was soon to come.

By 11 February Sir Redvers Buller had reassembled his force at Chievely, the base from which he had started a month earlier. Morale was low. In two months of fighting, Buller had involved his troops in a series of bungled battles: the beating he had taken at Colenso in December and his defeat at Spion Kop were widely regarded as the most badly managed episodes of the war. He seemed to have no idea of what was needed to combat the swift-moving Boer commandos. 'The fault of this and all other battles,' wrote J. B. Atkins after the most recent reversal, 'was the cumbrous nature of our transport. How should it be otherwise than that jam and pickles should be at a disadvantage against biltong [strips of dry meat carried by the Boers]?' To add to the depression was the knowledge that time was fast running out. News from Ladysmith made it clear that the garrison could not hold out much longer. The daily bombardments, outbreaks of enteric and dysentry had all taken their toll; the death rate was rising alarmingly. Food supplies were almost exhausted. 'If a Relief Column takes a day and a half to march a yard and a half,' quizzed the siege journal, 'how much longer will the price of eggs be 10/- per dozen?'

The ebullient Churchill, however, was unaffected by the prevailing gloom. Confident that Ladysmith would be successfully relieved, he was enjoying himself immensely. His job as a war correspondent was sheer delight. He knew everyone worth knowing and, so far, had managed to get to the front of every battle. The sunshine, Buller's ample provisions and the thrill of dodging an occasional bullet made him relish every minute of his outdoor life. It was a far cry from the frustrations of the Staatsmodelskool. What was probably more important, he had been assured that his despatches to the *Morning Post* were read by 'a wide and influential public'. There was no longer any chance of his being forgotten. Now that he had been joined by, and could lord it over, his brother Jack, his cup seemed pretty well full. 'I looked forward to showing him round and doing for him the honours of war,' he said. Unfortunately, this particular pleasure was soon to come to an abrupt end.

Sir Redvers Buller, having failed to cross the Tugela west of Colenso, decided to try a north-easterly approach to Ladysmith. On 12 February a cavalry contingent went out to reconnoitre the line of advance. Their immediate object was Hussar Hill, some 6 or 7 miles to the east. Both the Churchill brothers were included in the expedition. They left camp at eight in the morning and, arriving at Hussar Hill, had little trouble in driving off the small Boer patrol occupying it. All seemed so quiet that the infantry and field guns bringing up the rear were sent back.

At noon Sir Redvers Buller arrived. He surveyed the surrounding country with his telescope, announced his satisfaction, and ordered the withdrawal. There was a little skirmishing when the advance pickets returned but the enemy snipers who had engaged these pickets were too far away to be a serious threat. It was not until the last of the retiring troops rode down the slope of the hill that a sizeable Boer force revealed itself. These burgers had concealed themselves in a near-by dip and now rushed out, lined the top of the hill, and sent a hail of bullets into the rear of the departing columns. Churchill, who had been riding in the rear with Colonel Byng, made a dash for the nearest ridge, dismounted, and began to return the enemy fire. All along the ridge the South African Light Horse was spread in open order;

they were quickly joined by two infantry regiments who had turned back at the sound of the firing. The attack was well under way when Churchill, hurrying along the line, happened to see his brother lying on the ground. 'As I approached,' he says, 'I saw him start in the quick, peculiar manner of a stricken man. I asked him at once whether he was hurt, and he said something—he thought it must be a bullet—had hit him on the gaiter and numbed his leg. He was quite sure it had not gone in, but when we carried him away we found—as I expected—that he was shot through the leg.' The doctor assured him that the wound was not serious and that chloroform would make the extracting of the bullet painless. However, it meant a month in hospital for the unlucky Jack. Musing on this a little later, Churchill was to marvel at 'the strange caprice which strikes down one man in his first skirmish and protects another time after time'. An answer of sorts was supplied by J. B. Atkins, who had evidently been thinking along the same lines. 'Mr Jack Churchill was hit in the leg,' reported Atkins. 'He had just arrived from England, and this was the first day's fighting he had seen. It seemed as though he had paid his brother's debts.'

The cavalry completed a successful withdrawal and Jack Churchill was packed off to Durban. Inevitably he was taken on board the *Maine*, where he became one of the first (but not *the* first, as Winston fondly imagined) of his mother's patients. Although he missed his brother, Winston was not altogether sorry to see him go. When he had arranged for Jack to come out to South Africa, he had firmly believed that the worst fighting would be over before his brother arrived. Now, with another battle for Ladysmith still to be fought, he was, as he told his mother in a letter, glad to have Jack out of harm's way for a month. The same could not be said for Jack. He greatly resented having to leave the front so early. After a few days on the *Maine*, however, he seems to have found that the role of a battle-scarred warrior had its compensations. 'I saw young Jack Churchill, very pleased with his wound . . .' says Lord Rossyln, who visited the ship. 'He had done capitally during the short time he was at the front.'

Winston went on to relieve Ladysmith. It was tough going. The Boers contested every step of the way. On 16 February, Sir Redvers Buller ordered a general advance to start at dawn the following morning. By the evening of 18 February he was in possession of the range of hills on the British side of the Tugela and the Boers had started to retreat across the river. Churchill sent a cable to the *Morning Post* declaring success was in sight. But when Buller started crossing the Tugela he was again met by a determined Boer force entrenched in the hills facing him. So fierce was the resistance that no advance was possible; despite this Buller continued to pour men across the river until the pile-up was so great that the front troops were immobilized. An attempt to relieve the pressure by attacking the flanking hills resulted in a further disaster and added considerably to the mounting British losses. Churchill, watching the action from Hlangwane Hill on the other side of the river, began to regret his optimistic cable.

The following morning the cavalry brigade was ordered across the Tugela to assist in another diversionary attack. The attack began at twelve-thirty that afternoon: by nightfall, after a desperate charge and the loss of some 500 men, the enemy was still firmly entrenched. The bloody stalemate continued for four more days. Not until 27 February—the anniversary of Majuba—was Buller able to effect his long-sought breakthrough. It was achieved by a full-scale offensive along the entire front. For the first time Buller brought the whole of his army into play. Hill after hill was attacked and the Boers were given no time to reinforce their weak positions. The most obvious tactics succeeded where months of futile manoeuvring had failed: in the space of six hours the British were in possession of the Tugela heights.

That evening, passing through Sir Charles Warren's camp, Churchill happened to notice a row of Boer prisoners. There were forty-eight of them—about the same number as those who had been captured on the armoured train. 'Looking at these very ordinary people,' he wrote, 'who might, from their appearance, have been a knot of loafers round a public house, it was difficult to understand what qualities made them such a terrible foe.'

Four days later the relieving army made its triumphal entry into Ladysmith. As they advanced across the open plain in front of the town, they saw the last of the tented Boer wagons disappearing in the distance. The entry itself was a somewhat solemn affair. As the columns of soldiers marched along the main street, on their way to their camp on the other side of the town, they were watched by the hollow-eyed inhabitants of Ladysmith who showed surprisingly little enthusiasm at the sight of their deliverers. They had decked themselves out in their best clothes and dutifully lined the sides of the road, but most of them looked weary to the point of apathy. The only spontaneous display of emotion came from the relieving troops, who broke into cheers and waved their helmets as they passed the Town Hall where Sir George White, Ladysmith's commanding officer, was taking the salute. Churchill tried to make the best of the poor show—describing the tattered, dust-begrimed soldiers as 'a procession of lions'—but others who had expected to be met with wild rejoicings were frankly disappointed. 'I have been greeted with as much ardour in an afternoon in London by a man with whom I had lunched two hours before,' complained J. B. Atkins. He was told later, by one of the defending officers, that had they arrived two months earlier the town might have welcomed them as they expected; now the garrison was too exhausted to indulge in any such demonstrations. Of all the besieged towns, Ladysmith had undoubtedly fared the worst.

That evening the war correspondents descended upon Sir George White for interviews. The first to get in was the newly arrived Lord Rosslyn, who held a roving commission for the *Daily Mail*. 'I caught Winston Churchill up as we both rode to see Sir George White,' he says, 'but he took the front door carelessly, as one who knows he is expected, while I, seeing saddled horses, galloped to the back. For once speed stood me in stead. The General saw me and Winston did not see the General!' But later that night Churchill managed to get Sir George alone and listened while the General complained bitterly about the criticism that was being levelled at him for allowing himself to be bottled up. Walking back to his tent, Churchill could not help comparing this criticism with the cheers raised by the troops earlier that day.

With Ladysmith relieved and reported, there was not much for Churchill to do in the town. He knew that the *Maine* was shortly due to sail for England, so he hurried down to Durban to spend a few days with his mother before she left.

*

After her sons had left for the front, Lady Randolph had spent an extra day in Pietermaritizburg, visiting hospitals and discussing the war with the Governor of Natal. She would have stayed longer but a telegram from the *Maine* informed her that the first patients were on their way from the front. Catching the next train to Durban, she arrived in time to receive eighty-five sick and wounded men. Most of them had to be carried or helped up the gangway and she was pleased, as well as a little surprised, to see how competently her orderlies had mastered their 'litter drill'. A few days later another ten officers and ninety men arrived, which made the ship fairly full. The crowded conditions were not helped by the swarms of visitors who flocked on board and got in everyone's way. 'They meant so well,' she says, 'it seemed hard to turn them away, but to one tactful *bona-fide* visitor who had someone to see, twenty idlers would come careering all over the ship. . . . The practice had to be put a stop to and certain days and hours fixed.'

It must have been before the second batch of patients arrived that Lady Randolph achieved her ambition to visit the front. The military supplied her with a pass and the Governor of Natal lent her his own railway carriage. 'Provided with much food,' she says, 'armed with kodaks and field glasses, not to mention a brown holland dress (my substitute for khaki), in case we should meet the enemy and wish to be invisible, we started on our journey.' She was accompanied by Miss Warrender and the officer commanding the *Maine*. They travelled by night in a train crowded with soldiers returning to the front and were thrilled when, upon reaching Estcourt, the carriages were searched and two suspected spies arrested. When they arrived at Frere, at 5 a.m., a young army officer invited Lady Randolph to a cup of coffee in his tin hut. Still half asleep, she clambered down from the carriage looking so dishevelled that the officer tactfully suggested that she go back for her hat and shoes. The coffee turned out to be cocoa served in an enamel mug, but drinking it and watching the dawn break over the distant hills was an experience she long remembered. Her greatest thrill, however, came soon after the train had started again. 'About twenty minutes from Frere,' she says, 'we slowed down, and the friendly guard, knowing who I was, rushed to tell me we were passing the place of the armoured train disaster—and sure enough there it was lying on its side, a mangled and battered thing, and within a few yards, a grave with a cross—three sentries mounting guard—marked the place where were buried the poor fellows who were killed in it. I thanked God my son Winston was not there. Chievely—the train went no further—we were at the front.'

They were given a conducted tour of the camp at Chievely and they heard the guns bombarding Ladysmith. On the outskirts of the camp, they sat down to rest close to a naval gun which bore the name 'Lady Randolph Churchill'—painted in big white letters. For the first time the war seemed terrifyingly real. Through their field glasses they could see the white tents of Colenso which was then in enemy hands. 'It was thrilling,' declared Lady Randolph. 'I longed to be a man and take some part in the fighting, but then I remembered my red cross.'

When Lady Randolph came to write her account of this visit for the *Anglo-Saxon Review*, she claimed that the men were very depressed by the news of the retreat from Spion Kop which had taken place 'the night before'. This is either a mistake or deliberately misleading. For the retreat from Spion Kop occurred three days before the *Maine* arrived at Durban. Winston, who had been at Spion Kop, had been waiting to meet his mother when her ship docked but, in his own account, he gives the impression that he did not visit the *Maine* until after Jack was wounded. It might well be that neither of them was anxious to broadcast the fact that the correspondent of the *Morning Post* had left the front at a critical stage in the fighting.

It was on her return from Chievely that she received Sarah's answer to the cable she had sent from Cape Town. And it was probably at this time that Jack arrived with his wounded leg. Indeed, the retreat that was depressing the men at Chievely was most likely the retreat that had followed Jack's first engagement. From now on Lady Randolph was kept fully occupied. Although she was not a trained nurse, she found more than enough to do in comforting the men, writing their letters and supervising the domestic arrangements of the wards. Outside the wards, however, things were still far from perfect. 'Lady Randolph showed me over the wards and everything was beautifully clean and comfortable,' wrote Lord Rosslyn after his visit to the *Maine*; 'but she is not an ideal ship for a hospital, as there is so much lumber on her decks that the men get little space and opportunity to move about in the fresh air, and her 'tween decks are very low.'

On 27 February, when General Cronjé surrendered to Lord Roberts at Paardeberg and Buller captured the Tugela heights, the *Maine* joined in the general rejoicing. 'The band played itself tired,' wrote Lady Randolph, 'and the men sang themselves hoarse; and at last, after a bouquet of fireworks, we went to bed. The next day Durban was *en fête*; the whole harbour dressed; everyone wreathed in smiles. We dined at the Royal Hotel to celebrate the event.' Then came the relief of Ladysmith. There were more excited demonstrations: this time outside the Town Hall, where Winston had addressed the crowd a few weeks earlier. The speakers on this occasion were unable to make themselves heard; 'But,' says Lady Randolph, 'we took it for granted that all they said was appropriate.' And finally, on 4 March, Winston arrived and the family circle was complete.

For the first few days Winston was kept busy catching up with his despatches to the *Morning Post* and preparing his earlier despatches for publication in book form. Once this had been done, he was able to devote his time to his mother. As a farewell treat, he arranged to take Lady Randolph on a sight-seeing tour to Ladysmith. Sir Redvers Buller obligingly supplied the necessary passes. Miss Warrender was again in the party, as was one of the officers discharged from the *Maine*. They travelled up-country by night; arriving at Colenso at six o'clock in the morning, where, after an unappetizing breakfast of bully beef, they crossed the Tugela on a flimsy plank bridge. From here on Winston took over: explaining the fighting, pointing out landmarks and emphasizing the difficulties which Buller's army had had to overcome. Lady Randolph filled the pauses by 'kodaking' everything in sight. The railway beyond the river was still intact but no trains were running, so they started for Ladysmith on an open trolley pushed by a gang of Africans. 'It was an excellent way of seeing everything,' says Lady Randolph, 'as the whole fighting of the last two months has been along the line. We could see and understand everything with the help of Winston's graphic tongue.'

Outside the town they transferred to a Scotch cart, drawn by six mules. Ladysmith gave the appearance of a ghost town: hot and dusty, with shuttered houses, and a few wraith-like pedestrians flitting about the streets. The newcomers found themselves completely ignored. Failing to find a room for the night, they drove to the convent where Sir Redvers Buller had his headquarters. Here things were brighter. Sir Redvers was in high spirits and offered the two women beds, although he was unable to promise sheets. A spider was put at their disposal and a sergeant of the South African Light Horse drove them to Winston's camp where they were 'regaled with tea out of bottles and tin mugs'. Having been on the go since daybreak, the women were too exhausted to change for the dinner which Sir Redvers had waiting for them in his tent. But the General himself was on top form. He appears to have learnt little from his past experiences; his remarks to Lady Randolph were characteristic. 'He told me,' she says, 'that he expected one more big fight, and it would be the following week, if he could get his commissariat up, but the line was hopelessly blocked at present.'

Leaving Sir Redvers fretting about his baggage, Lady Randolph returned to Durban on a Red Cross train the following morning. Winston, whose leave was up, remained at Ladysmith and was unable to see the *Maine* sail from Durban at the end of March, cheered by every ship in the harbour. However, he fully expected to see his mother again soon. At last it looked as if the war was about to end. Two weeks before the relief of Ladysmith, British troops had arrived at Kimberley and ended the siege there. On 13 March, Lord Roberts had occupied Bloemfontein, the capital of the Orange Free State, and was shortly expected to enter the Transvaal. Only one blot marred the pattern of the British advance. Away to the north-west—far removed from Lord Roberts's intended route—the irritating town of Mafeking was still besieged.

CHAPTER SIXTEEN

'The Good Genius of the Siege'

THE SHELLING of Mafeking continued throughout February, but it became less and less predictable. Creaky was moved from one position to another and there was no telling when a bombardment would begin and end. The town was often lulled into a false sense of security. Sarah tells how, at the beginning of the month, she was deceived by a peaceful day and took a stroll through town towards evening. Just as she was passing the Post Office a shell crashed into the building and she found herself running through an avalanche of débris to the nearest shelter. 'For a moment I thought I was killed,' she said, 'but my trembling limbs and chattering teeth soon convinced me to the contrary.'

Every bit as nerve-shattering was the increased activity of the Boer sharpshooters. In spite of Baden-Powell's efforts to dislodge them, the enemy still occupied trenches in the Brickfields on the eastern outskirts of the town. From here and other vantage points snipers were able to harass the townsfolk as they walked about the streets. Most of Sarah's time was now taken up with her work among the convalescents at the convent and in helping at the hospital. 'It was practically impossible to walk from one building to the other,' she reported, 'without being shot at.' Another hazard had been added to the trials of the depressed civilian population.

'Days roll into weeks and weeks into months, but our life here goes on without much change or variation,' wrote Sarah; 'and yet there is a sort of change visible from the highest to the lowest. People are graver, there is a tired expression on most countenances, the women look paler, the children more pinched.' Thomasina Cowan agreed with her: 'Everybody, more or less, has the blues,' she noted, 'and is getting tired of it all.'

'THE GOOD GENIUS OF THE SIEGE'

Only Baden-Powell remained as bright, as active and as optimistic as ever. Sarah did her best to back him up. Although, at times, she felt as weary as everybody else she tried not to let it show. 'Inside Mafeking,' wrote Vere Stent, Reuter's correspondent, 'it is no hyperbole or flattery to say Lady Sarah was a star of merry reassurance and cheerfulness under increasing difficulties . . . she was a comfort and a very present help.' It was Vere Stent who first called her 'the good genius of the siege'.

She was to be seen everywhere: distributing prizes at the Sunday sports, accompanying Baden-Powell on his rounds and visiting sick civilians as well as sick soldiers. 'Lady Sarah Wilson showed us great kindness,' wrote one of the nuns, 'often visiting our sick sisters and bringing them delicacies.' The psychological effect of these Lady Bountiful activities was fully appreciated by Baden-Powell. Sarah might not, with her brusque manner and sardonic tongue, be the bank clerk's *beau ideal* of a gracious titled lady, but her name and social position did impart an air of normality—an almost villagey cosiness—to a far from ordinary situation. 'Throughout the whole siege she showed splendid pluck and fortitude,' said Baden-Powell. 'She kept up her vivacity and high spirits from the start to the finish, and, apart from the useful work she did, she set a valuable example of cheerfulness and courage to the other women.'

But all the cheerfulness in the world could not conceal the fact that the enemy was on their doorstep. Even the entertainments were overshadowed by the thought that when relaxed they were particularly vulnerable to attack. This was dramatically illustrated at the festivities organized by Baden-Powell on 11 February. The town had just learned from Lord Roberts that there was little hope of relieving Mafeking until the middle of May. To offset the inevitable gloom, Baden-Powell arranged an afternoon concert, to be followed by a 'Beleaguered Bachelors' Ball'.

The concert started at five o'clock and was a huge success. Baden-Powell was at his sprightliest. As a highlight he gave his hilarious impersonation of 'Signor Paderewski'—a tousle-haired pianist. 'Colonel Baden-Powell on the stage is simply inimitable,' wrote Sarah; 'in his quite extempore sketches he held the hall entranced or convulsed with laughter, and no one would have thought he had another idea in his mind beyond the nonsense he was talking. He certainly, by so thoroughly amusing them, put everyone on good terms with themselves.'

Spirits were still high at eight o'clock that evening when the guests began to arrive at the Masonic Hall for the Bachelors' Ball. The officers in their dress uniforms and the ladies in their bright, if dated, finery, brought a breath of the *beau monde* to the modest tin-roofed hall. Jet, ostrich plumes and outsized bunches of Parma violets more than made up for the shabbiness of the setting. When the band of the Bechuanaland Rifles, under the baton of the jovial Captain Cowan, struck up 'Rule, Britannia' it was greeted by enthusiastic cheers. The dancers, according to Thomasina Cowan, were an assorted crowd: 'Lords, Earls, Lady Sarah, Colonels and Majors, down to ourselves and all whirling away . . .'

They did not whirl for long. The ball had hardly got under way before a sudden crash of gunfire stopped the dancing. There were a few dazed seconds; then a stampede into the street. Officers left their partners gaping and went dashing to their posts. The streets—which had emptied once the ball had started —quickly filled with anxious, chattering crowds. Orderlies galloped past the hall sounding the general alarm. Soon it was known that the Boers were attacking from the Brickfields. Surprise gave way to utter confusion as the men ran home for rifles and ushered the women to safety.

That this disturbed dance should be compared to the famous ball given by the Duchess of Richmond on the eve of Waterloo was perhaps to be expected. The citizens of Mafeking, now proudly conscious of their historic role, were quick to draw parallels. 'It was just like Waterloo,' noted one guest, 'all the officers had to go, and left civilians to console the ladies.' Another was quite sure that the exodus from the Masonic Hall would prove 'just as remarkable to posterity' as the earlier occasion.

But the battle of the Brickfields was no Waterloo. After a night of sporadic gunfire and early-morning shelling, activity gradually decreased until, by noon the following day, it had ceased altogether. However, for the next few weeks the Brickfields became the centre of operations, with attackers and defenders jostling for these advanced positions.

*

'THE GOOD GENIUS OF THE SIEGE'

Armchair strategists tend to be scornful of the siege of Mafeking. They can make out a good case for their derision. Tactically the siege was ill-advised; incredible gaffes were made by the military on both sides; the hardships endured in Mafeking were debilitating but not excessive compared with those suffered in other sieges; and the schoolboy antics of Baden-Powell undoubtedly left him wide open to ridicule. For all that, this is not how it appeared to the civilians of Mafeking at the time. They were not responsible for the siege; most of them had little understanding of the military situation; they were not in a position to make comforting comparisons; and they were only too glad of the boost given to their morale by the commanding officer. Isolated by miles of hostile veld, it mattered not to them that the town was not completely encircled or that the Boers had reduced the besieging force. They were only conscious of their helplessness, of the women and children dying daily from diphtheria, typhoid and smallpox, of the incessant shelling, of the diminishing hope of relief and the limit to the time they could expect their supplies to last.

It was during the month of February that the white population of Mafeking was brought face to face with the spectre of any siege—the possibility of starvation. For some time past there had been an acute shortage of food in the overcrowded Baralong *stad*. As early as December one inhabitant had noted: 'The Kaffirs dig up dead horses and eat them, and sit picking on the rubbish heaps. Some of them are starving.' But, racial attitudes being what they were, this was not considered unduly serious. In the town itself there had been little concern about food. There were few who doubted that their provisions would last for many months. At the beginning of February Sarah was able to write to the *Daily Mail*: 'There is plenty of farinaceous foodstuffs to last three months on our present rations.' Less than two weeks later, however, her reports had become more guarded. 'As regards foodstuffs,' she wrote, 'the town can hold out for some time, if required, but only with the greatest economy.'

This change of tone was due, in part, to Lord Roberts's telegram. Once they knew for certain that they would have to hold out until the middle of May, they did some serious stocktaking. This showed that supplies were scarcely enough to last until the end of April. There was an immediate tightening of belts. Rations were reduced and new restrictions imposed.

It also became obvious that something would have to be done about the rising death rate among the Baralongs. Baden-Powell ordered soup-kitchens to be set up in the *stad* and the refugee camp. A horse-meat factory was started which, besides producing soup for the kitchens, provided sausages and brawn for the town. The soup kitchens, organized by Gordon Wilson and started towards the end of February, were expected to feed nearly 1,000 Baralongs daily. Ostensibly the soup was concocted from horse flesh; in fact, any stray animal—dogs, mules and mangy chickens—went into the cauldrons. Every effort was made to keep the ingredients of the soup a secret, but the more observant quickly caught on. 'Soup kitchens opened to feed the natives,' noted one of the troopers. 'Dogs not licensed are to be destroyed. Sound suspicious . . .' For this highly suspect fare the Baralongs were charged threepence a bowl; but it is only fair to note that those who could not afford to pay were supplied free. All the same, rumours about the organization of the kitchen put even some of the most destitute against them. 'Soup, composed of horse-flesh and of meal, is sold to the well-to-do and given free to the indigent,' Sarah reported, 'but some die of starvation owing to their prejudice against horseflesh.'

Sarah's reports on the soup kitchens earned her criticism. She made the mistake of explaining to the readers of the *Daily Mail* exactly how the kitchens were supplied. When her despatch was published, on 6 March, it appeared under the lurid heading: NOW EATING STRAY DOGS. This led to the accusation that she had sent 'alarming reports as to the condition of Mafeking in February'. But her reports are relatively moderate compared with those of other correspondents. Certainly they were not as pessimistic as those of Angus Hamilton, for instance. Hamilton, who is usually regarded as one of the more realistic recorders of the siege, had written to *The Times* a week or so earlier and had this to say about the food situation:

'Mafeking at last is siege-weary—and, oh, so hungry! It seems months since anyone had a meal which satisfied the pangs that gnaw all day. We have been on starvation rations for so many weeks that time has been forgotten, and now there seems the prospect of no immediate help forthcoming! We are sick of it, so tired of the malaria, diphtheria, and typhoid that claim a list almost as great as that caused by the enemy's shell and rifle fire! We ask, when will the end be? and then we shrug our shoulders and begin to swear; for we have such sorrows in our midst, and such suffering women and such ailing children as would turn a saint to blasphemies!'

Despite Baden-Powell's fooling, it was not all fun in Mafeking.

*

The news of the relief of Ladysmith reached Mafeking on 13 March. It was heartening, but not as heartening as it might have been. There was a sneaking suspicion among civilians that events in South Africa were bypassing them: they had been the first to be besieged, now it looked as if they would be the last to be relieved. 'News of the relief of Ladysmith was received yesterday,' reported Sarah on 14 March, 'but, while giving the greatest satisfaction, it must be confessed that all the more civilian portion of the garrison feel disappointed at there being no immediate prospect of the relief of this town.'

Nevertheless, the tide having taken a favourable turn, Baden-Powell siezed the opportunity of riding it. He put on his most ambitious show. On 19 March the *Mafeking Mail* announced that a 'Siege Exhibition' would be held at the Masonic Hall the following Sunday. A variety of events were listed which included a contest for the best model of a siege weapon or any of the forts, a competition for the best lace or fancy work made during the siege and a prize offered for 'the quaintest or most original curio constructed of shells or bullets fired into the town by the enemy'. Sarah was on the panel to judge the best original song or poem and, on her own account, offered £5 for the 'best Trimmed Lady's Hat. The hat and material to have been purchased in Mafeking during the Siege.' Everyone agreed that the show was a tremendous success. 'It had a beneficial effect, this artificial method of killing time,' reported a war correspondent, 'and it realised some £50 for the hospital.' Once again Baden-Powell had managed to ward off despondency.

As if to reward him there came, a few days later, news that Lord Roberts had marched into the Orange Free State and occupied Bloemfontein. At the same time rumours swept the town that Colonel Plumer's force (which had been separated from Baden-Powell at the beginning of the siege) was advancing towards Mafeking and that relief could be expected within a matter of days. Telegrams were even received from London congratulating the garrison on its release.

Excitement reached a peak on 31 March. Early that afternoon cannon and rifle fire was heard beyond the Boer lines. Baden-Powell, who usually did not man his look-out post until evening, was seen to be on watch at midday. A considerable Boer force was said to have left the laager, headed in a northerly direction. Weight was given to the rumours when Baden-Powell ordered a mounted squadron to make a diversionary attack on Game Tree Hill.

But as hopes rose, so they fell. Plumer had indeed been within six miles of the town but his approach had been little more than a tactical move. He had been engaged in skirmishes ever since his force hived off from Baden-Powell and for some time past he had been in fairly constant contact with Mafeking. Now, hearing that a relief column was on its way, Plumer had centred his men at Ramathlabama and then marched towards the besieged town. His intention had been to draw off Snyman's force to the north; but he had been outnumbered and forced to retire. The following day Snyman sent a letter to Mafeking announcing that the battlefield was strewn with British dead and giving permission for them to be buried. 'Happily,' said Sarah, 'his language was more forcible than accurate.' Nevertheless, out of a force of 350 men, Plumer suffered forty-nine casualties.

After this failure, Baden-Powell instructed Plumer to make no further attempt until he was sure the relief column was drawing near. At the same time he tried to put the nearness of Plumer's force to good use. He asked Plumer to send some cattle into the town and to assist in getting out some of the starving Baralongs.

The evacuation of the Baralongs, which was only partly successful, was a dangerous business. 'The natives have been sent out in batches,' noted one of the inhabitants. 'They are not armed and have to walk through the Boer lines, at the risk of being shot. They must not return. It does seem hard lines. But of the two evils, the risk of being shot at is the simpler as it would mean starvation living here.' Faced with these dreadful alternatives, over a thousand Baralongs managed to reach Plumer's advanced post. But the attempt to drive a herd of cattle into the town was a complete failure.

A new and bizarre source of food did penetrate the enemy lines at this time, however. A flight of locusts descended upon the town in such numbers that they blackened the surrounding veld. These insects, long considered a delicacy by the Bushmen of the Kalahari, were immediately seized upon by the Africans. The Bushmen were in the habit of cramming live locusts into their mouths, but this practice did not appeal to Mafeking's Africans. They preferred them boiled. Once the idea caught on, the townsfolk came to appreciate these insects. They were described as being rather like tasteless prawns. Sarah, of course, was among the first to try the new *hors d'œuvre*. She pronounced upon it favourably. Her taste was not shared by everybody. 'I ate the head of a shrimpy looking locust, and felt its eyes staring at me for four days afterwards,' said Thomasina Cowan. 'Lady Sarah Wilson has tasted all these dishes. She will be quite the lioness when she returns to Society.'

By April food had become a vital consideration. Even the optimistic were doubtful as to how long they could hold out. A further stocktaking revealed that, even under the new system of rationing, provisions would not last beyond 22 May. This fell far short of the new date of expected relief. This date had been given by Lord Roberts in a message which arrived on 20 April. Owing to unexpected delays, he explained, the relief column might not reach the town until mid-June. Only by reducing rations to a mere subsistence level could the garrison hope to last that long. And how, it was asked, could the troops be expected to defend the town under starvation conditions? They were even further alarmed when, on 24 April, it was learned that President Kruger's impetuous grandson, Sarel Eloff, had arrived from Pretoria with reinforcements and orders to take Mafeking at all costs. To the besieged garrison, Lord Roberts's tardiness seemed as frightening as it was inexplicable.

Yet, regardless of increasing hardships, the determination to hold out remained undiminished. There were still a few cheering compensations. On 1 April, Queen Victoria had sent a second message of encouragement to Baden-Powell: 'I continue watching with confidence and admiration,' she wired, 'the patient and resolute defence which is so gallantly maintained under your ever resourceful command.' On 11 April, there was a great sigh of relief when Creaky, after firing its last shot—which, ironically, hit the Dutch church—was sent back to Pretoria. At Easter the churches were full for the Holy Week services and Sarah noticed how, in contrast to earlier days, the rain now fell freely through the roof of the Anglican church. Hot-cross buns were made by stamping the meagre bread ration with a cross.

Sarah bustled about the town as briskly as ever. The siege had done nothing to mellow her sharp, commanding manner. 'Lady Sarah Wilson,' noted the ever-jealous Thomasina Cowan, '... called several times on Mrs Minchin and self, always accompanied by one of the Staff Officers whom she "left about" wheels—forward marches, at her will.' For all her aggressiveness, Sarah could still attract more than her share of male attention. On Sunday canters to and from the Recreation Ground, there was always a group of officers eager to escort her. And her bearing in the saddle won her a host of secret admirers. 'She was a cool and calm sort of woman,' remembered John Nicholson, one of the young refugees in Mafeking, 'but when she was on a horse, I tell you, she was something to look at.'

Much of Sarah's time was spent consoling those who had lost their homes or their livelihood. She had been concerned with this problem for some time. At the beginning of March she had written to her sister, Georgiana, describing the plight of the townsfolk and asking her to launch a fund for their benefit. In the letter to *The Times*, Georgiana had described the 'heartrending accounts of the sufferings of Mafeking that I have received from my sister Lady Sarah Wilson.' On Sarah's behalf, she appealed for subscriptions to a relief fund which would supplement any Government compensation. 'She implores me,' explained Georgiana, 'to take active measures to bring before the generous British public the destitute condition of the nuns, refugees and civilians generally in Mafeking. She writes with authority, having witnessed their sufferings herself, and, indeed, having shared equally with them the anxieties and privations of this prolonged siege.' The response was immediate. Donations poured in. Sarah's modest expectation of £2,000 to £3,000 was soon surpassed. When the appeal eventually closed, over £29,000 was sent to Mafeking. One of the first subscribers was the Princess of Wales. Sending Georgiana £100 she wrote: 'I hope very soon, however, they will be relieved, and I trust your poor sister Sarah will be none the worse for all she has gone through during her enforced captivity.'

By this time Mafeking was everyone's concern. As the British troops marched across South Africa, attention was riveted on the tiny town which had become the 'ewe lamb of the Empire'. Lord Roberts's advance seemed painfully slow. Every report coming from the besieged garrison emphasized the need for a speedy relief. Perhaps nothing depicted the plight of the defenders more succinctly than did a telegram from Sarah to Georgiana. It was published in the middle of April and read: 'Breakfast today, horse sausages; lunch minced mule, curried locusts. All well.'

*

And then, quite suddenly, the end seemed to be in sight. At the beginning of May, Baden-Powell heard that a relief column commanded by Colonel B. T. Mahon was about to approach the town from Kimberley. No official announcement was made in Mafeking, but the town was soon abuzz with rumours. Everyone seemed to sense that the long months of confinement were drawing to a close. 'As we near the end of the siege,' wrote Sarah on 11 May, 'our conditions in the little town are perhaps becoming more cheerful. The rainy season is apparently over, and the weather is splendid; consequently the fever epidemic is diminishing . . . I have had conversations with the ladies of Mafeking, and they, as much as the men, are determined that the Boers shall not come in here while a particle of food remains.'

She spoke too soon. The ladies might be determined to hold out, but President Kruger's grandson was equally determined to come in. Having been suspiciously quiet for the past few days, Sarel Eloff now decided to carry out his orders and take the town at all costs.

At four o'clock on the morning of 12 May, Sarah was suddenly woken by the sound of rifle fire. Hurrying out of her room, she was met by the noise of bullets swishing past the canvas blind at the end of her stoep. She quickly shut the door, lit a candle, and scrambled into her clothes. Outside everything was pitch dark; from the darkness came sounds of the town springing to life. Footsteps hurried to and fro, an occasional lantern was to be seen flashing between the houses. In a matter of minutes, the sound for which Sarah had been waiting drowned the rifle fire. The alarm bugle echoed through the streets, followed by the slow tolling of the bell of the Roman Catholic Church. It was the signal that a general attack was in progress. For the past seven months Mafeking had been living in fear of this happening.

As Sarah stood on the stoep wondering what to do, a man came running along the street. He told her that everything was under control. He had just left Baden-Powell and his staff drinking hot coffee at their headquarters. The first signs of an attack had come from the area of the Brickfields, but this was thought to be a feint; the real business was expected to start shortly on the opposite side of the town—near the Baralong *stad*. By this time a group of women from near-by houses had gathered on the stoep and together they strained their eyes, trying to make out what was happening. Not for long were they left wondering. From the direction of the *stad*, tongues of flame pierced the darkness. 'Even then,' says Sarah, 'one did not realize what was burning; someone said: "A big grass fire commenced yesterday." At the same time a din of confused cries, unmistakably native ejaculations, was borne to us by the breeze along with the smell of burning thatch and wood. "The Boers are in the stadt!" This dread sentence seemed to grow in volume till to one's excited fancies it became a sort of chant to which the faint yells of the natives, the unceasing rattle of musketry, the ping-pong of the bullets, formed an unholy accompaniament.' Then, quite close, they heard a cheer. There was no mistaking what it meant. The Boers had broken through.

There was surprisingly little panic. From the stoep the women watched their men walking calmly to the nearest cover and settling down with their rifles. One of the Town Guard crossed over to reassure them. The Boers had already rushed a fort, he said, 'but we will keep them there—they will never get out.'

As it grew lighter, Sarah resolved to go to the hospital. There was nothing she could do at the house. When she told Ben Weil this, he tried to dissuade her. The worst firing was coming from that direction. In fact the road she would have to take ran between the enemy and the defenders and was a gauntlet of cross-fire. 'You will be shot for a certainty,' said Weil. But Sarah refused to be put off. She was needed at the hospital. Sending for Gordon's batman to accompany her, she snatched up a few things of value and started off. Running along the road, they twice had to flatten themselves against a wall as bullets whizzed over their heads. Once Sarah tripped and fell; the batman, thinking she had been hit, rushed to pick her up and hurried her to the next place of shelter. Not until they had reached the hospital trench were they able to stand upright and cover the last 500 yards in comparative safety.

The hospital was in a state of chaos. From the beginning of the attack hospital wagons and stretcher parties had been arriving with wounded men. The harassed staff soon had to attend to enemy casualties as well as their own. Shortly after Sarah arrived, three Boers were brought in. 'The first prisoners Mafeking can claim,' observed Sarah. Then an African, with his arm shattered to the shoulder, arrived. It was whispered that he had acted as a guide for the attacking party. He was quickly attended by the doctors. One of the more pathetic cases was a young private of the Cape Police who had been found bleeding to death. He had been shot near the heart while taking a message to one of the forts. Sarah sat with him for hours, dabbing his head with eau-de-Cologne and brushing away the flies. Just before he passed into unconsciousness, he said: 'Tell the Colonel, Lady Sarah, I did my best to give the message, but they got me first.' He died shortly afterwards.

The firing continued all day. Sometimes there would be a burst lasting for ten minutes or more, then it would die down. From time to time the siren-like whistle of the high-velocity gun and the sound of shells exploding in the streets could be heard in the hospital wards. Conflicting reports came from the town. 'Now the Boers had possession of the stadt; again, they were murdering the women and children in the laager; a little later, they would never surrender the seized fort which, was amply provisioned; as soon as night fell large Boer reinforcements would force their way in.'

But the reinforcements did not arrive. Snyman had been half-hearted in his agreement to support the attack. Only a small force of burgers—including German and French volunteers—had assisted Sarel Eloff to capture the Police Fort on the western side of the town. Once in possession, the invaders had imprisoned the fort's commander and settled down to await Snyman's promised support. But Snyman's efforts were no less confused than they had been throughout the siege. Baden-Powell had little difficulty in repulsing his ineffectual attacks. After bravely defending the fort throughout the day, Eloff was forced to surrender at six o'clock that evening. Baden-Powell met the prisoners as they were marched into the Market Square, 'Good evening, Eloff,' he said, extending his hand. 'You are just in time for dinner.'

News of the surrender was immediately telephoned to the hospital. Shortly afterwards came the sound of cheering in the town. The wounded men added their feeble voices to the cheers. 'It was,' says Sarah, 'a pathetic sound.'

Most of the Boer prisoners were housed in the Masonic Hall. That evening Sarah and two of the nurses slipped out to have a look at them. 'Not till I had seen them with my own eyes,' reported Sarah, 'did I realize the marvellous success the Mafeking garrison had had. A motley crew they were—in the dim light of a few oil lamps—the greater part laughing, joking, singing even—all smoking the inevitable pipe—representatives of many nationalities, the few Boers *pur et simple* holding themselves somewhat doggedly aloof, but the whole community giving one the idea of a body of men who knew they had got out of a tight place and were devoutly thankful still to have whole skins.' Unlike some of the other inhabitants, she was not unduly put out at the sight of the French and German volunteers who formed part of the Boer force. To many, peering into the Masonic Hall, the presence of these outsiders was extremely puzzling. 'I couldn't help feeling,' remarked one bewildered Britisher, 'it wasn't their quarrel, and why they wanted to shove their nose into it we all fail to understand.' But magnanimity won through in the end. 'However,' he concluded tolerantly, 'the poor devils can't help being foreigners.'

At six o'clock the following morning, the town was again awakened by the sound of shell fire. The bursting of three shells, one after the other, was followed by an eerie silence. Sarel Eloff, who had been lodged at Mr Weil's house, explained to Sarah what they meant. They were, he said, an arranged signal which, had the Boers been in possession of the town, was to be answered by a volley of rifle fire.

As it happened, they were the last shells fired into Mafeking.

'THE GOOD GENIUS OF THE SIEGE'

Before setting off to take Mafeking, Sarel Eloff had encouraged his men with an optimistic message. 'We leave for Mafeking tonight,' he had said; 'we will breakfast at Dixon's Hotel tomorrow morning.' In fact, Eloff and three of his officers breakfasted at Ben Weil's. Sarah, who sat opposite the President's grandson, was able to get a closer look at Mafeking's visitors. She found Eloff's stream of complaints against Snyman somewhat off-putting. To her, loyalty was a primary virtue. Eloff was anxious to explain why his attack had failed. He said that having left the laager with a force approaching 400 men, he had been amazed to find, on reaching the *stad*, only 240 remained. An additional 500 men who should have come in once the fort was taken had failed him completely. This failure, on top of Snyman's feeble efforts, had left him extremely bitter. In sharp contrast to Eloff's attitude was the nonchalant conversation of an aristocratic French officer who sat next to Sarah. Chatting away gaily, he confined himself to observations on the African climate, the weather, and the recently opened Paris Exhibition. 'It was,' says Sarah, 'one of the most curious meals at which I have ever assisted.'

That afternoon the officers were packed off to the gaol where they were to be kept until a suitable house had been prepared for them. While they were still in the gaol they were interviewed by various war correspondents. Vere Stent asked Sarel Eloff why the Boers had released Sarah from the laager. 'Who could possibly have shot anyone so good-looking?' replied Eloff gallantly.

For the rest of the day Sarah was occupied in writing a despatch on the attack for the *Daily Mail*. It was one of the few reports she wrote that did not reach London. The runner carrying it was shot that same night. A few days later it was discovered in the Boer laager exactly as she had sent it—except that the siege stamps had been carefully cut from the envelope. In the evening Sarah attended a thanksgiving service organized by the Anglican minister. The little church was packed and the jubilant congregation turned the thanksgiving into a burst of self-congratulation. 'We were rather mad,' explained one of them, 'and it gave us a pleasant feeling to sing nice fighting psalms and hymns, because whichever way you look at it we are perfectly convinced out here that it is a righteous war.'

Eloff's bold but fruitless attack proved to be the Boers' last effort. The following Tuesday news arrived that Mahon's relief column had already passed Vryburg. That same morning Colonel Plumer and his somewhat depleted force joined the column. Together the combined force of almost 2,000 men headed towards Mafeking.

At the news of Mahon's approach, the inhabitants of the town roused themselves. Clambering on to the rooftops they watched as dust clouds blurred the distant horizon. Even then there were cynics who tried to dismiss the whole thing as a false alarm. Although horsemen were seen scurrying to and fro, there was no sign of the besieging force dispersing. Throughout Tuesday afternoon and for most of the following day, the crowds watched and waited. Every drift of dust seemed to tell a different tale; now it seemed as though the Boers were being reinforced, now it seemed as if the relief column was drawing nearer. At about two o'clock on Wednesday afternoon, the sound of artillery fire could be heard to the north-west and there were signs of a definite withdrawal from the Boer lines. Excitement was caused shortly afterwards when Gordon Wilson scrambled down from Baden-Powell's new look-out on the railway sheds and shouted orders for a contingent of horsemen to saddle up. As soon as they were mounted, they were joined by Baden-Powell and Major Panzerra with artillery guns. When the party returned later that afternoon, it was learned that they had tried to head off an enemy detachment but had been foiled by the gathering dusk. Then, just as the sun was about to set, a heliograph twinkled from the now visible mass of horsemen in the veld. 'From Colonel Mahon's force—How are you getting on?'

Baden-Powell replied: 'Welcome.'

Sarah was about to sit down to dinner that evening when she heard a feeble cheer. Rushing to the Market Square, she grabbed the arm of the first man she saw—a dusty, khaki-clad soldier.

'Has anyone come in?' she asked.

'We have come in,' replied the man casually. 'Major Karri-Davis and eight men of the Imperial Light Horse.'

Mafeking had been relieved.

It seemed too incredible to be true. Here at last were the men they had waited for so long. But there was no triumphant

Winston Churchill at Hlangwana Hill, Natal, shortly before the relief of Ladysmith. His companion is Lord Basil Blackwood

Africana Museum, Johannesburg

'The Tables Turned'—a contemporary drawing of the release of the captive British officers in Pretoria. Winston Churchill and the Duke of Marlborough are on horseback, centre

march, no bands playing, no hoarse-throated crowds: 'merely a score or so begrimed figures, each holding a tired and jaded horse, and a few women on the outskirts of the circle with tears of joy in their eyes.'

Later that night Sarah was taken in a pony-cart to the Recreation Ground. Here in the brilliant moonlight she joined the crowds watching the relief column march into camp. But the sense of anti-climax persisted. A Boer force, under their brilliant commander, De la Rey, had put up a determined opposition to the column's entry into Mafeking. Weary after the day's fierce fighting, the soldiers slumped down beside the assembled wagons and slept.

For the rest of the night Sarah was kept busy at the hospital tending the wounded.

'Men of all sorts and conditions, trades, professions and ranks, relievers and relieved,' wrote a reporter, 'slept that night in and about Mafeking, with a restless sleep, thinking of what England would think, and we knew and were sorry we couldn't hear what they said.'

*

In fact, it was almost impossible to hear what England was saying. All comment was drowned in the wild rejoicing that swept the nation. A Reuter's message telling of the relief reached England at about 9.30 p.m. on Friday, 18 May 1900. From the Mansion House, where it was first announced, the news was proclaimed from every lighted window of the delirious capital. News-boys raced along the streets giving away the special editions that were being churned out from Fleet Street. In music-halls and theatres performances were stopped as the audience rose to cheer and sing 'God Save the Queen'. Frantic crowds surged along Pall Mall, Piccadilly and Regent Street, singing, shouting, blowing whistles, waving flags and hoisting banners. Lamp-posts were scaled, top hats flung into the air, rockets fired into the night. From West End to East End, from Park Lane to the Bank, one could hardly move for the press of near-hysterical people. A new verb was added to the English language that night: 'to maffick—to exult riotously'.

In Grosvenor Square the mob swarmed about a tall, red-bricked corner house on the south side. It was here, said a report, 'that Lady Sarah Wilson's little boys are staying with their grandmother'.

The following morning all other news was swept aside. The papers plastered their pages with pictures of the defenders—Baden-Powell, Lord Edward Cecil, Colonel Plumer and Lady Sarah Wilson—all grouped under the triumphant headline: MAFEKING RELIEVED!

CHAPTER SEVENTEEN

Marching to Pretoria

ON THE day that Mafeking was relieved, Winston Churchill had just arrived at the little town of Lindley in the Orange Free State. He was accompanying one of the flanking columns of Lord Roberts's force which was then advancing towards the Transvaal. Once again he was officially a non-combatant. To get to the Orange Free State he had had to take leave from the South African Light Horse and fall back on his role of war correspondent. The column to which he was attached was commanded by General Ian Hamilton and Churchill was pleased to be in such good company. Not only was Ian Hamilton an old friend but, as events had shaped over the past few weeks, he was one of the few British generals favourably disposed to the controversial correspondent of the *Morning Post*. The sad fact was that, after leaving the congenial Redvers Buller in Natal, Winston Churchill had fallen foul of the military hierarchy. He was no longer regarded as the hero who had escaped from Pretoria but as an interfering newspaper man who needed to be kept firmly in his place.

This had been entirely his own doing. Like his father, he was never very good at toeing the party line and, as in the case of Lord Randolph, his dislike of conformity tended to land him in a great deal of trouble. He was now beginning to discover this. He had been dabbling in things which were widely considered to be none of his business. Not content with fighting and reporting the war, he had been tempted to try his hand at peace-making. The tide had turned for the British; the military campaign seemed to be drawing to a close; political considerations now loomed larger than enemy opposition. As a budding politician, Churchill had thought it opportune to voice his opinions about any future settlement of hostilities.

He had begun making his views known before he left Natal. Before quitting Ladysmith he had written a long letter to a Natal newspaper, expressing himself forcibly on what was then an explosive issue. It concerned the so-called Colonial 'rebels'. Both the Cape and Natal were British colonies but many of the colonists were kinsmen of the Boers and had openly, naturally, and often actively sympathized with the Republics. Many English-speaking colonists, incensed by what they considered 'traitorous conduct', were now demanding vengeance. There had been meetings, both in the Cape and Natal, at which angry speakers had insisted that the Colonial 'rebels' be taught a lesson. An example, it was said, must be made of those who had deserted the British cause. 'Our turn now', became the cry. Churchill found this hysterical attitude despicable. He fully agreed that a firm policy must be adopted: the Transvaal and the Orange Free State must be annexed and British supremacy established in South Africa. But there was nothing to be gained by persecuting individuals. 'It is the spirit of revenge,' he wrote. 'It is wrong, first of all because it is morally wicked; and secondly because it is practically foolish. Revenge may be sweet, but it is also most expensive. Let me urge material considerations first.' Threats would only make the recalcitrant Boers reluctant to lay down their arms and might prolong the war indefinitely. 'Beware of driving men to desperation,' wrote Churchill. 'Even a cornered rat is dangerous. We desire a speedy peace and the last thing in the world we want is that this war should enter a guerrilla phase. Those who demand "an eye for an eye and a tooth for a tooth" should ask themselves whether such barren spoils are worth five years of bloody partisan warfare and the consequent impoverishment of South Africa.'

Much the same sentiments were expressed in his despatches to the *Morning Post*. 'The wise and right course,' he declared, 'is to beat down all who resist, even to the last man, but not to withhold forgiveness and even friendship from any who wish to surrender.' None of this went down well with the Tories in England or the military die-hards. Young Jack Churchill, who had been left behind in Natal, wrote to his mother to report the opposition roused by Winston's 'Peaceful telegrams'. It was thought that, rather than persuading the Boers to lay down their arms, they would encourage them to continue fighting. The

Morning Post, a Conservative newspaper, was extremely embarrassed by its correspondent: while publishing his despatches, it took care to dissociate itself from his views. Natal papers replied with long, disparaging leading articles.

This was only part of the trouble. As far as Churchill was concerned, it was not his present indiscretions but his past sins that had given rise to his immediate problems. Having obtained leave from the South African Light Horse, he had then applied to the *Morning Post* to get him accredited to Lord Roberts's force in the Orange Free State. He had left Natal at the end of March, travelled to Cape Town, booked in at the Mount Nelson Hotel, and had waited for an answer to his application to the *Morning Post*. While he was in Cape Town he was entertained at Government House by Sir Alfred Milner, who sympathized with his plea for leniency towards the 'Boer rebels' but thought it unfortunately timed. There were other diversions to be found at the Cape and the few days he spent there passed pleasantly: but the pleasantness went on too long. There was no response to his application. A little worried, he wrote to Ian Hamilton and another friend at Bloemfontein in Lord Roberts's force and asked them to make enquiries. Their replies were not encouraging. It seemed that neither Lord Roberts nor his Chief of Staff, Lord Kitchener, were at all anxious for Churchill to join them. His free-flowing pen, he was now informed, had, on separate occasions, succeeded in offending the two most important officers in South Africa.

Lord Kitchener's resentment was of long standing. It dated from the Egyptian campaign two years earlier. Not having wanted Churchill in Egypt in the first place, Kitchener had objected strongly to criticisms of the campaign that had appeared in *The River War*. Lord Roberts's objections were more surprising. The Commander-in-Chief had good reason to look upon Churchill with indulgence. He had been friendly with the Churchill family for many years. Lord Randolph had been responsible for Roberts's appointment as Commander-in-Chief of the Indian Army and he had watched Winston grow up. However, all this had been cancelled out by an outspoken despatch which Churchill had sent to the *Morning Post* in February. The despatch had been written on the Sunday after his return to the Tugela with his brother Jack. At a church parade, attended by some 5,000 soldiers, he had listened impatiently to a meaningless sermon preached by an army chaplain on the siege and fall of Jericho. Nothing could have been more inappropriate. Spion Kop had just been lost, a new offensive was about to be launched, and the army was treated to a discourse on the 'peculiar and unconvincing tactics' of the Israelites. Churchill, recalling the inspiration gained from a Roman Catholic priest at Omdurman, had made some pointed remarks about the foolish formality of this sermon. His report had caused an ecclesiastical stir. The idea of losing the war to the Boers was as nothing compared with the threat of losing the army to Rome. Several preachers had volunteered for the front immediately. But the devout Lord Roberts felt that his chaplains had been slighted; he was still nursing his grievance when Churchill's application arrived. It took all the efforts of Churchill's friends to persuade the Commander-in-Chief to relent. When permission eventually arrived for Churchill to proceed to Bloemfontein it was emphasized that Lord Roberts was only allowing him to come for his father's sake.

He discovered just how reluctant Roberts was to have him soon after his arrival. On his first afternoon in the Free State capital, he was talking to some officers in a club facing the market-square. Suddenly the conversation stopped and all eyes were focused on a small, upright, grey-haired man walking across the square. 'No one doubted his identity for an instant,' says Churchill, 'and I knew I was looking at the Queen's greatest subject, the commander who had in the brief space of a month revolutionized the fortunes of war, had turned something like despair into almost inordinate triumph.' Churchill saluted. But Roberts disdained to notice him. He passed him as if he were a stranger.

*

Lord Roberts's march up through the Cape and into the Orange Free State had changed the pattern of the war. The formidable obstacles encountered by the British army in December had been overcome, Kimberley had been relieved, the Boer General, Cronjé, had been forced into surrender at Paardeberg and finally Bloemfontein had been occupied. This had not been achieved without cost. All the way, Roberts had been conscious of the vulnerability of his long line of communications and, at a critical stage of the march, Christiaan De Wet, the daring Boer guerrilla leader, had successfully attacked a transport column, depriving the British force of 1,600 oxen and some 200 supply wagons. On arriving at Bloemfontein the army was exhausted: men and horses were starved, supplies uncertain and enteric fever rife. Time was needed to strengthen the troops and to bring up reinforcements. For this reason Roberts was forced to a long halt at Bloemfontein, before attempting his advance to the Transvaal.

But while the British were licking their wounds, the Boers had sprung into action. 'I shall be here another fortnight at least,' Roberts wrote to Sir George Forrest on 7 April, 'I trust then nothing will prevent my moving steadily on. . . . Meanwhile we are being a good deal worried; the Boers are spreading over the country in small parties, cutting off supplies, turning the people against us, and threatening the line of the railway.' A new aspect had entered the war: the great set battles were over and the guerrilla phase, foreseen by Churchill, had begun.

To deal with the harassment of his supply lines, Roberts had continually to despatch troops to the threatened areas. Churchill's first weeks in the Orange Free State were spent accompanying these detachments. 'Equipped by the *Morning Post* on a munificent scale with whatever good horses and transport were necessary,' he says, 'I moved rapidly this way and that from column to column, wherever there was a chance of fighting.' Constantly on the move and revelling in the excitement and danger of it all, he was again enjoying life. Not all the Generals welcomed his presence with their columns. Word had got round that this cocksure subaltern-cum-war-correspondent was frowned upon by the Commander-in-Chief, that he could be very critical and commanded a large audience and that he was not to be trusted. However, this did not worry Churchill unduly. He was more than willing to brave military disapproval for the sake of a good story. It was important for him to be at the centre of things.

There were occasions when he was welcomed by the army with enthusiasm. One such time was when he joined General Brabazon's column at Dewetsdorp, some fifty miles southeast of Bloemfontein. Brabazon was an old friend. As the commanding officer of the 4th Hussars he had been instrumental in obtaining a commission for Churchill in the regiment and had since then taken an active interest in his protégé's career. Now, at the age of fifty-seven, he was commanding the Brigade of Imperial Yeomanry and certainly had no objections to receiving a little publicity.

Brabazon's column was approaching Dewetsdorp when Churchill joined it. As they drew near to the town the advance patrols were fired on from the surrounding hills. A few skirmishes developed but Brabazon was dissuaded by one of his officers from making a frontal attack. Such attacks invariably resulted in heavy casualties and were not favoured by Lord Roberts. It was decided to wait for reinforcements. But, after gathering a force of nearly eleven thousand men, Brabazon himself began to have doubts about the attack. He wired to Roberts for orders. A reply came from Bloemfontein the following morning telling Brabazon to postpone the attack for at least another day. To fill in time, the cavalry was sent to reconnoitre the enemy's left flank. Churchill went with them.

Approaching a small hill on the outskirts of the town, they sighted a force of about two hundred Boers, some mounted and some on foot. They opened fire and the Boers took cover behind the hill. At the same time, a new mounted Boer force appeared, riding across the open plain and heading towards another hill on the cavalry's right. Captain Angus McNeill, the officer commanding Montmorency's Scouts, immediately asked permission to ride after this second force in the hopes of heading it off. Permission was given and McNeill shouted to Churchill to join the sortie. 'So,' says Churchill, 'in the interests of the *Morning Post*, I got on my horse and we all started—forty or fifty scouts, McNeill and I, as fast as we could . . .'

The Boers had got a good start and Churchill despaired of catching them up: he shouted to the others that it could not be done. But the chase was under way and to give up would be to admit defeat. The scouts pounded on; Churchill, bent over his horse's neck, stuck with them. On reaching the crest of the hill they found their way barred by a wire fence. They dismounted and the soldiers began cutting the wire. Then, with startling suddenness, the heads and shoulders of a dozen Boers—'grim, hairy and terrible'—appeared among the rocks behind the fence.

There was an electrifying pause before McNeill shouted: 'Too late; back to the other koppie. Gallop!' Immediately bullets began to whistle about their heads. Churchill made a grab for his horse. But as he put his foot in the stirrup the terrified animal reared and began to prance and circle. He tried to jump into the saddle, but the saddle slipped from the horse's back and the animal broke loose and bolted. By this time the rest of the scouts were some two hundred yards away. Once again Churchill found himself the lone target for Boer bullets.

He started to run. The nearest cover was a mile away. 'Here at last I take it,' he thought. Then, out of nowhere, a horseman appeared. It was one of the scouts: 'a tall man, with skull and crossbones badge, and on a pale horse. Death in Revelation, but life to me!' He shouted and, to his surprise, the rider stopped. This time there was no fumbling as, in a running jump, he sprang on to the horse behind the scout. As they rode off, they were followed by a hail of bullets and the horse was hit. Churchill, with his arms round the scout's waist, gripping the horse's mane, found his hand covered in blood. But the wounded animal outpaced the bullets and brought them to safety.

It was a terrifying experience. In a letter to his mother a few days later, Churchill declared that it was the nearest he had ever been to death. However, the scout, Trooper Clement Roberts, was more concerned about his wounded horse than he was with saving Churchill's life. His distress over the animal was such that he was hardly aware that he had become a hero. 'All the officers were agreed that the man who pulled up in such a situation to help another was worthy of some honourable distinction,' Churchill wrote to the *Morning Post*. 'Indeed, I have heard that Trooper Roberts—note the name, which seems familiar in this connection—was to have his name considered for the Victoria Cross.'

But evidently the authorities were not appreciative of having the *Morning Post*'s correspondent restored to them. Trooper Roberts did not receive the Victoria Cross, nor any other distinction. Not until seven years later when Churchill—then Secretary of State for Colonies—succeeded in obtaining for him a Distinguished Conduct Medal, was the trooper's bravery officially recognized.

On 2 May Lord Roberts resumed his march on the Transvaal. Ten days later he occupied Kroonstad, the second largest town in the Orange Free State. Churchill did not accompany the main body of the army on this march. He had decided that Ian Hamilton's flanking column, which was advancing on a parallel route some forty or fifty miles to the east, offered him pleasanter company. For, although his choice cut him off from the centre of operations, it at least kept him away from the disapproving gaze of the Commander-in-Chief. He was not, in any case, unduly worried at being kept out of the limelight for a while. By this time he knew that he was quite capable of attracting attention if and when he wanted it. 'Although there is a considerable under-current of hostile and venomous criticism,' he wrote to his mother on 1 May, 'upon the whole I have gained considerably by what has passed since I have been in South Africa.'

He was not the only member of his family attached to Hamilton's column. When he had arrived back in Bloemfontein, after his adventure at Dewetsdorp, he had found his cousin, the Duke of Marlborough, languishing in the Free State capital. Marlborough, who had arrived in South Africa shortly after Jack Churchill, had been appointed assistant Military Secretary to Lord Roberts. Unfortunately his appointment had resulted in some pointed criticism from the Radical press in England. Lord Roberts had a number of dukes on his staff; it was suggested that the aristocracy was being favoured. This had led to a shedding of noble aides by the Commander-in-Chief and 'Sunny' Marlborough had been one of the first to be dropped. When orders for the advance on the Transvaal had been issued, Lord Roberts's new Military Secretary had found that he was expected to remain in Bloemfontein. Somewhat discouraged, Marlborough had appealed to his cousin for help; Churchill—always adept at family wire-pulling—had persuaded Ian Hamilton to take them both on the flanking march. They had joined Hamilton's column in Churchill's newly acquired four-horse wagon, lavishly provisioned with 'the best tinned provisions and alcoholic stimulants which London could supply'.

The Boers in the Orange Free State put up only a token resistance. They were aware that the invading army was not equipped to occupy the country. By allowing Hamilton to advance with comparative ease, the commandos could close in behind him and harass his rearguard. This is what happened at Lindley. Hamilton took the town after a brief skirmish, but he was forced to evacuate it immediately in order to continue his northward drive. As soon as he had left the Boers reoccupied the town. This weakness was only too apparent to those accompanying Hamilton. During the short stay in Lindley, for instance, Churchill went in search of potatoes to replenish his stock. He was directed to an English trader who was reported to have twelve sacks. The Englishman greeted him enthusiastically. 'You can't think,' he said, 'how we have looked forward to this day.' Churchill asked him if he had been ill-treated by the Boers and he was forced to admit that, apart from having some of his property commandeered, he had little cause for complaint. However, his hatred for the Boers was only too evident. It worried Churchill. 'This instinctive dislike which the British settler so often displays for his Dutch neighbour,' he wrote to the *Morning Post*, 'is a perplexing and not very hopeful feature of the South African problem.' On arriving at the man's house he was even more concerned, for over the door there hung a Union Jack. Churchill advised him to take it down. He explained that Hamilton's column would soon be leaving and there was no telling what might happen after they had gone. On hearing that there was little hope of troops arriving to garrison the town for at least another week the man was dumbfounded. When Churchill left him he was feeling very unhappy about his premature enthusiasm. He had good reason to be. During the next three months Lindley was to become the centre of some very fierce fighting.

As the advancing columns neared the Transvaal, Lord Roberts ordered Hamilton to move from the eastern flank to the west of the main army. Roberts expected the Boer force occupying Johannesburg to retreat into the western Transvaal and felt the need to reinforce his western flank. He also hoped that a powerful offensive to the west of Johannesburg would make it unnecessary for his own force to launch a costly frontal attack. But Louis Botha, knowing that Roberts would avoid a frontal offensive if he could, was ready for the attack from the west. When Hamilton joined General French, who was commanding the western flank, their combined force met with fierce opposition. The decisive battle for Johannesburg was fought in the vicinity of Doornkop—the very place where the Jameson Raiders had been captured. The Boers had secured themselves amid the rocks of a line of ridges and had to be dislodged by a determined bayonet charge. This charge fell to the Gordon Highlanders; it was successful only after the loss of a hundred killed and wounded. Towards the end of the action, Churchill rode up to the ridges and, blinded by the smoke of a grass fire, stumbled into a nest of Boer snipers. Once more bullets sang about his head as he turned his horse and careered back to safety.

Churchill's main concern, once the ridges had been captured, was to report the action to his newspaper. But this was not easy. The telegraph wires lay on the other side of Johannesburg and, as the town was still occupied by the Boers, the only way of getting a message through was by making a detour of some eighty miles through rough, hilly country. The morning after the battle Ian Hamilton sent despatches to Lord Roberts but it was thought that, if they got through at all, these despatches would not reach the Commander-in-Chief until late. Such a roundabout means of communication seemed both irritating and unnecessary to Churchill. The most direct, the most obvious, way of reaching the main army and the outside world was through Johannesburg. He needed only a little encouragement to risk a crossing of the enemy-occupied town.

The encouragement came from a Frenchman named Lautré. M. Lautré had been employed on one of the gold mines and had come out of Johannesburg to meet the British. He assured Churchill that, despite rumours to the contrary, the Boers were evacuating the town and there were not many of them left. The chances of a stranger being stopped and questioned at this stage of the evacuation were extremely remote. This was all Churchill needed to know. When Lautré offered to lend him a bicycle and act as his guide he accepted at once. He persuaded Ian Hamilton to write another despatch, then he changed into civilian clothes and, accompanied by M. Lautré, set off for Johannesburg.

On the outskirts of the town they met a British scout cautiously reconnoitring the area. He told them that the correspondent of *The Times* had passed him, headed for Johannesburg on a horse, two hours earlier. Lautré was extremely sceptical about this: anyone on a horse, he assured Churchill, could not hope to escape notice. They pushed on without incident until they reached the centre of Johannesburg. Churchill was rather apprehensive of the surly-looking citizens gathered in groups at street corners and was on the point of turning back when an armed Boer patrol crossed the road in front of them, but his companion remained astonishingly cool. They had agreed to speak only in French and Lautré, taking his promise to act as a guide seriously, chatted away, pointing out public buildings and places of interest.

After leaving the centre of the town, the road ran uphill and they had to dismount and push their bicycles. They were trudging along like this when they heard a steady trot of a horse behind them. It took all Churchill's will power to prevent himself from looking back. '*Encore un Boer*,' grinned Lautré. The rider drew alongside and pulled his horse into a walk. Out of the corner of his eye, Churchill saw that it was an armed burger carrying a full campaign kit. 'I looked at his face and our eyes met,' he says. 'Then he turned away carelessly. Presently he set spurs to his horse and cantered on. I breathed again freely. Lautré laughed.'

As they approached the outskirts of the town, the streets became more and more deserted until finally they found themselves quite alone. It began to grow dark. At any moment they expected to be pulled up by Boers picketing the approaches to Johannesburg; but the road that led them into the country was unguarded. They began to look for Lord Roberts's troops, who, if things had gone according to plan, should by this time have been advancing towards the town from the south. But the only person they encountered was a shabbily dressed old man sauntering aimlessly along the road. He seemed harmless enough, so they took a chance and questioned him. The news he gave them was reassuring: five minutes earlier he had seen British sentinels on the top of a near-by hill.

Cycling for another two hundred yards, they were surprised to meet three unarmed British soldiers walking casually towards the town. These men were not the advance pickets they had expected, but three hungry troopers who had come on ahead in search of food. Churchill warned them not to go any further as they were bound to run into an armed Boer patrol. This 'extraordinary possibility', he says, impressed the soldiers sufficiently to make them abandon their search and turn back.

Soon afterwards the fires of British encampments became visible. Pushing on through the darkness, sometimes carrying their bicycles across ditches or hauling them over wire fences, they eventually arrived at Lord Roberts's headquarters. They were given a great welcome. When Roberts heard that they had come direct from Ian Hamilton he insisted upon seeing them personally. They were ushered into a small room of a deserted farmhouse where the Commander-in-Chief and his staff were finishing dinner. Roberts sprang from his chair and shook their hands. His eyes were twinkling. He wanted to hear about their crossing of Johannesburg and of the action that had been fought the previous day. For Churchill it was a personal, as well as a professional, triumph. 'Then,' he says, 'while being most hospitably entertained, I gave a full account of the doings of General Hamilton's force to my father's old friend and now once again my own.'

*

Lord Roberts entered Pretoria on 5 June 1900. For days the Boer capital had been in a state of chaos. At the end of May, as the British approached Johannesburg, President Kruger, accompanied by some senior officials, had left for the eastern Transvaal where they hoped to establish a new seat of government. With the going of the President, the situation in Pretoria had deteriorated. Wild rumours were spread, food stores were looted and the small police force found it impossible to maintain order. When Louis Botha and his army retreated to Pretoria a few days later, they were forced to pass 'with sad hearts and empty stomachs through the ungrateful capital'.

The lawlessness in the town had infected the British prisoners-of-war. The officers had been moved from the Staatsmodelskool three months after Churchill's escape; now they were housed in a prison camp on the outskirts of Pretoria. They were fully aware of Lord Roberts's approach and at midnight on 4 June they had boldly arrested the camp commandant and compelled him to dismiss the escort which had been sent to take them from the town. But the camp was still guarded and the officers waited on tenterhooks for their rescuers. 'Great was the anxiety,' wrote one of them, 'with which next day we scanned the horizon for signs of the troops, as we could not feel safe till the latter were in occupation of the town. When at last two of our deliverers, the Duke of Marlborough and Mr Winston Churchill, appeared at the gallop, wild was the enthusiasm, and, amidst cheers that "made the welkin ring" the Transvaal flag was exchanged for the Union Jack.'

Churchill and his cousin had entered Pretoria with the advance troops. Their first thought had been for the prisoners. Knowing that the Staatsmodelskool had been evacuated, but not sure where the officers were now imprisoned, they had stopped a mounted burger and persuaded him to guide them to the camp. They rode for three-quarters of a mile and then came in sight of a long tin hut surrounded by wire entanglements. Churchill recognized it immediately. Waving his hat, he let out a loud cheer. An answering cry came from inside the hut; within seconds the prisoners came rushing into the yard, shouting, cheering and waving to the Churchill cousins. The Duke of Marlborough demanded a surrender, the guards threw down their rifles and the gates were thrown open. Someone produced a home-made Union Jack. 'The Transvaal emblem was torn down,' reported Churchill, 'and, amid wild cheers, the first British flag was hoisted over Pretoria. Time 8.47, 5th June.'

He could hardly have staged a more spectacular return to the scene of his captivity. The only thing that marred this dramatic finale was the absence of two important members of the cast. Neither Captain Haldane nor Sergeant Brockie was among the cheering prisoners. With remarkable ingenuity, they had arranged their own release some three months earlier.

When it had been learned that the officers at the Staatsmodelskool were to be transferred to the prison camp, Haldane, Brockie and another officer, Lieutenant Le Mesurier, had hit upon a new escape plan. Since Churchill's departure had effectively prevented them from scaling the wall, they had been obliged to examine a number of alternative schemes. The most promising had been a tunnel which they had started to burrow under the floor of their dormitory. To get under the floorboards had been easy enough for they had discovered a trapdoor conveniently situated in their room. However, their digging operations had run into a number of unexpected difficulties and they had been on the point of giving up when the announcement of the move from the school had given them a new idea. Haldane had suggested that they hide under the floor until the building was evacuated and then emerge and make their escape. This they did. Two days before the move was expected to take place they 'went to earth' and were duly reported missing. The alarm went out, their descriptions were posted throughout the Transvaal and reports that they had been 'recaptured' began to appear in the local press. One or two of their fellow prisoners had been let into the secret and were able to keep them posted as to what was happening above ground. Unfortunately, the move from the Staatsmodelskool was postponed and instead of spending two days under the floorboards they were forced to remain there for over two weeks. For all that, the plan was an undoubted success. When the school was finally evacuated on 16 March, 1900, the three men came out of hiding and, with the outcry over their disappearance having died down, they were able to make their way to Delagoa Bay. Haldane and Le Mesurier followed much the same route as Churchill and were, in fact, assisted by the redoubtable Mr Howard and his friends at the Transvaal and Delagoa Bay Colliery. Brockie became separated from his companions but was able to join up with them again at Lourenço Marques. As it happened, this shortened their captivity by only three months but their feat became a legend which Churchill was later pleased to report.

The absence of his friends in no way lessened Churchill's thrill at being instrumental in freeing the British prisoners. As soon as the camp commandant and his guards had exchanged places with their captives, there was a stampede to the centre of the town. Here, at two o'clock in the afternoon, Lord Roberts took the salute as his army occupied the Boer capital. 'For over two hours,' says Conan Doyle, 'the khaki waves with their crests of steel went sweeping by. High above their heads from the summit of the Raad-saal the broad Union Jack streamed for the first time. Through months of darkness we had struggled onwards to the light. Now at last the strange drama seemed to be drawing to its close.'

And so thought everyone. Writing to his mother four days later—in a letter headed 'Pretoria Again'—Churchill announced that he was preparing to return home. South Africa had served its purpose and served it well. He was now ready to take advantage of his experiences.

CHAPTER EIGHTEEN

The Leave Taking

SARAH ALSO was planning her return to England. Once order had been established in Mafeking she was anxious to get away. A few days after the relief of the town her maid, Metelka, joined her from Setlagole and there seemed no good reason for them to delay their departure. On 18 May Sarah had written her last despatch to the *Daily Mail*, making a further appeal for contributions to the Mafeking Relief Fund. 'May I now plead with the generous English public for subscriptions for refugees and sisters of the convent,' she wrote. 'Both have rendered great and valuable services, and have incurred the loss of all their property, while the refugees are mostly destitute . . . I am leaving for England when the line is open.'

But it took longer to open the line than she anticipated. By the end of May, although supply trains were arriving from the north, there was little hope of the rail to the south being repaired. It was estimated that it would take some weeks. The only way to reach Cape Town on this route was by trekking to Kimberley and taking the train from there. It was a long and tedious journey and one which did not appeal to Sarah. The only other possibility was to travel through the Orange Free State via Pretoria and Johannesburg, but this was considered to be out of the question. The country between Mafeking and Pretoria was still occupied by the enemy and, until it had been cleared, Baden-Powell would not hear of a woman taking such a route. The troops were preparing to advance on the area—Colonel Plumer heading for Zeerust, Baden-Powell taking a force to occupy Rustenburg—but it looked like being a lengthy business.

As reports came in that the Boers were laying down their arms and returning to their farms, Sarah became more and more impatient. Whatever the risk, she was determined to chance her luck and make for Pretoria. Among the first arrivals at Mafeking had been Mrs Godley—Sarah's erstwhile ally, who had been ordered to Bulawayo at the start of the siege. A woman very much of Sarah's calibre, Mrs Godley immediately fell in with the plan to evade the authorities and trek through enemy country. Their husbands, who were to accompany Baden-Powell to Rustenburg, could do nothing to dissuade them. 'They were wise enough not to ask for leave,' says Major Godley, 'which would almost certainly have been refused.'

On Sunday morning, 4 June, the two women packed Ben Weil's Cape cart and, accompanied by the long-suffering Metelka and an African driver, set out for Pretoria. It was a day of blue skies and bright sun, with just enough breeze to prevent it from being too hot. As the little cart trundled past the outworks of the town, Sarah found it difficult to believe all that had happened to her during the last few months. Snyman's headquarters could be seen in the distance, standing exposed and alone; beyond it, on a slight rise, stood the field hospital where she had been kept a prisoner. In spite of the memories evoked by these places, Sarah found she was torn between relief at being on the move again and a strange sadness at leaving the place which had played such an important part in her life. Taking her last look at Mafeking she had, she said, 'a curious feeling of regret and of gratitude to the gallant little town and its stout citizens; to the former for having been a haven in the midst of fierce storms during all these months; to the latter for their stout arms and their brave hearts, which had warded off the outbursts of the same tempests, whose clouds had hung dark and lowering on our horizon since the previous October.'

They stopped for lunch at a corrugated-iron hotel in the hamlet of Otto's Hoop. Word that they were on their way had been telephoned through and they were welcomed by some officers of the Imperial Light Horse. Their arrival created a small sensation. After months of isolation, the sight of these well-dressed women calmly eating lunch in hostile country was as improbable as it was unexpected. The German proprietor of the hotel, remarked Sarah, 'could do nothing but stare at us while we were eating'.

THE LEAVE TAKING

Their light-hearted jaunt was brought to an abrupt halt a few miles beyond Otto's Hoop. Across their path raged the waters of a swollen river. Nothing daunted, and egged on by the two women, the driver turned the horses' heads towards it and plunged straight in. As the waters began to rise over the cart, submerging their luggage, the leading horses took fright and headed back to the bank. The driver kept his head and managed to turn the cart and they were brought back, wringing wet, to the spot from which they had started. Uncertain what to do next, their problem was solved by the arrival of a trooper of the Imperial Light Horse. Mounting a loose horse, he managed to drag the leading animals forward to face the rushing stream. Once again their luggage was submerged but this time they arrived safely on the opposite bank.

As the sun was setting, they met Major Weston-Jarvis and a dust-begrimed squadron of the Rhodesian Regiment a few miles outside Zeerust. The soldiers took them in charge and escorted them into the little town. They had arrived well in advance of Colonel Plumer's force, which was supposed to be occupying Zeerust. Once again their unexpected presence caused considerable surprise; this time to their own forces. 'Charlie Fitzclarence riding with the scouts of our advance guard,' reports Major Godley, who heard of the incident later, 'observing every military precaution and peeping cautiously round the corner of a kopje, was rewarded by the sight of two ladies, one with a red parasol, and Weston-Jarvis in a red balaclava cap, sitting outside a Boer farmhouse and indulging in a hearty dinner.'

They stayed at Zeerust for two days. Then, hearing that Lord Roberts had occupied Pretoria, they hired a new cart and set off for the Transvaal capital. They had not gone far before a message from Baden-Powell caught up with them. Lord Roberts's line of communication had been interrupted, he told them, and they were to go no further. Even this intrepid pair could not ignore such definite instructions and so, reluctantly, they returned to Zeerust. However, on hearing a few days later that Baden-Powell had occupied Rustenburg, they decided to chance their luck again. This time they tried a different route. Heading their cart to the north, they passed through the pretty, mountainous country, softened by orange groves and sleepy farmsteads, which bordered the road to Rustenburg. That evening they were somewhat alarmed to learn of an outbreak of smallpox at the wayside store in which they slept, but otherwise their journey was uneventful.

At Rustenburg they were told that Baden-Powell and his staff had left for Pretoria to confer with Lord Roberts. Hardly waiting to rest their horses, they set off in hot pursuit. Two days later, entering the valley which led to the Boer capital, they watched heliograph messages flashing from the surrounding hills. By five o'clock that evening they had joined the stream of stragglers and camp followers making their way through the outskirts of Pretoria. They had accomplished the last stage of their journey—over 135 miles—without stopping to change horses.

This ride through enemy country was no mean feat: not so much for what happened, but for what might have happened. In fact, it was considered remarkable enough to earn Sarah and Mrs Godley a special mention in the history of the Imperial Light Horse. 'These daring young ladies,' it was noted, 'succeeded in driving from Mafeking to Pretoria, a distance of some 230 miles, and were not molested by anyone—a strange contrast between the powerful column, seeing an enemy behind every bush and the sprightly young ladies (well known in the fox-hunting world) caring nothing for all the Boers in Christendom. . .'

The centre of Pretoria bore all the marks of an occupied town. The streets were crowded with troops; carts and gun-wagons blocked the entrance to the main square and the shouts of the soldiers were to be heard everywhere. There was hardly a civilian to be seen.

Nowhere was the bustle of the occupation more apparent than in the crowded hotels. When Sarah and Mrs Godley drove up to the Grand Hotel, they found the place swarming with British officers. To Sarah, after her months of confinement, it seemed as if all the inhabitants of England had been trasported to Pretoria *en masse*. When they asked for a room, the hotel manager threw up his hands in despair. The idea of accommodating two respectable women amid the crush of soldiers was too much for him. However, he eventually pulled himself together. Hurrying along the corridors, with Sarah and Mrs Godley in his wake, he hunted desperately for a suitable room. Then an idea struck him. He conducted them to an apartment which, he explained, would be free in a few hours' time: the gentleman occupying it was due to leave that evening and was already packing his belongings. Arriving at the room, he threw open the door and they were greeted by the sight of a young man busily stowing away his clothes and papers. To Sarah's amazement, the startled guest was none other than her nephew Winston Churchill.

Her astonishment was matched by that of the hotel manager. Difficult as were rooms to come by, the sight of one of the new arrivals clasping the departing guest in her arms must have seemed to be carrying gratitude too far.

What Winston thought of this meeting with his 'catty' aunt is not recorded. However, he played the dutiful nephew. Not only did he give up part of his suite, but he postponed his departure for another twenty-four hours in order to entertain Sarah.

*

The following morning, Baden-Powell—now promoted to Major General—was due to leave Pretoria and return to Rustenburg. With him were going Gordon Wilson and Major Godley. Sarah and Mrs Godley, having just been reunited with their husbands, were up early to bid them goodbye. Winston went along to report the departure for the *Morning Post*.

The troops were given a special send-off by Lord Roberts. As a mark of respect for the defender of Mafeking, the Commander-in-Chief had agreed to ride with Baden-Powell to the outskirts of Pretoria. The procession, says Sarah, was an 'imposing sight'. Headed by a company of turbaned Indians, the soldiers made their way slowly through the streets, followed by Lord Roberts and Baden-Powell, riding side by side. To Sarah's delight, the two officers stopped when they came abreast of Mrs Godley and herself; Lord Roberts came over to have a word with them. He expressed surprise at seeing them there and complimented them on their daring. They were, he said, the first Englishwomen to enter the town. Sarah modestly explained that the roads had seemed quiet and that they had been treated with respect by the Boers they had met. 'That,' said Roberts, turning to Baden-Powell, 'is thanks to you, General.' All the same, his tone indicated that he by no means approved of their having made such a journey. Having just reconciled himself to the unruly Winston, the sight of yet another disobedient

Churchill in Pretoria was obviously not welcome. Sarah could not escape the feeling that she had been given a polite reprimand. 'On reflection,' she said, 'I decided, rather from what Lord Roberts left unsaid than from his actual words, that if we had asked leave to travel via Pretoria, it would have been refused.'

That afternoon Sarah and Mrs Godley were conducted about the town by Winston. He took them to the prison camp, from which he and the Duke of Marlborough had released the British officers, and then took them on a tour of inspection of the Staatsmodelskool. Sarah was able to view the former prison with an experienced eye. 'These quarters,' she remarked, after listening to Winston explaining how he had escaped, 'must have been a particularly disagreeable and inadequate residence.'

In the evening a group of army officers entertained Winston to a farewell dinner. Sarah, who was also invited, was delighted with the progress made by her precocious nephew. No longer was he the sulky youngster who had to be bossed about, but an enterprising young man who obviously commanded respect. The likeness to his father was striking. 'Winston . . .' she wrote, 'although he had been but a short time, comparatively, with Lord Roberts's force, had contrived therein to acquire influence and authority. The "bosses," doubtless, disapproved of his free utterances, but he was nevertheless most interesting to listen to, and a general favourite.'

Winston left Pretoria by train early the next morning. Sarah and Mrs Godley were at the station to see him off. It was all very different from his hurried departure from the same town six months earlier.

*

Churchill was once again a civilian. He had reported his final action as a uniformed war-correspondent shortly before leaving Pretoria. This was the battle of Diamond Hill: one of the last major pitched battles of the war.

Louis Botha and Koos de la Rey, two of the most distinguished Boer generals, had rallied a force of 6,000 burgers and positioned them along a range of hills some fifteen miles east of Pretoria. Lord Roberts personally commanded the force that had attacked them. The action lasted for two days and ended indecisively with

THE LEAVE TAKING

the Boers making a tactical withdrawal. Churchill, who had accompanied Ian Hamilton's column, distinguished himself by undertaking a single-handed scouting operation—which Hamilton was later to describe as 'an exhibition of conspicuous gallantry . . . for which he has never received full credit.' But once the battle was over he was obliged to say goodbye to his old friends. 'I had determined to return to England,' he wrote; 'but it was with mixed feelings that I watched the departure of the gallant column in whose good company I had marched so many miles and seen such successful sights. Their road led them past Lord Roberts's headquarters, and the old Field-Marshal came out himself to see them off . . . all streamed by, grew faint in the choking red dust, and vanished through the gap in the southern hills.' His cousin, the Duke of Marlborough, went with them.

Churchill, unlike many others, had no illusions about the war being over. In fact, on his return to England, he made a point of emphasizing that the fighting would continue. His decision to leave South Africa was a political one. A General Election was expected to take place that year and he was determined to fight it. Shortly after his escape from Pretoria he had been offered the nomination for the Conservative candidacy at Southport but, despite pressure from local officials, his heart was still set on winning Oldham. Only by returning now could he hope to be in a position to contest the seat.

The journey to the Cape was not without its excitement. The country was far from settled; Boer guerrillas, hoping to cut Lord Roberts off from his supplies in the south, were constantly menacing the railway line. Bridges had been destroyed, the tracks repeatedly disrupted and some trains attacked. Civilians travelling across the Orange Free State were warned before they set out of the risks they took. The train in which Churchill was travelling met no trouble until it was 100 miles south of Johannesburg. Then it was brought to an abrupt halt. Churchill and the Duke of Westminster—who had been breakfasting together—jumped from their carriage to find out what was happening. As they stepped on to the track, a small shell thudded into the embankment opposite them. They could see a wooden bridge in flames a hundred yards ahead. The train was taking troops to the Cape and when the shooting started the soldiers leaped from their carriages. There were no officers in sight and nobody seemed to be in charge. Churchill's experience of train-wrecking made him fully alive to the situation. Ignoring the confusion he ran along the line, climbed into the cab and ordered the driver to blow his whistle. Then, standing on the footplate, he shouted to the men to return to the train. As he stood there, he noticed a party of Boers crouching in the dry river bed under the burning bridge. He opened fire at them with his Mauser pistol. They scattered and disappeared without shooting back. 'These,' he says, 'were the last Boers I was to see as enemies.'

Once the men had reboarded the train, Churchill instructed the driver to shunt back for three miles to the nearest station. Here they were told what was happening. The train before them had been attacked at the next station along the line. Fighting was still in progress. The rails had been torn up to prevent reinforcements from reaching the embattled train. Not until the following day did they hear that the Boers had been beaten back, at the cost of 60 or 70 British casualties. As there was no hope of the rails being repaired for several days, Churchill and his friends had to borrow horses and ride through the night until they reached the other side of the disrupted line. This proved to be the last of Churchill's South African adventures.

At Cape Town he was entertained at Government House by Sir Alfred Milner, and Cecil Rhodes's brother, Frank, gave him lunch at Groote Schuur. He had plenty to keep him occupied. The Duke of Westminster organized a jackal hunt on Table Mountain and he was able to catch up with his mail. He was pleased to learn that his latest literary venture was proving a success. This was a book which he had compiled from his despatches to the *Morning Post*. Entitled *London to Ladysmith via Pretoria*, it told of his experiences in South Africa up to the relief of Ladysmith. It had been published with astonishing speed. Completed in March, it had been sent to England and was in the bookshops by the beginning of May. He had demanded a £2,000 advance and now, less than two months after publication, he was informed that 11,000 copies had been sold, which, he calculated, would bring him a further £720. Already he was busy with a second volume, *Ian Hamilton's March*, which was intended to complete his South African saga.

A cable, which he received from his mother, he found rather

puzzling. In it Lady Randolph broke the news that she intended marrying George Cornwallis-West at the end of July. But this was offset by a report in the *Cape Times*. A Reuter's cable, published in the newspaper, stated that Lieutenant Cornwallis-West was about to return to South Africa and that the marriage had been postponed. He was still uncertain as to his mother's plans when, on 4 July, he boarded the *Dunottar Castle*—the ship that had brought him to South Africa—and sailed for home.

*

It took a few days for Sarah to obtain a railway pass enabling her to travel to Cape Town. However, permission having finally been granted, she said goodbye to Mrs Godley and, accompanied by two army officers and Metelka, set off for the coast. Her journey, although not as hazardous as Winston's, was not entirely uneventful.

They had not got far beyond Johannesburg when it was announced that the train with which they were due to link up had broken down. At the next station they were bundled on to the platform and told to expect a delay of at least four hours. Sarah quickly tired of looking at the battle-scarred surroundings and retired to the general waiting room with a book. She was deeply absorbed in her reading when the door was thrown open and she was brought face to face with the Duke of Marlborough. 'We exchanged a surprised greeting,' she says, 'being totally unaware of each other's whereabouts. Except for meeting Winston in Pretoria, I had not seen the face of one of my relations for more than a year, but so many surprising things happen in wartime that we did not evince any great astonishment at this strange and unexpected meeting.' Marlborough explained that he had just arrived on a train from Heidelburg with General Ian Hamilton, who had recently fallen from his horse and broken his collarbone. They were on their way to Pretoria. Sarah was taken to see the injured General and was surprised to find him lying on a rough couch in a cattle-truck. Many years later Hamilton was to remember Sarah's visit and the blue bird's-eye dress she was wearing.

The Cape Town train did not arrive until long after Marlborough had left. It was dark before Sarah climbed into her carriage. 'Sleep with your head away from the window,' she was advised as she settled in, 'in case of a stray bullet.' Luckily, no bullets were fired at the train but the passengers were kept on edge until they passed Kroonstad in the Orange Free State, when it was judged that they were out of the danger zone. There was plenty of evidence that the war was still in progress. At wayside halts, groups of soldiers stood huddled over campfires; bridges that had been dynamited sagged into overflowing rivers; army encampments, flanked by Red Cross tents, lined the railway embankments; all the main stations were crowded with soldiers and congested traffic, adding to the interminable delays. The journey took several days and it was an exhausted, travel-stiff Sarah who eventually staggered on to the platform at Cape Town station.

For the few days that she was in Cape Town, Sarah stayed at Groote Schuur, where she was well looked after by Frank Rhodes. She was kept extremely busy. Not only did she have a host of friends to see, but her time was taken up with the Mafeking Relief Fund. Money from the fund was now arriving in South Africa and a committee had been set up in Mafeking to allocate the large donations to deserving cases. To Sarah fell the task of acting as liaison officer between the London and Mafeking committees. Her work was not made easier by the attacks on the Relief Fund made by correspondents to the Cape Town papers. She answered these attacks at length and, by the time she left South Africa, she had the satisfaction of knowing that her organization was running smoothly.

Busy as she was, she did find time to pose for a rather striking photograph. Always a lover of fancy dress, she had had made— either in Pretoria or Cape Town—a uniform which suited her role as an intrepid war correspondent. Tailored in khaki serge, it consisted of a tunic and skirt, white silk cravat, and a wide-brimmed military-style hat. Now, with a binocular case slung across one shoulder, a malacca cane gripped in her right hand, and her left foot planted mannishly on a studio rock, she faced a Cape Town photographer with her level stare. She looked every inch a Churchill. For years to come this photograph was to feature in books evoking the Anglo-Boer war period and her family regarded it with pride. 'At Rolleston,' wrote Viscount Churchill, 'there was a dashing photograph of Cousin Sarah, belted, high-collared and wasp-waisted in her African outfit.'

It was very much what the public in England expected of her. 'Sally Wilson of Mafeking' was already a popular heroine. 'When the history of the South African Campaign comes to be written,' declared one newspaper, 'there is one Englishwoman whose wonderful pluck and valour in face of terrible and depressing difficulties will need no fine language to enhance the glory of that simple record of fact. That Englishwoman is, we need hardly say, Lady Sarah Wilson, "the heroine of heroic Mafeking".' Suitably attired, she now felt ready to face the tremendous welcome that was waiting for her.

Both Gordon Wilson and the Duke of Marlborough managed to join Sarah for the homeward voyage. They sailed from Cape Town, on the s.s. *Briton*, two weeks after Winston Churchill had left.

*

The cable that Winston had received from his mother in Cape Town proved to have carried the correct information. Despite opposition from the bridegroom's family and some of her friends, Lady Randolph was married to George Cornwallis-West on 28 July 1900. Among those who disapproved of the match was Lady Randolph's old admirer, the Prince of Wales. Although the Prince gave the bride a personal gift the day before the wedding, he would not allow his name to appear on the list of present-givers and refused to attend the ceremony, which took place at St Paul's Church, Knightsbridge. But, despite the absence of the Prince and the bridegroom's family, the wedding was no hole-in-the-corner affair. Both the Jerome and Churchill families rallied to Lady Randolph's support and the church was packed by a large section of fashionable society.

There was no escaping the fact that it was a war-time wedding. Several members of the congregation were in uniform; the bridegroom and his best man, Lieutenant H. C. Elwes, were both regular soldiers; and when the bride entered the church, shortly after 11 a.m., she did so on the arm of the Duke of Marlborough, who had returned from South Africa only a matter of days before. For the crowd waiting outside the church, however, the most colourful reminder of the war was the arrival of the bride's famous son and sister-in-law. Winston Churchill had arrived at the church before his mother, with a Churchill aunt on each arm. Lady Georgiana Curzon was well known to the public for her work with the Yeomanry Hospitals and the Mafeking Relief Fund, and Lady Sarah Wilson was perhaps the most celebrated woman in England at that time. The sight of the two well-known ex-prisoners of war entering St Paul's Church arm in arm sent a flutter of enthusiasm through the crowd. It more than made up for the absence of royalty. More than all the current rumours of peace, this reunion of the Churchill clan, who had played such a prominent part in the war, seemed to promise an early end to hostilities. It might soon be possible to forget the unpleasantness in South Africa and to embark on a new, more forward-looking way of life.

It did not work out quite like that. The war continued for almost two years after the Churchills left Africa. But for them, at least, the wedding at St Paul's Church marked the end of an important phase in all their lives: a phase in which Africa had figured largely and significantly.

Epilogue

ONE DOES not automatically associate the Churchills with Africa. Yet there can be no doubt about the importance of the continent—particularly its southern part—in the lives of at least three members of the family. It was not merely that Africa provided the background for their colourful adventures, but that those adventures had considerable bearing on their careers.

Lord Randolph's decision to visit Mashonaland in 1891 reawakened public interest in his erratic career. Had it not been for his illness the visit could, as was hoped, have marked the beginning of his political comeback. For although the controversy it aroused was unfavourable, it provided the very atmosphere in which the turbulent Lord Randolph had previously flourished. If he had been able to follow up his South African venture with a vigorous political campaign (and, despite moments of pessimism, it was clearly his intention to do so) he would undoubtedly have re-established his parliamentary prominence. But this was not to be. His fatal disease was already beginning to sap his physical powers and was soon to put an end to all hopes of his return to high office. The South African expedition, therefore, instead of heralding his political resuscitation, represented the end of his active political career. It marked his last controversial fling.

For Sarah, South Africa provided a brief and unexpected burst of glory. But although her public career was short lived, its influence on her life was profound. It took her out of the ranks of conventional society women and established her in the eyes of her contemporaries as an adventurous and exciting personality. She did nothing to cultivate this reputation and, by neglecting it, allowed herself to be forgotten. Those who knew her well were amazed at her subsequent modesty. Sonia Keppel, for instance, was to remember Sarah playing with her as a child and classed her among the legendary figures of her youth. 'I put Lady Sarah Wilson in the same category as Miss Florence Nightingale...' she says. 'Both ladies had been heroines and as such were awe-inspiring... [but] Lady Sarah seemed cheerfully forgetful of her former heroism and content to let it lie in lavender.' For all that, Sarah was undoubtedly proud of her association with South Africa. She paid three more visits to the country and each time was received as a returning celebrity. It was her experiences at the Mafeking hospital that inspired her to undertake the organization of field hospitals in France during the First World War, a task she embarked on a few days after Gordon Wilson (then Lieutenant-Colonel) was killed while leading his men into action at Ypres. She worked unsparingly throughout the war but, once it was over, she again drifted back into comfortable anonymity. 'Lady Sarah Wilson,' commented a journalist, when she died on 22 October 1929, 'affords a striking example of a woman whose name was on everyone's lips rather more than a generation ago, but who lapsed into almost complete obscurity. Cynical people may add that, considering she was an aunt of Mr Winston Churchill, this was even more curious.' But perhaps this was the reason: like the rest of her family, Sarah was completely eclipsed by her brilliant nephew.

Africa was the launching ground for Winston Churchill's momentous career. It could have started anywhere, but it was South Africa that happened to provide him with his first break. His previous experiences—in Cuba and in India—demonstrated his determination to carve a name for himself; in South Africa he succeeded. Until his escape from Pretoria he had been regarded as Lord Randolph's pushing and unpredictable son; ever afterwards he was to be known as the pushing and unpredictable Winston Churchill. His experiences in South Africa seem in many ways to have set the pattern for his future course. All the ingredients are there: patriotism, ambition, courage, rebelliousness, bombast and humour. It is possible to recognize the man who could inspire others by his own defiance; who could alienate his colleagues by his wilfulness and soften his enemies by his generosity; who could seek public acclaim and at the same time refuse to run with the horde; who could be greeted with hosannahs and shortly afterwards have to fight for recognition. 'Success,' he once said, 'is the result of making many mistakes, and learning from experience.' The contributory causes of his own success were very much in evidence in South Africa.

Africa continued to play a prominent part in his life. He won his election at Oldham and took his seat in Parliament on 14 February 1901. His maiden speech was concerned with the continuing Anglo-Boer War and he startled his own side by his famous observation: 'if I were a Boer I hope I should be fighting in the field.' His magnanimity towards his former foes won him many friends among the Boers; friends such as Louis Botha and Jan Smuts, who were to prove firm allies during the two world wars. His first ministerial appointment, as the Liberal Under-Secretary for the Colonies in 1906, again involved him in South African affairs. It fell to him to pilot through the House of Commons measures granting responsible government to the Transvaal and the Orange Free State and to pave the way for the eventual unification of South Africa in 1910. All of this helped to consolidate his friendship with the men who then ruled the country. 'During 1912–13 I made a tour of the Empire, lasting seventeen months,' says Sir Evelyn Wrench, 'but only in South Africa . . . did I find much interest taken in Churchill.' Unfortunately, the men who accepted Churchill's hand of friendship were to find that it earned them the distrust of their fellow Afrikaners. Not everybody could afford Churchill's generous sentiments.

There were to be other associations with Africa. A tour of East Africa in 1908 resulted in his travel book, *My African Journey*; the campaigns of the Second World War brought him into close contact with North Africa; there were the painting expeditions to Marrakesh after the war. . . . But these are episodes which belong to another era in the life of the man; they bear no relation to those formative years when Churchill first responded to the impact of Africa.

There are reminders of the Churchills throughout South Africa. Lord Randolph's tempestuous journey has left few traces although one or two of the houses in which he spent a few days still stand. The re-built Keeley home at Mosita, in which Sarah Wilson drove the family to near distraction, still crowns a rise above the shimmering veld and the Setlagole store is still an oasis in the dust of the Vryburg–Mafeking road. Mafeking itself is full of mementoes of the days of the Siege. But, not unnaturally, it is Winston's trail that has been most clearly marked. At Chievely the motorist on the road between Durban and Johannesburg will see a stone by the roadside commemorating the spot where the armoured train was derailed. A plaque set into the wall of the Durban Post Office (the former Town Hall) depicts, in low relief, the young Churchill addressing the assembled citizens. Near Witbank in the Transvaal another plaque is affixed to the skeleton of the disused Transvaal and Delagoa Bay Mine in which Churchill spent those anxious nights. The Staatsmodelskool, that Victorian red-brick building from which he made his famous escape, has been proclaimed a historical monument.

Nor did Churchill himself forget his association with the country. In 1955, when Pretoria celebrated its centenary, a richly characteristic message was received by the organizers of the centenary celebrations: 'It is my privilege,' wrote Sir Winston Churchill, 'as one not unacquainted with Pretoria's hospitality, to offer the City my heartiest congratulations . . .'

Bibliography

UNPUBLISHED SOURCES

Thomasina Cowan's Diary. In the possession of Mrs S. Minchin, Mafeking, South Africa.

The Mafeking Convent Papers. Convent of Mercy, Rosebank, Johannesburg, South Africa.

The Keeley Family Papers. In the possession of Mrs E. M. Johnstone, Setlagole, South Africa.

Miss Crauford's Diary. In the possession of Mrs C. Cassidy, Maseru, Lesotho.

Trooper Fuller's Diary. In the possession of Mr J. Fuller, Johannesburg, South Africa.

Baden-Powell's Staff Diary. In the possession of Mr W. Hillcourt, North Brunswick, U.S.A.

PUBLISHED SOURCES

Aitken, W. Francis, *Baden-Powell: The Hero of Mafeking*. S. W. Partridge, London, 1900.

Amery, L. S., *Days of Fresh Air*. Jarrolds, London, 1939.

— (ed.) *The Times History of the War in South Africa*. Low-Marston, London, 1905.

Andrews, Allen, *The Splendid Pauper*. Harrap, London, 1968.

Atkins, J. B., *Incidents and Reflections*. Christophers, London, 1947.

— *The Relief of Ladysmith*. Methuen, London, 1900.

Badenhorst, Alida, *Tant Alie of the Transvaal* (Translated by Emily Hobhouse). Allen & Unwin, London, 1923.

Baillie, F. D., *Mafeking: A Diary of the Siege*. Constable, London, 1900.

Balsan, Consuelo, *The Glitter and the Gold*. Heinemann, London, 1953.

Brain, Sir Russell, *Diseases of the Nervous System*. Oxford University Press, 1956.

Bonham-Carter, Lady Violet, *Winston Churchill as I knew him*. Eyre & Spottiswoode, London, 1965.

Butler, Jeffrey, *The Liberal Party and the Jameson Raid*. Clarendon Press, Oxford, 1968.

Churchill, Lord Randolph, *Men, Mines and Animals in South Africa.* Sampson Low, London, 1892.
Churchill, Lady Randolph, *Letters from a Hospital Ship. Anglo-Saxon Review,* London, 1900.
Churchill, Randolph S., *Winston S. Churchill: Youth 1875–1900.* Heinemann, London, 1966.
— *Winston S. Churchill: Young Statesman 1901–1914.* Heinemann, London, 1966.
— *Companion Volume 1 to Winston S. Churchill Parts 1 and 2.* Heinemann, London, 1967.
Churchill, Sarah, *A Thread in the Tapestry.* André Deutsch, London, 1967.
Churchill, Viscount, *All My Sins Remembered.* Heinemann, London, 1947.
Churchill, Winston, *The Story of the Malakand Field Force.* Longmans, London, 1898.
— *The River War.* Longmans, London, 1899.
— *London to Ladysmith via Pretoria.* Longmans, London, 1900.
— *Ian Hamilton's March.* Longmans, London, 1900.
— *Lord Randolph Churchill.* Macmillan, London, 1906.
— *My Early Life.* T. Butterworth, London, 1930.
— *Thoughts and Adventures.* T. Butterworth, London, 1932.
— *Frontiers and Wars.* Eyre & Spottiswoode, London, 1962.
Cole, P. Tennyson, *Vanity Varnished.* Hutchinson, London, 1931.
Collier, Joy. *The Purple and the Gold.* Longmans, London, 1965.
Creswicke, Louis, *South Africa and the Transvaal War.* T. C. & E. C. Jack, Edinburgh, 1902.
Currey, R., *Rhodes: A Biographical Footnote.* Carmelite Press, Cape Town (N.D.).
Dennison, Major C., *A Fight to the Finish.* Longman, London, 1904.
de Souza, C. W. L., *No Charge For Delivery.* Books of Africa, Cape Town, 1969.
De Waal, D. C., *With Rhodes in Mashonaland.* Juta, Capetown, 1896.
Doyle, A. Conan, *The Great Boer War.* Nelson, London, 1903.
Dugdale, E. T., *Maurice De Bunsen: Diplomat and Friend.* John Murray, London, 1934.
Eade, Charles (ed.), *Churchill: By His Contemporaries.* Hutchinson, London, 1953.
Field, Julian O., *Uncensored Recollections.* Eveleigh Nash, London, 1924.
Finlason, C. E., *A Nobody in Mashonaland.* G. Vickers, London, 1894.
Fitzpatrick, J. P., *Through Mashonaland with Pick and Pen.* Johannesburg, 1892.
Fletcher, J. S., *Baden-Powell of Mafeking,* Methuen, London, 1900.

BIBLIOGRAPHY

Forrest, Sir George, *The Life of Lord Roberts*. Cassell, London, 1915.
Fort, G. S., *Chance or Design? A Pioneer Looks Back*. Robert Hale, London, 1942.
Gardner, Brian, *Mafeking: A Victorian Legend*. Cassell, London, 1966.
Godley, Sir Alexander, *Life of an Irish Soldier*. John Murray, London, 1939.
Graham, A. J. P., *The Capture and Escape of Winston Churchill*. Edinburgh Press, Salisbury, Rhodesia, 1965.
Guedalla, Philip, *Mr Churchill: A Portrait*. Hodder & Stoughton, London, 1941.
Gutsche, Thelma, *No Ordinary Woman*. Timmins, Cape Town, 1966.
Haldane, Sir Aylmer, *A Soldier's Saga*. Blackwood, London, 1948.
— *How We Escaped From Pretoria*. Blackwood, London, 1901.
Hamilton, J. Angus, *The Siege of Mafeking*. Methuen, London, 1900.
Harris, Frank, *My Life and Loves*. Obelisk Press, Paris, 1926.
Hofmeyr, A., *The Story of My Captivity During the Transvaal War 1899–1900*. Edward Arnold, London, 1900.
Hutchinson, H. G. (ed.), *Private Diaries of the Rt. Hon. Sir Algernon West*. John Murray, London, 1922.
Howard, Lord Esme, *Theatre of Life*. Hodder & Stoughton, London, 1935.
James, Robert Rhodes, *Lord Randolph Churchill*. Weidenfeld and Nicolson, London, 1959.
Johnson, Frank, *Great Days*. G. Bell, London, 1940.
Keppel, Sonia, *Edwardian Daughter*. Hamish Hamilton, London, 1958.
Kruger, D. W., *Paul Kruger*. Afrikaanse Pers, Johannesburg, 1963.
Kruger, Rayne, *Goodbye, Dolly Gray*. Cassell, London, 1959.
Le May, G. H. L., *British Supremacy in South Africa 1899–1907*. Oxford University Press, 1965.
Leslie, Anita, *The Fabulous Leonard Jerome*. Hutchinson, London, 1954.
— *Mr Frewen of England*. Hutchinson, London, 1967.
— *Jennie: The Life of Lady Randolph Churchill*. Hutchinson, London, 1969.
Lewsen, Phyllis (Ed.), *Selections from the Correspondence of John X. Merriman*. Van Riebeeck Society, Cape Town, 1963.
Lippert, Marie, *The Travel Letters of Marie Lippert 1891*. (Translated by Eric Rosenthal) Friends of the South African Library, Cape Town, 1960.
Magnus, Sir Phillip, *Kitchener*. John Murray, London, 1958.
Martin, Ralph, *Lady Randolph Churchill*. Cassell, London, 1969.
Michell, Lewis, *The Life of the Right Hon. Cecil John Rhodes* Edward Arnold, London, 1910.

Milne, Duncan-Grinnell, *Baden-Powell at Mafeking*. Bodley Head, London, 1957.
Milner, Viscountess, *My Picture Gallery*. John Murray, London, 1951.
Neilly, J. Emerson, *Besieged with B.P.* Pearson, London, 1900.
Pakenham, Elizabeth, *Jameson's Raid*. Weidenfeld & Nicolson, London, 1961.
Phillips, Lionel, *Some Reminiscences*. Hutchinson, London, 1924.
Poel, Jean van der, *The Jameson Raid*. Oxford University Press, 1951.
Ransford, Oliver, *The Rulers of Rhodesia*. John Murray, London, 1968.
— *The Battle of Spion Kop*. John Murray, London, 1969.
Raymond, E. T., *Portraits of the Nineties*. T. Fisher Unwin, London, 1921.
Reitz, Deneys, *Commando*. Faber and Faber, London, 1929.
Ronan, Barry, *Forty South African Years*. Heath Cranton, London, 1923.
Rosslyn, Earl of, *Twice Captured*. Blackwood, London, 1900.
Rowse, A. L., *The Later Churchills*. Macmillan, London, 1958.
St Helier, Lady, *Memories of Fifty Years*. Edward Arnold, London, 1909.
Sencourt, Robert, *Winston Churchill*. Faber and Faber, London, 1940.
Serle, P. (Ed.), *Dictionary of Australian Biography*. Angus and Robertson, 1949.
Storr, Anthony (and others) *Churchill: Four Faces and the Man*. Penguin Press, London, 1969.
Stratford, Esme Wingfield, *Churchill: The Making of a Hero*. Gollancz, London, 1942.
Taylor, J. B., *A Pioneer Looks Back*. Hutchinson, London, 1939.
Thomson, Malcolm, *The Life and Times of Winston Churchill*. Odhams Press, London, (N.D.).
Wallis, J. P. R., *Fitz: The Story of Sir Percy Fitzpartick*. Macmillan, London, 1955.
Weir, Charles, *The Boer War: A diary of the Siege of Mafeking*, Spence and Phimister, Edinburgh, 1900.
West, Mrs George Cornwallis, *The Reminiscences of Lady Randolph Churchill*. Edward Arnold, London, 1908.
West, George Cornwallis, *Edwardian Hey Days*. Putnam, London, 1930.
Williams, Basil. *Cecil Rhodes*. Constable, London, 1921.
Williams, W. W., *The Life of Sir Charles Warren*. Blackwell, London, 1941.
Wilson, H. W., *With the Flag to Pretoria*. Harmsworth, London, 1941.

BIBLIOGRAPHY

Wilson, Lady Sarah, *South African Memories.* Edward Arnold, London, 1909.
— *The Transvaal War: A Woman's Reminiscence of 1899. Book of Beauty*, Hutchinson, London, 1902.
Wolff, Sir Henry Drummond, *Rambling Recollections.* Macmillan, London, 1908.
Young, Filson, *The Relief of Mafeking.* Methuen, London, 1900.

NEWSPAPERS AND PERIODICALS
South African: Cape Times, Cape Argus, Eastern Province Herald, Diamond Fields Advertiser, Johannesburg Star, Pretoria News, Rand Daily Mail, South African News, De Volksstem, Natal Mercury, Natal Witness, Natal Times, Standard and Diggers' News, Bulawayo Chronicle, Pretoriana, Outspan.
British: London Times, Morning Post, Daily Graphic, Daily Mail, Daily Telegraph, Financial News, Newcastle Leader, Phoenix, South Africa, Illustrated London News, The Speaker, Punch, Anglo-Saxon Review, Strand Magazine.

References

CHAPTER ONE

p. 4. 'There is Fort Tuli . . .' Churchill R., *Men, Mines and Animals in South Africa*.

p. 5. 'He has grown a beard . . .' *Graphic*, 18 April 1891; 'Lord Randolph said many imprudent . . .' Rhodes James *Lord Randolph Churchill*.

p. 8. 'Tory Democracy . . .' Guedalla, *Mr Churchill*; 'I found it . . .' Drummond Wolff, *Rambling Recollections*; 'The career of Lord Randolph . . .' Raymond, *Portraits of the Nineties*; 'It is remarkable . . .' Rhodes James *Lord Randolph Churchill*; 'Marshall and Snelgrove . . .' and 'lords of suburban . . .' Raymond *Portraits of the Nineties*.

p. 9. 'The forest laments . . .' Guedalla *Mr Churchill*.

p. 10. 'I forgot Goschen' St Helier *Memories of Fifty Years*; 'He made the clever man's . . .' Raymond *Portraits of the Nineties*; 'We may notice with satisfaction . . .' quoted in *South Africa* 4 April 1891.

pp. 11–12. Interview with *South Africa*, *South Africa* 7 March 1891.

pp. 12–13. Moreton Frewen and the gold crusher, see Andrews *The Splendid Pauper* and Leslie *Mr Frewen of England*.

p. 13. The Churchill syndicate, *South Africa* 18 June 1892.

pp. 14–15. Members of the expedition, see *Graphic* and *South Africa* March–April 1891; Captain Giles' report, *South Africa* 18 April 1891.

p. 16. Reports on farewell dinners, *South Africa* 18 April 1891, *The Times* 20 April 1891.

p. 18. 'While wishing him . . .' *Manchester Examiner* quoted in *South Africa* 14 March 1891.

REFERENCES

CHAPTER TWO

Lord Randolph Churchill's letters from southern Africa were republished in his book *Men, Mines and Animals in South Africa*. Unless otherwise stated the quotations in this chapter are taken from this book.

p. 20. 'Grandolph is in our midst . . .' Lewsen *Correspondence of J. X. Merriman*; Churchill at The Grange, *Cape Argus Weekly* 27 May 1891 and Currey *Rhodes*.

p. 22. 'The immediate occupation . . .' *Cape Argus Weekly* 24 June 1891.

p. 27. 'Wealth cannot break law . . .' Williams *Cecil Rhodes*.

p. 30. 'At De Beers Mine . . .' *Graphic* 21 July 1891; Reactions to Churchill's letters quoted *South Africa* 25 July 1891.

p. 32. Johannesburg reception *Star* 6 June 1891.

p. 33. 'It was only when his lordship . . .' *Eastern Province Herald* 3 Aug. 1891.

p. 34. 'His Lordship was asked out . . .' *Eastern Province Herald* 16 September 1891.

p. 35. 'Poor man! I think his health . . .' Phillips *Some Reminiscences*.

p. 36. Churchill and Beit at Irene *Star* 30 June 1891.

p. 37. 'From all sorts and kinds . . .' *Graphic* June 1891.

p. 38. 'The wonderful thing was . . .' Fitzpatrick *Through Mashonaland with pick and pen*.

p. 39. Denial by Transvaal Government of Churchill's accusations, *Cape Times*, 12 September 1891; 'In a flash the hotel-keeper . . .' *De Volksstem* 14 July 1891.

p. 40. Visit to farm, Fitzpatrick *Through Mashonaland*.

CHAPTER THREE

Quotes from *Men, Mines and Animals* except as follows:

p. 42. 'capacious enough to hold the great king . . .' *South Africa*, 16 May 1891.

p. 45. 'The first day of trekking . . .' Fitzpatrick *Through Mashonaland*.

p. 46. 'a striking rather picturesque figure' Fort *Chance or Design?*

pp. 46–7. Attack on catering of *Grantully Castle*, *Graphic*, 15 June 1891; Reactions to Churchill's letters, *South Africa*, 20 June 1891, 27 June 1891, 4 July 1891 and 11 July 1891; Testimonial to cook, *South Africa*, 22 August 1891.

CHURCHILLS IN AFRICA

pp. 48–9 Comments on Lord Randolph's letters were made throughout his tour of southern Africa; a representative selection has been given. 'If the Boers have not . . .' *Cape Times*, 10 October 1891; Interview with Pasteur, *Graphic*, November 1891; interview with Kaiser, *South Africa*, 30 January 1891; 'Lord Randolph Churchill's "fairies" *South Africa*, 5 December 1891.

pp. 49–50. Skit at Gaiety, *Graphic*, 10 October 1891; 'Everyone laughed . . .' *South Africa*, 17 October 1891; Winston Churchill's reactions, R. Churchill *Companion Volume I* and Rhodes James *Lord Randolph Churchill*.

p. 51. 'in Pall Mall . . .' Lewson *Correspondence of J. X. Merriman*; 'Randolph at Random' *Star*, 14 September 1891; 'We have written . . .' Bloemfontein *Express* quoted in *Eastern Province Herald*, 14 September 1891.

p. 52. 'The hasty, ill-tempered . . .' *De Volksstem*, 5 September 1891; Description of effigy burning, *Cape Times*, 8 September 1891, *Star* 7 September 1891, *Eastern Province Herald*, 9 September 1891 and *De Volksstem*, 8 September 1891; 'Lord Randolph will evidently . . .' *Eastern Province Herald*, 9 September 1891; 'the spoor of the Cape sorcerer . . .' *Standard and Diggers' News*, September 1891.

p. 56. 'He had met Lord Randolph Churchill . . .' *Cape Times*, 22 September 1891.

p. 57. 'started with antagonistic . . .' Johnson *Great Days*.

p. 58. 'Randolph Churchill has been . . .' Lippert *Matabele Travel Letters*; 'Besides his lisp . . .' Fitzpatrick *Through Mashonaland*.

p. 59. 'As money was plentiful . . .' Johnson *Great Days*.

p. 60. 'What between that fool . . .' Lippert *Matabele Travel Letters*.

p. 61. 'He was besieged . . .' Michell *Life of Rhodes*; 'After supper . . .' De Waal *With Rhodes in Mashonaland*.

p. 64. 'But if you can take me . . .' De Waal *With Rhodes*; 'At two o'clock in the afternoon . . .' De Waal *With Rhodes*.

CHAPTER FOUR

Quotes from *Men, Mines and Animals* except as follows:

p. 66. 'The general opinion here . . .' *Cape Times*, 3 October 1891.

REFERENCES

pp. 68–9. 'much pleased with Bechuanaland . . .' *Cape Times*, 25 Nov. 1891; Guest of Alfred Beit, *Cape Times*, 26 November 1891; Churchill's letter to wife, W. Churchill *Lord Randolph Churchill*; move to Rhodes's house, *Cape Times*, 18 December 1891.

p. 70. 'certain claims adjoining . . .' *Cape Times*, 7 January 1891; 'looked more out of tune . . .' Howard *Theatre of Life*; 'There is only one position . . .' Currey *Rhodes*; 'My dear fellow . . .' Howard *Theatre of Life*.

pp. 71–2. 'Had written in bitter . . .' De Waal *With Rhodes*; Rhodes' accident, *Cape Argus Weekly*, 24 December 1891 and *Cape Times*, 23 December 1891; 'a number of people . . .' *Cape Times*, 24 December 1891.

p. 72. Churchill's arrival at Southampton *South Africa*, 9 January 1892 and Churchill *Companion Volume 1*.

p. 73. 'Everyone makes fun . . .' *South Africa*, 16 January 1892; 'There is not the slightest doubt . . .' *South Africa*, 2 January 1892.

p. 74. Churchill's illness, Rhodes James *Lord Randolph Churchill*, W. Churchill *Lord Randolph Churchill* and R. Churchill *Companion Volume 1, Part 1*.

p. 75. 'He is travelling . . .' Dogdale *Maurice De Bunsen*.

pp. 77–8. Doctor's reports on Churchill's illness, Churchill *Companion Volume 1, Part 1*. See also Leslie *Jennie* 'as to be apparent only . . .' Brain *Diseases of the Nervous System*.

p. 78. 'If he cannot say anything . . .' Michell *Life of Rhodes*.

p. 79. Account of Churchill syndicate, *South Africa*, 18 June 1892; 'For this capital . . .' *Land and Water* quoted in *South Africa*, 18 June 1892; Churchill's deep-level shares, W. Churchill *Lord Randolph Churchill*.

p. 82. 'to get at the truth . . .' *Cape Times*, 10 October 1891.

CHAPTER FIVE

Lady Sarah Wilson recorded her impressions of South Africa in her book *South African Memories*; unless otherwise stated, quotes in this chapter are taken from this book.

p. 87. 'I had a letter . . .' Hutchinson *Private Diaries of Sir A. West*; 'complete, full-blown . . .' Rowse *Later Churchills*.

p. 88. 'At luncheon rows of . . .' West *Reminiscences of Lady Randolph Churchill*.

p. 89. 'When I look round . . .' Leslie *The Fabulous Leonard Jerome*; 'She lived for nobody . . .' St Helier *Memoirs of Fifty Years*

p. 91. 'wept large tears . . .' Martin *Lady Randolph Churchill*.

p. 92. 'her brother possessed . . .' *The Times*, 15 October 1929.

p. 93. Winston and Sarah, Churchill *Companion Volume 1 Part 1*.

p. 94. 'Then Sarah tittered . . .' and 'Sarah Wilson—a Churchill . . .' Balsan *The Glitter and the Gold*.

p. 103. 'and the town resounded . . .' *Eastern Province Herald*, 6 January 1896.

CHAPTER SIX

Quotes from *South African Memories* except as follows:

p. 104. 'Your Excellency . . .' *Eastern Province Herald*, 6 January 1896.

p. 105. 'Old Jameson has upset . . .' Williams *Cecil Rhodes*; 'In times of political . . .' *Diamond Fields Advertiser*, 13 January 1896.

p. 108. 'One lady Rhodes liked . . .' Interview with Charles Rickson *Outspan*, 9 December 1944.

CHAPTER SEVEN

p. 121. 'Sensible people will wonder . . .' *Newcastle Leader*, 7 December 1895; 'You know what Papa . . .' Churchill *Companion Volume 1, Part 1*.

p. 123 'I would far rather have been . . .' W. Churchill *My Early Life*; 'If ever I began . . .' and 'All my dreams . . .' W. Churchill *My Early Life*.

p. 124. 'I read industriously . . .' W. Churchill *Thoughts and Adventures*.

p. 125. 'The future is to me . . .' Churchill *Companion Volume 1, Part 1*.

p. 126. 'the courage and resolution . . .' Churchill R. *Winston S. Churchill Vol. I*.

p. 127. 'quite a grown up' W. Churchill *My Early Life*.

p. 128. 'You must work Egypt . . .' Churchill *Companion Volume 1, Part 2*.

p. 129. 'If there is anything . . .' W. Churchill *My Early Life*.

p. 130. 'It is a vy strange . . .' Churchill *Companion Volume 1, Part 2*; 'Those of us, who . . .' W. Churchill *My Early Life*.

REFERENCES

p. 131. 'While we watched, amazed . . .' W. Churchill *The River War*; 'The sight was . . .' W. Churchill *My Early Life*.
p. 132. 'Talk about Fun! . .' W. Churchill *My Early Life*.
p. 133. 'Well, I don't exactly . . .' W. Churchill *My Early Life*.
p. 134. 'magnificent folly' Magnus *Kitchener*; 'for certain and two . . .' Churchill *Companion Volume 1, Part 2*; 'To keep our Empire . . .' R. Churchill *Winston S. Churchill Volume 1, Part 1*.
p. 137. 'There is no way out . . .' Le May *British Supremacy*.
p. 138. 'I am sending a line . . .' Kruger *Goodbye, Dolly Gray*.
p. 139. 'He was slim . . .' Atkins *Incidents and Reflections*.
p. 141. 'You were not concerned . . .' Chaplin *Winston Churchill and Harrow*; 'We pitched our tents . . .' Chaplin *Winston Churchill and Harrow*; 'During the present campaign . . .' *South Africa News*, 16 November 1899.
p. 142. 'He showed me some . . .' Atkins *Incidents and Reflections*.

CHAPTER EIGHT

Quotes from *South African Memories* except as follows:
p. 143. 'The Nineties were . . .' Raymond *Portraits of the Nineties*.
p. 145. 'charming . . . somewhat eccentric . . .' Churchill *Companion Volume 1, Part 1*.
p. 146. 'Lady Sarah struck me . . .' Cole *Vanity Varnished*.
p. 147. 'Café Chantant . . . Geisha Tea' *Bulawayo Chronicle*, 2 Sept. 1899.
p. 148. 'Lady Sarah Wilson arrives . . .' Milner *My Picture Gallery*.
p. 149. 'I little thought . . .' *Daily Mail*, 3 November 1899. 'On arriving here . . .' *Ibid*.
p. 151. 'There are in town . . .' Hamilton *The Siege of Mafeking*.
p. 152. 'There is no rush . . .' *Bulawayo Chronicle*, 20 October 1899; 'Every effort . . .' Hamilton *The Siege of Mafeking*.
p. 154. 'Both wished to remain . . .' Godley *Life of an Irish Soldier*; 'So that afternoon . . .' Badenhorst *Tant Alie of Transvaal*.
p. 155. 'The troop of donkeys . . .' Wilson *The Transvaal War*.
p. 158. 'acted as chief medium . . .' Hamilton *Siege of Mafeking*; 'Sometimes they got through . . .' Interview with Baden-

Powell *Daily Telegraph*, 23 October 1929; 'were handed by the natives . . .' Dennison *A Fight to the Finish*.

CHAPTER NINE

p. 162. 'Meanwhile we wait . . .' W. Churchill *London to Ladysmith*; 'Day after day . . .' Haldane *How we escaped from Pretoria*.
p. 163. 'puffed and trundles . . .' Amery *Days of Fresh Air*; 'The garrison is utterly . . .' W. Churchill *London to Ladysmith*.
p. 164. 'very unpopular . . .' Amery *Days of Fresh Air*; 'The talk was all . . .' Atkins *Incidents and Reflections*.
p. 165. 'That is perfectly true . . .' Atkins *Incidents and Reflections*.
p. 166. 'I do not wish . . .' Haldane *A Soldier's Saga*.
p. 167. 'splattered on the . . .' W. Churchill *My Early Life*; 'Buck up a bit . . .' *Morning Post*, 12 December 1899.
p. 170. 'In an idle moment . . .' *Pretoria News*, 19 January 1965; 'Botha listened in silence . . .' W. Churchill *My Early Life*.
p. 171. Doubt concerning Botha story, A. M. Davey quoted in R. Churchill *Winston S. Churchill*; 'He also refused . . .' Telegram in South African Government Archives; 'So they were not cruel men . . .' W. Churchill *London to Ladysmith*; 'It was plain to me . . .' Haldane *How we escaped*.
p. 172. 'A crowd of rough looking . . .' Haldane *How we escaped*. 'Here we flung ourselves . . .' W. Churchill *London to Ladysmith*.
p. 173. 'Selecting a corner . . .' Haldane *How we escaped*; 'Ah, but it was worse . . .' Atkins *The Relief of Ladysmith*; 'telegraph to England . . .' Haldane *How we escaped*; 'Men stood on the footplate . . . Keep cool . . .' Atkins *The Relief of Ladysmith*.
p. 174. 'a distinct glimpse . . .' Amery *Days of Fresh Air*; 'Sir, The railwaymen . . .' *South African News*, 20 November 1899; 'Capt. Wylie who . . .' *Cape Times Weekly*, 22 November 1899.
p. 175. 'I am sorry to say . . .' *Morning Post*, 12 December 1899; 'Mr Winston Churchill is a prisoner . . .' *Illustrated London News*, 25 November 1899.
p. 176. 'Those are our . . .' and 'Beleaguered Ladysmith . . .'

REFERENCES

W. Churchill *London to Ladysmith*; 'Churchill, needless to say . . .' Haldane *How we escaped*.
p. 177. 'I have the most vivid . . .' Haldane *How we escaped*.
p. 178. Churchill's discussion with Boer guard. W. Churchill *London to Ladysmith*.
p. 179. 'He knew that such . . .' Haldane *How we escaped*; Churchill's conversation with Ferrand, *Standard and Diggers' News* 20 November 1899; 'Now for the first time . . .' W. Churchill *London to Ladysmith*.
p. 180. 'We know and care . . .' Haldane *How we escaped*; 'They looked up . . .' W. Churchill *London to Ladysmith*.

CHAPTER TEN

Quotes from *South African Memories* except as follows:
p. 181. 'Anxieties crowd upon . . .' *Daily Mail*, 8 December 1899; Story of Sarah and vegetable patch, Private Information Mrs E. M. Johnstone (née Keeley) of Setlagole.
p. 189. 'Several of the native . . .' Dennison *A Fight to the Finish*; 'skirting the Kalahari' *Standard and Diggers' News*, 21 November 1899.
p. 190. 'A carrier pigeon hovering . . .' *Standard and Diggers' News*, 21 November 1899.
pp. 191–6. Another account of Sarah and the Boer occupation of the store is given in Wilson *The Transvaal War*.

CHAPTER ELEVEN

p. 197. Reports of Churchill's arrival in Pretoria, *Standard and Diggers' News* and *De Volksstem*, 20 November 1899; 'Mr Winston Churchill declares . . .' *Standard and Diggers' News*, 21 November 1899.
p. 198. 'I understand that the son . . .' de Souza *No Charge for Delivery*, see also Churchill *Companion Volume 1, Part 2*; 'they might as well . . .' Kruger D. W. *Paul Kruger*.
p. 199. 'His name was Winston . . .' Reitz *Commando*; 'The days I passed . . .' W. Churchill *London to Ladysmith*.
p. 200. 'not exactly . . .' Haldane *How we escaped*; 'He is a short . . .' Hofmeyr *The Story of My Captivity During the Transvaal War 1889–1900*.
p. 201. 'a foul and objectionable . . .' W. Churchill *London to*

Ladysmith. 'The Secretary of State . . .' *Ibid.*; 'almost anything . . .' Haldane *How we escaped.*

p. 202. 'quite unsuitable . . .' and 'Our daily routine . . .' Haldane *How we escaped.*

p. 203. 'probably the most astounding . . .' W. Churchill *London to Ladysmith.*

p. 205. 'Suppose this thing . . .' W. Churchill *My Early Life.*

pp. 205–10. Both Churchill and Haldane wrote private accounts of the circumstances surrounding Churchill's escape. These accounts were published in *Companion Volume 1, Part 2* of Randolph Churchill's *Winston S. Churchill.* The story told here is an attempt to relate these two accounts in a continuous narrative.

p. 206. 'Up to this time . . .' Haldane *How we escaped.*

p. 208. 'I had to pause . . .' W. Churchill *My Early Life.*

p. 209. Inquiry into Churchill's escape. Davey *Pretoriana.*

p. 210. 'I was at large . . .' W. Churchill *My Early Life.*

p. 211. 'some fat first-class . . .' and 'Then I hurled myself. . .' W. Churchill *My Early Life.*

p. 213. 'The garden of this house . . .' Haldane *How we escaped*; 'Thank God you have come . . .' W. Churchill *My Early Life.*

p. 214. 'It's all right . . .' W. Churchill *My Early Life*; 'Dewsnap shook Churchill's hand . . .' *Star,* 8 March 1966; 'Viewed from the velvety . . .' W. Churchill *My Early Life.*

CHAPTER TWELVE

Quotes from *South African Memories* except as follows:

p. 220. 'When Lady Sarah arrived . . .' Aitken *Baden-Powell.*

p. 223. 'What shall I do . . .' de Souza *No Charge for Delivery.*

p. 224. 'Lady Sarah wrote saying . . .' Baden-Powell's Diary in possession of W. Hillcourt, New Bruswick, U.S.A.

p. 225. 'she had too many . . .' and 'In a mad moment . . .' Thomasina Cowan's Diary in possession of S. Minchin, Mafeking; 'Wrote to Genl Snyman . . .' Baden-Powell's Diary. 'I have rejected . . .' de Souza *No Charge For Delivery.*

p. 226. 'Will it be . . .' *Daily Mail,* 9 December 1899; 'The Queen was full . . .' West *Reminiscences of Lady Randolph Churchill.*

p. 230. 'Please, please send me . . .' de Souza *No Charge For Delivery.*

REFERENCES

p. 231. '... altho. Lady Sarah Wilson ...' Baden-Powell's Diary; 'We should have liked ...' Emerson Neilly *Besieged with B-P.*

p. 232. 'A common prisoner ...' Weir *The Boer War*; 'I am of course ...' de Souza *No Charge For Delivery.* 'It speaks volumes for ...' quoted in *Cape Argus Weekly*, December 1899.

p. 233. 'He, I fancy ...' Baillie *Mafeking: A Diary of the Siege.*

CHAPTER THIRTEEN

p. 235. Soldier servant and dummy figure Haldane *How we escaped*; 'Sorely afraid of losing ...' Hofmeyer *My Captivity.*

p. 236. Search for Churchill, Hofmeyr *My Captivity*, Haldane *How we escaped*; Churchill's letter to de Souza, Churchill *Companion Volume 1, Part 2* and *Standard and Diggers' News*, December 1899.

p. 237. 'The popular impression is ...' *Standard and Diggers' News*, 14 December 1899; Search and arrests in Pretoria. Hofmeyr *My Captivity* and Mrs T. J. Rodda *Pretoriana.*

p. 238. 'the bold escape ...' *Standard and Diggers' News*, 14 December 1899; 'recaptured in a Transvaal ...' *Ibid*; 'Mr Winston Churchill ... has been ...' *South African News*, 19 December 1899.

pp. 238–9. Commandant Opperman and Churchill's escape, *Standard and Diggers' News*, 14 December 1899, Hofmeyr *My Captivity* and Davey *Pretoriana*; 'For a time ...' Haldane *How we escaped*; 'Seeing that a parole ...' de Souza *No Charge For Delivery* and Churchill *Companion Volume 1, Part 2.*

p. 240. 'Zal hy de ...' Davey *Pretoriana*; 'The idea! ... Hofmeyr *My Captivity*; 'Right airily the officials ...' *Ibid.*

p. 241. 'good authority ...' *De Volksstem*, 14 December 1899; 'the melodramatic descendant ...' *Standard and Diggers' News*, 14 December 1899.

p. 242. 'The three days ...' W. Churchill *My Early Life*; 'When the native ...' Howard *Star*, 11 Dec. 1923; Churchill's advice to his children, Sarah Churchill *A Thread in the Tapestry*; 'Mr Churchill remained ...' Howard *Star*.

p. 243. 'As the office boy ...' Howard *Star*, 22 December 1923.

p. 244. 'I was present ...' Burnham *Star*, 22 December 1923; 'I didn't want him ...' W. Churchill *My Early Life.*

p. 245. 'Smokes were taboo ...' Howard *Star*, 11 December

CHURCHILLS IN AFRICA

1923; 'While dining at . . .' Burnham *Star*, 22 December 1923.
p. 246. 'He surveyed me . . .' and 'with as much . . .' Burnham *Star*, 22 December 1923.
p. 247. 'As we rumbled . . .' W. Churchill *My Early Life*; 'From that moment . . .' W. Churchill *My Early Life*; 'Am now writing . . .' *Standard and Diggers' News*, 23 December 1899.
p. 248. 'It might almost be said . . .' W. Churchill *Strand Magazine* 1923; 'Marlbook in a Coal Truck . . .' *Standard and Diggers' News*, 25 December 1899.
p. 249. 'Although the Boers are . . .' *Times of Natal*, 26 January 1900.
p. 250. Churchill's arrival at Durban, *Natal Mercury*, 23 and 25 December 1899 and *Times of Natal* 25 December 1899 and *Cape Times*, 25 December 1899.
p. 251. 'I was nearly torn . . .' W. Churchill *My Early Life*.
p. 252. 'Nothing would content them . . .' W. Churchill *Strand Magazine* 1923.
p. 253. Churchill's congratulatory messages, W. Churchill *London to Ladysmith* and Churchill *Companion Volume 1, Part 2*.
p. 254. 'Winston Churchill was established . . .' Wingfield-Stratford *Churchill: The Making of a Hero*; 'order his execution' *Phoenix*, 23 November 1899; 'I don't see why . . .' *South African News*, 30 December 1899; 'Our poor gaoler could not . . .' Hofmeyr *My Captivity*.

CHAPTER FOURTEEN

Quotes from *South African Memories* except as follows:
p. 255. 'We are sure . . .' *Mafeking Mail*, 7 December 1899; 'To capture a lady . . .' *Mafeking Mail*, 11 December 1899; 'In treating this lady . . .' *Mafeking Mail*, 11 December 1899.
p. 256. 'Colonel Baden-Powell has inspired . . .' *Daily Mail*, 20 March 1900; 'She was a most remarkable . . .' Interview in *Daily Telegraph*, 23 October 1929; 'much resembles . . .' *Daily Mail*, 20 March 1900.
p. 257. 'It is I think . . .' *Daily Mail*, 20 March 1900.
p. 258. 'The siege of Mafeking is . . .' *Daily Mail*, 20 March 1900.
p. 259. 'I suppose we are . . .' Baillie *Mafeking: A Diary*; 'with

REFERENCES

the knowledge . . .' Emmerson Neilly *Besieged with B-P*.
p. 260. 'All luxuries are eaten . . .' Thomasina Cowan's Diary.
p. 261. 'Lady Sarah Wilson was flirting . . .' Thomasina Cowan's Diary; 'We had a great feast . . .' Godley *Life of an Irish Soldier*.
p. 264. 'The authorities in Pretoria . . .' Hamilton *The Siege of Mafeking*.
p. 265. 'She ran some considerable . . .' *Daily Telegraph*, 23 October 1929; 'Lady Sarah regarded . . .' *Illustrated London News*, 4 August 1900.
p. 266. 'She was a lady . . .' Private Information Mother Columba, Convent of Mercy, Rosebank, Johannesburg.
p. 268. Capture of Mr Hellawell, *Daily Mail*, 4 January 1900; 'No doubt book . . .' *Daily Mail*, 20 March 1900.

CHAPTER FIFTEEN

p. 271. 'All I could hear . . .' West *Reminiscences of Lady Randolph Churchill*.
p. 272. 'It is proposed . . .' Leslie *Jennie*; Donation of *Maine* by Bernard Baker, *Illustrated London News*, 4 November 1899.
p. 273. 'It would be useless . . .' West *Reminiscences*; 'the Fund now stands . . .' *South African News*, 20 Nov. 1899; 'Perhaps the most comfortable . . .' *Times of Natal*, 26 Jan. 1900; 'I never realized before . . .' *Letters from a Hospital Ship*, *Anglo-Saxon Review*, June 1900.
p. 274. 'In the hurry of departure . . .' *Letters from a Hospital Ship*; 'indeed the real thing', 'the absence of news', *Ibid*.
p. 275. 'it was very pleasant . . .' and 'All we wanted . . .' *Letters from a Hospital Ship*.
p. 276. 'Luckily they were hailed . . .' *Letters from a Hospital Ship*.
p. 277. 'There was no fresh . . .' *Letters from a Hospital Ship*; 'He really is . . .' Churchill *Companion Volume 1 Part 2*; 'You will have to . . .' W. Churchill *My Early Life*.
p. 278. 'I know he sits . . .' Atkins *The Relief of Ladysmith*; 'The vast amount . . .' W. Churchill *London to Ladysmith*.
p. 279. 'Ah, horrible war . . .' W. Churchill *London to Ladysmith*; 'Spion Kop . . . was the key . . .' Atkins *The Relief of Ladysmith*.
p. 280. 'I saw it from below . . .' Atkins *The Relief of Ladysmith*; 'For God's sake Levita . . .' *Life of Sir Charles Warren*.
p. 281. 'Who is this man . . .' Williams *Life of Sir Charles*

Warren; 'The General Officer . . .' Williams *Life of Sir Charles Warren.*
p. 282. 'Better six good battalions . . .' W. Churchill *My Early Life*; 'We descended the hill . . .' Reitz *Commando*; 'Sir Charles Warren made his . . .' Atkins *The Relief of Ladysmith.*
p. 283. 'It was hard . . .' *Letters from a Hospital Ship*; 'The fault of this . . .' Atkins *The Relief of Ladysmith*; 'If a Relief Column . . .' Kruger *Goodbye, Dolly Gray.*
p. 284. 'I looked forward . . .' W. Churchill *My Early Life.*
p. 285. 'As I approached . . .' W. Churchill *London to Ladysmith*; 'the strange caprice . . .' *Ibid*; 'Mr Jack Churchill was hit . .' Atkins *The Relief of Ladysmith*; 'I saw young Jack Churchill . .' Rosslyn *Twice Captured.*
p. 286. 'Looking at these . . .' W. Churchill *London to Ladysmith.*
p. 287. 'I have been greeted . . .' Atkins *The Relief of Ladysmith*; 'I caught Winston Churchill up . . .' Rosslyn *Twice Captured.*
p. 288. 'They meant so well . . .' *Letters from a Hospital Ship*; 'Provided with much . . .' *Ibid*; 'About twenty minutes . . .' *Ibid.*
p. 289. 'It was thrilling . . .' *Letters from a Hospital Ship*; 'Lady Randolph showed me . . .' Rosslyn *Twice Captured.*
p. 290. 'The band played . . .', 'we took it for . . .' and 'It was an excellent way . . .' *Letters from a Hospital Ship.*
p. 291. 'regaled with tea . . .' and 'He told me that . . .' *Letters from a Hospital Ship.*

CHAPTER SIXTEEN

Quotes from *South African Memories* except as follows:
p. 292. 'For a moment I thought . . .' *Daily Mail*, 21 February 1900; 'Days roll into weeks . . .' *Daily Mail*, 20 April 1900 (despatch written 16 February 1900); 'Everybody more or less . . .' Thomasina Cowan's Diary.
p. 293. 'Inside Mafeking it is . . .' *Cape Argus*, 23 October 1929; 'Lady Sarah Wilson showed . . .' *Mafeking Convent Papers* at Convent of Mercy, Johannesburg; 'Throughout the whole siege . . .' *Daily Telegraph*, 23 October 1929; 'Colonel Baden-Powell on the stage . . .' *Daily Mail*, 20 April 1900.
p. 294. 'Lords, Earls, Lady Sarah . . .' Thomasina Cowan's Diary; 'It was just like . . .' *Ibid.*
p. 295. 'The Kaffirs dig . . .' Thomasina Cowan's Diary; 'There

REFERENCES

is plenty of . . .' *Daily Mail*, 21 February 1900 (despatch written on 9 February); 'As regards foodstuffs . . .' *Daily Mail*, 16 March 1900 (despatch written 20 February).

p. 296. 'Dogs not licensed . . .' Diary of Trooper W. Fuller in possession of J. Fuller, Johannesburg; 'Soup, composed of horse-flesh . . .' *Daily Mail*, 26 March 1900; 'alarming reports . . .' Aitken *Baden-Powell: The Hero of Mafeking*; 'Mafeking at last . . .' Hamilton *The Siege of Mafeking*.

p. 297. 'News of the relief . . .' *Daily Mail*, 26 February 1900; 'It had a beneficial effect . . .' Hamilton *The Siege of Mafeking*.

p. 298. 'The natives have been sent . . .' Thomasina Cowan's Diary.

p. 299. 'I ate the head . . .' Thomasina Cowan's Diary.

p. 300. 'Lady Sarah Wilson . . . called . . .' Thomasina Cowan's Diary; 'She was a cool . . .' Private Information John Nicholson of Mafeking.

p. 301. 'As we near the end . . .' *Daily Mail*, 22 May 1900.

p. 303. 'Now the Boers had possession . . .' *Daily Mail*, 19 June 1900.

p. 304. 'Good evening Eloff . . .' Grinnell-Milne *Mafeking*; 'Not till I had seen . . .' *Daily Mail*, 19 June 1900; 'I couldn't help feeling . . .' Baillie *Mafeking: A Diary*.

p. 305. 'We leave for Mafeking . . .' Grinnell-Milne *Mafeking*; 'Who could possibly . . .' *Cape Argus*, 23 October 1929; 'We were rather mad . . .' Baillie *Mafeking: A Diary*.

p. 306. 'From Colonel Mahon's . . .' Grinnell-Milne *Mafeking*.

p. 307. 'Men of all sorts . . .' Hamilton *The Siege of Mafeking*.

p. 308. 'that Lady Sarah Wilson's little boys . . .' *Daily Mail*, 21 May 1900.

CHAPTER SEVENTEEN

p. 310. 'It is the spirit of revenge . . .' *Natal Witness*, 29 March 1900; 'The wise and right . . .' W. Churchill *My Early Life*.

p. 312. 'peculiar and unconvincing tactics' W. Churchill *My Early Life*; 'No one doubted . . .' W. Churchill *Ian Hamilton's March*.

p. 313. 'I shall be here another . . .' Forrest *The Life of Lord Roberts*; 'Equipped by the . . .' W. Churchill *My Early Life*.

p. 314. 'So in the interests . . .' W. Churchill *My Early Life*.

p. 315. 'Here at last . . .' and 'a tall man . . .' W. Churchill *My*

357

Early Life; 'All the officers were agreed . . .' Churchill *Winston S. Churchill*.

p. 316. 'Although there is . . .' Churchill *Companion Volume 1, Part 2*; 'the best tinned provisions . . .' W. Churchill *My Early Life*.

p. 317. 'You can't think . . .' and 'This instinctive dislike . . .' W. Churchill *Ian Hamilton's March*.

p. 319. 'I looked at his face . . .' W. Churchill *Ian Hamilton's March*.

p. 320. 'Then while being. . .' W. Churchill *My Early Life*; 'Great was the anxiety . . .' Rosslyn *Twice Captured*.

p. 321. 'The Transvaal emblem . . .' W. Churchill *Ian Hamilton's March*.

p. 322. 'For over two hours . . .' Conan Doyle *The Great Boer War*.

CHAPTER EIGHTEEN

Quotes from *South African Memories* except as follows:

p. 323. 'May I now plead . . .' *Daily Mail*, 28 May 1900.

p. 324. 'They were wise enough . . .' Godley *Life of an Irish Soldier*.

p. 325. 'Charlie Fitzclarence riding . . .' Godley *Life of an Irish Soldier*.

p. 326. 'These daring young ladies . . .' quoted Godley *Life of an Irish Soldier*.

p. 329. 'I had determined . . .' W. Churchill *Ian Hamilton's March*.

p. 330. 'These were the last . . .' W. Churchill *My Early Life*; publication of Churchill's books and his mother's telegram, Churchill *Companion Volume 1, Part 2*.

p. 332. 'At Rolleston there was . . .' Viscount Churchill *All my sins remembered*.

p. 333. 'When the history . . .' *Illustrated London News*, July 1900; Account of Lady Randolph's wedding, *The Times* and *Daily Mail*, 30 July 1900.

EPILOGUE

p. 336. 'I put Lady Sarah Wilson . . .' Keppel *Edwardian Daughter*; 'Lady Sarah Wilson affords . . .' *Daily Telegraph*, 23 October 1929.

REFERENCES

p. 337. 'During 1912–13 I made . . .' Wrench in *Churchill by His Contemporaries.*
p. 338. 'It is my privilege . . .' *Rand Daily Mail,* 26 January 1965.

Index

Adams, John, 243, 244
Alexandra, Princess of Wales, 300–301
Amery, L. S., 163–164, 165, 173–174
Amphitryon Club, 16, 32
Anglo-Saxon Review, The, 271, 289
Ascroft, Robert, 136
Asquith, H. H., 16
Atbara, Battle of, 127, 128
Atkins, J. B., 139, 140, 141, 142, 164, 165, 173–174, 277, 279, 280, 282, 283, 285, 287

Badenhorst, Alida, 154
Bailey, Abe, 112
Baker, Bernard N., 272
Baker, Herbert, 100
Balfour, Arthur, 7, 16–17, 68, 70
Bangalore (Madras), 122, 126
Beira, 21, 60
Beit, Alfred, 12, 13, 17–18, 28–29, 33, 36, 37, 38, 45, 57, 69, 79, 80, 87, 97, 98, 100, 101, 106, 107, 176
'Black Week,' 249, 274, 275
Bladon (Oxfordshire), 75
Blandford, Marquis of, *see* Marlborough, 8th Duke
Blenheim Palace, 6, 75, 87, 88, 89, 219
Blood, Sir Bindon, 125

Blow, Mrs, 271
Boaz (African runner), 158, 182, 189
Borthwick, Sir Algernon, 13
Borthwick, Oliver, 130, 138
Boshof, Mr, 201
Botha, Commandant, 221
Botha, Gen. Louis, 170, 249, 278, 282, 317, 320, 328, 337
Brabazon, Major-Gen., 313–314
Bradley's Hotel (Mafeking), 267
Breteuil, Marquis of, 13
Bridges, Trooper, 206
Briton, s.s., 333
Brockie, Sergeant-Major, 178–179, 180, 200, 205, 206, 207–208, 209, 211, 215, 237, 321–322
Bulawayo (Rhodesia), 144, 146, 147, 148, 149, 154, 324
Buller, Gen. Sir Redvers, 139, 140, 141, 162, 249, 274, 276–284, 290, 291, 309
Burnham, Charles, 243, 244, 245, 246, 247
Buzzard, Dr Thomas, 74–75, 77, 78
Byng, Col., 277, 284

Cahill, Trooper, 206
Cairo, 129, 135
Cambridge, Duke of, 15, 83
Campbell, Hon. William, 92

360

INDEX

Cape *Argus*, 22
Cape *Times*, 20, 22, 48–49, 61, 69, 70, 331
Carrington, Major-Gen. Sir Frederick, 125
Cecil, Lord Edward, 146, 151, 231, 233, 308
Chamberlain, Joseph, 16, 137, 138–139, 140, 144, 176
Charter, Fort (Rhodesia), 55
Chievely (Natal), 166, 283, 289, 338
Chronicle, Daily, 125
Churchill, Lady Georgiana Spencer, *see* Curzon, Lady Georgiana
Churchill, John Strange Spencer (Jack), 7, 72, 275–276, 283, 284–285, 289, 310, 311, 316
Churchill, Lady Randolph, 6, 12, 13, 17, 50, 72, 75, 77, 88, 89, 91, 121–122, 125, 128, 129, 174, 199, 226, 270, 271–276, 285, 288–291, 330–331, 333–334
Churchill, Lord Randolph Henry, discusses visit to Mashonaland with Rhodes, 3–4; prepares for Mashonaland visit, 4–5, 11–17; early career of, 5–7; and Fourth Party, 7–9; in office, 9; resignation, 9–10, 91; forms gold-prospecting syndicate, 13; accepts *Daily Graphic*'s commission, 14; addresses his constituents, 16; farewell dinner to, 16–17; leaves for South Africa, 17–18; arrives at Cape Town, 19–21; supports Rhodes against Portuguese, 21–22; views on South African situation, 23–25; Uitlanders' hopes of, 27–28; arrives at Kimberley, 28–29; views on diamond industry, 29–30; arrives in Transvaal, 31–32; in Johannesburg, 32–35; in Pretoria, 36–39; meets President Kruger, 38; visits Transvaal farm, 40; arrives in Mashonaland, 43; at Fort Tuli, 4, 44–46; attacks catering on *Grantully Castle*, 46; criticized in England, 47–49; satirized in Gaiety skit, 49–50; criticized in South Africa, 51–52; hunts in Mashonaland, 53–54; at Chartered Company settlements, 55; arrives at Fort Salisbury, 56; invests in Matchless Mine, 57; criticized in Mashonaland, 58; holds auction at Fort Salisbury, 59; races horse at Fort Salisbury, 63; visits Mazoe valley with Rhodes, 61–63; quarrels with D.C. de Waal, 61–63; leaves Fort Salisbury, 63; at Fort Victoria, 63–65; returns to Fort Tuli, 66; in Bechuanaland, 67–68; at Mafeking, 68; returns to Cape, 69; invests in mine on Witwatersrand, 69–70; second stay in Cape Town, 70–72; arrives at Southampton, 72–73; publishes *Men, Mines and Animals in South Africa*, 73; declining powers of, 74; attempts world tour, 75; death of, 75; effects of his South African visit, 76; nature of his last illness, 77–78; results of his South African investments, 79; his relationship with Rhodes and Beit, 80; his political views on South Africa, 80–83; his telegram to his sister Sarah, 83
Mentioned: 87, 88, 89, 90–91,

INDEX

93, 94, 95, 97, 109, 111, 113, 114, 115, 121, 123–124, 129, 134, 136, 138, 139, 140, 141, 148, 172, 174, 176, 177, 197, 198, 206, 229, 240, 272, 309, 335, 336, 337

Churchill, Lady Sarah Spencer, see Wilson, Lady Sarah

Churchill, Sarah, 242

Churchill, Winston Leonard Spencer, and the Jameson Raid, 119, 122; in Cuba, 121, 124; in India, 122–127; relationship with his father, 123–124; seeks adventure, 125–127; attempts to join Kitchener's Expeditionary Force, 125, 128–129; published *The Story of the Malakand Field Force*, 126; arrives in Egypt, 129–130; contracts to write for *Morning Post*, 130; at Omdurman, 131–134; returns to England, 134; leaves army, 134–135; publishes *The River War*, 135; contests Oldham by-election, 136; commissioned by *Morning Post* to cover war in South Africa, 138; sails to South Africa, 138–140; arrives at Cape Town, 140; travels to Natal, 140–141; arrives at Estcourt, 141–142; reports from Estcourt, 162–164; agrees to travel on armoured train, 164–165; and armoured train incident, 165–168; taken captive, 169–171; asks for interview with Joubert, 171–172; at Colenso station, 172–173; reactions to his capture, 174–175; at Boer camp, 176–177; travels to Pretoria, 178–180; arrival at Staatsmodelskool, 180; protests against his imprisonment, 197–199; suspected of being armed when captured, 198–199; views on his gaolers, 200–201; depressed by captivity, 202–203; and plan for mass escape, 204–205; and Haldane and Brockie's escape plan, 205–206; escapes from Staatsmodelskool, 207–210; boards train to Delagoa Bay, 211; follows railway track, 212–213; arrives at Transvaal and Delagoa Bay Collieries, 213; hidden in mine, 214–215; reactions to his escape, 235–241, 253–254; his life underground, 241–242; hidden in mine store-room, 243–244; on train to Delagoa Bay, 245–247; at Lourenço Marques, 247–249; calls for reinforcements, 249; at Durban, 250–253; meets his mother, 276; joins the South African Light Horse, 277; accompanies Buller's advance troops, 278–279; and the battle of Spion Kop, 280–282; returns with Jack to the front, 283; and the battle of Hussar Hill, 284–285; and the relief of Ladysmith, 286–287; accompanies his mother to Ladysmith, 290–291; offends military authorities, 309–312; arrives at Bloemfontein, 312; and battle at Dewetsdorp, 313–315; with Ian Hamilton's column, 316–317; and battle for Johannesburg, 318; crosses Johannesburg, 318–320; reconciliation with Lord Roberts, 320; and the release of officers in Pretoria, 321–322; meets his aunt

INDEX

Sarah, 327; at farewell dinner in Pretoria, 328; and battle of Diamond Hill, 328–329; journey to the Cape, 329–330; publishes *London to Ladysmith via Pretoria*, 330; prepares *Ian Hamilton's March* for publication, 330; leaves South Africa, 331; at his mother's wedding in London, 334; significance of South Africa in his career, 336–337; later associations with Africa, 337; message to Pretoria centenary celebrations, 338
Mentioned: 7, 13, 22, 34, 50, 72, 74, 78, 81, 93–94, 151, 158, 185, 257, 270, 274, 275, 276, 289
Claridge's Hotel (London), 273
Cockran, William Bourke, 203
Cole, P. Tennyson, 145–146
Coleman, Arthur, 157, 159, 183–185
Colenso (Natal), 163, 170, 171, 172, 173, 175, 249, 278–289, 290
Connaught, Duke of, 273
Coventry, Hon Charles, 44
Cowan, Captain, 260, 294
Cowan, Thomasina, 225, 260, 261, 292, 294, 299, 300
Crauford, Miss, 263, 265
Cromer, Lord, 135
Cronjé, Gen. Piet, 220, 232, 290, 312
Cronjé, Mrs, 232
Cuba, 119–120, 124, 336
Currey, Henry L. (Harry), 21, 71, 101
Currey, J. B., 101, 102
Currie, Sir Donald, 20, 47
Curzon, Lady Georgiana, 88, 89, 300, 301, 334

Curzon, Viscount, 89

Davis, Major Karri, 306
De Beers (Mining Company), 28–30, 71, 101
de Bunsen, Sir Maurice, 75
de Koker, Veld-Kornet, 194–196, 216, 217, 218, 221
Delagoa Bay, 21–22, 96, 210, 211, 244, 247, 248
De la Rey, Gen. Jacobus H., 307, 328
Delpoort, Jeffrey, 225
Delpoort, Mrs, 216, 221, 223, 224
Dennison, Major C., 158, 189–190
de Souza, L., 197, 201, 236, 238, 249
de Waal, D. C., 61–65, 71
De Wet, Gen. Christiaan, 313
Dewetsdorp (Orange Free State), 313–315, 316
Dewsnap, Dan, 214, 215, 243, 244
Diamond Hill, battle of, 328–329
Dietrich (Boer guard), 192–193, 194, 195
Disraeli, Benjamin, 6, 7, 92
Dixon's Hotel (Mafeking), 68, 150, 151, 260, 305
Dormer, F. J., 60
Doornkop (Transvaal), 318
Doyle, Dr Conan, 148, 322
Drake, Spencer, 229–230, 231
Dunottar Castle, R.M.S., 138, 139, 140, 141, 274, 331

East London, 140
Eckstein, Friedrich, 33
Eckstein, Hermann, 33, 36
Edward, Prince of Wales, 6–7, 84, 203, 273, 333
Edwardes, George, 50

INDEX

Eloff, Veld-Kornet Sarel, 299, 301, 303, 304, 305, 306
Elwes, Lieut. H. C., 333
Estcourt (Natal), 141, 142, 162, 163, 165, 166, 172, 173, 197, 199, 288

Ferrand, Commandant, 179
Field, Julian O., 77
Fitzclarence, Capt. Charles, 150, 325
Fitzpatrick, James Percy, 36, 37, 38, 40, 45, 58
Forrest, Sir George, 317
Fourth Party, the, 8, 16, 17, 68
Frankland, Lieut. T., 169, 200
Fraser, Mrs, 155, 187, 188, 191, 192, 216
Fraser, Mr, 155, 187, 188, 192–193
French, Gen. J. D. P., 317
Frere (Natal), 165, 166, 288
Frewen, Moreton, 12–13, 17, 126

Gaiety Theatre (London), 49–50
Gallwey, Lieut., 200
Game Tree Hill (Mafeking), 262–263, 264, 265, 298
Garth Castle, R.M.S., 11
Giles, Major George, 14, 15, 20, 37–38, 44, 57, 73
Gillespie, Dr James, 243
Gladstone, William Ewart, 7, 8, 23, 24, 48, 80, 82
Godley, Major Alexander, 154, 324, 325
Godley, Mrs, 152, 154, 324–328, 331
Goldman, Mr, 33
Goold-Adams, Major H., 43, 153, 267
Gordon, Gen. Charles, 127
Gorst, John, 7

Goschen, George, 10
Graepon, Mr, 225
Grand Hotel (Pretoria), 326–327
Grange, The, (Cape Town), *see* Groote Schuur
Grantully Castle, R.M.S., 20, 21, 24, 46, 47, 50, 73
Graphic, Daily, 14, 15, 21–22, 23, 29, 30, 34, 37, 43, 44, 46, 48, 49, 50, 52, 61, 62, 63, 64, 70, 78, 80, 87, 95, 113, 121, 124
Grimshaw, Lieut., 209
Groote Schuur (Cape Town), 20, 21, 24, 69–72, 100–101, 106, 107, 145–146, 148, 330, 332
Gunning, Dr J. W. B., 201, 236, 237–238

Haldane, Capt. Aylmer, 127, 164, 165, 166, 167, 168, 169, 170, 171, 172, 175, 177, 178, 180, 198, 200, 201, 202, 205–210, 213, 215, 235, 237, 239, 240, 321–322
Hamilton, Angus, 152, 158, 296
Hamilton, Gen. Sir Ian, 309, 311, 316, 317, 318, 320, 329, 331
Hammond, John Hays, 78
Harmsworth, Alfred, 138
Harris, Frank, 77
Harrow Gazette, the, 50
Hartley Hill (Rhodesia), 57
Havana (Cuba), 121, 272
Hawkesley, Bourchier, 17
Heaney, Major, 144
Hellawell, Mr, 158, 161, 268
Heyman, Capt., 21
Hill, Miss, 259, 263
Hirsch, Baron Moritz, 13
Hlangwane Hill (Natal), 286
Hofmeyr, Rev. Adrian, 200, 209, 210, 235–236, 237, 239, 240, 254
Howard, Esme, 70

364

INDEX

Howard, John George, 213, 214, 241–245, 322
Hutchinson, Sir Walter Hely, 253, 276

Ian Hamilton's March, 330
Induna, s.s., 249, 250, 251

Jameson, Dr Leander Starr, 60, 61, 63, 98, 102–103, 104, 105, 106, 108, 109, 110–111, 119, 121, 144, 151, 153
Jameson Raid, the, 97–98, 101–116, 119, 136, 143, 146, 178, 179, 253
Jarvis, Major Weston, 325
Jerome, Clara, 12, 272
Jerome, Jennie, *see* Churchill, Lady Randolph
Jerome, Leonard, 6, 17
Jerome, Mrs L., 6, 12
Jerome, Leonie, *see* Leslie, Mrs Leonie
Jeune, Lady, *see* St Helier, Lady
Johnson, Frank, 57, 58, 59
Jooste, Lieut., 190
Joubert, Gen. Petrus J., 164, 171, 172, 176, 197, 198, 226, 236, 239, 240, 248, 255

Keeley, Mr, 156, 157, 159, 160, 181–182, 186–187, 190, 193, 195
Keeley, Mrs, 157, 159, 160, 161, 183, 186–187, 190, 195
Keppel, Sonia, 336
Khama, Bangmanwato Chief, 68
Khartoum (Sudan), 127, 134
Kitchener, Gen. Lord, 125, 127–129, 130, 131–132, 134, 135, 274, 275, 311
Komatipoort (Transvaal), 238, 246
Kroonstad (Orange Free State), 316, 332

Kruger, President Stephanus Johannes Paulus, 26–27, 38, 52, 81, 96, 97, 98, 99, 102, 103, 106, 112–113, 114, 115, 137, 143, 146, 148, 152, 176, 198, 202, 205, 226, 232, 299, 301, 320

Labouchere, Henry, 47, 48, 82
Laing's Nek (Natal), 102
Lamb, Mr, 193, 194
Lautré, M., 318–320
Lawson, Harry, 106, 108
Lawson, Mrs H., 107, 108
Lee, Hans, 44, 53, 54
Le Mesurier, Lieut. Frederick, 321, 322
Leslie, Mrs Leonie, 93, 272
Levita, Capt., 280–281
Lindley (Orange Free State), 309, 317
Lobengula, Matabele King, 42–43, 46, 67
Loch, Sir Henry, 60, 69
London to Ladysmith via Pretoria, 330
Londonderry, Lady, 277
Long, Col. Charles James, 164, 165
Lonsdale, Capt., 209
Lourenço Marques, 210, 244, 246, 247–249, 271, 322

Macequece (Mozambique), 21, 22, 63
McHenry, John, 214, 243
McKenna, Joe, 214, 242, 243
McKinley, President, 273
Maclean, 92
McNeill, Capt. Angus, 314–315
Mafeking Mail, 255, 261, 268, 297
'Mafeking Night', 307–308

INDEX

Mafeking Relief Fund, 300–301, 323, 332, 334
Maggersfontein, 207, 249
Mahmoud, Emir, 128
Mahon, Col. B. T., 301, 306
Mail, Daily, 138, 150–151, 158, 161, 181, 226, 268, 287, 295, 296, 305, 323
Maine, s.s., 272, 276, 285, 287, 288, 289, 290, 291
Majuba, battle of, 23, 24, 25, 26, 48, 52, 102, 139, 178, 249, 286
Malan, Veld-Kornet, 201, 236–237, 240–241
Manchester, Duke of, 254
Manchester Guardian, 15
Marjoribanks, Edward, 90
Majoribanks, Mrs Fanny, 90, 91
Marks, H. H., 13
Marks, Sammy, 35
Marlborough, 1st Duke of, 6, 87, 241
Marlborough, 7th Duke of, 6, 7, 87, 88
Marlborough, 7th Duchess of, 50, 87, 88, 89, 90, 91
Marlborough, 8th Duke of, 6, 50, 89, 94
Marlborough, 8th Duchess of, 272
Marlborough, 9th Duke of, 94–95, 316, 321, 328, 329, 331, 333
Marlborough, 9th Duchess of, 94–95, 272
Matchless Mine (Rhodesia), 57, 79
Matjesfontein (Cape), 28
May of Teck, Princess (Queen Mary), 91
Mazoe River (Rhodesia), 56–57, 61–62
Men, Mines and Animals in South Africa, 73, 83

Merriman, J. X., 20, 51, 71–72
Metcalfe, Sir Charles, 17–18, 28, 33, 72
Metelka (Lady Sarah Wilson's maid), 144, 153, 156, 160, 217, 227, 323, 324, 331
Milner, Sir Alfred, 137, 138, 140, 146, 224, 226, 274, 276, 311, 330
Minchin, Mrs, 300
Moncrief, Lieut., 233
Morley, John, 122, 135
Morning Post, 13, 130, 134, 135, 138, 141, 142, 162, 174, 249, 253, 271, 272, 277, 284, 286, 290, 309, 310–311, 313, 315, 317, 327, 330
Mosita (British Bechuanaland), 156–161, 181–186, 187, 189, 193, 196, 337
Mount Nelson Hotel (Cape Town), 275
My African Journey, 337
Mzilikazi, Matabele King, 41–42

Natal Mercury, 250, 251
Neumann, Sigismund, 13
New York, 121
Nicholson, John, 300
Nightingale, Florence, 336
North, Col., 13
Nylstroom (Transvaal), 39

Oldham (Lancs), 136, 214, 253, 329, 337
Omdurman (Sudan), 127, 130, 131, 132, 134, 135, 312
Oosthuizen, Veld-Kornet, 171–172
Opperman, Commandant, 200, 206, 236, 238–239, 254
Otto's Hoop (Transvaal), 324, 325

INDEX

Paardeberg (Orange Free State), 290, 312
Paddington South, 9, 10, 15, 36, 49, 56, 74
Palapye (Bechuanaland), 68
Pannonia, s.s., 276
Panzerra, Major F. W., 306
Pasteur, Louis, 48
Patterson, Mr, 204
Pearson, J. E., 188, 189, 190
Penn Symons, Gen. Sir W., 139, 140
Perkins, Henry Cleveland, 15, 33, 56–57, 59, 63, 67, 69, 79, 111
Peshawar (N.W. Frontier), 127
Philadelphia (U.S.A.), 254
Phillips, Lionel, 33, 35, 106
Pietermaritzburg (Natal), 141, 162, 163, 165, 175, 253, 254, 288
Pioneer The, 125, 126
Plumer, Lieut.-Col. Herbert, 148, 298, 306, 308, 323, 325
Portuguese East Africa, 19, 21–22, 59, 60, 96, 210
Powell, Col. Robert S. S., Baden-, 146–147, 148, 149, 150, 151, 152, 153, 158, 186, 190, 193, 216, 217, 219, 221, 223, 224, 231, 232, 233, 255 et seq, 292 et seq, 323, 324, 325, 326, 327
Punch, 9, 49

Radziwill, Princess Catherine Maria, 145
Ramatlhabama (Bechuanaland), 147
Raymond, E. T., 8
Rayner, Dr Hugh, 14, 36, 44
Reform Committee, the, 102, 104–105, 106, 112, 143, 179
Reitz, Deneys, 199, 282
Reitz, F. W., 198

Ressano Garcia (Mozambique), 246
Rhodes, Col. Frank, 330, 332
Rhodes, Cecil John, 3–4, 11, 12, 15, 17, 18, 19–22, 24–25, 26, 27, 28, 36, 40, 42, 52–53, 57, 58, 60–64, 68, 69, 71–72, 76, 78–79, 80, 97, 98, 99, 100–101, 105, 106, 107–108, 109, 115, 121, 143–146, 176, 201, 269, 330
Rhodes's Drift (Rhodesia), 43
River War, The, 134, 135, 311
Roberts, Arthur, 49–50
Roberts, Trooper Clement, 315
Roberts, Field Marshal Lord, 274, 275, 276, 290, 291, 293, 295, 297, 299, 301, 309, 311–312, 313, 314, 316, 317, 318, 319, 320, 322, 325, 326, 327–328, 329
Robinson, Sir Hercules, 106, 107, 109
Robinson, Lady, 107
Rosebery, Earl of, 135
Roslin Castle, R.M.S., 109, 113
Rosslyn, Earl of, 237, 285, 287, 289
Rothschild, Baron, 16
Rothschild, Messrs, 15
Rustenburg (Transvaal), 38, 323, 324, 326

St Helier, Lady, 89, 128, 129
St James's Gazette, 31
Salisbury, Fort (Rhodesia), 56–60, 61, 63, 68, 78
Salisbury, Marquess of, 9, 10, 22, 27, 91, 129
Sampson, Aubrey Woolls, 112
Sapte, Major, 21
Scot, s.s., 72–73
Scott, Capt. Percy, 252, 276
Setlagole (Bechuanaland), 153,

INDEX

154–156, 158, 186, 187–196, 221, 222, 223, 228, 323, 338
Shaka, Zulu King, 41
Silvers, Messrs, 15, 37
Smuts, Gen. Jan Christiaan, 337
Snyman, Assistant Commandant-Gen. J. P., 195, 196, 216, 220–222, 223–225, 227, 228, 230, 231, 232, 233, 248–249, 255, 256, 264, 298, 303–304
South Africa, 11, 13, 49
Speaker, The, 30, 47
Spectator, The, 30
Spion Kop, battle of, 279–282, 283, 289, 312
Standard and Diggers' News, 197, 241, 247
Stanhope, Mr, 47
Star, The (Johannesburg), 27, 32, 33, 34, 51, 60
Stent, Vere, 293, 305
Stormberg (Cape), 207, 249
Story of the Malakand Field Force, The, 126, 129
Stratford, Esme Wingfield, 253–254
Sullivan, W., 47

Tantallon Castle, R.M.S., 96, 98, 99, 102
Taylor, J. B., 36, 37
Teck, Duchess of, 91
Telegraph, Daily, 14, 106, 126, 134
Theron, Capt. Danie, 171
Thorneycroft, Col. A. W., 281–282
Times, The (London), 4, 11, 49, 91, 152, 163, 296, 300, 318
Tory Democracy, 8, 9, 10, 15, 68, 135
Transvaal Hotel (Pretoria), 36
Truth, 82

Tuli, Fort (Rhodesia), 4, 36, 44–46, 53, 54, 60, 66–67, 148

Umtali (Rhodesia), 61

Vanderbilt, Consuelo, *see* Marlborough, 9th Duchess
Vernon, Capt. Ronald, 261, 262, 263
Victoria, Fort (Rhodesia), 55, 57, 59, 63–65, 66
Victoria, Queen, 6, 92, 186, 226, 269, 273, 299
Victoria, R.M.S., 107, 109–111, 122, 144
Viljoen, Petrus, 223, 224, 225, 228, 231, 232, 233, 264
Volksstem, De, 23, 27, 33, 39, 51–52, 197, 202, 207, 241
Vryburg (British Bechuanaland), 22, 31, 160, 182–185, 187, 188, 192, 195, 268, 306, 338

Wagner, Charles, 167, 174, 175, 203
Walden, Thomas, 44, 138, 174–175, 199
Warde, Major, 13
Warren, Gen. Sir Charles, 278, 279, 280, 281, 282, 286
Warrender, Miss Eleanor, 276, 288, 290–291
Waterval Boven (Transvaal), 238, 244
Waterval Onder (Transvaal), 245
Weil, Benjamin, 152, 234, 256, 257, 260, 261, 262, 263, 302, 304, 305, 324
West, Lieut. George Cornwallis, 272, 275–276, 331, 333
Westminster, Duke of, 329, 330
Whales, Mr, 268
White, Gen. Sir George, 287
Wilhelm II, Kaiser, 48, 227

INDEX

Wilhelm (Zulu servant), 153, 156, 186, 217, 219
Williams, Capt. Gwynydd, 14, 28, 33, 56
Willoughby, Sir John, 122
Wilson, Alan Spencer, 94, 144
Wilson, Capt. Gordon, 83, 91–93, 100, 101, 105, 106, 107, 108, 109, 110–111, 112, 144, 146, 147, 148, 150, 153, 154, 158, 223, 224, 233, 255, 259, 261, 262, 265–267, 268, 296, 303, 306, 327, 336
Wilson, Randolph Gordon, 94, 144
Wilson, Sir Samuel, 92, 93
Wilson, Lady, 92
Wilson, Lady Sarah, marriage of, 83, 92–93; arrives in Cape Town, 87, 100; childhood of, 87–89; personality of, 90; interest in her brother's career, 90–91; meets Gordon Wilson, 91–92; relationship with Winston Churchill, 93–94; early married life of, 94–95; sails for South Africa, 95, 96; on board *Tantallon Castle*, 97–99; meets Cecil Rhodes, 100–101; at Kimberley, 101–104; returns to Cape Town, 105–106; in Rhodes's confidence, 107–108; sails for Durban on *Victoria* 109–111; meets Dr Jameson, 111; travels to Johannesburg, 111; in Pretoria for first time, 112; returns to England, 113–115; friendship with Rhodes and Jameson, 143–144; in Rhodesia before Anglo-Boer war, 144; Rhodes's guest at Groote Schuur, 145–147; accompanies her husband to Bulawayo, 147–148; arrives in Mafeking, 149; reports for *Daily Mail*, 150–151; ordered out of Mafeking, 152–153; at the Setlagole store for first time, 154–156; leaves for Mosita, 157; sends messages to Mafeking, 158; life at Mosita, 158–161, 181–182; reports about in London papers, 181; plans trip to Vryburg, 182–183; arrives at Vryburg, 184; life in Vryburg, 184–185; returns to Mosita, 185; leaves for Setlagole, 186; life at Setlagole on her second stay there, 187–188; visits armoured train wreck, 188–189; sends carrier pigeon to Mafeking, 190; and the arrival of Boer party at Setlagole, 191–194; put under detention, 194–196; decides to leave Setlagole, 216; journey to Boer laager, 217–220; interview with General Snyman, 221–222; imprisoned in laager hospital, 222–223; negotiations for exchange of, 223–226, 228, 230, 231; Queen Victoria's opinion of, 226; exchanged for Petrus Viljoen, 233; arrives back in Mafeking, 233–234; welcomed by *Mafeking Mail*, 255; builds bomb-proof shelter, 256–257; reports conditions in Mafeking, 258; life in Mafeking, 259–260; organizes children's Christmas treat, 260–261; and battle of Game Tree Hill, 262–263; takes charge of convalescents, 263; her views on Game Tree Hill, 264; work at Railway Institute, 265–266; moves to convent, 266; near escape from shell, 267; as

INDEX

correspondent to *Daily Mail*, 268–269; replies to Lady Randolph's telegram, 270; and the perils of Mafeking, 292; tributes to her courage, 293; her reports on food situation in Mafeking, 295–296; and the 'Siege Exhibition', 297; and attempt to relieve Mafeking, 298; eats locusts, 299; starts Mafeking Relief Fund, 300; and the relief of Mafeking, 301–307; assists at hospital, 302–303; and captured Boer prisoners, 304; decides to leave Mafeking, 323; sets out for Pretoria, 324; at Zeerust, 325; at Rustenberg, 326; arrives in Pretoria during occupation, 326; meets Winston Churchill, 327; meeting with Lord Roberts, 327–328; says goodbye to Winston, 328; journey to Cape Town, 331–332; photographed in 'Mafeking outfit,' 332; leaves for England, 333; at Lady Randolph's wedding, 333–334; later career of, 335–336; death of, 336
Mentioned: 13, 17, 83, 121, 289, 308
Wimborne, Lord and Lady, 13
Witbank (Transvaal), 212, 245, 338
Wolff, Sir Henry Drummond, 7 8, 16, 119
Wood, Sir Evelyn, 128–129
Woodgate, Gen. Sir Edgar; 279–280
Wrench, Sir Evelyn, 337

Zeerust (Transvaal), 228, 323, 325
Zimbabwe (Rhodesia), 64
Zululand, 41